Japan's Gre

Japan's Green Monsters

*Environmental Commentary
in Kaiju Cinema*

SEAN RHOADS *and*
BROOKE MCCORKLE

McFarland & Company, Inc., Publishers
Jefferson, North Carolina

LIBRARY OF CONGRESS CATALOGUING-IN-PUBLICATION DATA

Names: Rhoads, Sean, 1985– author. | McCorkle, Brooke, 1980– author.
Title: Japan's green monsters : environmental commentary
in Kaiju cinema / Sean Rhoads and Brooke McCorkle.
Description: Jefferson, North Carolina : McFarland & Company, Inc.,
Publishers, 2018. | Includes bibliographical references and index.
Identifiers: LCCN 2017058867 | ISBN 9781476663906 (softcover :
acid free paper) ⊗
Subjects: LCSH: Monster films—Japan—History and criticism. | Monsters
in motion pictures. | Environmentalism in motion pictures. | Ecology in
motion pictures. | Monsters—Symbolic aspects. | Environmentalism—
Japan. | Motion pictures—Social aspects—Japan.
Classification: LCC PN1995.9.M6 R46 2018 | DDC 791.43/67—dc23
LC record available at https://lccn.loc.gov/2017058867

BRITISH LIBRARY CATALOGUING DATA ARE AVAILABLE

ISBN (print) 978-1-4766-6390-6
ISBN (ebook) 978-1-4766-3134-9

Front cover illustration by Mike Bonanno (iStock)

Printed in the United States of America

*McFarland & Company, Inc., Publishers
Box 611, Jefferson, North Carolina 28640
www.mcfarlandpub.com*

For Banno Yoshimitsu,
March 31, 1931–May 7, 2017

Table of Contents

Preface

On November 3, 1954, the world changed. A massive prehistoric creature irradiated by nuclear testing rose from the ocean's deep abyss and devastated Tokyo. The monster crushed trains and tanks with his massive feet and rained fiery destruction on the Japanese metropolis with his radioactive breath. Thousands perished, millions more were displaced. In the decades since, this creature and other similar manifestations continued to plague not only Japan but the entire world. It is imperative that humankind understand these monsters—their origins, their motivations, and the reasons behind their implacable fury.

This is a book about *daikaijū eiga*, or Japanese giant monster movies, abbreviated throughout this text as *kaijū eiga*. The genre of Japanese monster films is so vast that we could not possibly cover it in its entirety with any specificity; we are therefore limited by necessity and design. Our intent and focus is not to provide an extensive, comprehensive survey of Japanese *kaijū* ("monsters") and films, but rather present an intensive examination and new interpretation on a set topic within the genre.

In this book, we focus on environmental commentaries and social history as overarching themes in *kaijū eiga*. We analyze these topics in their common and widest possible understandings, intentionally casting a wide net. Not only are these topics themselves fairly broad, but each of these major areas can be broken down into many smaller fields as well. For example, some issues examined throughout this book include: nuclear testing, radiation and fallout, monstrosity, feminism and nature, industrial waste, biological invasion, and genetic engineering and biotechnology, among others. An analysis of environmental messaging in these films illustrates many other social, political, economic, and cultural issues.

We base our analysis in the field of ecocriticism, also known as green studies, when making our environmental interpretation of *kaijū eiga*. It is important to note that because we are examining popular media, we use the common understanding of environmentalism. Therefore, we discuss a wide range of pressing ecological issues that were present in the popular mindset at the time of each film's creation. We also consider other issues relating to nature and pollution from a more theoretical point of view. For this reason, we include an analysis of economics as part of our broader environmental discussion. In their purest forms, environmentalism (the preservation of nature and wildlife) and capitalism (the private ownership of property and production) are diametrically opposed and therefore intrinsically linked. An ecocritical reading of *kaijū eiga* must necessarily contain economics as a factor.

1

Throughout our book, we scrutinize monster films from three different franchises: Tōhō Studios' Godzilla and Mothra films, and their competitor Daiei Company's Gamera series. We chose these three franchises because they are among the most prolific and influential of Japanese *kaijū* creations, and each franchise's respective monster has appeared in multiple iterations over several decades. We examine a number of films beginning in the immediate postwar era through the end of the 20th century, concentrating on works that we consider to have particularly strong or unique environmental messages. We selected films representative of different eras in Japanese history and our analysis proceeds, with minor exception, chronologically.

The title of this work is *Japan's Green Monsters*. We chose this title for several reasons, implying different themes found throughout this book. As the title indicates, this is a book about Japanese giant monster cinema, but what does the "green" signify? First, the title hints at the monsters' appearances. Godzilla and Gamera are often depicted as green, and Mothra hatches from an enormous celadon egg. Second, we use the term "green" in its modern, environmental sense, implying that the monsters and films embody ecological messages. Third, we analyze *kaijū eiga* as cultural artifacts that have an undeniable connection to business and profit; in this sense, "green" signifies the importance of money and capitalism.

In addition to our argument regarding environmentalism in *kaijū eiga*, this book has a secondary aim. Many have previously viewed the genre of Japanese monster movies as frivolous kitsch lacking in serious content. Authors continually critique shortcomings in special effects and production values. They assume a simulacrum of realism is the goal of these films. It is not. We contend that beneath a fantastic façade, *kaijū eiga* contain a kernel of the serious and can be interpreted as important sources of environmental, social, and political critiques.

Among the three leading monsters we discuss, Godzilla looms as the most well-known, popular, and prolific *kaijū* on the Japanese monster scene. From 1954 through the time of this publication, the radioactive dinosaur has starred in more than thirty feature films, though the exact number is fluid, depending on if or how one counts edited foreign versions or international productions. Godzilla is a common household name not only in Japan but around the world, and even those unfamiliar with the films likely recognize the monster's moniker and silhouette. That the suffix "-zilla" has come to denote any number of things large, powerful, and angry in the English language indicates the monster's ubiquity.

Scholars have largely ignored Mothra, an enormous, brightly-colored moth. A Tōhō Studios monster, she is perhaps most well-known for her encounters with Godzilla. However, Mothra began her career as an independent monster franchise in 1961, and only later matched wits and strength against Godzilla. She returned to star in her own trilogy in the 1990s in addition to renewing her battle with the radioactive dinosaur of the deep. Mothra's films differ from Godzilla's in many ways, and her deep connection with nature, music, and the feminine contribute to her relevance to this book.

Finally, Tōhō was not the only Japanese studio to produce monster films. Many major Japanese studios tinkered with *kaijū*, and the runner-up to Tōhō's Godzilla was certainly Daiei's Gamera. Although the Gamera franchise, centered around a flying, fire-breathing turtle, never reached the storied heights of the Godzilla series, the monster remains quite popular with fans of *kaijū eiga* and equally worthy of intellectual study. By examining the Gamera series, we reveal that environmental commentary is widespread throughout Japanese monster movies and not confined to productions from a single company.

Before we proceed to our analysis, it is important to make a few brief points about this book in general. First, this book is cowritten by two authors. We make no distinctions between the authors of individual chapters—we therefore both take full credit (and accept full blame) for this book in its entirety. We use the term "we" in order to present our joint thoughts and opinions. Everything of value in this book belongs to both of us equally, and all criticisms should be directed at us jointly.

As a corollary, we must note that our critical analysis is based on the original Japanese-language versions of the films addressed. Unlike several prior studies, we do not focus on the Americanized versions or English-language dubbed edits of the pictures. All film quotes are translations made or confirmed by the authors from the original Japanese dialogue. We have both spent a significant amount of our academic lives on Godzilla studies and portions of this book have appeared as Bachelors theses at Dickinson College and the University of Oklahoma, respectively, as Masters theses at the University of Pennsylvania, in *G-Fan* magazine, the peer-reviewed journal *Horror Studies*, and as academic conference papers and presentations.

Due to copyright and trademark restrictions, our access to images for this book is limited. We have done our best to find images, production and publicity stills, and other photographs suitable for publication. We suggest that if you are unfamiliar with the appearance of these creatures, a quick internet image search would lead to far more visuals than we could ever possibly hope to include in a physical printed book (at least without denuding the planet's forests). Or better yet, we recommend viewing the discussed films, as it would lead to an even deeper understanding and appreciation of *kaijū eiga* and this study.

Next, we come to the question of how to refer to the monsters we discuss in this book. The Japanese language rarely uses gendered pronouns, which complicates the discussion of monsters and their gender identification. How does one refer to Godzilla, Mothra, and Gamera when their sex is unclear? We have decided to follow the general convention of those that have written on these topics before us, and also by following our "gut feeling" of each monster's gender identity. Throughout this book, we therefore refer to both Godzilla and Gamera with the masculine "he" and "his," and Mothra with the feminine "she" and "her." Moreover, we do not force a gender binary on creatures clearly falling outside such a problematic system—others like the robotic Mechagodzilla and the androgynous blob Hedorah earn the neuter "it" and "its." The topic of gender and *kaijū eiga* could easily provide substantial material for a book, and while we touch on gender briefly, the issue is for the most part beyond the purview of this study.

There is another issue regarding linguistics. Obviously, we have written an English-language book that is about Japanese-language "texts." This creates several predicaments. For the sake of accessibility, we use the common English names for the films and monsters, after first providing each film's original Japanese title. Several films have been released in various versions with differing titles over the years, and when possible, we have chosen to use the English title that more accurately reflects the Japanese name for the film. For example, when Mothra and Godzilla first faced off against each other, the original release in North America was titled *Godzilla vs. The Thing*. Later the same picture was retitled *Mothra vs. Godzilla*, a far more appropriate name, and therefore the one we use throughout this book.

In the Japanese language, surnames are placed before personal names. This order is often inverted when Japanese names are translated into English-language texts, but the practice is far from consistent. We will therefore follow the Japanese style for each name throughout our text, except for those that have published extensively in English under the reverse order. Moreover, the Japanese language utilizes many long vowel sounds that are often noted in English through the use of diacritical marks, such as the one in *kaijū*. Like many scholars of Japan before us, we have chosen to eliminate the use of these marks from common city names like Tokyo and Osaka, but maintain them in other words less familiar to a general English-language audience.

Finally, we would like to mention the enormous debt we owe to others who have helped make this book possible. In addition to academics like William Tsutsui, Susan Napier, Yoshikuni Igarashi, Anne Allison, and Chon Noriega who have promoted *kaijū eiga* in scholarly discussion, we would also like to thank others for their help and inspiration. Special thanks to Alex Bates, Shawn Bender, Frank Chance, Linda Chance, Elyssa Faison, Yoshiko Fukushima, Noriko Horiguchi, Ayako Kano, David Strand, Alexander Bazes, Frank Clements, Keri Fisher, Brett Homenick, Erik Homenick, Christopher Napolitano, and J.D. Lees. We especially want to thank Michael Lee who provided us with invaluable insight on monster cinema during our writing process. Lastly, we would like to acknowledge and thank our anonymous peer reviewers for their helpful comments and suggestions.

With these important details out of the way, we now proceed to our discussion and film analysis. We proceed with a chronological and topical selection of films within each series, considering both historical and theoretical foundations. In some instances, the environmental commentary is overt, whereas in others we rely on subtextual analysis in our interpretation. We examine storylines, dialogue, visual imagery, and musical elements to arrive at our environmental analyses. Japan changed dramatically over the latter half of the 20th century. From the deprivations of the postwar era through the boom years of the high-speed economic growth period and the eventual Lost Decade at the close of the millennium, Japanese society transformed. In this book, we argue that although Japanese monsters evolved concomitant with their country of origin, a strong undercurrent of ecological commentary unites the genre of *kaijū eiga*.

1

Japanese Giant Monster Movies

In this introductory chapter, we lay the groundwork for the themes and ideas that appear throughout this book and situate the subject of Japanese monster cinema within a broader academic context. First, we discuss the relevance of the fantasy, horror, and science fiction genres to *kaijū eiga*. Second, we examine early examples of monster cinema, especially the original *King Kong* (1933) and its significance to the *kaijū eiga* genre. In particular, we analyze why monster films appeared as a natural creative choice for the Japanese film industry given Japan's history of monsters in both theater and mythology. Third, we present an overview of scholarship concerning the three monster franchises we focus on in this book: Godzilla, Mothra, and Gamera.

Fantasy, Horror and Science Fiction

It may seem obvious, but it is important to keep in mind that monster films do not take place in our universe. Instead, they are set in a universe very much like our own where the conventions and tropes of the fantasy, horror, and science fiction genres hold sway. These three genres are all branches of the larger field known as speculative fiction and their components, conventions, and conceits appear throughout the Godzilla, Mothra, and Gamera franchises. Therefore, before we embark on an exploration of Japanese *kaijū eiga*, we must first navigate our way through some of the theoretical and theatrical underpinnings of these genres.

This book is grounded in film studies, thus we focus our discussion on cinematic rather than literary examples. Recognizing Hollywood's global influence on the genres of fantasy, horror, and science fiction, we make some general observations regarding generic conventions.[1] Therefore, many of the examples in this chapter draw on American or international cinematic productions. We wish to examine the tropes of the genres in order to better understand how creators of *kaijū eiga* adapted the components of fantasy, horror, and science fiction to suit Japanese audiences.

Fantasy films contain fantastic or supernatural elements, locations, and characters. Folklore, mythological and phantasmagorical creatures, exotic locales, magic, and the extraordinary dominate the fantasy genre. Fantasy films tend to rely on the use of vivid, contrasting colors and stunning visual effects. One of the earliest fantasy feature films was the enormously influential *The Wizard of Oz* (1939), notable for its distinctive story, music, and striking use of Technicolor. Many readers may also correctly think of either Peter Jackson's *The Lord of the Rings* trilogy (2001–2003) or the Harry Potter films (2001–2011) as exemplary series planted firmly in the world of fantasy.

Generally, fantasy films are filled with non-diegetic music, that is, music that does not have an on-screen source. Composers often use non-diegetic music, also known as an underscore, to indicate magical or fantastic characters and events. Max Steiner, composer for *King Kong*, many other film music composers of his generation, as well as John Williams and his coterie decades later, drew on styles and aesthetics established in melodrama and opera. German opera composer Richard Wagner and his tetralogy of myth-based operas, the Ring Cycle, particularly influenced future cinema scores. Among the most common techniques borrowed from Wagner was the use of leitmotif, or using a specific melody or instrument to represent a character, object, or feeling. This approach to film music composition appears in all the genres we discuss to varying degrees, but it is perhaps most easily identified in fantasy-genre films.

Japan has a deep connection with fantasy that stretches through folklore and traditional dramatic arts. However, the anime (short for *animeshon*, or "animation") productions of Studio Ghibli embody the flower of the fantasy film in contemporary Japan.[2] Indeed, the illustrated worlds created by Miyazaki Hayao's company tend to use brilliant colors and emphasize magic and the otherworldly, definitive traits in the fantasy genre. Two relevant examples of Studio Ghibli's works, *Majo no Takkyūbin* (*Kiki's Delivery Service*) (1989) and *Mononoke-hime* (*Princess Mononoke*) (1997), fuse fantasy with Japanese values and aesthetics. In the former film, the young witch Kiki and her talking black cat, Jiji, fly on a broomstick delivering packages and sundries to earn a living; in the latter picture, a youthful warrior-prince becomes involved in an epic struggle between medieval Japan's forest deities and the proto-industrial forces of Irontown. *Princess Mononoke*'s emphasis on fantasy, Japanese mythology, and nature echoes many common themes of the *kaijū eiga* genre.

Monsters—broadly defined as animals or plants of abnormal, strange, or terrifying shape and size—fall largely within the fantasy realm, where other fantastic creatures like dragons, merfolk, and unicorns reside. Yet in practice the lines between fantasy, horror, and science fiction are often hazy, and not all monsters can be categorized as merely one or the other. Let us take, for example, the universally-recognized Frankenstein's monster—he is the product of scientific experimentation, taking us into the realm of science fiction, but his murderous killing spree frightens viewers, thus *Frankenstein* (1931) crosses the boundary into horror as well.

Monsters are not the only elements of fantasy prominent in *kaijū eiga*. Throughout the films we discuss in this book, there are numerous examples of other fantastic creatures and characters. The Mothra franchise's fairy duo and the extraordinary, paranormal psychic abilities displayed by the clairvoyant character Miki in Godzilla films of the late 1980s and 1990s also illustrate elements of fantasy in *kaijū eiga*. Similarly, the revelation that monsters inhabit a special isle off the coast of Japan, known as Monster Island, hints at the old fantasy trope of mystical lands occupied by dragons. Although deeply but not exclusively rooted in fantasy, these characters and places demonstrate the porous boundaries between fantasy and other domains within speculative fiction.

Unlike fantasy pictures, horror films represent a genre of cinema that typically plays on an audience's primal fears. Horror works inspire darker emotional responses, like terror, alarm, and anxiety. The horror genre tends to rely on the use of somber colors and darkness, starkly contrasting with the colorful fantasy genre. In film, editors and directors of horror often manipulate the tempo of shots and cuts to build a sense of foreboding. One effective decision common in horror is to withhold the image of the monster; the audience sees only characters' reactions at first, leaving their imaginations free to envision something far more terrible than any filmmaker could create. Scores for horror movies can range from the operatic to the distressingly dissonant or even the eerily quiet.

Some well-known archetypes illustrating the diversity of horror cinema include F.W. Murnau's *Nosferatu* (1922), Roger Corman's *House of Usher* (1960), William Friedkin's *The Exorcist* (1973), and more recently *The Witch* (2015) by Robert Eggers. These and other horror films also contain monsters, but of a more sinister, macabre variety. Common monsters and creatures found in horror films include demons, werewolves, vampires, ghosts, and zombies, to name but a few. Such beasts and ghouls are almost always portrayed as evil or bloodthirsty (at least initially), stoking the audience's deepest revulsions and fears of the unknown. The spectacle of death features prominently in nearly all horror films.

In Japan, the horror genre follows many of the same conventions as Hollywood productions, while frequently incorporating the additional dimension of Japanese folklore. One of Japan's earliest and most revered films including horror motifs is undoubtedly Daiei Company's *Ugetsu Monogatari* (*Ugetsu*) (1953), a ghost story period film.[3] The later *Kaidan* (*Kwaidan*) (1964) released by Tōhō Studios is a collection of four traditional ghost stories with an eerie, sound-effects driven score by the well-established Japanese composer Takemitsu Tōru. More recently, the well-known psychological horror film *Ringu* (*Ring*) (1998) gained popularity not only in Japan but around the globe. *Ring*, based on a novel which draws on a Japanese folktale, tells the story of a journalist ensnared in a series of deaths all linked to a cursed video tape. The film features the dark colors, sense of foreboding, and spectacle of death that have come to define the horror genre.

Of course, the light-hearted *kaijū eiga* of the 1960s and 1970s may not cross the frontier into the horror realm, but others certainly do, most notably the original *Gojira* (*Godzilla*) released in 1954. In his first appearance on the silver screen, the monster Godzilla terrified Japanese moviegoers, reminding them of the recent horrors of World War II and the omnipresent specter of the atomic bombings and nuclear testing. The film's weighty themes, coupled with the literal darkness of the black-and-white picture, allow us to categorize the work as functioning within the horror domain.

Alternatively, science fiction films exhibit speculative phenomena and technologies that lie beyond accepted, contemporary mainstream science. Some common tropes and elements found in the science fiction genre include: futuristic devices and computers, robots, spaceships, interplanetary travel, cyborgs, and aliens. When considering science fiction, most readers will likely imagine *Forbidden Planet* (1956), Gene Roddenberry's Star Trek franchise, Stanley Kubrick's watershed film *2001: A Space Odyssey* (1968), or the vast world of George Lucas's Star Wars. Authors and artists often use science fiction to explore relevant social, political, and philosophical issues. The genre provides an allegorical framework for artists to comment on otherwise taboo or controversial issues of the day. Science fiction is an extremely flexible category, thus its generic boundaries are fluid.

Japanese science fiction examples share many traits with Hollywood. *Chikyū Bōei-gun* (*The Mysterians*) (1957), one of the earliest Japanese science fiction films, featured the use of new widescreen filming and stereophonic sound technologies. Tōei Company's *Uchū kara no Messeeji* (*Message from Space*) (1978) infamously sought to capitalize on the preceding year's *Star Wars: A New Hope* (1977). In the big-budget Tōhō Studios production *Sayonara Jupitaa* (*Sayonara Jupiter*) (1984), humanity's population has expanded around the solar system, and scientists plan to ignite Jupiter as a second sun to help foster human habitation of distant planets.[4] A few years later, anime crossed paths with science fiction in *Akira* (1988), a cyberpunk subgenre tale set in post-apocalyptic Tokyo, where rival biker gangs battle for supremacy and survival.[5] *Akira* proved a transformational film for the anime medium and Japanese science fiction—it was the highest-grossing film in Japan in the year of its release, gained critical acclaim internationally, and "can be seen as the film that started the anime boom in the West."[6]

Readers familiar with *kaijū* cinema might most easily connect it to the science fiction tradition. Many of the common tropes and motifs of the genre pervade the Godzilla, Mothra, and Gamera franchises. Aliens, space exploration, time travel, robots, and many other science fiction elements abound in the world of Japanese monster movies, including in some examples we discuss in later chapters. Moreover, the environmental themes and issues we explore in this book are deeply connected to technology, a concept at the heart of the science fiction genre.

Just as science fiction as a genre melds tropes from fantasy and horror, so too does the music for many of these films. For example, John Williams's score for the Star Wars series is rooted in a Wagnerian aesthetic, while Jerry Goldsmith's score for *Planet of the Apes* (1968) is atonal; that is, the music lacks a tonal center, making it sound unstable, a quality normally a bit off-putting for listeners accustomed to the more common lush, harmonious underscore. The use of atonal music and shocking dissonant chords (also called stingers) frequently appear in scores for horror as well as science fiction with horror leanings. Beyond this, it is worth noting a specific sound prominent in many science fiction films of 1950s and 1960s: electronic music. Sounds produced from electronic means, whether emanating from a synthesizer, modulator, or theremin, came to indicate both the technologically-advanced as well as the uncanny in classic science fiction films, such as the aforementioned *Forbidden Planet*.

Theoretically, there are clear lines between the fantasy, horror, and science fiction genres, but in practice a different tale emerges. The reality of the matter is that all three branches of speculative fiction merge into a single multi-layered continuum. Many cinematic examples complicate the boundaries between the three seemingly discrete genres and hint at myriad subgenres. For example, science fiction horror films like *The Thing from Another World* (1951), Ridley Scott's *Alien* (1979), and Paul W. S. Anderson's *Event Horizon* (1997) all feature space travel and aliens but also play on the audience's deep fears and anxieties. *Fiend Without a Face* (1958) equally blurs the boundaries between horror and science fiction; in its case the monsters are the result of scientific experimentation gone awry. These crossovers utilize the stark, gloomy color palette of the horror genre, though they are set within the framework of a science fiction storyline. Meanwhile, films like *Barbarella* (1968) and *Krull* (1983) blur the lines between fantasy and science fiction; both portray magical abilities and fantastic creatures set on exotic worlds connected by interplanetary travel. *Buffy the Vampire Slayer* (1992) and the later television series of the same name blend horror elements with fantasy (and comedy)—vampires, werewolves, and other creatures coexist in a world infused with magic and the occult, set in an otherwise mundane California town. Many other films and franchises mix the various genres of speculative fiction, leaving a nebulous boundary between realms.

The porosity between fantasy, horror, and science fiction does not always remain within the realm of speculative fiction. Sometimes films strike even farther afield. Joss Whedon's *Serenity* (2005), set in the universe popularized by the short-lived TV series *Firefly* (2002), combines elements of science fiction with the Western. Len Wiseman's *Underworld* (2003) commingles the tropes of the horror and action genres, in order to tell the tale of an epic, interminable battle between vampires and werewolves in a stylized modern world. The popular *Twilight Saga* (2008–2012) capitalized on a blending of horror and romance, a combination rooted in the genre's Gothic sources. Finally, another Ridley Scott film, *Blade Runner* (1982), crosses the frontier between science fiction and film noir, detailing the story of a hard-boiled detective tracking genetically-engineered "replicants" through a futuristic, dystopian Los Angeles.

This is all to say that although we understand and examine movies through the lens of genre, films very rarely limit themselves to the conventions of a single generic mode. Like many of the films mentioned above, *kaijū eiga* also blend aspects and elements of the fantasy, horror, and science fiction genres. Japanese monster pictures do not fit neatly into any particular branch of speculative fiction, and these movies often find their motivation in other genres as well, from mysteries to spy thrillers to morality plays. This combination results in *kaijū eiga*, a different form of cinema in its own right. Rather than being limited to a single genre, these films exist in a murky amalgam of domains within the celluloid medium. *Kaijū eiga* should be examined and analyzed within the creative scope of fantasy, horror, and science fiction, keeping in mind the flexibility of the genres and their evolution over time. Throughout our analysis, we contemplate the development of monster films and examine why they provided a suitable vehicle for Japanese film studios to comment on topics like nature, pollution, and environmental degradation.

King Kong, *Monsters and the Japanese Tradition*

Any discussion of monster cinema would be incomplete if it did not note the enormous debt owed to the original *King Kong* (1933) produced and directed by Merian C. Cooper and Ernest B. Schoedsack.[7] The cinematic *tour de force* tells the story of ambitious film director Carl Denham (Robert Armstrong) who takes his cast and crew, including the lovely starlet Ann Darrow (Fay Wray), aboard the ship *Venture* to the mysterious Skull Island located somewhere in the Indian Ocean. The island's natives present sacrifices to an enigmatic creature—Kong—that lives beyond an ancient wall behind their village. After spying the alluring blonde Darrow, the natives abscond with her and present her to Kong, a massive fifteen-meter (fifty-foot) gorilla. Denham and his men pursue Kong through the island's jungles, with nearly all perishing in their encounters with dinosaurs, other creatures, and Kong himself. The *Venture*'s first mate, Jack Driscoll (Bruce Cabot), rescues Darrow and flees with her back to the village, with Kong in pursuit. Kong bursts through the wall's gate, ravages the village, and is gassed by the foolhardy Denham. The *Venture* transports the enchained Kong back to New York City, where he is displayed as a theater attraction. He escapes, wreaks havoc, and climbs the Empire State Building with Darrow in hand, only to be gunned down and killed by biplanes. As one of the first and most influential monster movies, *King Kong* represents a zenith of giant monster cinema.

In addition to the influential plot of *Kong*, the movie addresses themes that reverberate throughout later monster movies, most notably a tension between nature and humanity (or perhaps more accurately human science and technology). Denham and the ship's crew use "modern" weapons to massacre dinosaurs and capture Kong and transport him to New York City. Humanity utilizes technology, from high-powered rifles to gas grenades to armed aircraft, to overcome the forces of nature. When the giant ape escapes, he climbs atop the Empire State Building, a glittering symbol of human progress and ingenuity, only to be toppled by modern war machines. While humanity's attempts to control nature end poorly for both parties, nature invariably suffers more. This theme, prevalent in *King Kong*, persists in countless fantasy, horror, and science fiction features, and Japanese *kaijū eiga* exemplify *Kong*'s enduring legacy.[8]

An interesting wrinkle in *King Kong*'s commentary on the modern world is the film's similar treatment of both Skull Island's forest primeval and New York City's concrete jungle. Both locales are portrayed as brutal, but in different ways. Whereas on Skull Island nature itself is savage and unforgiving, it is the human world of skyscrapers, elevated trains, and theater attractions that is equally barbarous and merciless.[9] In 1933, *King Kong*, despite the titular monster, critiqued the exploitive horrors of the human world—particularly the deprivations of the Great Depression—and Kong himself is less a monster to be feared than a creature to be pitied.

But what was it about *Kong* that so enthralled audiences around the world, including those in Japan? In addition to the compelling narrative that combines adventure and romance within a humanity versus nature framework, the special effects for *King Kong* astounded audiences both in 1933 and in 1952, one of many times the classic was re-released worldwide.[10] Through American productions like *King Kong* and *The Beast from 20,000 Fathoms* (1953), Japanese producers saw the potential for the monster cinema genre in Japan.[11]

The spectacle and story of *Kong* resonated in Japan on a singular level. Theatrical effects in combination with mythological (and often vengeful) creatures pervade traditional theater in Japan. The special effects used in traditional stage theater provided film studios a clear segue for monster cinema to gain a foothold among Japanese audiences. Indeed, the influences and aesthetics of both Nō, Japan's ancient dramatic art, and Bunraku, Japanese puppet theater, can be found in *kaijū eiga*.[12] Furthermore, Japanese studios also drew on the special effects concept of *tokusatsu* (literally "special filming"), the earliest origins of which trace themselves to Japan's third traditional dramatic

Kong battles a dinosaur in the original *King Kong* (1933). Ann Darrow (Fay Wray) watches from the tree bough on the right. Unlike Japanese *kaijū eiga* productions that relied on suitmation and puppetry, special effects master Willis O'Brien brought Kong to life with stop-motion animation (RKO Radio Pictures Inc./Photofest).

art, Kabuki. Finally, Japan's ancient mythology, legends, and indigenous religious tradition, Shintō, bolster the historical underpinnings of monsters within Japanese culture. We will look at the relationship between these elements and *kaijū* cinema in turn.

The earliest origins of Nō theater can be traced to festivals at Shintō shrines devoted to the native spiritual tradition of Japan.[13] There, performers would move as if possessed by spirits, their actions supposedly willed by the gods.[14] Nō developed over time from a religious performance to a theatrical art, largely arriving at its present-day form in the 14th century, during the early rule of the Ashikaga shōguns (1336–1573).[15] Many Nō dramas feature monsters, ghosts, and demons—revealing the art's mythological roots—but the aesthetics of the theatrical tradition also lend themselves in less obvious ways to the visual appearance of Japanese monster movies.

Nō actors wear elaborate masks and loose-fitting costumes, concealing the performers' faces and shapes but not completely removing their presence from the audience. Similarly, Japanese studios relied on the concept of suitmation (actors dressed in monster costumes surrounded by miniature sets) to bring their *kaijū eiga* to life. Unlike *King Kong* and *The Beast from 20,000 Fathoms*, where special effects teams relied on the use of stop-motion animation, Japanese monster movies produced during the 20th century predominantly utilized such rubber suits and puppets during their production.

Even at their best, the special effects of Japanese monster movies require some suspension of disbelief on the part of the viewer. In several cases, it is difficult to ignore that the respective beasts are not just actors in rubber suits crushing model buildings—we acknowledge this, but consider it to be one of the genre's many charms. Like Nō performers, *kaijū* actors are never fully removed from the gaze of the audience.

Furthermore, Nō productions are known for their austere severity—a bare wooden stage, an overhanging roof, and a simple image of a pine or cedar tree are the theater's only set. Nō backgrounds depict the Yōgō Pine, a tree located at Nara's Kasuga Shrine, a site where the gods supposedly descend to the earth and instill their spirit in Nō performers.[16] The *mise-en-scène* (a film term for scenery, setting, costumes, etc.) of certain *kaijū eiga* scenes recall the spartan Nō stage, while the barrenness of many *kaijū* battle sequences replicate this aesthetic connection. In both Nō and *kaijū eiga*, sometimes it is the presence of the actors (be it in masks or rubber monster suits) more than the setting and literal believability of the special effects that commands the audience's attention.

Bunraku puppet theater is another of Japan's traditional dramatic arts, dating in its largely current form to the early 19th century when the most famous of Bunraku theaters opened its doors in Osaka. Puppet theater existed in differing forms throughout Japan prior to this period, but scholars trace the development of Bunraku's golden age to this era.[17] Bunraku plays feature large wooden puppets controlled by three puppeteers: the principal operator, an operator for the left hand, and an operator for the puppet's feet. Unlike the two subordinate puppeteers, who conceal their faces behind black hoods, the face of the principal operator is visible. Despite the puppeteers' obvious appearance on-stage, as Japanologist Donald Keene notes, "How, I wondered privately, could one forget the operators when they seemed so much more alive than the puppets? [...] after the first few minutes of uncertainty I found myself being drawn into the world of puppets, and if I looked at the operators' faces afterwards it was by deliberate choice."[18] So it is with *kaijū eiga* as well—like Bunraku, when the audience is drawn into the universe of monsters, they can forget the performers manipulating the monster puppets and costumes, and enjoy the story untroubled by the mechanics of the special effects.

Another intriguing correlation between Bunraku and *kaijū eiga* also exists. In both forms of theater, the puppets and the monsters are literally voiceless. Godzilla, Mothra, Gamera, and other *kaijū* emit noises ranging from the musical to the animalistic that convey certain emotions to the viewer, but they are unable to present complex thoughts or ideas.[19] Like the speechless, wooden Bunraku puppets, Japanese monsters require an intermediary to speak on their behalf; in short, a narrator. In Bunraku, this narration function is fulfilled by the *tayū*, the traditional storyteller recounting the play's events and background to theatergoers. The same is true of *kaijū eiga*, wherein the film's human cast must speak to the audience for the voiceless *kaijū*, interpreting their motivations and observing their destructive fury. As author Jason Barr notes in his wide-ranging study of the *kaijū eiga* genre: "The characters often narrate the battle and comment on the proceedings, sometimes expressing chagrin at a particular *kaijū*'s failures."[20]

In Nō, Bunraku, and Kabuki, as with other live theatrical performances, characters differ in physical appearance due to changes in actors, costumes, and the passage of time. Yet, stock characters remain recognizable across years and performances. Similarly, although the physical appearances of the monsters change over time in *kaijū eiga*, the creatures nevertheless represent the same character in the eyes of viewers. Many commenters have noted the physical alterations made to the monster costumes used in *kaijū eiga* productions.[21] As prominent Japan historian and Godzilla expert William Tsutsui has noted: "After the two more serious films of the 1950s, the Godzilla costumes were stripped of their forbidding fangs [...] The suit was given a friendly, more mammalian look over the course of time, with the hint of an upturned smile."[22] Similar changes occurred in the Mothra and Gamera franchises, leading to monsters that looked dramatically different by the turn of the 21st century when compared to their original incarnations. However, like traditional Japanese theatrical productions (and stage theater more generally), there is seemingly no requirement in *kaijū eiga* that monster costumes remain static—like a new actor filling in for a retired performer, or a change in wardrobe at a different venue, moviegoers themselves do not dwell on the physical changes.

Historically, much of Japanese theater features supernatural legends and mythological creatures. These creatures, known as *yōkai*, appear in scores of guises and forms throughout innumerable Japanese legends and plays.[23] Some of the most well-known include eldritch creatures like *kappa* (mischievous turtles), *oni* (malevolent demons), and *kitsune* (shapeshifting foxes). Other legendary beasts imported from mainland East Asia, like the water dragon, which made its way from China to Japan sometime during the 6th century, also deeply influenced Japanese mythology.[24] Dragons, demons, and other creatures then appeared regularly in Nō productions, and later massive monsters like "giant octopi, giant snakes, and giant toads" became common in Kabuki theater as well.[25]

In addition to their roots in Japanese lore and theater, monsters like Godzilla can also be connected to the native religion of Japan, Shintō.[26] Some of the earliest Shintō texts and Japanese folk tales, such as the *Nihon Shoki* (*Chronicles of Japan*), compiled in the 8th century, include stories of dragons. These hoary tales are commonly cited as inspiration for monsters like Godzilla.[27] Moreover, Shintō is a religious tradition that is deeply concerned with the natural world. Shintō shrines themselves typically feature an innate connection with nature. One Shintō scholar has declared: "No amount of artificial beauty is an adequate substitute for the beauty of nature. Throughout the country the most beautiful spot in any community is generally the site of a shrine."[28] In fact, Shintō spirits and deities, known as *kami*, are often believed to inhabit conspicuous examples of natural beauty, from massive trees to majestic mountains to monumental boulders, further connecting Japanese religious traditions with themes of monsters and nature. Mark Justice, writing for *G-Fan* magazine, even states: "Godzilla becomes a great and evident manifestation of Shintō symbolism shown through the image of a monster."[29]

Finally, although Nō, Bunraku, Kabuki, and Japan's mythological and Shintō religious traditions represent discrete elements of Japanese history and culture, they nonetheless overlap in many ways. Nō is a theatrical tradition, but its roots delve into its ancient origins as a religious performance, influencing not only its visual aesthetics but the plot devices of many Nō dramas. Bunraku, despite lacking the clear religious origins of Nō, nonetheless continues a similar aesthetic tradition in another form of

Japanese theater, wherein the puppeteers remain obvious to the viewer. Many Kabuki plays copy or draw on earlier Nō works, continuing their inclusion of monsters and the otherworldly while adding new theatrical effects.[30] Lastly, the history of Japan's indigenous tradition of Shintō is intertwined with legendary and mythological tales, which themselves reappear on stage in Nō, Bunraku, Kabuki, and other performances. All the while, monsters, spirits, and the supernatural pervade these and other elements of Japanese tradition, creating a cultural pastiche that embraces such tales and creatures in other media.

Japanese monster movies did not emerge from a void in 1954, nor did they merely copy or imitate Hollywood monster-on-the-loose films like *King Kong*. Instead, *kaijū eiga* and their aesthetics draw from a font of inspiration anchored in Japanese theater, mythology, and religious traditions with deep roots in Japanese society and culture. At the same time, this history and mythology also provides an abiding connection between the Japanese people and nature, a connection that, we argue, *kaijū eiga* continues. An examination of published scholarship regarding the three franchises we consider in this book prepares the way for our environmental analysis and critique of Japan's green monsters.

Godzilla, Mothra and Gamera

In 1954, Tōhō Studios released *Godzilla*, a new kind of film with the potential for environmental, social, and political commentary. In *Godzilla*, a giant, irradiated dinosaur rises from the depths of the Pacific Ocean and destroys great swaths of Tokyo. Many scholars and fans have long understood *Godzilla* as a commentary on modernity, nuclear warfare, the horrors of the Asia-Pacific War (1937–1945), and the Allied Occupation of Japan (1945–1952).[31] Although the original *Godzilla* raised many serious issues, according to most commentators the series of films that followed generally failed to sustain the original's profundity. Many deride the post–1954 Godzilla series as an accumulation of politically and socially meaningless films, or what William Tsutsui has called a "B-movie morass."[32]

Tsutsui has written on Godzilla both in English and Japanese, and his monograph *Godzilla on My Mind* remains at the forefront of intellectual engagement with *kaijū eiga*. In it, Tsutsui addresses some of the deeper issues present in the Godzilla series. Early in the book, Tsutsui makes his intentions clear: to dispel the widely held belief that there are no serious Godzilla films.[33] Tsutsui elevates the original 1954 *Godzilla* while largely disparaging the remainder of the series:

> There was a dead-serious Godzilla movie. Well before the series degenerated into big-time wrestling in seedy latex suits, well before Godzilla had a laughably unlikely son, well before a giant technicolor moth was passed off as a gruesome monster, well before Tokyo was besieged by rapacious aliens or vengeful undersea civilizations (all fluent in Japanese, of course), [*Godzilla*] was a solemn affair, an earnest attempt to grapple with compelling and timely issues.[34]

In this vein, Tsutsui's purpose is similar to our own, but he strives to show the merits of the original *Godzilla* alone, without considering the underlying symbolism embedded in other *kaijū eiga*. Tsutsui also co-edited an important collection of academic essays, *In Godzilla's Footsteps*, contributing greatly to other areas of scholarly inquiry of Japanese monster cinema.[35] Tsutsui forged a path for those interested in studying *kaijū eiga* as a serious academic topic, and while we disagree with some of his statements, we aim to supplement his scholarship rather than supplant it.

Although Tsutsui is one of the most prominent of Godzilla scholars, one of the earliest writers to grapple with Godzilla's symbolism was film scholar Chon Noriega in his influential essay "Godzilla and the Japanese Nightmare: When *Them!* is U.S." published in 1987. Noriega attempts to interpret the Godzilla franchise through a psychological framework, analyzing the state of Japanese-American relations in the aftermath of World War II, the atomic bombings, the Allied Occupation, and continued nuclear testing in the Pacific.[36] Noriega concludes his analysis by discerning that Godzilla symbolizes both the Japanese Self and the American Other.

Like Noriega, Yoshikuni Igarashi discusses Godzilla's monstrosity and his relationship to Japanese war memory. In his landmark book *Bodies of Memory* Igarashi states, "monstrous forms that defy human comprehension were burdened with the mission to represent memories of war loss."[37] Igarashi considers how Godzilla in the 1954 film represents the destructive power of nuclear warfare and the United States. In addition to discussing the problematic postwar relationship between Japan and America, Igarashi extrapolates Godzilla's representation of Japan's war dead. He asserts: "Not only memories of loss but also the loss itself—the souls of the war dead—return to Tokyo in the form of Godzilla."[38] Igarashi posits that although the Japanese destroy Godzilla in the first film of the franchise, monsters continue to plague Japan in sequel films "as long as postwar Japanese society exists under the aegis of the United States and keeps forgetting the war dead."[39]

Throughout the 1960s, Igarashi contends, Godzilla films were forced to change with Japan, leaving behind the somber anti-nuclear commentary and jarring war imagery of the original 1954 film. The new order of the 1960s and the increased tensions of the Cold War called for a new kind of hero-monster to defend Japan.[40] Opposed to Tsutsui's assertion that the series immediately fell into a period of worthless cinema fare, Igarashi views the Godzilla movies of the 1960s as relevant cultural artifacts. However, he concludes his analysis of the series with the final film of the 1960s, leaving a vast swath of *kaijū eiga*—Godzilla and otherwise—beyond the purview of his book.

Anthropologist Anne Allison presents a different view on Godzilla's origins and international metamorphosis in her monograph *Millennial Monsters*. She comments on various themes present in *Godzilla* which diverge from historical fact and how these changes affected the film's marketing and reception abroad. Allison declares:

> The story of [Godzilla], however, is a retelling of the war with a twist. In [*Godzilla* producer] Tanaka's version, the Japanese bear no responsibility for the destruction wreaked upon their land. Rather, the aggressions in the tale rest entirely with the monster and with the nuclear fallout provoking his transformation and rage. [Godzilla] signifies World War II as a travesty of nature brought on by the atomic blasts of the Americans. For Japanese audiences, then, [Godzilla] provided a vehicle for reliving the terrors of the war relieved of any guilt or responsibility—solely, that is, from the perspective of victim. In this sense, [*Godzilla*] was a fantasy.[41]

Allison's analysis of the film clarifies the necessity of re-editing *Godzilla* for a global market. In order to sell the monster in the United States and other Allied countries, the film needed to be stripped of its World War II commentary, which resulted in a dilution of *Godzilla*'s environmental and anti-nuclear messages. In 1956, an American studio released a cut and dubbed version called *Godzilla, King of the Monsters*. Marred by illogical changes, additional scenes, and poor translation, this version contributed to the movie's infamy as a "camp phenomenon."[42] *Godzilla, King of the Monsters* dissociated the creature from the film's original intent, leading to a misunderstanding of the Godzilla series globally.

Susan Napier offers an alternative theoretical framework in her seminal article "Panic Sites: The Japanese Imagination of Disaster from *Godzilla* to *Akira*." Napier's article represents the most influential academic essay dealing with the nature of Godzilla. In it she discusses the evolution of Japanese science fiction vis-à-vis a shifting sense of Japanese national and cultural identity. Napier compares three landmark Japanese science fiction works: *Godzilla, Nippon Chinbotsu (Japan Sinks)* (1973), and *Akira* (1988).[43] The essay examines how these works represent a shift in the sensibilities of Japanese society regarding disaster and dystopian imagery.

In her cartography of postwar Japanese science fiction, Napier maps out the specific relationships between each of her case studies and the decade they represent. Her analysis of the causal events which led to the production of *Godzilla, Japan Sinks*, and *Akira* reveal elements similar to those we discuss regarding the evolution of *kaijū eiga*'s environmental commentary over time. Napier claims:

> This continuum [of films] spans over three decades, starting in the early 1950s which spawned both *Godzilla*'s nuclear anxiety and its easy moral certainties, through the 1970s ambivalence toward Japan's own success that characterizes [*Japan Sinks*], and ends with *Akira* in the late 1980s, a decade of tumultuous change, both in Japan's conception of itself and its relationship with the rest of the world.[44]

Aside from stressing the importance of contextualizing the films within the framework of Japanese history and society, Napier also stresses the intrinsic flexibility of science fiction as a genre and a medium when she states:

> In fact, science fiction is a particularly appropriate vehicle for treating the complexities of the Japanese success story. The very vocabulary of the genre—that of technological, social, and cultural advancement—reflects the cultural instrumentalities that characterize modern capitalism. These instrumentalities include the rapidity of change, the ideology of progress toward some anticipated "future," and the omnipresence of the machine. All of these elements are treated in Japanese science fiction, usually in a way that emphasizes the darker side of modern Japanese society.[45]

Regarding *Godzilla*, Napier considers it in the context of its immediate postwar production, discussing the film's sense of nuclear anxiety, moral certainty, and Japanese nationalism.[46] These themes are relatively evident: American nuclear testing creates Godzilla, he sinks several Japanese ships and decimates Tokyo, and an "oxygen-destroyer" developed by a Japanese scientist slays the monster. Napier highlights that science as a whole is not demonized in *Godzilla*. While American science inadvertently creates Godzilla, it is a Japanese scientist who defeats Godzilla and saves the Japanese people from imminent annihilation. These themes lead Napier to label *Godzilla* as a film of "secure horror," a genre in which "the collectivity is threatened, but only from the outside, and is ultimately reestablished, usually through the combined efforts of scientists and the government. It is a fundamentally optimistic genre in which it is possible [...] 'to imagine successful human intervention.'"[47]

Aside from scholarly books and articles, many journalists and film critics have discussed the meaning of Godzilla. Over time, the films of the Godzilla franchise changed dramatically and reviews of the films diverged accordingly. We will not visit every critical review and interpretation of the monster here. However, David Milner, a staff writer for *Cult Movies* magazine, presents an interesting interpretation of Godzilla's symbolism in the original film. In a 1995 interview, Milner succinctly declared: "He represents death."[48] While other authors have heretofore connected Godzilla with atomic anxiety, Japan's war dead, and lingering memories of the horrors of World War II, Milner offers a more metaphysical interpretation. Godzilla not only brings death, destruction, and carnage—he is the avatar of death itself.

Finally, the most prominent Japanese scholar of Godzilla is Takahashi Toshio of Waseda University. Takahashi has written several volumes on Godzilla concentrating on the nature of the monster, his origins, the tale's meanings, and technical and theatrical aspects of the film series.[49] Takahashi frequently comments on the original *Godzilla* film and even its American release *Godzilla, King of the Monsters*. However, like many others who seek to analyze Godzilla, Takahashi focuses his examinations on the earlier films of the franchise.

In sum, the perceived symbolism of Godzilla presents a complex and contradictory dilemma. Scholars, journalists, critics, and fans alike have weighed in on the monster's meaning over the many decades since the original film's debut in 1954. We have not presented every understanding and interpretation of Godzilla, only a varied cross-section, and we will visit more views on Godzilla's saurian majesty throughout this book. The historiography of Godzilla analysis shows that interpretation of the monster is subjective, and that the monster himself changes over time and place. Obscuring the issue further are the many different cuts and edits of Godzilla films that have appeared throughout the world, with altered plots, missing scenes, and poorly dubbed dialogue.

Few scholars and critics have paid heed to other *kaijū*, even those produced by Tōhō Studios, such as Mothra. Mothra, a massive, brightly-colored moth, first appeared on the silver screen in 1961, to protect the inhabitants of her island home from nuclear testing and greedy evildoers. Little more than a surface survey of the franchise has been written on Godzilla's flying adversary, delving nowhere nearly as deeply as the intensive studies of Godzilla. Although some writers applaud Mothra's unique place within the *kaijū eiga* genre, Tsutsui largely sums up the wider view of Mothra when he states: "Mothra repeatedly appears as a selfless goody-goody."[50] We intend to do justice to the Mothra franchise, providing a detailed examination of her relationship to our themes, in particular Mothra's inherent connection to nature and the franchise's unique use of music and sound to convey its environmental messaging.

Tōhō's main competitor Daiei produced the Gamera series, which has also received scant attention in the scholarly realm. The first Gamera film premiered in 1965, and the gargantuan turtle became a mainstay of *kaijū eiga* productions throughout the remainder of the 1960s and into the 1970s. Daiei pictures often suffered from constraints different than Tōhō films, especially in regards to financing, production values, and talent. For this reason among others, Gamera was widely rebuked by critics as a poor imitation of Godzilla. In his exhaustive study of Japanese science fiction films, Stuart

Galbraith sums up the wider view of Daiei's premier monster franchise: "The Gamera pictures were geared for the most undemanding of children in Japan."[51] As a result of the franchise's perceived weaknesses, no detailed examinations of the Gamera films have previously been written. With this information in mind, we embark on an eco-critical examination of the films of the Godzilla, Mothra, and Gamera franchises.

2

Nuclear Terror
and Radioactive Landscapes

The first Japanese giant monster films focused on one predominant environmental and social issue: nuclear testing and radioactive fallout. In this chapter we will examine the history of nuclear testing and the atomic bombings of Hiroshima and Nagasaki. We look at the science and history of nuclear weapons as well as the effect of atomic tests and radiation on nature and the environment. Finally, we will explore Japan's singular and conflicted relationship with harnessing the power of the atom—despite a total renunciation of warfare and nuclear weapons in the postwar period, Japan began relying extensively on nuclear power for peaceful purposes, in part due to its new alliance with the United States.

"Trinity," Hiroshima and Nagasaki

On the early midsummer morning of July 16, 1945, American, British, and Canadian scientists carried out the first successful atomic test in the history of the world on the high desert plateau of New Mexico.[1] The United States and its closest allies had harnessed the power of the atom, and they had every intention of using that terrifying power in a few short weeks. Although Nazi Germany lay defeated, World War II raged on, and Imperial Japan steadfastly resisted the ever-increasing might and matériel of the Allied forces.

This successful test, codenamed "Trinity," was the first tangible result of the Allied Manhattan Project to develop a functional atomic bomb. Trinity was a relatively low-yield fission device, producing a blast of a little under twenty kilotons, or about 2000 tons of TNT. The detonation left a crater in the earth five meters (twenty-five feet) deep in the center, and melted the desert sands around the blast site into a radioactive translucent grey-green glass, named "Trinitite." The first Trinitite fell to the ground immediately following the detonation as a molten rain, an atomic slag that gave scientists and soldiers alike their first experience with radioactive fallout. The mushroom cloud resulting from the world's first successful nuclear detonation reached just under thirteen kilometers (eight miles) in height, and the flash and blast caused by the explosion could be seen and felt hundreds of kilometers away.[2]

The U.S. government carefully orchestrated the timing of the test to occur before the start of the Potsdam Conference, set to begin just outside of Berlin in occupied Germany the following day. President Harry S Truman wanted to ensure the full functionality of the new weapon so he could inform both British Prime Minister Winston Churchill and Soviet Premier Joseph Stalin of the efficacy and availability of the atomic bomb.[3] At the same time, the American, British, and Nationalist Chinese governments issued an ultimatum to Japan promising its "prompt and utter destruction" without an immediate unconditional surrender.[4]

Despite the Allied ultimatum, the war continued. Although internal politics within Japan were far more complicated, with many senior politicians pushing for a negotiated peace against a resistant army general staff, to the Allies it seemed Japan had no interest in surrendering. President Truman was aware of a peace movement within the Japanese political establishment, but he questioned their sincerity and intentions. Even within the peace movement, few people supported the terms of the Potsdam Declaration— unconditional surrender was not an option even the Japanese peace instigators were willing to accept.[5]

Slightly less than three weeks after the successful Trinity test in the New Mexican desert, Truman authorized the U.S. military to unleash a "special bomb" against the Japanese.[6] Truman's goals were likely multi-tiered: first and foremost, he wanted to end the war as quickly and bloodlessly as possible; second, the president wanted to force Japan's surrender before the Soviet Union entered the war and launched a planned invasion of Japan's northernmost main island of Hokkaidō; finally, he would demonstrate the power of the atomic bomb to the entire world, with an eye toward the increasing American-Soviet tensions as the end of World War II developed into the simmering Cold War.

It is useful to examine a chronology of the final days of the Asia-Pacific War, including the atomic bombings, the Japanese surrender, and the beginning of the Allied Occupation. Although the atomic bombings and end of World War II reverberated around the globe, their impact was obviously magnified many times for the Japanese people themselves, especially the citizens of Hiroshima and Nagasaki. To date, Japan remains the only nation ever attacked by nuclear weapons, and the atomic scars on the Japanese psyche continue to influence Japanese society, politics, culture, and arts, including *kaijū eiga*.

On the morning of August 6, 1945, the U.S. Army Air Force B-29 "Superfortress" *Enola Gay* dropped an atomic bomb nicknamed "Little Boy" on the Japanese city of Hiroshima. Like Trinity, Little Boy was a simple fission device yielding approximately fifteen kilotons of explosive force, about seventy-five percent of the strength of the first nuclear test.[7] Unlike Trinity, however, Little Boy was a uranium-based weapon, compared to the plutonium-based bomb used in the test in New Mexico.[8] By utilizing different radioactive elements, the bomb's designers and creators could evaluate the efficacy and usefulness of both materials, even as a weapon during wartime.

Little Boy exploded in the air above Hiroshima, and the temperature at the center of the fireball instantly reached approximately 3800 degrees Celsius (over 7000 degrees Fahrenheit). The circle of immediate destruction radiated about two kilometers (one-and-a-quarter miles) from the epicenter of the blast, instantaneously incinerating thousands of men, women, and children, leveling concrete and wooden buildings alike, and obliterating the entire downtown core of central Hiroshima. Japan historian James McClain recounts the devastation that followed: "Radiation was everywhere. Firestorms ravaged the city, and moisture collecting on rising ash came back to earth as radioactive 'black rain.'"[9] Four hours after the explosion, a separate flight of B-29s equipped with cameras attempted to photograph what remained of Hiroshima, but the fires that still engulfed the city obscured it with heavy smoke.[10] No exact figures exist for the death toll of the Hiroshima bombing, but a conservative estimate places the number of lives lost at a minimum of 90,000, with a high estimation of approximately 166,000.[11]

Three days later, the Soviet Union declared war on Japan. While Soviet forces were pouring over Japan's Kwantung Army on the Asian mainland, the United States dropped a second atomic bomb.[12] At 11:01 a.m. that same day, August 9, 1945, the B-29 bomber *Bockscar* dropped an atomic bomb nicknamed "Fat Man" on the Japanese city of Nagasaki on the southernmost home island of Kyūshū. Fat Man was a plutonium-implosion style weapon, like the original Trinity device, and yielded slightly more than the original test—about twenty-one kilotons. Despite the higher yield, cloudy weather caused *Bockscar* to drop Fat Man over a kilometer off-target, and hills protected much of downtown Nagasaki from the fireball and shock wave, limiting the damage. However, the results of the second—and last—use of a nuclear weapon in wartime proved similarly catastrophic, and between 39,000 and 80,000 Japanese perished in the bombing.[13]

One question commonly asked surrounding the atomic bombings is: why Hiroshima and Nagasaki? Before the bombs were even fully developed, the U.S. military convened a "Target Committee" to determine the best sites for deploying the atomic bomb against Japan, should the need arise. The committee weighed several criteria when determining which cities to select, ranging from the size of the urban area, geography that would allow effective damage, major military headquarters and installations, and a variety of other military and psychological factors. In the end, the committee recommended that atomic bombs be used against the following Japanese cities: Kyoto, Hiroshima, Yokohama, Kokura, and Niigata.[14] The U.S. Secretary of War, Henry L. Stimson, convinced President Truman to order the removal of Kyoto from the target list, given its cultural, architectural, and historical significance. Truman ordered the military to remove Kyoto from the list, replacing it with Nagasaki, noting in his diary that the United States could not "drop that terrible bomb on the old capital [Kyoto] or the new [Tokyo]."[15]

With Kyoto saved from perdition by Stimson and Truman, Nagasaki was moved into the approved target list. When the *Enola Gay* lifted off from its airbase on Tinian Island near Guam on the morning of August 6th, Hiroshima's fate was not yet entirely sealed. Along with the *Enola Gay*, other B-29s reconnoitered the weather conditions above not only Hiroshima, but Kokura and Nagasaki as well. The aircrew of the *Enola Gay* received the weather reports from the other aircraft, and determined to strike Hiroshima.[16] Three days later, a similar series of events led to the salvation of Kokura and the destruction of Nagasaki. Kokura, located on the Straits of Shimonoseki between the southern island of Kyūshū and the main island of Honshū, was spared by cloudy weather and smoke from a nearby firebombing the prior day.[17] *Bockscar* diverted to nearby Nagasaki, which was still partially obscured by clouds, but not enough to save the B-29's secondary target from destruction.

Although the Japanese government and military had attempted to develop their own nuclear weaponry during the war, they were nonetheless shocked that the United States had succeeded where they had failed.[18] Even before the bombings the Japanese political elite saw the writing on the wall—they knew that defeat was inevitable—but they could not bring themselves to accept the Potsdam Declaration and allow any chance of the dismemberment of the imperial institution, the Japanese polity, or a foreign occupation of the home islands.[19] A combination of the bombings of Hiroshima and Nagasaki, as well as the Soviet declaration of war, forced the Japanese government to reconsider capitulation and offer the Allies their unconditional surrender.

The Japanese government signaled its surrender to the Allies on August 15, 1945. The Shōwa Emperor, better known in the West as Hirohito, cast the deciding vote in a supreme council meeting accepting the conditions of the Potsdam Declaration.[20] At noon on August 15th, the emperor spoke to the Japanese nation via a recorded radio message, known as the "Jewel Voice Broadcast," announcing the empire's unconditional surrender to the Allied Powers. In his speech, the emperor noted the destruction of Hiroshima and Nagasaki, asserting that the United States had employed "a new and most cruel bomb, the power of which to do damage is, indeed, incalculable, taking the toll of many innocent lives" and that the Japanese people must now "endure the unendurable" humiliation of defeat.[21] Japan signed the terms of surrender to the Allied forces on-board the battleship USS *Missouri*, anchored in Tokyo Bay, on September 2, 1945, paving the way for the Allied Occupation of Japan (1945–1952).

Castles, Dragons and Distant Isles

With the war concluded, the United States needed a new proving ground for its atomic weaponry. The U.S. military found its ideal test site at Bikini Atoll. Bikini, a small coral atoll in the Marshall Islands chain, was suitable for a variety of reasons: first, it was under American control, the military having seized it from the Japanese during the war; second, it had a small population that could be easily relocated; third, it was both remote and isolated, minimizing possible radioactive contamination of large population centers.[22]

The natural geography of Bikini made it ideal for a new series of nuclear tests. The United States, having already proved the effectiveness of atomic bomb strikes against land targets, wanted to test the deadliness of nuclear weapons on naval targets, particularly large concentrated fleets of warships. Bikini's extended coastline and geography provided both a safe anchorage for a large fleet of vessels, but also a shallow one—divers would easily be able to inspect submerged ships sunk as the result of any atomic tests. There is a longstanding connection between ships, nuclear testing, and monsters in *kaijū eiga*, so it is worth considering the U.S. atomic tests at Bikini Atoll in greater detail.

The U.S. military planned a series of three atomic bomb tests to take place in July 1946, almost exactly one year after the first successful Trinity test in New Mexico. The three planned tests were part of Operation Crossroads, which would assess naval vessels' resilience to atomic blasts deployed by various means. The first experiment, Able, would feature an atomic blast above the surface of the lagoon; the second test, Baker, would test a device suspended thirty meters (ninety feet) underwater beneath a target ship; the third planned blast, Charlie, would detonate a bomb placed deep underwater on the far side of Bikini's lagoon.

Before the Operation Crossroads tests could be carried out, a fleet needed to be assembled at Bikini Atoll. The U.S. Congress initially authorized the U.S. Navy to use up to thirty-three warships as floating "guinea pigs," but the military eventually outfitted ninety-four vessels as targets. In all, the U.S. Navy gathered a vast array of warships and noncombatant vessels—five battleships, two aircraft carriers, four cruisers, twelve destroyers, eight submarines, two oilers, nineteen attack transports, forty-one landing craft, and a floating dry-dock.[23]

Although a vast majority of the target ships deployed to Bikini were retired, mothballed, or otherwise surplus U.S. Navy vessels, the defeated Axis powers were also represented. Two Japanese warships and a solitary German one were steamed or towed to Bikini for Crossroads: the German heavy cruiser *Prinz Eugen*, and the Japanese battleship *Nagato* and cruiser *Sakawa*. There was little symbolism involved in the choice of *Prinz Eugen*.[24] When asked years later if he ever felt there was any deeper meaning attached to the use of his ship at Bikini, German sailor Otto Schötzow replied that *Prinz Eugen* "was tested to see which one is a better ship and which one will survive an atom bomb attack [...] one can be proud of being tested, of the durability of the material people built."[25] One can hardly disagree with Schötzow's assessment, according to some. David Bradley, American radiation monitor (and later congressman) wrote in his 1948 book *No Place to Hide* that the captured Nazi vessel was "graceful [and] beautiful [and] as sleek and cavalier a ship as ever sailed the seas."[26]

On the other hand, the selection of the *Nagato* was rife with symbolism for both the victorious Americans and the defeated Japanese. From a fleet of ten battleships that the Imperial Japanese Navy possessed at the outbreak of the war, the *Nagato* was the only remaining afloat when Japan surrendered in 1945. Mainly a bombed-out floating hulk when the Americans captured her in Tokyo Bay, the *Nagato* had once served as Admiral Yamamoto Isoroku's flagship as well as a major operational planning site for the Pearl Harbor attack. Maritime Archaeologist James P. Delgado opines on the use of the *Nagato* in the Crossroads tests: "The use of Japanese warships as atomic targets was a 'symbolic killing' of the enemy's ships with the same weapon that had forced his capitulation [...] [s]inking the same battleship [where Pearl Harbor was planned] with an atomic bomb now ritually 'destroyed' the Imperial Japanese Navy."[27]

The U.S. military utilized symbolism frequently during Japan's capitulation and subsequent occupation. During the Japanese surrender ceremony aboard the USS *Missouri*, the U.S. Navy displayed two American flags saturated with meaning: first, the very banner flying at the White House on the day of the Pearl Harbor attacks; and second, the ensign flown by Commodore Matthew Perry's infamous "black ships" when he forced Japan to open its doors to the West in 1853.[28] A few weeks after Japan's surrender, on September 27, 1945, U.S. General Douglas MacArthur, who had been appointed to oversee the occupation as the Supreme Commander for the Allied Powers (SCAP), posed with Emperor Hirohito for what became the most famous photograph of postwar Japan. MacArthur, meeting with the emperor in his own headquarters, wore a casual uniform and stood in a relaxed position, towering over the formally attired, statuesque emperor. According to Japan historian Andrew Gordon: "A master of the sparing and symbolic use of his own image [...MacArthur's photograph] conveyed the subordinate position of the Japanese state and people with shocking force to the entire population."[29]

The importance of sinking the *Nagato* during the Bikini tests cannot be overemphasized. The U.S. Navy went to great—indeed, extraordinary—lengths to make sure the *Nagato* would not founder before the nuclear tests. When American forces captured the *Nagato*, she was in shambles; after participating in several major naval engagements in 1944, the battleship was never fully repaired and instead consigned to coastal defense in Tokyo Bay, where U.S. Navy aircraft later bombed her in July 1945.[30] Several American support vessels were moored alongside the leaky *Nagato*, and American sailors supplemented her remaining Japanese crew for the long journey south to Bikini Atoll. "The Nasty Naggy," as the Americans stationed aboard called her, was a floating house-of-horrors: although she could make steam to propel herself, she could not supply her own running water or electricity; citizens of Tokyo were rounded up daily to remove garbage and debris scattered about the derelict before she departed, while others clamored alongside to beg for scraps; and, by far worst of all, her remaining crew were forced to wear gas masks in certain parts of the ship, for as many as a hundred dead Japanese sailors were left aboard, decomposing for over a year since the last American attack on the ship.[31]

Compared with his assessment of the *Prinz Eugen*, Bradley's description of the *Nagato* is decidedly derisive: "This many-storied, buttressed pile of junk looks as though it had been thrown together without plan or purpose out of odds and ends of American

The dilapidated battleship *Nagato* at anchor off Yokosuka in 1946, shortly before departing for Bikini Atoll. The *Nagato* was captured by the Allies at the conclusion of World War II and used as part of the "guinea pig" fleet for the Crossroads nuclear tests. The irradiated hulk of the battleship remains on the bottom of Bikini's lagoon (Naval History and Heritage Command, Archives Branch).

scrap iron."[32] Unlike other target ships at Bikini, the *Nagato* had very few instruments or test animals aboard and was only given a cursory examination by U.S. Navy divers after the tests. It would have been far easier for the U.S. Navy to simply scrap or scuttle the *Nagato*; on the way from Tokyo Bay to Enewetak and then Bikini, she ran out of fuel, blew a boiler, took on a heavy list to port, and needed to be towed by tugs for several days.[33] However, like a condemned prisoner on suicide watch, the *Nagato* was not allowed to die until the U.S. Navy conducted the execution.

To the United States, there was no use performing a symbolic extinguishing of Imperial Japan if it was kept secret, so the Crossroads tests were opened to the public, the press, and foreign nations. Over one hundred American journalists and ten foreign correspondents attended Crossroads, as well as official observers from several foreign nations, including the Soviet Union. Leading up to the tests in July 1946, hundreds if not thousands of articles appeared in newspapers, magazines, filmstrips, and radio broadcasts around the globe.[34] In fact, the hype surrounding the tests at Bikini Atoll turned the name itself into part of global popular culture—French engineer and designer Louis Réard chose to name his new swimsuit creation, announced to the world on July 5, 1946, after the irradiated Pacific isle, to the delight of beachgoers and swimming enthusiasts ever since.[35]

The first Crossroads test, Able, was carried out on July 1, 1946. Like at Hiroshima and Nagasaki a year prior, a B-29 dropped the atomic bomb, nicknamed "Gilda" (after the eponymous Rita Hayworth film) on Bikini Atoll. Gilda exploded at a height of just over 150 meters (500 feet) above the target fleet, sinking five ships and seriously damaging numerous others. However, for those expecting the instantaneous incineration of the entire armada, disappointment reigned. Some commentators were particularly disheartened that Bikini had not been reduced to "Nothing Atoll."[36] Although the U.S. Navy had not expected Gilda to vaporize the entire fleet, the results were nonetheless lackluster, and over one-quarter of the press corps present at the Able test departed before Baker later that month.

The Baker detonation proved far more unpredictable than the Able test. On July 25, 1946, the world's fifth nuclear device—and the first one placed underwater—detonated. The bomb was suspended thirty meters (ninety feet) underwater, beneath the hull of *LSM-60*, a mid-size amphibious assault craft. Baker generated a supersonic hydraulic shock wave that crushed the hulls of nearby ships, carving a crater ten meters (thirty feet) deep and 600 meters (2000 feet) wide in the bottom of the lagoon. Meanwhile, an expanding gas bubble created a dome of water that burst into the air like a geyser traveling over twice the speed of sound. The blast created a hollow column of water 1800 meters (6000 feet) tall and 600 meters (2000 feet) wide, spraying two million tons of seawater and sand into the air.[37]

Baker vaporized *LSM-60* instantly (not a single piece of the craft was ever located), and sank nine other vessels, including the Japanese battleship *Nagato*. Radioactive fallout from the spray, sand, and other detritus volleyed into the air by the explosion coated the floating remnants of the fleet. Following the Able test three weeks earlier, radiological monitors had determined that it was safe to re-enter the Bikini lagoon the afternoon of the test.[38] Baker would provide the U.S. Navy with a much more complex problem, for which they were wholly unprepared.

Operation Crossroads nuclear test carried out by the United States Navy at Bikini Atoll in July 1946. This photograph depicts the underwater Baker detonation from a distance of over five kilometers (three miles) away. The Japanese battleship *Nagato* is the large black silhouette positioned immediately to the right of the base of the water column (George Washington University, National Security Archive).

Although the officers overseeing Crossroads knew that water falling from any Baker-induced mushroom cloud would contaminate vessels, they did not expect the explosion to douse almost the entire target fleet.[39] Of the ninety-four vessels moored in Bikini Atoll for Crossroads, all but nine were either sunk or too badly irradiated to be salvaged. Navy personnel attempted to decontaminate the radioactive ships, but water, lye, intensive scrubbing and other extensive attempts all failed. The radiation would not dissipate. To make matters worse, the support vessels carrying the Crossroads staff (numbering some 42,000 military personnel, scientists, and civilians at its high-water mark), slowly became contaminated by the radioactive lagoon.

The fallout from Baker irradiated not only the "guinea pig" ships, but the plant and animal life of Bikini as well. U.S. Navy divers recovered a surgeonfish that was so radioactive it was able to leave an X-ray image of itself on metal plates, without the normally required machine. Despite intensive efforts to neutralize the radioactive fallout, Admiral W.H.P. Blandy, the Crossroads commander, was forced to end the operation and cancel the final planned Charlie test.[40]

The United States military continued to test and refine nuclear weapons into the 1950s at Bikini Atoll, other sites throughout the Pacific, and in the western United States. The American atomic monopoly ended on August 29, 1949, when the Soviet Union detonated its first nuclear weapon, nicknamed "Joe 1" in the West, after Soviet Premier Joseph Stalin. With the ever-increasing tensions of the escalating Cold War, from the Berlin airlift to the start of the Korean War, the pace of nuclear weapons testing increased dramatically in the 1950s. At the same time, the explosive power of atomic energy increased exponentially, with the development of thermonuclear weapons, also known as hydrogen bombs (or H-bombs).[41]

The most powerful H-bomb test ever conducted by the United States was carried out at Bikini Atoll on March 1, 1954. The second test of Operation Castle, it is most commonly called Castle Bravo. H-bombs like Castle Bravo were, quite literally, an entirely different order of nuclear weapon than the relatively simple atomic bombs used and tested less than a decade earlier. Atomic bombs, like Hiroshima, Nagasaki, and Operation Crossroads, relied on nuclear fission (the breaking apart of atoms) to create their explosive power. Contrariwise, Castle Bravo and other thermonuclear weapons depend on a primary nuclear fission detonation to set off a secondary hydrogen fusion (the joining together of atoms) explosion, like the sun itself. Unlike atomic bombs, thermonuclear weapons have no theoretical limit to their destructive potential, and for this reason many of the original scientists employed at the Manhattan Project in the creation of the atomic bomb opposed the later development of H-bombs.[42]

The scientists responsible for the design of Castle Bravo were shocked by the explosive magnitude of the weapon. Although they predicted the yield of the device to be approximately five megatons, the bomb yielded an explosive force of fifteen megatons of TNT, tripling their previous estimates and unleashing a blast more than 1000 times that of Little Boy when it was dropped on Hiroshima. The detonation instantly gouged a massive crater in Bikini's reef, and the resulting fireball was almost five kilometers (three miles) in diameter.[43]

The miscalculations over Castle Bravo's yield had disastrous consequences, as nuclear fallout in the form of radioactive coral vaporized by the blast began to fall as a snow-like atomic ash on nearby islands and vessels. Rongelap, a populated island about 160 kilometers (100 miles) away from Bikini, experienced a loud explosion followed by ground tremors a few minutes later. Within hours, a radioactive powder poured down from the heavens contaminating the drinking water and food, while children played in the accumulating fallout. When the islanders were evacuated the following day, many already had severe burns and were beginning to experience hair-loss, both signs of acute radiation exposure.[44]

Slightly closer to the blast, Castle Bravo highly irradiated the Japanese trawler *Daigo Fukuryū Maru* (more commonly known as the *Lucky Dragon No. 5*).[45] Like on Rongelap, the fishing boat was coated in radioactive fallout in the form of an ash-like powder, material that had been forced up from Bikini's coral reef and carried great distances in the upper atmosphere by the prevailing winds.[46] Ōishi Matakichi, a crewman aboard the *Lucky Dragon No. 5*, later described what the crew experienced that morning: "A yellow flash poured through the porthole [...] bridge, sky and sea burst into view, painted in flaming colors [...] white particles were falling on us, just like sleet."[47] Later that evening, the ship's crew began to notice burns and hair-loss. When the *Lucky Dragon No. 5* reached port two weeks later, a Geiger counter (a device used for measuring radiation) detected radiological contamination emanating from the vessel from nearly thirty meters (100 feet) away. A few weeks later, the trawler's radio operator died from liver complications brought on in part by his treatment for radiation poisoning.[48]

Even today, many decades after Castle Bravo and scores of other nuclear tests in the Pacific, many islands remain uninhabitable due to the residual radiation from years of nuclear testing. Nuclear testing peaked in 1962 and gradually declined throughout the remainder of the Cold War era, with the five acknowledged nuclear powers—the United States, the Soviet Union (later the Russian Federation), the United Kingdom, France, and the People's Republic of China—all agreeing to cease nuclear testing in the 1990s. The cavalier attitude of the United States toward H-bomb testing and the resulting radiation is perhaps best encapsulated in a statement made by General Curtis LeMay, the former commander of the U.S. Strategic Air Command, in 1968: "I've seen a film of Bikini Atoll after twenty nuclear tests, and the fish are all back in the lagoons, the coconut trees are growing coconuts, the guava bushes have fruit on them, the birds are back [...] [the crustaceans] get minerals from the soil, I guess, through their shells, and the land crabs are a little bit hot [...but] the rats are bigger, fatter, and healthier than they ever were before."[49] Despite LeMay's "reassurances," the native residents of Bikini Atoll have never been able to return to their island, and radiological contamination of the atoll's plant and animal life has only slowly dissipated over a long period of time, still remaining at unsafe levels.[50]

Ships and Monsters

The cases of both the *Nagato* and the *Lucky Dragon No. 5* exemplify the association of nuclear weapons with ships in Japanese monster cinema. In their respective films, Godzilla, Mothra, and Gamera all sink numerous Japanese vessels. Moreover, the origins of all three monsters are steeped in nuclear testing imagery and history. In *Gojira* (*Godzilla*) (1954), Godzilla destroys a Japanese fishing trawler (nearly identical to the *Lucky Dragon No. 5*) in the opening scene of the film after being awakened and irradiated by nuclear testing. In *Mosura* (*Mothra*) (1961), the titular monster crushes a ship while swimming from her island home, a place ecologically devastated by atomic tests, to Japan. Finally, in *Daikaijū Gamera* (1965), an accidental nuclear blast awakens the giant turtle Gamera; he then sinks a Japanese icebreaker on a scientific expedition in the Arctic Ocean. Throughout the *kaijū eiga* genre, monsters destroy legions of ships, submersibles, and submarines. The propensity of Japanese monster cinema to reenact the destruction of Japanese vessels indicates the topic's significance. Because of this, we delve into both the role of the *Nagato* and the *Lucky Dragon No. 5* in the history of nuclear testing and monster cinema in Japan.

Today, both the *Nagato* and the *Lucky Dragon No. 5* serve as monuments to the nuclear testing conducted at Bikini Atoll. The battered hull of the *Nagato* lies submerged in the Bikini lagoon, where it has become a popular diving site for intrepid tourists.[51] James P. Delgado made several dives on the sunken warship, examining the wreckage in a way never performed by U.S. Navy divers after the battleship sank unnoticed in the night, two days after the Baker test in 1946. Delgado describes his final dive on the *Nagato*: "Like other ships with famous pasts that served as settings for great and terrible events, the *Nagato* has an almost ghostly presence. World War II, with all its drastic consequences, began for Japan on the *Nagato*. In certain measure, it also ended there."[52] Although the *Nagato* is now a popular dive site, the interior of the ship remains largely inaccessible, and divers are limited to exploring the exterior of the sunken battleship. The vessel sank slowly after taking on seawater following the Baker test, and lies upside-down in about fifty-five meters (180 feet) of water, with the main superstructure lying to one side of the capsized warship.

As discussed in Chapter 1, Yoshikuni Igarashi posits one possible explanation for Godzilla's origin in his book *Bodies of Memory*—the monster represents the ghosts of Japan's war dead returning home.[53] Igarashi presents a compelling case: Godzilla and the war dead he embodies are enraged and irradiated by U.S. nuclear testing in the Pacific, particularly at Bikini Atoll; the war dead then return to wreak havoc on Japan. The souls of the war dead target postwar Japan due to the country's newfound alliance with the United States. Here, Igarashi presents both a salient and politically charged interpretation of *Godzilla*.

Yet what deceased soldiers were irradiated by U.S. nuclear testing and might have a vendetta against the Japanese people? The answer lies on the bottom of Bikini lagoon, in the bowels of the battleship *Nagato*. Forgotten during the war and forsaken by their homeland, the human remains of as many as one hundred Japanese sailors remain entombed within the hull of the warship unceremoniously sunk by American atomic testing. George Culley, a quartermaster on the U.S. Navy cruiser *Topeka* who sailed on the *Nagato* during her final voyage to Bikini, recounted years later that the crew found a compartment "that was filled with dead Japanese [...] the crew had to wear gas masks, but [...] the stench was too overpowering and they had to seal up the compartment."[54] The sailors had likely been killed during U.S. airstrikes near the end of the war, and in the turbulent weeks that followed had been forgotten, never provided with the honorable funerals they deserved. No one seemed to care about the war dead left aboard the *Nagato*'s battered hulk—who but these lost souls would fit better into Igarashi's allegory? If any of Japan's war dead could be directly connected to U.S. nuclear testing in the Pacific, and Godzilla's wrath when attacking Japan, it can only be the irradiated, entombed remains of the unfortunate Japanese sailors trapped aboard the *Nagato*.

We can carry this analogy one step further. Over the course of Tōhō's franchise, Godzilla was not only irradiated by atomic testing, he is attracted to nuclear material in all its forms.[55] What lured Godzilla to Tokyo Bay? In November 1945, the American occupation forces destroyed a wide array of Japan's "war-related" material, including two RIKEN laboratory cyclotrons, devices used for nuclear experimentation and the enrichment of uranium.[56] After cutting apart the apparatuses with blowtorches, the Americans dumped the pieces into Tokyo Bay. Later, outrage from the international community forced American officials to release a statement of regret, but not until after dealing a blow to Japanese scientific endeavors.[57] Perhaps Godzilla was not only created by American nuclear testing at Bikini Atoll, but also drawn toward Japan's capital by the dismembered cyclotrons submerged on the bottom of Tokyo Bay.

Unlike the subtextual analysis of the *Nagato* and the RIKEN laboratory cyclotrons, an overt reference to the *Lucky Dragon No. 5* incident appears in *Godzilla*. The film's creators used the furor surrounding the incident as inspiration. In fact, "seizing upon the clamor over the fallout-poisoned fishermen, [*Godzilla* producer] Tanaka Tomoyuki used newspaper clippings about the *Lucky Dragon* incident to show [Tōhō executives] that the time was right for a gigantic monster, stirred from an eons-long sleep by rampant atomic testing, to come ashore and trample Tokyo."[58]

In the opening scene of the 1954 film, Japanese sailors aboard a fishing boat, the

The *Lucky Dragon No. 5* at an exhibition hall in Tokyo's Yumenoshima Park in April 2017. The infamous irradiation of the trawler by the Castle Bravo thermonuclear test provided inspiration for Tanaka Tomoyuki during the development of *Godzilla*. The fishing boat has been on display since 1976 (photograph courtesy Keri Fisher).

Glory No. 5, are exposed to a blinding flash of light before their ship catches fire and burns. Like the actual fishermen aboard the *Lucky Dragon No. 5*, the crew of the *Glory No. 5* see what could be described as "the sun rising in the west."[59] At first, the viewer is uncertain if the flash is indeed a nuclear blast, discovering only later that Godzilla is responsible for the ship's conflagration. In an earlier draft of *Godzilla's* script, director Honda Ishirō planned an even more direct connection to the *Lucky Dragon*—having the irradiated, derelict trawler drift back into port "like the death ship in *Nosferatu*."[60] However, Tōhō's executives found that version to be *too* provocative. The timing of the film, released later the same year as the *Lucky Dragon* incident, as well as the similarities between the trawlers and their names, reveal the direct connection between nuclear testing, Godzilla, and the destruction of the fishing ship—both the concrete and the fictitious.

Compared to the remains of the Imperial Japanese Navy's last battleship in the shallows of Bikini lagoon, the *Lucky Dragon No. 5* serves as a far more accessible memorial to the human cost and environmental toll paid for the pursuit of atomic and thermonuclear testing. After continuing to serve as a fishing boat for a few years under a new name, the trawler was almost scrapped in 1967, before being restored as the centerpiece of an exhibition on nuclear testing in 1976. Since then, the *Lucky Dragon No. 5*, along with other artifacts belonging to the ship and its crew, has been on display to the public at an exhibition hall in Yumenoshima Park, in Tokyo's Kōtō ward. Tourists and schoolchildren frequently visit the site and have decorated the hall with thousands of origami cranes, as a prayer for peace and an end to nuclear testing.[61] Nearby, in the museum's book shop, a model Godzilla stands guard like a silent sentinel.[62]

Nuclear Power and Nuclear Protests

Given Japan's intimate and unique experience with nuclear weaponry, one might think that the Japanese people would shun nuclear energy in all its forms. However, the opposite is true. Although Japan eventually banned nuclear weapons and all military uses of atomic power, in the postwar period the Japanese built an extensive and powerful system of nuclear reactors to provide energy to the war-torn nation. Contrary to popular misconceptions, the anti-nuclear weapon movement did not begin in earnest in Japan immediately following the atomic bombings in August 1945. The Allied Occupation lasted from the 1945 surrender until April 28, 1952, when the Treaty of San Francisco restored Japan's sovereignty. During the occupation, a military government led by General MacArthur's SCAP administration ruled Japan. The United States and the Allied nations assigned SCAP with several duties, ranging from demilitarizing Japan to democratizing the Japanese polity, including drafting a new postwar constitution for the Japanese people that was promulgated and adopted in 1947. However, part of SCAP's military occupation of Japan also included censorship of art, film, news, literature, and other media.[63]

SCAP's censorship campaign included a ban on Japanese media depicting the atomic bombings of Hiroshima and Nagasaki or publishing interviews with survivors. Early in the occupation, SCAP sent the Japanese government a "Memorandum Concerning a Press Code for Japan," that stipulated what information would be censored from Japanese media for the duration of the occupation.[64] Among other things, the code banned nearly all discussions of the atomic bombings and the human casualties caused by radioactivity associated with the nuclear events and resulting infernos. Although some local papers in Hiroshima published prose and poetry on the bombing, most writings on the subject were severely suppressed.[65] One historian of the Japanese anti-nuclear movement notes that the "censorship was so effective that ordinary Japanese people were prevented from learning about the real horror of the atomic bombing."[66]

Despite stringent censorship, some nascent anti-nuclear movements did begin to appear in Japan by the early 1950s. For the most part, Japanese anti-nuclear politics in the early postwar era centered on petition movements as their primary locus of support. From 1950 through 1953, peace groups and labor unions gathered over six million signatures in Japan in support of the Stockholm Appeal, an initiative launched by French physicist Frédéric Joliot-Curie that called for an absolute, worldwide ban on nuclear weapons.[67] In 1951, a University of Kyoto student group created the world's first atomic bomb exhibit, featuring images of the destruction of Hiroshima and Nagasaki as well as victims of radiation poisoning, which began its run near Kyoto Station and later traveled throughout the greater Kyoto and Osaka areas.[68]

The anti-nuclear movement developed in the years that followed thanks to two events: first, the end of the Allied Occupation and its censorship; and second, the previously discussed Castle Bravo nuclear test and resulting irradiation of the *Lucky Dragon No. 5*. In August 1952, mere weeks after the last occupation forces were required to depart, Japanese newspapers began running articles and special issues on the true horrors of the atomic bombings. Finally unleashed from SCAP's censorship, the *Asahi Gurahu* (*Asahi Picture News*) published photographs of the destroyed cities and their victims.[69]

On the seventh anniversary of the atomic bombing of Hiroshima, August 6, 1952, the film *Genbaku no Ko* (*Children of the Atomic Bomb*) premiered in Japan.[70] The film focuses not on the events of the atomic bombing itself, but on its aftermath and the effects of radiation on the survivors. Among other notable members of the cast and crew, the film was scored by Ifukube Akira, only two years before his work on *Godzilla*. Ifukube's work on *Children of the Atomic Bomb* adumbrated the similar anti-nuclear messages presented in the original Godzilla film.

The Castle Bravo detonation and the irradiation of the *Lucky Dragon No. 5* pushed the Japanese anti-nuclear movement into overdrive in 1954. The news of the trawler's radioactivity and the crew's radiation sickness hit Japanese newspapers two days after the ship returned to port in March 1954, when the *Yomiuri Shinbun* (*Yomiuri News*) scooped the story.[71] The following day, the *Asahi Shinbun* (*Asahi News*) declared that Japan had now been victimized by the atomic bomb for a third time, asserting: "Twenty-three members of the [*Lucky Dragon No. 5's*] crew are the victims of the third atomic disaster in Japan."[72]

The Castle Bravo calamity also led to a food crisis in Japan, after the Ministry of Health and Welfare determined that 856 Japanese fishing vessels were exposed to radiation from the test and irradiated tuna and other seafood entered Japan's food chain. Geiger counters were used at Tokyo's Tsukiji and other fish markets, and approximately seventy-five tons of tuna were confiscated and destroyed by the authorities.[73] Initially, the Japanese government believed that the radiation could be washed from the seafood making it safe to consume, but a Japanese research vessel soon discovered radioactive contamination in the organs of many fish caught in the South Pacific.[74] The price of tuna rapidly plunged, as millions of Japanese refused to consume seafood potentially contaminated by Castle Bravo's fallout. For a time, even the emperor foreswore consuming the fish.[75]

Strident anti-nuclear movements began to appear throughout Japan in the toxic political fallout that followed the Castle Bravo crisis. As the Japanese rainy season in the spring of 1954 carried radiation-laced downpours throughout Japan, the winds of change followed.[76] Like the fledgling Japanese anti-nuclear movement in the early 1950s, the response to Castle Bravo also appeared in the form of petition movements. After the establishment of several local and regional petition groups throughout Japan, the national "Petition Council against Atomic and Hydrogen Bombs" coalesced in August 1954. Within weeks of the Petition Council's first meeting that month, over ten million Japanese submitted petitions by early September. By the end of 1954, over twenty million signatures had been gathered, and by the summer of 1955 the number collected reached thirty million—over one-third of Japan's population at the time.[77]

The potent political force of the Petition Council led to the adoption of the "Three Principles of Atomic Energy" by the Japanese government. The petitioners did not reject nuclear power in all its forms, only its military and destructive uses. The thoroughly pro-science "Three Principles" directed that all Japanese nuclear research, development, and use should be conducted in accordance with the principles of openness, democracy, and independence.[78] The Japanese did not shun all nuclear power, and in fact embraced it as a form of peaceful, abundant energy.

The Japanese Diet passed the government's first budget for nuclear power research in March 1954, allocating ¥235 million for the project. Shortly thereafter, largely as a result of the petition movement, the government formally adopted the "Three Principles" in Japan's Atomic Energy Basic Law.[79] At the same time, President Eisenhower's administration in the United States was conducting an international public relations campaign, known as "Atoms for Peace," promoting the non-war uses of nuclear power and contributing to the Japanese government's decision to pursue an ambitious atomic energy program.[80] Japan's first test reactor went online in 1957, and the country quickly constructed nuclear reactors throughout the archipelago. By the early 21st century, Japan was operating fifty-four of the world's 442 nuclear power plants, providing approximately 30 percent of the nation's electric power.[81]

In November 1954, *Godzilla* premiered in Japan, less than a decade after the atomic bombings of Hiroshima and Nagasaki, and following scores of nuclear and hydrogen bomb tests in the Pacific. When the first *kaijū eiga* debuted, the Japanese anti-nuclear petition movement was rapidly expanding, reaching a fever pitch the following year. Given this background, it becomes easy to see why a monster film about a radioactive dinosaur devastating Tokyo would play to the nuclear fears of the Japanese audience at that time, and why the film's producers utilized *Godzilla* to convey an environmental message to a mainstream audience.

3

Godzilla, Nature and Nuclear Revenge

On November 3, 1954, Japanese cinema changed forever.[1] A new form of science fiction horror film emerged from the social ether of postwar Japan—*Godzilla,* the original Japanese giant monster movie. *Godzilla* unleashed the potent force of *kaijū eiga* on not only Japan but on the entire movie-going world. Thanks to *Godzilla's* success, Japanese monster films—and their common underlying thread of environmental and ecological commentary—reached a global audience.

In this chapter, we first provide a brief overview of the original *Godzilla,* both to properly situate the film and to explain some of the differences between it and its more widely known American iteration *Godzilla, King of the Monsters.* We will examine the original film's narrative anti-nuclear commentary and other visual environmental cues. Finally, we will analyze *Godzilla's* soundtrack. The music, by composer Ifukube Akira, along with the sound design reinforce the film's strong science versus nature motifs as well as its connection to environmental messaging. In *Godzilla on My Mind,* William Tsutsui asserts: "Some students of environmental studies have begun to reflect on science fiction films from an ecological standpoint, which certainly might be a revealing way of examining the Godzilla series."[2] We agree.

A Monster Is Born, a Legend Arises

Godzilla's success was not preordained. Instead, the film's critical acclaim and enduring appeal developed as a direct result of the insight and ingenuity of the monster's creator, Tōhō's young up-and-coming producer, Tanaka Tomoyuki. According to Godzilla's origin myth, which is recounted in numerous publications, Tanaka conceived of Godzilla somewhere over the South Pacific on a dispirited flight home from Indonesia in the spring of 1954.[3] Tōhō Studios gave Tanaka a tall order—after the collapse of his prior project, he had six short months and a budget of slightly over ¥60 million (approximately $175,000 in 1954 U.S. dollars) to produce a box office hit.[4]

Tanaka later avowed that his epiphany was a moment of true inspiration: "The thesis was very simple. What if a dinosaur sleeping in the Southern Hemisphere had been awakened and transformed into a giant by the bomb? What if it attacked Tokyo?"[5]

Despite Tanaka's claim, in reality *Godzilla*'s plot involved only a sprinkling of the truly original, with a great heaping scoop of elements borrowed from other science fiction and monster films. In addition to the obvious references to *King Kong*, Tanaka also drew from other more recent films, in particular *The Beast from 20,000 Fathoms* (1953). The true tale is therefore less one of total inspiration and more one of amalgamation and adaptation, but the result nevertheless produced a masterpiece in its own right.

Tanaka chose the working title "The Giant Monster from 20,000 Miles Beneath the Sea" for his project long before any concrete plans were in place. Next, Tanaka met with Tōhō executives and convinced them that the time was right to produce his film—he even included newspaper clippings of the Castle Bravo test and *Lucky Dragon No. 5* incident (discussed in Chapter 2) to bolster his pitch. Tōhō sent Tanaka to meet with Tsuburaya Eiji, their special effects maestro, to determine if the studio had the technical wherewithal to produce the film. After meeting with Tsuburaya and selecting Honda Ishirō to direct, Tanaka convinced Tōhō to greenlight the film in April 1954, under the new codename "Project G."[6]

Special effects director Tsuburaya initially planned to bring Godzilla to life through the use of stop-motion animation, like the great Kong. However, Tōhō did not have the infrastructure or staff to feasibly produce these special effects in any reasonable amount of time; Tōhō's executives demanded that the film debut before the end of the year. Faced with this conundrum, Tsuburaya decided to work with rubber monster costumes and utilize Tōhō's extensive expertise in model construction instead.[7] Although the use of suitmation and puppetry were not Tsuburaya's first choices, they nonetheless found their roots in traditional Japanese dramatic arts and proved effective.[8]

As the project moved forward, Tōhō needed to devise a name for their new monster. Several conflicting stories exist surrounding the inception of the name "Godzilla," and Tōhō has never officially confirmed the origin of the monster's name. First and foremost, it is important to note that in the original Japanese, Godzilla is more appropriately transcribed as "Gojira." According to numerous recollections and assessments, Tōhō selected the name Gojira as a portmanteau of the Japanese words *gorira* (gorilla) and *kujira* (whale). Another tale ascribes the moniker to a burly Tōhō employee transferred to the irradiated dinosaur as an inside joke, but according to director Honda's widow this apocryphal story is likely more fiction than fact.[9]

Regardless of its exact origins, the name stuck, and it became "Godzilla" in English thanks to the transcribing style popular in the 1950s. Tsutsui notes: "That Godzilla sounds so appropriate in English, evoking the grandeur, mystery, and saurian nature of the monster, was more the result of dumb luck than shrewd planning."[10] Indeed, before *Godzilla, King of the Monsters* was released in the United States in 1956, there was no standardized way to transcribe the original Japanese name, and eminent Japanologist Donald Richie chose to render the monster's name as "Gojilla" in his 1954 *Japan Times* review of the original film.[11]

Tsuburaya Eiji brought in his old colleague Toshimitsu Teizō to construct the original Godzilla costume based on the drawings of Watanabe Akira. The costume melded characteristics of three dinosaurs: the Tyrannosaurus, the Iguanodon, and the Stegosaurus.[12] The final suit weighed in at 100 kilograms (220 pounds), and featured alligator-textured skin that resembled the keloid scars prevalent among survivors of the atomic bombings. In addition to the full suit, Toshimitsu also designed and built a puppet, to be used for close-up shots of the monster and his radioactive breath.[13]

Principal photography for *Godzilla* began in August 1954, only three months before the film's release. Honda and Tsuburaya shot all of *Godzilla*'s footage in just over two months, leaving only a few weeks for editing and post-production to complete the finished film.[14] In the end, Tōhō's gamble paid off, and *Godzilla* proved to be a runaway critical and commercial success. Big things have small beginnings—who would have guessed that under such circumstances a cultural icon would emerge to take Japan and later the world by storm and become one of the most recognized movie franchises of all time?

Big Green Monster—Godzilla *(1954)*

As we discussed in Chapter 1, scholars and fans have pondered *Godzilla* since the film's debut. The monster Godzilla has been widely analyzed and dissected by academics, critics, and other writers over the several decades since the first picture premiered in 1954. Having already provided an overview of many of the interpretations expressed, we tackle the film's environmental commentary and consider how the soundtrack contributes to this theme

Godzilla begins with a shot of the glittering Tōhō logo, to the ominous sounds of the monster's heavy footfalls.[15] The title card quickly glides up to the center of the screen, with Godzilla's now universally recognized roar in accompaniment. The stomping and bellows continue as the credits begin, eventually accompanied by composer Ifukube Akira's March theme. The credits fade to the wake of a ship at sea, the *Eiko-maru* (*Glory No. 5*). The fishermen on the boat see a blinding flash, the sea begins to froth, and a wave of radiation pours over the crewmembers as the *Glory No. 5* erupts into flame and sinks. As we discussed in Chapter 2, this opening sequence directly corresponds to the accidental irradiation of the *Lucky Dragon No. 5* by American nuclear testing at Bikini Atoll. From its very first scene, *Godzilla* therefore reveals its sober and powerful anti-nuclear commentary.

Ogata Hideto (Takarada Akira), working for a marine salvage company, receives a phone call from the coast guard informing him of the *Glory No. 5*'s loss, forcing him to cancel his date with Yamane Emiko (Kōchi Momoko).[16] The coast guard sends a second ship to investigate the steamer's loss; it meets a fate similar to the previous one. Not only do these scenes mimic the irradiation of the *Lucky Dragon No. 5*, they also visually remind the viewer of Japan's heavy wartime losses and environmental degradation. During the war, Allied forces sank approximately 80 percent of Japan's entire seagoing fleet and the country's landscape itself was terribly scarred.[17] Some survivors are rescued from the sunken ship, having enough time to recount their tale before the third boat succumbs to the same fate as well. The source of the destruction remains a mystery to the viewer and the film's characters.

Meanwhile, on nearby Ōdo Island, the villagers consider the repeated shipwrecks. One of the lost fishing boat's crew washes ashore. After hearing the fisherman's story and witnessing the island's fisheries completely depleted, a village elder declares:

"Godzilla must have done it."[18] A helicopter arrives, carrying journalist Hagiwara (Sakai Sachio) to report on the continued crisis.[19] That night, the Ōdo Islanders perform a ritual Shintō-inspired exorcism ceremony (wearing masks strongly reminiscent of Nō theater) while the elder tells Hagiwara of the island's Godzilla legend.[20] He recounts that in the old days, a monster from the sea would come on land to feed on humans, and the islanders would sacrifice girls to appease it. Here, we see a connection between Godzilla and mythology—in the form of the Ōdo Island legend—as well as with earlier monster cinema, particularly the similar ideas of female sacrifice depicted in *King Kong*. Furthermore, the trope of female sacrifice to appease powerful monsters hints that the feminine possesses some power in tune with nature that the masculine lacks, an idea that becomes more apparent in the films of the Mothra franchise discussed in later chapters.

A violent storm strikes Ōdo Island during the night and Godzilla wades ashore. In a particularly interesting shot, the winds and rain shake the trees and *torii* gates of the island's Shintō shrine, providing in a single shot a visual connection between the approaching monster, nature, and Japanese mythology. The villagers hear Godzilla's footfalls (but they still do not see him), and the storm and an unseen force destroy seventeen homes and Hagiwara's helicopter; nine villagers also perish. Like the unseen forces of nature, Godzilla too possesses a hidden destructive presence.

Representatives from Ōdo Island travel to Tokyo to present their case for disaster relief to the Japanese Diet. The villagers raise concern about the mysterious force—more than just an ordinary typhoon—and Professor Yamane Kyōhei (Shimura Takashi), Emiko's father and an eminent paleontologist, testifies. The Diet authorizes Prof. Yamane to lead an investigative team to Ōdo Island to ascertain the true cause of the growing list of disasters. On their journey to the island, Ogata and Emiko discuss her betrothed, the reclusive scientist Dr. Serizawa Daisuke (Hirata Akihiko), adding an emotionally complex love-triangle to the film's plot. Visually, the scene harkens back once more to *King Kong*, notably the shipboard flirtation sequences between Ann Darrow and Jack Driscoll.

The team arrives on Ōdo Island, where Yamane and the other members discover signs of radiation, giant footprints, and a trilobite, a creature long-believed extinct. The hamlet's watchman begins to sound the alarm, and the investigation team and villagers scramble up into the hills to see the monster. As the group approaches the summit, Godzilla peers over the mountain roaring and everyone scatters. Godzilla returns to the sea, and Yamane and his team return to Tokyo to make their report.

Prof. Yamane presents his case to the Diet: Godzilla is an ancient dinosaur, an unknown intermediary between terrestrial and aquatic creatures, disturbed by "recent experimental nuclear detonations."[21] Debate erupts in the Diet, with a stodgy conservative legislator declaring that Yamane's information should be kept secret, and a seemingly left-wing female representative denouncing him for keeping vital information from public eyes. The bickering continues and insults fly. Maybe this scene simply showcases political differences in Japan in the postwar era, or perhaps it is a critique of Japan's recent "democratization" and nascent party politics.

Newspapers report the creation of a task force to counter Godzilla; the number of ships lost to the monster increases to seventeen. On a train, a woman complains to two fellow passengers: "Contaminated tuna and radioactive fallout, and now this Godzilla to top it off!"[22] The passengers continue to discuss what would happen if Godzilla entered Tokyo Bay. One states: "I guess I will have to find a shelter again soon," while the other replies, "Not the shelters again! That stinks!"[23] Here, the film directly positions Godzilla in relation to past events in Japan, reinforcing his monstrosity and impending horror. The film directly references the furor surrounding the *Lucky Dragon No. 5* incident, from contaminated seafood to nuclear fallout. Next, *Godzilla* provides a clear connection to the terror and deprivations of the war years, and the use of shelters during the widespread Allied bombings of Japan.

The Japanese Self-Defense Forces (JSDF) initiate a naval campaign to destroy Godzilla by dropping depth charges in the sea around Ōdo Island. Prof. Yamane, clearly depressed, tells his daughter Emiko that Godzilla should be studied, not destroyed. Later, he is called to the counter-Godzilla headquarters, where government officials ask him how Godzilla can be defeated. Yamane demurs: "Godzilla absorbed massive amounts of atomic radiation but still survived."[24] Emiko and the journalist Hagiwara travel to see Dr. Serizawa—Emiko to speak with him about her relationship with Ogata, Hagiwara to interview him about Godzilla for his newspaper. Hagiwara questions Serizawa about his current research, implying that it may be quite useful in Japan's fight against Godzilla, but Serizawa refuses to divulge any information. After Hagiwara leaves, Serizawa demonstrates his "oxygen-destroyer" to Emiko on a fish-filled aquarium; it is a device capable of rapidly killing underwater creatures. Before she leaves, Serizawa demands that Emiko keep the device secret, fearing that it will fall into the wrong hands. What non-destructive purpose such an invention could possibly have is left unanswered.

Godzilla emerges in Tokyo Bay. The JSDF open fire while civilians flee the city. Prof. Yamane, Ogata, and Emiko watch Godzilla's rampage through the city from a nearby hill. In a scene strongly mirroring *King Kong*, Godzilla derails a commuter train. He picks one of the train cars up in his mouth before tossing it to the ground. He continues to smash several buildings and bridges before returning to the bay.

International researchers arrive to assist the Japanese, and a government official declares that a massive electrified fence will be constructed along the coast; the military hopes to electrocute Godzilla.[25] A stirring sequence shows the JSDF forces deploying to construct defenses and prepare the giant barrier to keep the monster out of Tokyo. Certainly, a case can be made that Godzilla in this moment represents the United States—during the war, American forces consistently overwhelmed Japanese bases and fortifications in a series of island-hopping battles throughout the Pacific.[26] Before the atomic bombings, Japan was busy preparing a defense of the home islands from the planned final American invasion, codenamed Operation Downfall. In *Godzilla*, the JSDF must prepare Japan against an invasion by a monster created by American nuclear testing at Bikini Atoll, an island captured from the Japanese during that very same island-hopping campaign. As Chon Noriega notes, "the films transfer onto Godzilla the role of the United States in order to symbolically re-enact a problematic United States-Japan relationship that includes atomic war, occupation, and thermo-nuclear tests."[27]

Back at the Yamane residence, a dejected Prof. Yamane returns home, declaring: "All they can think about is killing Godzilla, why can't they try to study him from a radiological perspective?"[28] Ogata disagrees with Yamane, "Isn't Godzilla a product of the atomic bomb that still haunts many of us Japanese?"[29] After Yamane storms out, a radio bulletin announces that Godzilla has been spotted and the electric fence is being charged. Intriguingly, a close-up shot of songbirds confined in a birdcage dominates the screen as the radio announcer makes his pronouncement. Could there be some subtle environmental message here? We shall return to this question shortly.

Godzilla makes landfall; he immediately rips through the defensive electrical barrier, completely unharmed. Like the doomed sailors and soldiers of Japan's maritime empire during the Asia-Pacific War, Godzilla—like the United States military's island-hopping campaign—quickly overwhelms the Japanese fortifications. The JSDF units fire a devastating barrage at the monster, but he responds by using his radiation breath to burn huge sections of the city. In one particularly striking shot, Godzilla burns and irradiates a group of civilians on the street, in a scene eerily reminiscent of atomic blast footage, therefore making a clear visual connection to the atomic bombings of Hiroshima and Nagasaki.[30]

Godzilla continues his reign of terror across the metropolis, setting neighborhood after neighborhood on fire with his radioactive fury.[31] In one shot, Godzilla's head is seen in the background, mostly concealed behind a large aviary filled with birds in the foreground.[32] Along with the shot of a birdcage noted earlier, we can see a clear, if subtle, environmental critique. Humanity attempts to control or harness nature—like the caged birds or Serizawa's unfortunate fish—but such attempts are often futile and destructive. By first attempting and failing to corral Godzilla with an electric barrier, and later by superimposing an image of a bird-filled aviary in front of him, the film visually connects the monster with the unleashed forces of nature.[33] Immediately after this shot, Godzilla topples a building on a woman and two children, as the woman cries, "We'll be joining your father soon!"[34] This scene, one of the most poignant in the film, coupled with the birdcage imagery, further connects Godzilla's destructiveness to both nature and the lingering memories of World War II. After setting vast swaths of Tokyo ablaze, JSDF aircraft manage to drive Godzilla back into the sea.

The following morning, Tokyo lies in ruins. Casualties pour into hospitals, where a doctor examines a young child's radiation exposure with a Geiger counter.[35] From the expression on the doctor's face, the child's prognosis is not good. The hospital scenes undoubtedly reminded Japanese viewers in 1954 of the horrors of the Asia-Pacific War, especially the atomic bombings of Hiroshima and Nagasaki and the American fire-bombing of Tokyo, the single "deadliest air attack of World War II."[36] Overcome with grief, Emiko tells Ogata about Serizawa's oxygen-destroyer.

In a flashback sequence, the viewer sees Serizawa show Emiko his oxygen-destroyer: he drops a small object into an aquarium, and the fish inside quickly die and dissolve to nothing but bones. Serizawa's fish, like the encaged birds, reveal another angle of humankind's attempt to confine and control the natural world, leaving death and destruction in their wake. The power of Dr. Serizawa's device is clear: "A little piece of this, dropped into the water, could turn all of Tokyo Bay into a graveyard!"[37] A horrified Emiko asks Serizawa how he could make such an awful device, but the doctor refuses to accept accountability, stating that he only performs his work as a research scientist. Serizawa tells Emiko he cannot reveal his oxygen-destroyer, fearing it could be turned into a terrible weapon. The flashback ends by panning to Serizawa's experimental aquarium, now clouded and devoid of life.

Ogata and Emiko confront Dr. Serizawa. The three sit around a new decorative fish tank in his living space—notably absent from the same set in earlier scenes—debating the use of the oxygen-destroyer. After several attempts and a well-timed TV broadcast of Godzilla's destruction of Tokyo, Serizawa agrees to use his discovery to defeat Godzilla. However, to ensure that his device will not fall into the wrong hands, Serizawa burns his notes.

In *Godzilla*'s final sequence, Ogata and Serizawa descend into Tokyo Bay in diving suits to deploy the oxygen-destroyer. The two divers locate the monster, and Serizawa activates his invention. Ogata returns to the surface, but Serizawa cuts his own breathing line ensuring that the secret of the oxygen-destroyer will die with him. The device works; Godzilla's body dissolves. Although overlooked in other critiques of the film, it seems clear that all life in Tokyo Bay has been destroyed, saving Japan from Godzilla but creating a massive environmental catastrophe in return. As the film comes to a conclusion, Prof. Yamane intones: "If we keep conducting nuclear tests, it's possible that another Godzilla may appear."[38] *Godzilla* concludes with a shot of the sun reflecting off the surface of the now lifeless Tokyo Bay.

In his critical filmography, David Kalat muses that Godzilla represents not nature but modern technological society, and that the "monster is defeated by *even more* technology, and so the central conflict of the story is not so much society against nature as society against itself."[39] Kalat raises an interesting point, but nature nonetheless plays a strong role throughout the film. Perhaps what Kalat and others have missed is that in this "society against itself" conflict nature cannot be forgotten. Ultimately, it is nature that suffers. From the portrayal of atomic blasts irradiating humans and landscapes to shots of Yamane's caged birds and Serizawa's aquarium, the film hints at humanity's failed attempt to confine and control nature. In the end, Japanese science may indeed save Tokyo from Godzilla's radiological menace, but at what cost? Godzilla's death is not so clean and antiseptic as other studies have claimed—by killing the monster the film's heroes lay waste to all life in Tokyo Bay. Humans may be safe, at least for a time, but nature pays the ultimate price.

Since the premiere of *Godzilla*, many people have added their voices to deciphering what the monster Godzilla actually represents. Tanaka Tomoyuki himself melodramatically declared: "Godzilla is the son of the atomic bomb. He is a nightmare created out of the darkness of the human soul. He is the sacred beast of the apocalypse."[40] Perhaps we can only echo an earlier assessment that Godzilla is "a moving target, a constantly shifting metaphor, an unstable and contradictory icon, a chimera."[41] Godzilla—like the proverbial onion—has many layers, some complementary and others contradictory, but buried deep within the monster's radiation-scarred exterior lies a series of strong antinuclear and environmental messages.

Hearing the Self and the Other in Godzilla

Music is a key component in conveying *Godzilla*'s ecological message. Throughout the Godzilla series, Ifukube Akira's many scores stand out for their nuance and dynamism.[42] Ifukube's works also represent a union of Japanese and foreign music styles. The movie *Godzilla* reflects concerns about Self and Other relevant to the years immediately following the end of the occupation. What do we mean by Self and Other? We draw on Edward Said's *Orientalism* in examining this phenomenon of geographical identity. In Said's writing, he determines that the Orient (generally meaning the Middle East and Asia) is in this way "Orientalized" by the West, and in the process becomes to some extent the fictional object of the West's fantasy. We extrapolate the relationship described by Said to the more abstract concept of Self and Other. To very loosely summarize, the Other is defined by the Self's perception of it.[43]

While Said concentrates on Western perception of the East, we are more concerned with Eastern perceptions of other Others, particularly *kaijū eiga*'s frequent depiction of the South Pacific. Japanese monster cinema's portrayal of Pacific Islanders (and other indigenous peoples) relates directly to our environmental commentary. As David Mazel expounds in his essay in *The Ecocriticism Reader*, in "early environmental construction, natives were not part of the internal but the external sphere, quite in keeping with prevailing notions of native peoples as 'natural,' as 'children of the forest,' and so on."[44] This concept comes to the forefront in the films of the Mothra franchise, but is present in other *kaijū eiga* as well. Certainly, it was relevant to the Japanese experience in the immediate postwar era.

In the decade immediately following the war, Japan filtered its national identity through American Orientalisms of the island nation. But it also turned inward, looking to rebuild a national character looking at Others within its borders and within Asia. Japan in the post-occupation years inhabited a space between the "Orient" and the "Occident," between Self and Other.[45] Ifukube's score for *Godzilla* and his contributions to the sound design reinforce these issues of Self and Other during a key moment of national identity reconstruction in Japanese history. His music simultaneously engages with these binaries while opening up space for a more nuanced understanding of music and nation in the narrative. In order to appreciate Ifukube's aesthetic approach to film scoring, however, we first must consider his upbringing.

Ifukube was born on May 31, 1914, in a small village on the northernmost island of Japan, Hokkaidō.[46] Growing up in rural Hokkaidō exposed Ifukube to the music and aesthetics of the Ainu people. Racially different from the Japanese-Yamato people, the Ainu are culturally more similar to Siberian peoples.[47] The Japanese state annexed the Ainu homeland in 1869, colonizing their island with ethnic Japanese and persecuting the indigenous inhabitants.[48] Thus Hokkaidō became a locale of inter-racial interaction far from the cosmopolitan center of Tokyo.

From a young age, Ifukube was exposed to both Ainu and Japanese music. The difference in Japanese and Ainu musical style is striking, considering that the populations live side by side. According to music scholar Tanimoto Kazuki, "Ainu instrumental music is a stylization of animal cries and calls," and in individual music, "the melodies are characterized by personal traits, and each melody can be identified with a specific member of the tribe."[49] The musical impressionism of the natural world and identifiable leitmotifs (recurring melodies that represent places, people, things, or even ideas) often appear in Ifukube's *Godzilla* score. Although the Ainu are ethnically different from the Japanese, for Ifukube the Ainu can be perceived as a friendly Other, as Ifukube grew up on the cusp of these two different societies. Despite commonplace discrimination by Japanese against the Ainu, young Ifukube had many Ainu friends at the local school and his parents often invited Ainu guests over to their home.[50]

In this way, Ifukube was "inspired by a love of nature and the indigenous culture of his native Hokkaidō," declares Japanese music specialist Judith Ann Herd, "[and] his music is as spontaneous and joyful as the lively folk traditions of the Ainu people that influenced his compositional style."[51] In general, the use of folkloric elements would categorize Ifukube as a nationalist composer. However, we recognize that even his folkloric style derives not just from Japanese, but also from Ainu tradition. The inclusion of Ainu folkloric aspects instead of Japanese-Yamato folklorism prevents Ifukube's music as being heard as purely jingoistic. Indeed, "Ifukube's background was unconventional but appropriate for a passionate individualist."[52]

Thanks to his upbringing, Ifukube conceptualized the *Godzilla* score through Other means, such as the Ainu. Yet, the Ainu people and culture, as part of the Japanese archipelago, signify an Other not quite so foreign as the West. Essentially, they represent a middle ground between the two opposing ideas of Self and Other. As a result, we can identify elements in the film's narrative and soundtrack that complicate the distinction between foreign and native, Self and Other binaries.

Noriega points out that in most Hollywood films, the monsters are literally nameless.[53] This creates an impersonal sense of the monster as Other. Tsutsui relates: "The significant difference between *King Kong* and *Godzilla* is how we identify with the monster."[54] Godzilla "is a paradox of sorts—a horrible embodiment of the Bomb that created him, and yet a pitiable victim of it; a symbol of Japan's postwar regrets, and nuclear fears and alternatively, the nation's rage and retaliation."[55] In *Godzilla*, unlike the Western monster movies of the 1950s, the monster is named and identified with as both a Japanese (Self) and Western (Other) creation, signaling a dialectical synthesis.

The juxtaposition of native and foreign elements saturate *Godzilla*'s plot. The contrast between Ōdo Island (traditional-insider-Self) and Tokyo (modern-outsider-Other) settings is one example; this use of settings also comes into play in various guises. The elderly Prof. Yamane lives in a traditional Japanese home, complete with a *genkan* entrance and *tatami* floors. In contrast, Dr. Serizawa, a young scientist injured during the war, lives in a European-style castle and listens to Western classical music. The conspicuous absence of American military forces (historically stationed in Japan) and the substitute presence of the JSDF units illustrate a more subtle instance of Self and Other at play in the film. Even Godzilla represents a synthesis of native and foreign components. Godzilla is a legend among the people of Ōdo Island, similar to a *kami* spirit in Shintō or the legendary water dragon found throughout East Asian mythology.[56] Conversely, Godzilla is also a product of modernity, endowed with radioactive powers thanks to American nuclear tests in the South Pacific. In this way, "we have in Godzilla an entity that is simultaneously associated with 'authentic' Japanese tradition and 'alien' U.S. military might."[57]

Because *Godzilla* addresses intense themes of Self and Other within the safely cathartic guise of a *kaijū eiga*, Ifukube felt justified in accepting the job offer to score the film, despite warnings that he would be typecast as a *kaijū eiga* composer if he did so. Ifukube was impressed by the story, sharing:

When I first read the script, I first felt like the idea was one of anti-technology. During the war, I had been testing the strengths of woods. When MacArthur and the marines came and asked me what I had done during the war, I replied that I tested the strength properties of wood. I felt keenly aware of the difference in technology levels. Japan really lost the war due to such a disparity. Our building materials were few, our food supply couldn't meet demand, and we couldn't compare to America's growing technology and science. It was such a shock![58]

For many who lived through the war, the tension between technology and the old ways added to the anxiety of occupied Japan, and to the conflict of traditional (native) elements and modern (foreign) ones. The film depicts these anxieties via shots of Tokyo in the aftermath of Godzilla's attack; these images could just as easily be depictions of Tokyo after the devastating air raids of 1945. In the resolution of the film, though, it is technology that rescues Japan. It is likely that this outcome also influenced Ifukube's decision to score the movie. According to many scholars, as well as Ifukube, "Godzilla represents the unquiet souls of the soldiers and sailors who died in the Pacific during World War II, returning to Japan to wreak vengeance, to demand belated acknowledgement, and rekindle national spirit."[59]

If this is how Ifukube imagined Godzilla and interpreted the story, what kind of compositional techniques might he use to impress the image as well as meaning in the minds of viewers? For many fans, "It's impossible to imagine the film without the score ... the music sets the moods for the movie."[60] Tsutsui suggests that since "the film score was written in an incredibly short period of time (about a week), Ifukube was liberated from convention, and was allowed to write on impulse in the service of creativity."[61] This impulse encouraged Ifukube to incorporate autochthonous and foreign elements in his music. In each of the pieces—Godzilla sound effects, the March, the Horror theme, and the Requiem, along with two pre-existing works—the synthesis of East and West is made evident in the music by melodic, metric, formal, and textural factors. In this way, the music adds another dimension to Japanese monster cinema's trope of a conflict between science and nature.

Sound and Music in Godzilla

The first sound the audience hears in the movie is Godzilla's roar, accompanied by thundering footsteps. Ifukube played a key role in the development of both of these sound effects. Drawing on Western technology like magnetic tape and the techniques of *musique concrète*, or literally, "concrete music," that is, music created using recorded sounds as raw material, Ifukube conceived Godzilla's cry. Ifukube described the creation process:

At the time the sound effects and recording team were worried about the issue of what to do for Godzilla's roar and footsteps. At first, Godzilla's cry was made from a combination of lion, tiger, and elephant sounds; it sounded a bit like a condor, but it just didn't approach the image of a *kaijū* like Godzilla.[62]

Director Honda approached Ifukube for help. The composer suggested using a contrabass. He loosened the strings and rubbed them with a tanned leather glove covered with rosin. In doing so, he could change the sound based on the pressure he applied, thus creating an intricate and complex sound. This sound was then taped, and the revolutions were lowered, producing Godzilla's otherworldly roar.[63] In Godzilla's cry, Western elements coalesce with an Ainu-like musical stylization of an animal cry. This fusion creates a musical effect that becomes an example of successful integration of technology and recreations of nature. The successful navigation between ancient and modern demonstrates an achievement of Japan's postwar goals.

Ifukube also helped create the sound effect of Godzilla's footsteps. This effect, too, is a combination of acoustics and technology. While working on a previous project, Ifukube had stumbled off a wooden platform and a huge "boom" emitted from the nearby speakers. The microphone had picked up "spring reverb." Ifukube recalled this sound and suggested it for Godzilla's footsteps.[64] By means of Western instruments and technology, Ifukube was able to craft a sound that seems organic. So musical are his sound effects that they appear as tracks on many compilations of his *kaijū* film scores.

Film specialist Randall Larson describes the first tune: "The March is the primary theme for Godzilla, first heard during the main title, a fast-moving motif for see-sawing strings punctuated with drums and cymbals."[65] The music appears twice in its main title form in the movie; both scenes depict the Japanese military leaving to do battle with Godzilla, but the music, as much as the story, hints that these battles will not bode well for the human forces. When the music appears in an early battle sequence, the music accompanies shots of Godzilla approaching and reverse shots of faceless tanks raising their artillery. These shots and reverse shots suggest that the military and monster are one and the same.

The music reinforces this notion through melody, mode, and meter.[66] The tune is in Phrygian mode; that is, it uses a set of notes common in Western medieval music, but uncommon in music outside of a religious setting after the 16th century. It also features a driving descending repeating line, called an ostinato. The descents almost always occur on strong beats, such as one and three. This emphasis on descent combined with Phrygian modality sounds nothing like "Japanese exoticism" as perceived by the West (typically by the use of a five-tone scale).[67] It does, however, create a dark, doomed atmosphere recognized as sinister by both Western and Eastern ears. Although the March's melody seems relatively simple and straightforward, its meter is intricately thorny. Ifukube applied mixed meter to this march, alternating bars of four beats with bars of five beats. This pattern within the March confers on it an unsettled sense of time and space, one that the closing musical material emphasizes through accented offbeats. This displacement undermines the musical function of a march, to unify soldiers mentally and physically. The March conveys a feeling of futility that the military faces when battling Godzilla, and on a deeper level, the sense of military failure Japan experienced at the end of the war.

Some scholars suggest that this metrical displacement is a result of Ifukube's affinity for Russian composer Igor Stravinsky's *The Rite of Spring*, a work known for its driving pulse and allusions to primitivism.[68] This is evidenced by Ifukube's use of ostinato and syncopation, an asymmetrical emphasis on beats. However, it is possible that Ifukube picked up on ostinato technique long before hearing Stravinsky. Ainu music, too, is also filled with repeated patterns.[69] Therefore, in the March, Ifukube is not implementing ethnic exoticism. Ifukube stylistically alludes to both Stravinsky and Ainu music, seamlessly stitching together a new patriotic music. By using external sources that Ifukube personally identified with, the score audibly models Japan's portrayal of its struggle with nature and technology in the postwar era.

The next prominent melody that occurs in the movie is the Horror theme. Intoned on various occasions when Godzilla emerges, the leitmotif conveys the terror Godzilla and atomic weaponry represent, reinforcing the film's anti-nuclear commentary. The piece begins with low register tone clusters in the piano, insinuating something abnormal, sinister, and heavy. The bass trombone enters on C# with the theme, a mostly stepwise melody, with the largest range of all the motives, aurally signifying the monster's dreadful enormity. The tempo is deliberate and lumbering, with clear downbeats and phrasing. There is no doubt as to the threat Godzilla poses to Tokyo, and the music's transparency furthers this notion. The tempo, register, and orchestration of the Godzilla motif paint an aural portrait of the film's monster.

A third melody, the Requiem, plays a substantial role in the film's soundscape. The Requiem is first heard after Godzilla's Tokyo rampage. People are clearing the rubble, treating the wounded, and struggling to hang on to hope after such devastation. On the television, a girls choir sings, and the melancholy beauty of the song prompts the scientist Serizawa to allow his oxygen-destroyer to be used against Godzilla. The Requiem returns at the end of the film, in an underwater scene in which Serizawa sacrifices himself in order to defeat Godzilla and prevent anyone from ever discovering the weapon's secrets. Larson declares: "The Requiem really stands out as a unique and evocative piece of music, powerfully compelling the audience to an emotional involvement with the characters."[70] Ifukube employs a variety of methods to produce this emotional impact. The most obvious of these are the lyrics themselves, written by Kayama Shigeru, that intone a simple prayer for peace.[71]

The Requiem's tempo is slow yet even in its seeming simplicity aspects of rhythmic displacement remain, especially in its underwater version. Like the March, this cue eschews the more typical scales and harmonies of Western classical tradition. It also employs mixed meter, with Ifukube interpolating bars of four beats with bars of three. This play with musical time endows the Requiem with a sense of *rubato*, a temporary bending of time in service of expressivity. This in combination with the tempo, mode, and lyrics contributes to a sense of lamentation. When discussing the Requiem, Ifukube commented:

> The reason my music sounds like a requiem is because of the scales [...] In Japanese music, the one above the ending tone is a half tone. One below is a full note. This cannot be classed as a major key nor a minor key [...] I value our traditional sense of beauty. When Westerners hear my music, they think of church music of the Middle Ages; when Japanese hear it, it sounds Japanese but its tempo is slow like a requiem.[72]

Although the emotional impact is similar, the musical association with the Requiem depends on one's enculturation. The mutability of the Requiem, then, is imperative to the film. The synthesis of Western and Japanese music aesthetics mirrors the film's own approach to cultural co-mingling.

In addition to the three primary leitmotifs, there are two lesser motives, the cues Ōdo-shima Temple Festival and the Japanese Army March. We group these cues together because Ifukube excerpted both from pre-existing compositions. The Ōdo Island shrine motive derives from the second movement of *Japanese Rhapsody*, called *Matsuri* or "festival." The music is intoned during an exorcism ceremony meant to appease the local demon-spirit, presumably Godzilla. This motive is the most prominent moment of diegetic music in the film. It is also the motive that most closely resembles Japanese folk music; thus it is connected to Japan's mythological past, and hence nature.

The Japanese Army March cue is an excerpt of *Heishi no Jogaku*, a work Ifukube composed for the Japanese military during World War II.[73] It accompanies stock footage of the Japanese Self-Defense Forces conducting target practices. This brass band piece "uses duple time and sounds essentially cheerful, but it does not evoke the patriotic excitement typical of pre-war Japanese marches."[74] The piece undermines the militaristic aura of war marches, despite being commissioned as one. Ifukube makes this possible by subtly manipulating the rhythmic pulse to make it sound and feel off-balance (as he does in the earlier March theme). Furthermore, while the motive begins optimistically in C major, the melody ends in the relative key of A minor. The final note, a B, is the leading tone for C major, and the second scale degree of A minor. This provokes a sense of irresolution in the piece.

Music scholar Shuhei Hosokawa points out, "the whole motif lacks in functional harmony," and he suggests that maybe this was Ifukube's "personal resistance to military oppression."[75] Finally, because of this lack of resolution the cue itself can be repeated *ad nauseum*; it can basically function as a vamp, filling moments with music as the director and editor saw fit. In the case of this cue, the repetition reinforces the idea of history repeating itself in terms of the Japanese military battling a horrific foe. Yet it also emphasizes the banality of military life. In this way, Ifukube adopted the Western march style and used it not only to suit the needs of his government, or of a movie, but, in a small way, to give a single voice against militarism.

Altogether, the sound effects, the March, Horror, and Requiem themes, along with the Ōdo-shima Temple Festival theme and the Japanese Army March, endow *Godzilla* with an aesthetic cohesion that combines Japanese and Western musical values. Ifukube refined the tensions between Japanese insider, Ainu insider/outsider, and Western outsider elements to compose a film score that is neither specifically Western nor Asian. Like the film itself, it carries broad appeal the globe over. The strain between humanity and nature and the ancient and modern is embedded in the score and sound effects themselves. This synthesis of aesthetics defines Ifukube as an exceptional composer in the postwar era and contributes to the ecological subtext present in *Godzilla* and many other *kaijū eiga*.

Godzilla, King of the Monsters (1956)

Seventeen months after the premiere of *Godzilla* in Japan, Embassy Pictures distributed an edited version for American audiences.[76] This version changed the primary narrative from one concerned with morals of scientific weaponry to a monster-on-the-loose romp.[77] In order to attract a teenage market, the Embassy release omitted reflections on the tragic proliferation of nuclear weaponry and the conflict between technology, humanity, and the natural world. Several authors have examined the changes made to the original film to suit American tastes.[78] Some of these adjustments de-centered the narrative focus away from the Japanese wartime experience and concerns about environmental destruction.

Godzilla, King of the Monsters was the result of Tōhō's sale of *Godzilla*'s distribution rights to Embassy Pictures for $25,000.[79] The executive producer Joseph Levine, along with writer and director Terry Morse and others at Embassy together spearheaded a series of alterations to the original picture. Among these was the addition of the American journalist character Steve Martin (Raymond Burr).[80] The Americans oriented the film to portray the monster's attack on Tokyo primarily from Martin's point of view. In order to accomplish this, much of the original movie was re-edited, with additional scenes tucked into the film. It seems Embassy assumed that American audiences required an American protagonist with whom to empathize.

For example, *Godzilla, King of the Monsters* begins with a voiceover by Martin describing Godzilla's attack on Tokyo. Accompanying this are shots of a destroyed Tokyo, Ifukube's Requiem in the underscore. The voiceover establishes the setting and tells us what has happened, placing the audience *in media res.* Martin awakes trapped in rubble, though he is soon rescued and taken to a makeshift hospital where Emiko is working. They are acquaintances, and through some clever splicing and over-the-shoulder shots Martin and Emiko appear to have a conversation. The majority of the film then takes place in flashback, as Martin recollects the preceding days.[81] He explains he had come to Tokyo to visit his old college friend, Dr. Serizawa, while en route to Cairo. When several fishing boats are mysteriously attacked off the coast of Japan, Martin decides to remain in Tokyo to investigate.

With the help of an English-speaking security officer (Frank Iwanaga), Martin manages to join a scientific trip led by Professor Yamane to Ōdo Island. There Martin learns from the native islanders of an ancient legend of Godzilla and encounters the monster first-hand. Upon returning to Japan, Prof. Yamane reveals that Godzilla is an ancient beast that has awoken. In the film's single reference to nuclear testing, Yamane surmises that Godzilla was disturbed by hydrogen bomb tests. Despite attempts to prevent Godzilla's attack, the monster proceeds to destroy Tokyo and Martin is injured. Meanwhile, Emiko has learned of Serizawa's oxygen-destroyer. The flashback concludes, and Emiko tells Martin and Ogata about Serizawa's weapon. Like the original film, Serizawa initially refuses to deploy the weapon; he is worried about such a powerful weapon falling into the wrong hands. After observing the devastation Godzilla caused, though, Serizawa agrees to use the oxygen-destroyer. He and Ogata dive into Tokyo Bay to release the weapon. Serizawa sacrifices himself, while the rest of the cast looks on, mourning and saluting the tragic hero.

While the general plot of *Godzilla, King of the Monsters* is generally the same as the Japanese version, the otherwise drastic differences contribute to a dilution of the 1954 film's message. The frequent voiceovers align the audience with the American narrator Steve Martin. These voiceovers contribute to a sense of the American's omniscient knowledge and by extension, superior insight. They work to prevent viewers from deeply empathizing with the Japanese characters and situation. Adding to this distancing effect is the lack of subtitles with Japanese-language scenes and the poor dubbing when characters from the original film "speak" English. The English language subsumes the emotional power of the Japanese voice writ large.

In the American release, there are no references to World War II, international relations, or nuclear proliferation; indeed Godzilla seems to appear without any cause. There is little subtext in this version. Perhaps the most significant moment occurs when Serizawa expresses his concern about his weapon being abused; in *Godzilla* this comment hints at the possibility of the American government appropriating the oxygen-destroyer for its own purposes, while in *Godzilla, King of the Monsters* this seems to be directed at the Soviet Union. The American release also omits the most powerful statement of the original film, Yamane's conclusive warning about nuclear testing and the return of Godzilla. Instead, the film cuts away immediately prior to Yamane's somber comment; rather, Martin narrates a cheerful platitude about the world now being safe to wake up and live again. The cumulative result is a passable monster film that tells us more about Japanese-American relations than contemporary socio-political or environmental concerns.

Until relatively recently, *Godzilla, King of the Monsters* clouded scholarship (or lack thereof) on Godzilla.[82] Earlier scholars often had to rely on bootleg VHS tapes of Godzilla films due to the lack of officially released original versions outside of Japan.[83] Thanks to *Godzilla* and the American version of the film, as well as subsequent films in the series, the reptilian behemoth quickly became an international global icon, transcending national boundaries to develop a worldwide following. Although filmmakers in Japan produced Godzilla films without any contextualization for foreign moviegoers, or perhaps in some cases because of it, Godzilla acquired a fan following throughout not only Japan but the entire world. Viewed through this lens, *Godzilla* became an unmitigated success for Tōhō. Their film, originally intended to be a one-off feature, became one of the most powerful forces in cinema—the *kaijū* monster franchise.

Taking a cue from *Godzilla, King of the Monsters*, another American studio, Warner Brothers, released an extensive reworking of Tōhō's second Godzilla film, *Gojira no Gyakushū* (*Godzilla Raids Again*) (1955). Eager to keep their foothold in the burgeoning American monster film market, Tōhō again licensed the rights to Godzilla's encore with little concern about how the film itself would be transformed. The original plan by the American distributors was to cannibalize the special effects sequences and place them into an entirely new script called "The Volcano Monsters," which would tell the story of two dinosaurs discovered in suspended animation by an American expedition, transported to the U.S. West Coast, climaxing with a final showdown in San Francisco. Ib Melchior, one of the writers hired to pen the new script for "The Volcano Monsters," recalled in a retrospective interview: "I'm sure this was the studio's response to the success of [*Godzilla, King of the Monsters*], Ed [Watson] and I were asked to write this monster thing and to basically Americanize the Godzilla movies."[84] By licensing the rights to American studios, Tōhō became an accessory to Godzilla's dissection, not only approving the use of the footage for the "monster thing" but also agreeing to ship the Godzilla and Anguirus (Godzilla's nemesis in the 1955 picture) suits to the United States so additional scenes could be shot in Hollywood.[85]

However, "The Volcano Monsters" never came to fruition and *Godzilla Raids Again* instead launched in the United States in 1959 as *Gigantis, the Fire Monster*.[86] Unlike the initial plan for "The Volcano Monsters," the *Gigantis, the Fire Monster* edit of the film left the original footage largely intact. However, any *kaijū* connoisseur undoubtedly will be left feeling both disconcerted and confused after viewing this release of the film. Aside from inexplicably changing the title monster's name, the editing team also reversed the monsters' familiar roars and other sound effects. Godzilla's trademark roar is instead bellowed by his opponent Anguirus, while Gigantis (née Godzilla) emits Anguirus's haunting ululations. Following the earlier release of *Godzilla, King of the Monsters*, this film contributed to audience bewilderment of the Godzilla series in North America and around the world, but kept the cash flowing to Tōhō Studios from the international market.

The domestic success and international proliferation of *Godzilla* and its sequel helped spur other monster creations. Tōhō Studios continued funding the production of *kaijū eiga* and allowed creative teams to pursue multi-pronged messages of society, politics, and environmentalism in various guises. In the latter half of the 1950s, Tōhō debuted monster productions like *Radon (Rodan)* (1956) and *Daikaijū Baran (Varan the Unbelievable)* (1958). By the early 1960s, with the release of the first film of the Mothra franchise, the future appeared bright for sustained environmental commentary in *kaijū eiga*.

4

Mothra, Marx,
Mother Nature

Among Godzilla's many monstrous foes, few are more beloved than Mothra. More-over, the winged *kaijū*'s early appearances in the films *Mosura (Mothra)* (1961) and *Mosura tai Gojira (Mothra vs. Godzilla)* (1964) reveal a new angle on environmentalism in Japanese monster cinema.[1] Although both movies deal with nuclear testing and its disastrous effects (by this time *de rigueur* in *kaijū eiga*), these works expand and explore the underlying forces driving environmental degradation. No longer limited to critiques of American militarism, the films confronted contemporary issues concerning the environment, unchecked capitalism, women's liberation, and of course, nuclear proliferation, now within the context of the intensifying Cold War.[2] Mothra, in her title vehicle and her later heroic turn versus Godzilla, comes to represent both nature and the feminine. She is a monstrous symbol at odds with rapid postwar industrialization and the greedy pursuit of capital, activities destructive to nature and coded as masculine in the movies.

We first situate *Mothra* and *Mothra vs. Godzilla* within the context of 1960s Japan, with a particular focus on industrialization and gender roles. Then we expound on the films themselves, paying particular attention to the narratives, visual elements, and the role of music in effectively conveying these subtle commentaries. By examining the films' critiques of industrial expansion and its environmental repercussions we can better appreciate *Mothra* and *Mothra vs. Godzilla* as serious works contemplating concerns relevant to the era of their production.

Economic Miracle, Moral Doubts and Gender Troubles

Japan's emergence as a postwar economic powerhouse was nothing short of a miracle.[3] However, very little about this miracle had been left to chance. American as well as Japanese leaders had worked to maneuver Japan into a superior economic position, a position that was bearing fruit by the 1960s. Japan was a newly-risen phoenix that feasted on Cold War tensions, American wars in Asia, and a dubious affiliation between business and politics that echoed the *zaibatsu*, industrial and business conglomerates that had close ties with the imperial state before and during World War II. Although it was no longer a colonial power, Japan was starting to flex a different type of might, one of the financial kind.

As in many cases, material profit for the elite was the result of the manipulation of those with less power and wealth. Both of the Mothra movies address the hierarchical relationship between proletariat and bourgeoisie, though the earlier film implicates a foreigner, the latter a Japanese, in the role of capitalist villains. In the case of both movies, however, the victims remain the same: generally, the Japanese public, who bear the brunt of *kaijū* wrath, and specifically, non–Japanese Asians, as characterized by two diminutive ladies (also called the Twin Fairies) who serve as priestesses of Mothra and representatives for the natives of an imaginary Polynesian land called Infant Island.

Along with our earlier discussion of the frequent conflation of native peoples with nature, there is also a common connection between nature and the feminine. As Kate Soper relates in her essay "Naturalized Woman and Feminized Nature," the female and the feminine are often considered to be more "natural" than the male and the masculine.[4] At the same time, Soper relates, nature itself is described with terminology often reserved for the feminine. A particularly relevant example of this tendency appears in famed author Ōoka Shōhei's World War II novel *Fires on the Plain*, wherein the protagonist, a Japanese soldier based in the Philippines, describes the island chain's geography and vegetation in sexualized terms, contrasting nature with the novel's otherwise dark war imagery. He relates: "One low branch of the mountains extended to the left and formed a backdrop to the forest ahead of me; it was curved gently like the smooth back of a recumbent woman," "Then I realized that the palm trees that surrounded me were being transfigured [...] into the various women whom I had known and loved in the past," and "Somehow the contour of the hill reminded me of a woman's *mons Veneris*."[5] Soper argues that such conflations lead to "the antithetical equivalence: woman = reproduction = nature versus man = production = culture."[6] We will see these issues at play throughout the films of the Mothra franchise (and *kaijū eiga* generally), both through the Infant Islanders as well as Mothra's tiny priestesses.

Mothra's Twin Fairies simultaneously represent human, Japanese women and foreign, magical female fairies. This concentration of the little, the feminine, and the native/ foreign dichotomy embodied by these two characters begs us to consider gender roles more broadly in modern Japanese history. How did this conflation of qualities come to represent different facets of the female in postwar Japan? How does this play into our understanding of its connection to Mothra and environmental messages more generally? A brief excavation of gender in modern Japan will thus inform our interpretation of the movies.

Some scholars have argued that Japan was originally a matrilineal society, but the introduction and adoption of Buddhism and Confucianism in later centuries served to solidify patriarchal order in the island nation.[7] Although many things changed following the Meiji Restoration of 1868, the idea of a masculine public sphere and feminine private sphere did not. Indeed, while the Meiji government (1868–1912) issued promulgations ensuring equal childhood education, it also promoted a state ideology of "good wife, wise mother," those being the suitable roles for a woman. The imperial government implemented this policy through hard and soft ideological apparatus; female suffrage was out of the question and much of the popular literature depicted the ideal woman as one who submitted herself to her husband, family, and state. This imagined ideal became a rallying cry during the years of increased militarism of the 1920s and 1930s. Yet at that same time, a few young women attracted a lot of attention specifically for their rejection of the "good wife, wise mother" role. These women, called *moga* (a portmanteau of "modern" and "girl"), are often depicted with short stylishly bobbed hair, dressed in Western clothes instead of traditional kimono, and seemingly meant to represent a new kind of woman.

However, the *moga* were a flash in the crucible of modern Japanese history. With the increase in military expansion throughout the 1930s and 1940s, they and many others became cogs in the machinery of war. While women at home worked to aid husbands and sons, whether through moral support or physical labor, women in colonial territories were forced to serve a much darker role in the efforts of empire. George Hicks eloquently documented the plight of the "comfort women," or sexual slaves, particularly those of Korea and China.[8]

After Japan's defeat and the subsequent occupation, the government requested women of lesser means (typically non–Japanese Asians) to serve the nation (and service occupation personnel) in order to uphold the chastity of others. Although state-sponsored prostitution in the postwar period was quickly outlawed (not because of morals but because of rampant venereal disease), the use of women to achieve political ends remained common. Now private prostitutes adapted Western clothes and attitudes in an attempt to attract military men. Known as *pan-pan* girls, they were practical about the situation in the immediate postwar period.[9] They openly invited the male gaze and capitalized on their sexual allure and exotic (to American servicemen) qualities. The *pan-pan* girls were a kind of echo of the *moga* of earlier decades and the freedom they represented.

The occupation sought to ensure that women were no longer officially subjugated to men in postwar Japan. As part of the promotion of democracy by the Supreme Commander for the Allied Powers (SCAP), the (American) authors of Japan's postwar constitution added an equal rights clause, Article 14, and a women's civil rights clause, Article 24.[10] Under these clauses, women were guaranteed the right to vote and to decide whether or not to marry.[11] The occupation years were in many ways years of female liberation and empowerment, though soon after (and even before) the Americans departed a backlash was already rippling through society.[12] Although women had worked in factories, struggled to build their own businesses and their own lives, the notion of placing marriage and motherhood before one's own interests and desires was still very much in place (an idea that lingers into the 21st century).[13] The liberties promised by the constitution could not be revoked, but they could be contained. Societal pressures often compel women even today to leave the workforce once they become married or pregnant.[14] Although the maxim "good wife, wise mother" is no longer intoned, it implicitly reverberates through modern Japanese society to this day, and did so even more forcefully in the early 1960s.[15]

Housewives and intellectuals alike (sometimes one and the same) were debating ideas about domestic labor and compensation as early as 1960.[16] Moreover, communist and socialist parties, legalized by the postwar constitution, were presenting ideological platforms relevant to postwar Japanese women.[17] Marxist intellectuals questioned the valuation of domestic labor in an economy that was increasingly service-based. Generally domestic (women's) labor had "use value" but no "exchange value." In other words, female labor did not produce commodities.[18]

At this same time, many women were involved in grassroots political efforts addressing concerns about nuclear proliferation. These campaigns gathered steam as they promoted their anti-nuclear efforts as a desire to protect children and future generations.[19] The same year America and Japan committed to the Treaty of Mutual Cooperation and Security, in 1960, about 13,000 mothers converged on Tokyo to protest the renewal of an unequal treaty between the United States and Japan.[20] The treaty, despite sizable opposition, was ratified, with the promise from Prime Minister Ikeda "that personal incomes would double within the decade" thanks to American military activities on the continent.[21]

The combination of local organization and leftist leanings converged a decade later in Tanaka Mitsu's manifesto for women's liberation for the group "Fighting Women" (*tatakau onna*). Emerging out of student protests and activism that continued throughout the 1960s, the Fighting Women and other female groups found that even in student activism, a gendered divide remained.[22] There were also similar movements to generally increase political engagement by women led by Saitō Chiyo, founder of *Agora*, eventually "a resource centre where women could engage in consciousness-raising and assertiveness training, and gather information as a resource for feminist activity."[23] *Agora*, generally described as housewife feminism, addressed issues relevant to women based on their situation and locale. They, like their more leftist colleagues, were concerned with the same issues, such as pollution and nuclear proliferation.[24]

This is all to say, although perhaps the idea of an organized political group geared towards women's liberation did not truly take hold in postwar Japan until 1970, there were certainly seeds of it in the preceding decade in both politics and culture. Furthermore, a probing of the ideals espoused by the housewife feminists and leftist activists alike appeared in a most unlikely venue—*kaijū eiga*. This is not to say that many depictions of women in Japanese monster movies are at the surface derogatory, but they do transition over time. Typically, female characters in early *kaijū eiga* are mothers, sisters, or girlfriends of the male protagonists. But in certain cases, the stereotypical gender roles are turned sideways. In some instances, women are portrayed as empowered characters and sexual beings.[25] Perhaps an indirect result of women's liberation and political activism, *kaijū eiga* of the 1960s and 1970s occasionally interrogated gendered power structures.

While this chapter concentrates on two Mothra movies, other Tōhō Studios films explore gender roles in some interesting ways. For example, in *San Daikaijū: Chikyū Saidai no Kessen* (*Ghidorah, the Three-Headed Monster*), released in 1964, the same year as *Mothra vs. Godzilla*, a foreign princess acts as a conduit for a Venusian voice of reason amidst a panicking Japan.[26] This is contrary to the typical portrayal of women as illogical, over-emotional characters. In *Gojira tai Mekagojira* (*Godzilla vs. Mechagodzilla*) (1974), an Okinawan priestess summons the local monster deity, King Caesar, via song, a relationship with obvious parallels to the example of *Mothra*. In this film as in the Mothra movies, we see a connection between women and relatively benevolent monsters. In all these cases, a few common themes emerge. First, women tend to have access to the natural world and, by extension, the monstrous. Second, those who are connected to the monsters are often foreign, by which we mean non–Japanese. Third, the unbridled female and/or monster disrupts the nation-state. Whether this is to be applauded or deplored is left to the audience to decide.

In the remainder of this chapter, we will clarify our interpretation of the Mothra movies. Although there is some doubt about Mothra's sex, the general consensus is that Mothra is female. We believe this to be clear.[27] Mothra is a brightly-colored moth, elegant and, for lack of a better term, pretty. She is not a gnarly-skinned monster, a hairy ape, or prickly dinosaur. The design of Mothra clearly designates her as feminine, if not female. Nor is she a violent being; rather her attacks are often based on protecting others, not aggression. Additionally, Mothra lays eggs, an action biologically associated with female creatures. Finally, Mothra is inextricably connected to women in the movies, as we will see. For all these reasons, we contend that Mothra is undeniably female.

At first glance, *Mothra* and *Mothra vs. Godzilla* might seem misogynist and racist, especially to viewers today. Instead of simply chalking this up to histories of racial elitism and Confucian patriarchy, we invite readers to consider the interplay of the aforementioned societal themes and the movies' narratives and audiovisual elements. We understand these films not as masculine kitsch but rather as nimble commentaries on the increasingly complex nexus of gender, economics, and environmentalism in a Japan emerging from the shadow of defeat. In doing so, we discover a unique social commentary embedded in the Mothra films, a commentary as serious and as relevant as that of the original *Godzilla*.

Beauty and Beast: Mothra (1961)

Among all the Tōhō *kaijū*, Mothra is by far the most successful after Godzilla. In addition to her introduction in a stand-alone movie, Mothra appeared in four Shōwa-era Godzilla films, and five Heisei-era Tōhō productions including her own trilogy (as discussed in Chapter 11). She returned in three Millennium-era Godzilla films in the early 2000s. The majestic moth even made a cameo appearance in Hollywood's *Kong: Skull Island* (2017) and is rumored to appear in future productions of Legendary Entertainment's "MonsterVerse," including sequels to *Godzilla* (2014) scheduled to run into the 2020s.[28]

The vision of Mothra is said to have appeared to special effects artist Tsuburaya Eiji in a dream.[29] He submitted the idea to Tanaka Tomoyuki, who commissioned a three-part serialized story that served as the foundation for the *Mothra* script written by Sekizawa Shinichi.[30] The movie, directed by Honda and scored by Koseki Yūji, opened in Japan on July 30, 1961.[31] It became a box-office success. Koseki's participation in the film is an anomaly, given that Honda, Tsuburaya, and Tanaka were all *kaijū eiga* regulars at this point. Erik Homenick, Ifukube biographer, suggested that Ifukube's absence might be due to his concentration on completing *Ritmica Ostinata* for premiere in October of 1961 in addition to scoring *Musashi Miyamoto* and *Osaka-jō Monogatari* (*The Story of Osaka Castle*) that same year.[32]

Koseki had trained as a classical music composer and written several ballads in support of the military during the war years.[33] In the postwar era, he continued to work in the popular realm and was a long-time collaborator with the music duo The Peanuts (twins Itō Yumi and Emi), who appear in the Mothra movies as the Twin Fairies.[34] Koseki's musical language is distinct from Ifukube Akira's, but not jarringly so. Koseki's score owes more to Rodgers and Hammerstein's 1958 movie musical *South Pacific* than to Ifukube's heavy, motivic-driven scores. The result was a score that is lush with exoticist tropes but lacks in memorable themes aside from the crucial diegetic performance of the Mothra Song discussed later in this chapter. In this way, Koseki's score and the movie itself established musical and narrative motifs that appear throughout the Mothra oeuvre, such as concerns regarding women's roles, unchecked capitalism, and the conservation of nature.

Mothra begins with a typhoon causing a Japanese ship to capsize.[35] Four sailors survive the wreck and make it safely to shore, only to realize they are on Infant Island, an area infamously devastated by radioactive fallout from nuclear weapons testing by the imaginary nation of Rolisica. It is worth noting here that Rolisica, though again an imaginary nation, represents both Soviet Russia and the United States. "Ro" is an abbreviation of the Japanese *roshia*, for Russia, while the ending "ka" references the last syllable in "America."[36] The Rolisican flag depicted in the film borrows iconography from the Soviet and American flags, a golden star and curved sickle in the center between red and white stripes. Moreover, the cloak and dagger actions of the Rolisican government and its people, including antagonist Clark Nelson, imply a Russian connection.[37] Yet when we finally receive shots of Rolisica, they are clearly American, with sequences taking place at a cattle ranch and later New Kirk City. Establishing shots of New Kirk City are a combination of scale models of New York City and stock footage of Los Angeles. So, via its very name and its portrayal in the film, Rolisica represents both America and Russia. This is worth keeping in mind as *Mothra* is an early example of *kaijū eiga* commenting on global politics.[38]

From the description of Infant Island, we can clearly understand it as a stand-in for Bikini Atoll, albeit one infused with a Skull Island aesthetic borrowed from *King Kong*. Military personnel rescue the sailors, who are kept in quarantine in case they develop radiation sickness. However, the young sailors never become ill. The situation baffles scientists and excites the press; the newspaper reporters are eager to share information regarding a possible cure for radiation poisoning. It is in gestures like this one that we can still identify the lingering traces of postwar trauma. The discovery of a possible cure for radiation poisoning provides the impetus for a mission to Infant Island.

The scientists plan to limit reports on the sailors' condition until they can run more tests, but a determined team of reporters manages to sneak in, hoping to snag a scoop. Journalist Fukuda Zenichirō (Frankie Sakai) and photographer Hanamura Michiko (Kagawa Kyōko) of *Nitto News* discover that not only are the sailors immune to radiation, there are also natives still living on Infant Island.[39] The pair discover that the natives gave the sailors a red juice that protected them from sickness. The promise of this discovery prompts the Japanese government along with the Rolisican government to co-sponsor an expedition to Infant Island. Ostensibly the goal is to make contact with the native leaders, but the Rolisican Clark Nelson (Jerry Ito) has other plans. Nelson insists on no reporters joining the expedition, but accepts that the leading

Japanese radiation scientist Dr. Harada (Uehara Ken) and linguist Chūjō Shinichi (Koizumi Hiroshi) may come along.

As the expedition ship leaves its Japanese dock, well-wishers including the *Nitto News* team and Chūjō's little brother, Shinji (Tayama Masamitsu) bid them *bon voyage*.[40] Among the travelers, Nelson alone stands surly on the deck, waving goodbye to no one. This hints at his questionable character; he is singularly lacking normative social ties. His social isolation suggests an inherent self-interest, portrayed as a social evil that can potentially destroy an entire community.

Distracted by the departure and blaring brass band, Michiko loses Fukuda in the crowd as the ship departs. En route, the film shows the viewer a conversation between Chūjō and Dr. Harada; they are concerned about Nelson's secretiveness and his refusal to share scientific information with the academic community. After this, the movie reveals a shot of Nelson in his cabin searching a drawer containing several pistols. Nelson discovers Fukuda hidden in the room and threatens him with a gun. Chūjō, apparently intending to confront Nelson, enters and rescues his fellow countryman. By this point in the film, it is clear that Nelson is not an honest person; his foreign swarthiness and his lack of social connections are external manifestations of his polluted spirit. This spiritual pollution is not supernatural however (a case we will encounter in the Heisei Mothra series). In Nelson's case, monetary greed and a desire for power provide fertile ground for the fatal flaw.

The team finally arrives at Infant Island and sets out to explore, making sure to undergo a thorough check of their radiation suits before landfall. The group treks through a craggy landscape accompanied by Koseki's luscious underscore.[41] As they reach the peak, Chūjō and Fukuda are the first to discover an expansive green valley.[42] Glissando harps and blaring trumpet act as a stinger synchronized to the shot of the valley to emphasize its jarring placement on the desolate island.[43]

An oasis amidst a land infused with radioactive fallout, the valley shocks the expedition. Here we can already identify obvious resonances with Japan's contemporary situation. Although Infant Island is clearly meant to represent Bikini Atoll, in a way it also represents Japan, a Japan that dreams of a return to a vibrant green environment—a kind of "Ur-Nippon" that did not experience the atomic bombings, suffer radiation poisoning, or face a long bitter path to recovery. The valley is the opposite of concrete-smothered Tokyo; pristine, untouched by modernization, literally immune to the poisons of science, technology, and war. What we see here is the kernel of an unspoken idea that carries throughout both Mothra movies, that is, the portrayal of Infant Island and its people (the Other) is in some ways a portrayal of Japan and its people (the Self). This notion becomes more apparent as we progress through the two films.[44]

The team descends into the jungle; notably only diegetic sound accompanies them on their trek.[45] Chūjō becomes separated from the group and enters a mysterious cave. The soundtrack includes high strings, harps, and pizzicato in the low strings repeating a motif. Oboe and bassoon enter, playing a short sequential motif. The effect creates an aura of mystery. As Chūjō finds a stone inscription the sound of a non-diegetic Electone (electric organ) rises in the mix, an orchestrational choice that adumbrates the appearance of the Twin Fairies (Itō Yumi and Emi). As Chūjō makes his way back to camp, a tentacled flora attacks him. Just before he passes out, the Lilliputian-sized twins, drawn to his location by a distress beacon, appear and rescue him, an Electone accompanying their appearance. Chūjō catches a glimpse of them before passing out. He awakes in bed on the ship and describes the twins, whom Fukuda dubs "little beauties" (*shobijin*).

The following day, Chūjō tests a theory. He sets off his distress beacon on purpose, hoping to attract the fairies and speak with them. He is successful, though the beacon also brings the rest of the expedition to his location, among them Nelson. Chūjō explains that he realized the Twin Fairies are sensitive to sound. Though a comment made in passing, the idea is crucial to clarifying the connection between music and the little beauties. In this, *Mothra* (and later *Mothra vs. Godzilla*) follow the classical Hollywood model of scoring that film music scholar Claudia Gorbman lays out in her seminal text, *Unheard Melodies*.[46] Akin to Steiner's practices in *Kong*, the use of music in *Mothra* aligns nature, the feminine, and the foreign with music. Conversely, civilization, the rational, and the masculine are rarely treated with music.

A moment in the film clarifies this mode of signification—Chūjō, having lured the fairies out of hiding, attempts to converse with them.[47] The twins, wearing tan toga-like dresses and red flowers in their hair, seem to be singing, yet instead of words, a meandering, mostly stepwise line played on a solo Electone seems to emit from them. An excited Fukuda declares, "A song! They're singing!" Chūjō gently corrects him, "No, it's not a song. That's their language. It doesn't belong to any linguistic system. It's more of a code." Dr. Harada asks if Chūjō can understand them. Chūjō replies, "It seems like they're asking us not to harm their island."[48]

Fukuda chimes in: "Of course, they've had atomic and nuclear testing here before."[49] Behind the two main characters a Japanese team member continuously snaps photographs of the fairies, who nod in confirmation of Fukuda's comment. Chūjō promises that there will be no more nuclear testing. As the fairies smile and wave farewell after this guarantee, Nelson gestures to his crony, who grabs the tiny women. Fukuda and Chūjō challenge him, but Nelson declares the "rare specimens" to be valuable. Nelson's crony commands the little beauties to "Shut up!" As the fairies struggle, the Electone plays a definitive melodic line with clear cadential structure, foreshadowing the recurring motif of the Mothra Song described later in this chapter.[50] As the melody fades, the sound of drums and auxiliary percussion rises in the mix. It is the sound of emerging Infant Island natives (played by Japanese in blackface) beating stones and shells together in an ever-increasing tempo meant to intimidate Nelson into releasing the fairies. Nelson wants to fight the natives, but Dr. Harada overrules him, noting that violence has no place on a scientific expedition. The team coerces Nelson into releasing the twins. The percussion-playing natives immediately cease, and the twins again "sing" the Mothra Song as they depart.

We attend to this sequence in particular for a number of reasons. This moment sets up a definitive binary of woman/music/nature versus man/language/civilization, akin to Kate Soper's "antithetical equivalence" noted earlier.[51] More interestingly, it asks us to consider music as language, a concept still debated by music scholars today.[52] Like most of the general population, *Mothra* accepts music's expressive ability; all that is left is the need for a cipher to translate it. Just as Chūjō, an eminent linguist, interprets the fairies' sounds, so too can we interpret the musical choices made by Koseki and the rest of the movie's team. Of specific interest is the use of the Electone.

The Electone, an electric organ/synthesizer created by Yamaha in 1959, grew out of the popularity of music education in the postwar era.[53] It was one of the first instruments to create digital sound using transistors instead of vacuum tubes.[54] As such, the Electone (named because of its use of electricity to produce sound) represented a new accessibility in domestic music-making as well as an early Japanese foray into high technology. Most viewers, especially non–Japanese ones, might have missed the irony of using an Electone to make the fairies "speak," but the result is musical cogency.[55] The fairies are simultaneously incarnations of modern magic and a domestic dream.

In this sense, the Twin Fairies represent a new Japan, one of female mobility and modernity, but still kept at bay. The small size of the twins is not only a reference to a patriarchal desire to control; they can also be understood as representing Japan's perceived relationship with the United States, one typically characterized as hierarchical and gendered. Indeed women, from the stylish new flight attendants for Pan American Airlines to the traditional Kyoto geisha, came to symbolize Japan in iconography of the 1960s.[56]

The use of blackface in the portrayal of the Infant Island natives similarly indicates a complicated act navigating identities of Self and Other. Although blackface is unfortunately still used without regards to racial sensitivity in Japan, the act of painting actors' faces a different color cannot be ignored. Though the practice was not continued in *Mothra vs. Godzilla*, it is noteworthy. In donning blackface, the Japanese actors assumed a stereotyped mantle of Other-ness, one that is doubly reflected onto the bodies of the actors performing as natives. That is, they are Japanese (Other in relation to the West), but made to look like another Other (dark-skinned Pacific Islanders).[57] These natives, unlike the ones in *Mothra vs. Godzilla*, do not speak. They merely appear, banging rocks or coconut shells in an attempt to intimidate the expedition, or are shown worshipping Mothra. So in the original *Mothra*, the depiction of the Infant Island natives visibly and narratively distances them from their Japanese counterparts on Nelson's expedition. The Twin Fairies serve as intermediaries both between the "primitive" natives and the "civilized" Japanese as well as between Mothra and humanity. This digression informs our understanding of the rest of the movie.

After the first encounter with the islanders, Fukuda and Chūjō concur that it might be best to leave Infant Island alone, lest its fragile environment and people suffer even more. The team returns to Japan welcomed by a brass band, and Fukuda begins an investigation of Nelson. His past is incredibly shady; his birthdate, country of origin, and wartime activities are all unlisted. This serves to further characterize Nelson as a misanthropic outsider. Fukuda does discover Nelson's past endeavor to find beautiful women from the Amazon for entertainment purposes. This finding connects Nelson's desire to control women with his quest for capital. The linking of these two activities thus provides a transparent commentary on gender and economics. The two protagonists determine that Nelson is likely a dealer in artifacts on the black market. Trying to solve the mystery of Infant Island's preservation despite the nuclear tests, Chūjō shares with Fukuda some cave rubbings of strange hieroglyphs discovered there. Using a Polynesian dictionary as a guide, Chūjō determines a prominent glyph to be "Mosura." Its meaning, however, is unclear.

Nelson, with his cronies, secretly returns to Infant Island. He successfully captures the fairies while his henchmen mercilessly gun down approaching natives.[58] The blood-bath is shocking.[59] This sequence recreates the atrocities and horrors of the Asia-Pacific War on the part of both the Allies and Japan. Because of the jungle *mise-en-scène*, the depiction of natives, and the non–Japanese aggressors, the shots seem to evoke the Battle of Okinawa, a brutal combat that resulted in the deaths of tens of thousands of Japanese soldiers, American troops, and Okinawan civilians.[60] It is a disturbing moment of remembrance in the film at a time when most sought to forget and erase past atrocities. Moreover, the sequence is an uncanny premonition of America's escalating involvement in Vietnam. Watching it today, one cannot help but be reminded of numerous similar shots in films about the horrors of warfare in Southeast Asia. Despite the vagueness of this reference, the meaning itself is clear: capitalist greed is deadly to humanity's peaceful coexistence with the natural world.[61]

Nelson and his team, having slaughtered numerous islanders, abscond with the fairies. The film cuts to a dying native ascending a stone staircase to an altar with Grecian columns. The native rasps, "Mosura" before collapsing.[62] The orchestral underscore swells as the native falls to the ground. A wordless chorus enters the soundtrack as the camera focuses on a crumbling dirt wall that reveals a giant blue and yellow pastel egg. Glissando harps enhance the cue as the shot fades out.

Nelson is obsessed with creating a stage show centered on the little beauties, convinced that it will make him wealthy. He has completely forgotten that the original purpose behind the trip was to discover the secret cure for radiation sickness. Such a cure could be profitable, but its discovery would make for a more positive portrait of Nelson. Instead, Nelson creates an entertainment event called "The Secret Fairies Show" performed at a theater in the southeast portion of the Chūō district in Tokyo. Chūō is an area known as the main commercial center in Tokyo and it encompasses the famous shopping and entertainment neighborhood Ginza.[63] Crowds flock to see the show, which begins with a diegetic orchestral fanfare heralding Nelson's appearance on stage in a tuxedo.[64] He welcomes the audience and introduces the little beauties, declaring:

> We now live in the atomic age. But are miracles a thing of the past? Is mystery merely a word? No, miracles still exist. Mysteries are not just in dreams. Now, let me show you the modern-day mystery, the modern-day miracle that I have discovered after great hardships. Allow me to introduce my lovely fairies.[65]

Honda and his team packed a lot of information into this monologue and the following performance sequences. Nelson's speech is compelling. In a Japan increasingly facing the consequences of the atomic age and postwar modernization, the idea of miracles and mystery is an attractive one. The fairies in this sense are displayed as relics of a lost past untarnished by modern civilization. As Nelson concludes his speech he gestures to an upper corner of the theater. A tiny golden carriage emerges from behind a curtain and floats down to the main stage accompanied by what seems to be non-diegetic Electone. The carriage lands on the stage and audience members (including Fukuda, Chūjō, and his little brother Shinji) clamor for a view of the stage. Nelson opens the minute carriage door and the Twin Fairies emerge while drum, trumpets, flutes, and high strings (ostensibly diegetic given the shot of the pit orchestra earlier in the sequence) appear in the soundtrack. The twins step out, dressed in South Asian-inspired costumes, and proceed to sing the eponymous Mothra Song.

The Mothra Song begins with a low register drum beating a duple-meter pulse that remains constant throughout the tune.[66] Soon high brass, strings, and woodwinds enter with a flourish. In this context, the song is a showpiece of exoticism. The lyrics are in Malay, though sung thickly with Japanese pronunciation. They pray for Mothra to come help, metaphorically referring to her as a natural force, "like a wave."[67]

While the Twin Fairies sing, they perform a dance rich with gestures and movements reminiscent of traditional Thai dance. "Natives" (apparently Japanese hired by Nelson) encircle the fairies' platform and perform a rough imitation of a tribal dance. During this performance no one can take their eyes off the stage—the theater audience is entranced. Fukuda and Chūjō whisper during the song, Chūjō relating that the Rolisican government was not enthusiastic about the expedition and Nelson funded it without receiving government support. During all this they never glance at each other. The shot cuts from them to a long shot of the entire stage of dancers. Chūjō then recognizes the melody to the Mothra Song—it is the same one the fairies "sang" when captured by Nelson on the island. The camera moves to extreme close-ups of Fukuda and Chūjō, centered on their eyes. Interspersed with medium shots of the fairies we receive shots of the stage from the balcony that can be understood as a point of view shot from the pair of protagonists.[68] Following this shot, we receive a long shot of Infant Island, the drums disappearing from the mix and the fairies' voices echoing slightly to create a perception of distance.[69]

As that aural world fades a new one emerges in the soundtrack. This one includes drums, gong, and high flutes. Shots of Mothra's altar and "real" dancing natives appear concomitant with this music. The Infant Islanders sit in a circle clapping in time to what may or may not be diegetic music (no mouths appear to move in the shots of the islanders). A man and woman enter the center of the ring and dance seductively. Above them sits Mothra's giant egg. A mixed chorus appears in the soundtrack, repeating "Mosura." Though melodically more restricted than the fairies' song, the feel is the same. The female dancer shakes her hips in time to the music, punctuated by synch points in the brass and strings. As the sequence concludes, glissando harps dominate the underscore while the camera cuts to a shot of the egg. Back-lit lighting and the sound of thunder denote the end of the sequence as the mixed chorus holds its final chord. The sequence ends with a hard cut to the two fairies imprisoned and singing mournfully with human voices accompanied by Electone.[70]

This Mothra Song sequence is a significant moment in the film and to our argument. To begin with, it is the first time the Mothra Song appears in the *kaijū eiga* world. This scene establishes the Mothra Song as a cue connected to the fairies, the foreign, and the monster. Moreover, this sequence represents the first time the fairies have the ability to speak, albeit one that is rooted in the musical and the foreign. The choice to not provide translated subtitles for the song contributes to the exotic quality of the piece; despite having words the text does not seem to matter, at least not to the Japanese listeners (and by extension the movie audience). Yet we know that it has meaning—Chūjō says as much when he recognizes the song as being a plea for help. This ability to decipher the fairies' song and sympathize with them augments our understanding of Chūjō as protagonist. Conversely, Nelson clearly does not understand the song's purpose. If he did, he would forbid it. In this way, the movie esteems acts of musical interpretation. It depicts music as a vehicle for subversion; the fairies' song, its meaning lost on the antagonist and the entertainment-hungry masses, in actuality beckons Mothra and her wrath.

Additionally, the sequence provides a strange doubling. Viewers see Japanese dancers perform primitivistic movements on Nelson's stage soon followed by a recreation of this dance by the "real" natives of Infant Island. In other words, Nelson's Tokyo staging of primitivism is a reimagination of an already imagined Other. None of the Tokyo performers wear blackface, and their costumes, while bright and sparse, are more tailored than the costume design for the Infant Islanders. The Tokyo dancers' movements also seem more polished than those of the islanders. The "actual" ritual dance, with its *pas de deux*, displays a more intense sexuality than the sanitized version performed in the Tokyo theater.

But what can any of this tell us about Japan, nature, and its international positioning? The sequence provides us with a view of cinematic depictions of Asian Others during this specific point in Japanese history, a point when Japan was working to define itself against these Others. But simultaneously, there is an element of Self (Japaneseness) in these depictions; after all, the performers are in all likelihood Japanese. The movie also works to compel its viewers, along with Chūjō and Fukuda, to sympathize with and favor the natives. Watching the film, we almost feel shame for the Japanese audience clamoring to see Nelson's show. The audience does not question the show's dubious background, they merely seek entertainment. In this sense, the Japanese audience is similar to that for Kong in New York City. However, the *Mothra* audience is more middle-class than that in *Kong*. Nelson apparently made his tickets more affordable than Denham. This is interesting to consider—Nelson's show is entertainment for all, while Denham's is more akin to a high-class excitement.

The audience in *Mothra* gazes at the exotic stereotypes on-stage, completely absorbed by Nelson's false, immoral world. The shots of the audience, perhaps even more than those of the actual performance, clarify the filmmakers' message: uncritical consumption encourages and even propagates immoral acts in the name of profit. The critique of blind consumerism is equally pertinent to concern over fair trade practices and ethical sourcing, issues that resonate with global society of the 21st century.

Following the Mothra Song sequence, Chūjō, Fukuda, and Michiko confront Nelson and his gang about the fairies. Here Nelson, chortling in true evil-villain style, literally says: "My fairies do not understand speech."[71] Fukuda asks Nelson to "stop this inhumanity" and return the fairies to the island. Nelson's Japanese partner scoffs, "Inhumanity? Ridiculous! Strictly speaking, they're scientific data." Nelson goes one step further, chiming in, "Those fairies aren't human. They're merchandise." This scene makes plain the issues foreshadowed in previous scenes, issues concerning detrimental scientific testing and the treatment of cognizant beings as if they were goods. That the fairies are foreign, female, and the size of dolls all feeds into this understanding. It also seems evident that the fairies are in some way representative of Japan—foreign, female, doll-size—these are all characteristics Western entertainment would draw on (and in many ways still does) to depict Japan.[72] The film drives this home in a later performance sequence in which the Twin Fairies sing a Japanese song while wearing kimono (it turns out they do understand the language).

Nevertheless, Nelson is not wrong when he says the fairies are not human; they are something more than human. Though they appear to be cute, tiny humans, they are also aberrations, mystic representatives of an ancient and powerful monster, Mothra. The fairies, though small and seemingly helpless, are, by means of their mistress, Mothra, mightier than all humans and military technology combined.

Throughout the latter half of the film, the movie makes clear the superiority of Mothra, and through her, the fairies. As a larva, Mothra rampages through Japan, seeking to rescue her tiny priestesses. The Rolisican and Japanese governments are impotent in their attempt to destroy Mothra's cocoon, which is woven on the ruins of Tokyo Tower, itself a symbol of Japanese technology and mass media. It is only through the protagonists' efforts to free the fairies and return them to Mothra that the monster can be appeased. In this way, as David Kalat points out, *Mothra* is a unique movie in which the monster "wins."[73]

The original *Mothra* also clarifies a connection between the feminine and nature. The symbiotic relationship between the fairies and Mothra can be understood as representing two facets of the feminine: one, seemingly cute, weak, and domestic, the other beautiful and strong, with a power that reflects that of the natural world.[74] Mothra guards the delicate, verdant oasis on Infant Island. She is a protector and preserver of nature in the midst of technological destruction. Moreover, Mothra's attacks on Japan and Rolisica are at their core, natural disasters. The most compelling scene in the Japan attack is a flood from a broken dam; Fukuda risks his life to rescue a baby as waves crash into a crumbling bridge. In Rolisica's New Kirk City (a stand-in fusion of New York City and Los Angeles), Mothra uses her wind attack to destroy the metropolis. The shots of Tsuburaya's detailed miniatures being destroyed by deadly winds echo the movie's opening shots of the typhoon.[75] Indeed in this film and later ones, Mothra is connected to typhoons, storms that carry special weight in Japanese cultural history as both *kamikaze*, or god-winds, and as annual seasons of destruction.[76]

Mothra's very life cycle of birth, transformation, death, and rebirth mimics the natural world's tendency to bring life out of death.[77] Mothra is nature. In this she represents a stark contrast to Godzilla, a product of science gone amok. Unlike Godzilla, Gamera, and a host of other *kaijū*, Mothra is not created, awakened, or mutated by science—she simply exists. Mothra and the natives are immune to the radioactive poisons Godzilla simultaneously suffers from and spreads. The filmmakers in this way imply that a return to a more natural existence may ameliorate the conflicting and disastrous results of technology.

In the film's climax, Nelson and his gang escape to Rolisica, encasing the fairies in a soundproof box so they cannot telepathically call to Mothra for help. Mothra still manages to follow the evil-doers to New Kirk City and wreaks havoc until the fairies are released. Nelson, in his attempt to escape, is mobbed by Rolisicans who have realized that he is the true cause of their suffering. The rowdy crowd piles around Nelson's car. A series of shots and reverse-shots provides a glimpse of Nelson's point of view. Shots of the Rolisican mob are interspersed with shots of vengeful Infant Islanders.[78] Nelson tries to escape the crowd, but someone shoots him in the back.[79]

In the denouement, Chūjō, Fukuda, and Michiko arrive in New Kirk City in hopes of stopping Mothra's rampage. They piece together a plan using the local mission's bells to play the Mothra Song and thus beckon the monster to a safely cleared airstrip. There the team returns the Twin Fairies to the monster. The twins thank them, speaking in unison, and Chūjō promises that Infant Island will not be disturbed again. The fairies climb onto Mothra's back and together they fly away. The film's closing shots depict Infant Island and natives worshipping at Mothra's altar accompanied by orchestra and wordless chorus that, according to a concluding voice-over is "a prayer for peace and prosperity to last for all eternity."[80]

Mothra vs. Godzilla *(1964)—Nature vs. Capitalism*

The 1961 film *Mothra* establishes significant musical and thematic elements, most notably the Mothra Song, the association between nature and the feminine, and a critical examination of unchecked capitalism. The diametric opposition of environmentalism and capitalism is another core concept of ecocritical theory, placing the Mothra franchise's critique of unrestrained capitalism firmly within the environmentalist framework.[81] The 1964 sequel *Mothra vs. Godzilla* perfects these themes and weaves them into a tight narrative embellished with monster battles. The combination is compelling. Stuart Galbraith even refers to the film as "the apex of the *kaijū eiga* genre."[82] It is worth noting that Mothra's name receives top billing in the film's title, denoting her importance, whereas nearly every other film starring Godzilla features his name first.

While superficially the film is about the conflict between the monsters, the subtext shows us that the true conflict is between humankind and nature. Attending to the narrative and audiovisual elements makes this apparent.[83] The opening credits of *Mothra vs. Godzilla* are telling; after a shot of Tōhō's emblem accompanied by a resonating gong, the Godzilla theme used in this film (a version of the Horror theme in the original 1954 film but with added introductory material in the low brass) emerges in synchronization with the title card.[84] Already, it is clear that Ifukube's score will be more thematically driven than Koseki's. The rest of the opening credits are projected onto a background of a typhoon storm. The Horror theme elides into a new theme—one that we later find to be associated with Mothra. A stepwise descent characterizes this theme, which we designate the Mothra motif.[85] Along with the orchestral music, the sound effect of blowing wind and waves can be heard, with percussion and brass serving as musical sweeteners supporting the effect.[86] When the opening credits end, the movie provides us a full view of typhoon destruction on the shores of Kurata Beach. The sounds of the natural world, such as the wind, the waves, and crumbling wooden structures, ebbs and flows in the soundtrack's mix. In the first three minutes of the film the soundtrack presents the two monsters' leitmotifs and acoustically establishes the driving thematic concern with the relationship between nature and the human-made world.

A hard cut to a shot of giant pumps loudly clearing the typhoon's floodwaters drives this theme home. As locals work to clear the wreckage, two representatives of *Maichō Newspaper* arrive on the scene. A politician involved in the Kurata Beach Industrialization Project confronts the journalist Sakai Ichirō (Takarada Akira) and photographer

Nakanishi Junko (Hoshi Yuriko), complaining about the newspaper's report on the typhoon's effect on the project.[87] The filmmakers again find a clever way to insert this concern between industrialization and nature early on in the film.

They also depict the suspicious relationship between politics and industry. The assemblyman promises a group of reporters that the project will continue as scheduled, claiming "I've never told a lie," followed by a studied cackle; clearly the opposite is true.[88] What is interesting here is the subtle shift in antagonists. While the 1961 *Mothra* featured Nelson, a foreign capitalist, as the main villain, here the antagonists are unscrupulous Japanese businessmen in collusion with elected public officials. The shift reveals a growing social concern with internal corruption and detrimental industrial practices.[89]

Amidst the beachfront wreckage, Junko arranges an artful photo of the detritus. To Sakai's chagrin she dubs a shiny piece of rubbish "a ray of light on a scene of utter destruction."[90] Tremolo strings and a vibraphone accompany the shot of this "pretty" garbage, suggesting there is something significant and mysterious about it. Woodwinds join the underscore as Sakai lifts the metallic debris out of the lapping water.

The movie then cuts to a brief scene back in the newsroom, before shifting to a small fishing village. Villagers gaze at a large egg floating on the ocean's horizon, an ovoid Aphrodite. A cue featuring Electone and strings accompany the shots of the celadon egg. This is a clever orchestrational technique on Ifukube's part to create a cohesive *kaijū* sound world, signaling to viewers of the original movie the egg's connection to Mothra. Initially, the villagers fear the monstrous egg but a Shintō priest convinces them to tow it ashore. News of the egg graces the headlines of several newspapers and attracts scientists' attention. Note that all those concerned with the giant ovular jewel are men—first the local fishermen and priests, then scientists, newspaper reporters, and finally capitalists. This could be understood as a subtle critique of gender relations in 1960s Japan; that is, the feminine is subject to spectacle, study, and exploitation by men.

Sakai and Junko travel to the coast of Shizunoura to report on the egg. They encounter the scientist Professor Miura (Koizumi Hiroshi) taking samples of eggshell and attempt to interview him, but soon the venture capitalist Kumayama (Tajima Yoshibumi) interrupts them. Kumayama orders the professor to cease damaging the egg which is now owned by his company, Happy Enterprises. Astounded, Prof. Miura asks how Kumayama purchased the egg. Kumayama explains the process. He calculated that the egg is approximately 153,820 times larger than a chicken egg. Since chicken eggs have a market value of eight yen each, Kumayama offered the villagers ¥1,224,560 (8 × 153,820, but incorrectly). He even produces a receipt to verify the purchase.

The humor in this exchange lies in its absurd specificity. Kumayama monetizes the egg in a way that follows a certain kind of logic, albeit one that undercuts the egg's fantastic qualities. By putting a price on the egg, Kumayama attempts to harness the supernatural and bring the egg into the mundane world of capital exchange. Kumayama's approach is representative of the general relationship between capitalism and the environment. Humanity tends to monetize nature despite our lack of knowledge and despite its pricelessness.[91] Often it is only in hindsight that we regret our overconsumption of natural resources, our over-dependence on chemicals for growing food, our hunger for petroleum. As with the Ancient Romans who consumed all of the world's silphium, or the Māori of New Zealand that wiped out the giant moa, it falls on future generations to pay the heaviest toll.[92] In this way, the egg in *Mothra vs. Godzilla* is not only a stand-in for the female, but also for nature and the environment.

Sakai and Junko argue that the egg should not be privately owned and is of value to the scientific community. Kumayama responds that the egg will be open to the public for viewing during its incubation period, though onlookers must pay an admission fee. The sequence ends with him laughing and blowing cigarette smoke at Junko as she takes a photograph. Kumayama is clearly an unsavory character, but we soon learn that he is merely a front for the real mastermind behind Happy Enterprises, Torahata Jirō (Sahara Kenji).

Kumayama and Torahata meet at a nearby hotel following the confrontation on the beach.[93] Delighted, they estimate Happy Enterprises' profits far exceed the price they paid the fishermen. As they plan the Shizunoura Happy Center, a pair of high-pitched voices command, "You must not." Torahata, believing Kumayama spoke, orders him to not use such a weird voice.[94] Kumayama denies that it was him and the voices plead "Please return the egg."[95] The men, unable to see anyone, conclude the voices belong to corporate spies. They search the room, Torahata opening a cabinet full of money that catches Kumayama's attention. At that moment, the Twin Fairies appear on a mantle asking again for the egg's return. High-pitched alternating chords in a minor mode along with a subtle cyclic melody accompany the fairies' appearance.[96] The music abruptly stops when Kumayama tries to capture the little ladies and reappears as they escape. Sakai, who had been listening in, enters the room offering to help catch the nonexistent robbers, though it is obvious his real purpose was to discover the identity of Kumayama's business partner.

Outside the resort, Sakai, Junko, and Prof. Miura gather to discuss what to do about Kumayama and Torahata. Sakai relates that Torahata is the son of a prominent businessman and has powerful political connections. The fairies interrupt, and beg "Please return the egg."[97] Startled, the protagonists search for the voices' source. They discover the little women sitting on a tree branch. The earlier cue accompanies this shot of the fairies, thinning out to an instrumental version of what later becomes the diegetic cue Sacred Springs. This music underscores the fairies' narration of the events that led to the egg's arrival off the coast of Japan. They describe the dire ecological situation on Infant Island, a result of nuclear testing in combination with the recent typhoon. They relate that the egg belongs to Mothra.

Like the 1961 film, the fairies here speak in unison. When they speak of the typhoon, cymbals and low brass along with other sound effects appear in the soundtrack; they aurally emphasize the past event, shown in flashback. As the film returns to the present, the fairies beg for the return of the egg, asking the team if they can hear the voices of the native people. We receive a lengthy sound advance of a yodeling voice and percussion as the fairies "listen" to the distant islanders' prayer. This cuts to a scene of brown-skinned Infant Islanders, some in feathered headdresses, genuflecting and dancing. The music fades into the lament as the scene cuts back to the fairies and the protagonists.

The team sympathizes with the fairies, but feel there is little they can do to help.

They ask what will happen if the egg is not returned. The Twin Fairies explain that when the egg hatches, the larvae will be hungry and likely cause damage in their quest to find food and return to Infant Island. The fairies explain that Mothra also asks for the humans' help, pointing out that she is waiting nearby. A loud brass stinger appears in the soundtrack when Sakai catches a glimpse of Mothra behind some barren trees. It is here that we first receive Mothra's orchestral cue, or motif, in the movie proper.[98] As Mothra takes flight the cue likewise lifts off. Trumpets play a short, nine-note phrase in the upper registers. Below, harp glissandi add a textural impression of atmospheric gliding while simultaneously alluding to the exotic. The scene fades to black, the music lingering until the following sequence that features construction workers building the Shizunoura Happy Center.

In a nearby lounge, Sakai, Junko, and Prof. Miura confront Kumayama and Torahata about the egg, asking for them to return it to Infant Island. Kumayama argues that there is no proof of the egg's rightful owner. Sakai's explanation that the egg obviously belongs to Mothra gives the capitalists pause. But Torahata undercuts any thought of the serious consequences of refusal, jokingly asking if Sakai has power-of-attorney for Mothra. The protagonists then offer proof of the egg belonging to Mothra. Junko opens a lacquered travel box, revealing the Twin Fairies who emerge and again beg for the egg's return. Instead of listening to the little ladies, Kumayama offers to buy the fairies, upping his price at the team's appalled refusal. It is worth considering that this whole scene plays out without any music. Only the distant sound of construction and dialogue can be heard. Even the fairies' appearance is unscored. This judicious lack of music reinforces the depiction of the capitalist industrialist world as cold and mundane.[99] Moreover, like Nelson's character in *Mothra*, Kumayama treats the Twin Fairies not as living beings, but as property to be bought and sold.

Dejected, the fairies return home, flying on Mothra's back, again accompanied by the Mothra motif along with Mothra's cry, a kind of electronically-manipulated screech. Sakai and the team spread news of the fairies' plight, leading to negative publicity for Happy Enterprises. The fishermen who originally sold the egg demand payment, which a strained Kumayama rebuffs. Torahata refuses to help Kumayama, but offers to loan him money with the egg as collateral. This scene, though short, depicts the capitalists as driven by self-interest without concern for honoring business agreements or personal friendships. Sakai becomes dejected that the news articles had little effect. He argues with his boss, who expounds on the duty of the press to champion the common people. Despite the bad press, the capitalists push forward, artificially heating the egg to speed incubation.

Sakai and Junko receive an invitation to Prof. Miura's lab. Before they enter, they must decontaminate; Miura relates that they had been exposed to radiation. He reveals that the shiny metallic flotsam that Junko photographed earlier in the film is extremely radioactive. In a close-up of the trash, Miura waves a Geiger counter around, which is accompanied by a stinger, a shocking dissonant chord that in this case signifies the ominous danger the radioactive rubbish represents. The scene cuts to Sakai and Junko hiking through the once-flooded plain where they discovered the dangerous junk. The politician from the first scenes appears, basking in the success of the typhoon recovery efforts. When Miura explains that they are conducting a test for radiation the pro-industrialist politician becomes irate, demanding that they cease at once. In these little ways, the film conveys the perceived corrupt relationship between business and government. After this conversation, the earth begins to tremor and Miura's Geiger counter crackles. A giant lizard tail pushes out of the sand. The jagged, introductory brass cue for Godzilla appears in the soundtrack, followed by a variation on the Horror theme.[100] Destruction ensues.

Godzilla heads inland. The first structure he attacks is a smoke-belching factory, a subtle environmental message foreshadowing themes addressed here and later in the Shōwa series. After destroying the factory, Godzilla proceeds to the heart of Nagoya, a city known as a key industrial center. The monster crushes skyscrapers, a broadcast tower, and Nagoya castle, which at this point was freshly rebuilt after being destroyed in World War II. Godzilla's attack prompts Prof. Miura, Sakai, and Junko to take desperate action. Spurred by an off-hand comment from fellow reporter Nakamura, they decide to ask Mothra for help defending her egg (and by extension Japan) from Godzilla.

The following sequence on Infant Island is filled with music as expected, given the precedent set by the first film and the score's tendency to connect the foreign and fantastic with music.[101] This sequence more than any other clarifies the relationship between the exotic and the monstrous while simultaneously speaking to Japanese positionality in Asia and addressing recurring concerns about nuclear testing and the environment. An establishing shot of the island introduces the sequence. Instead of the lush orchestrated strings that appeared with this shot in *Mothra*, a solo horn followed by a solo flute plays a plaintive modal melody in the lower registers. The cue continues as Sakai, Junko, and Prof. Miura land on the island, dressed in bright yellow anti-radiation suits.

The desolate craggy landscape covered with skeletal remains shocks Sakai and Junko. Sakai wonders if people can truly live in such a place and Junko asks Miura, "Is this all a result of nuclear testing?" He replies, "In simple terms, it's an aftermath of radiation. This must have been a beautiful green island at one time."[102] Junko explains that she in a way feels responsible for the disaster and Sakai angrily notes that anti-nuclear demonstrations do not even make the news anymore. As they trek through the rocky landscape, shots of red-painted natives peering over the stones are intercut with those of the protagonists and an oboe joins in the underscore.

Just then, the team spots the natives, who emerge from hiding and surround them. The music stops instantly, the silence acting as a kind of "shock" moment. The natives, covered in red paint, round the group up and take them to the chief elder. Music reappears in the underscore in the form of flutter-tongued flute in a low register accompanied by violin harmonics and vibraphone, and later, piano and muted brass. Natives fill the meeting space. Although these people are not painted, the costume design signifies their alterity. Many of the male natives wear headdresses (an inspiration seemingly borrowed from Hollywood Westerns) while the women appear in dresses, some embroidered, and wear orchids in their hair. The costuming is a strange conflation of indigenous cultures of North America and South Asia. Tremolo strings enter the score as women bring cups of juice to the Japanese visitors (who are now stripped of their radiation suits). As the music fades, the chief commands, "Drink!" in the English language.[103] The natives echo his order. This use of English as a *lingua franca* is a fascinating depiction of American culture's ubiquity. Even more intriguing is that, after the team gulps down the juice, the chief begins speaking fluent Japanese. He explains that the juice will rid their bodies of radiation poisoning. In this, nature literally cures the ills brought on by technology and militarism.

The chief asks why the team came to Infant Island. They explain that they hope to ask for Mothra's help in defeating Godzilla. The chief refuses their request. He goes on, describing the history of the island, its peaceful, Edenesque existence ruined by "devil's fire."[104] The island has since become a place of suffering; he cannot trust in the benevolence of outsiders like the Japanese, who will not even return Mothra's egg. As the chief ends his speech, the Twin Fairies can be heard singing Sacred Springs off-screen. The team follows the sound of their voices to a hidden oasis of jungle on the island.[105] The tune has much in common with the Requiem from *Godzilla*. It is in a minor mode, has a slow tempo, and the voices sing alternatively in unison and in close harmony.[106] Instead of mourning a destroyed Tokyo, however, Sacred Springs laments the destruction of the natural world. The Filipino lyrics go untranslated for the film's characters and the movie's viewers, but those able to comprehend the song's words can hear a simple text inviting the visitors to sit and enjoy the oasis of natural beauty amid an island of ash.[107] Although the lyrics are pertinent to the scene, it is the music that takes on significance in this instance.

A short horn solo introduces the lament. The tempo of the piece is slow and the meter is manipulated for ultimate expressive effect. The harmony is predominantly in a Phrygian mode and a descending pattern characterizes the melody.[108] This all contributes to the piece's requiem-esque quality. Indeed, the cue in many ways fuses together the elements from *Godzilla*'s Requiem with those of the Mothra Song. Here, Sacred Springs achieves something significant—it compels the main characters, and thus the viewers, to empathize with the islanders' situation. And the compassion rings true, despite the trappings of exoticism.[109]

As the fairies conclude their song, the team asks for Mothra's help to defend Japan (as well as her egg) against Godzilla. The fairies refuse and the natives shake their heads. Junko makes an impassioned plea to the natives and the fairies. She recognizes that the natives have little reason to trust the outsiders, but that among them, many good people will lose their lives to Godzilla. "Even bad ones," she argues, "have the right to live."[110] She begs for help before tearfully turning to Sakai, weeping on his shoulder. Sakai continues Junko's speech, admitting the problems of society, but arguing that one must not give up hope and that they are working together towards something better. As he pauses awaiting a reply, Mothra's screech resonates through the soundtrack. The same non-diegetic cue that introduced the Infant Island sequence appears as the fairies lead them to Mothra. The underscore elides into a diegetic performance of the Mothra Song by the fairies.

Ifukube pared down the original tune from *Mothra* to simple vocals and subtle string accompaniment. This change in orchestration gives more of a sense of a prayer-like chant than an entertaining song. The overall effect is that of a powerful prayer; the minute ladies, it shows, are able to communicate to the powerful monster through music. We can understand the cue not only as a catchy tune, but also as a way of endowing seemingly helpless characters with a power that is both benevolent and superior to

Godzilla's strength. As the fairies conclude, fragments of the Mothra motif appear in the score. The little ladies explain that Mothra will use her remaining strength to help the Japanese; she is near the end of her life and does not expect to survive. The final shot shows Mothra resting on her altar, screeching her willingness to help as the full form of the Mothra cue swells in volume.[111]

As the Infant Island scene fades, the film returns to Japan and the JSDF preparing for Godzilla's attack. Sounds of machinery, mixed high in the soundtrack, accompany several shots of bulldozers preparing a defensive wall. These shots and effects emphasize the film's subtext: humanity's hubristic trust in industry and military is misplaced. Godzilla soon shows up to correct this misplaced faith, accompanied by the film's variation on the Horror theme. The motif serves as a sound bridge to a shot of Mothra's egg. The team of protagonists shows up, awaiting Mothra's arrival. They ask their colleague what happened to Kumayama. He explains that the fear of Godzilla drove him away.

The film does a hard cut to Torahata's hotel room, which Kumayama rudely enters and begins yelling at his financial backer. They fight over money lost in the Happy Enterprises venture, first with words and then with fists. Torahata claims it was just business, further upsetting Kumayama, who punches his face. Blood covers Torahata's nose and face, one of the few times in *kaijū eiga* we actually see human blood. It is worth noting that Godzilla is not the cause of this bloodshed, human greed and frailty has brought it on itself. Kumayama begins filling his jacket with stacks of yen from Torahata's safe. Again, this interaction is without musical accompaniment, which might be a surprise given the fight. The lack of music again stresses the banality of the capitalists' fight over money. As Torahata regains consciousness, he spies Godzilla approaching through the window. Music floods the soundtrack. It is the Horror theme, signifying the monster's relentless incursion. Torahata rifles around his desk and finds his handgun. He shoots Kumayama, scoops up as much yen as he can carry, and flees. Godzilla swipes his tail at the hotel, causing the building to cave in. Torahata cries out as a pillar collapses on him.

The final scene featuring the greedy capitalists is significant for the Godzilla and Mothra franchises. The movies rarely depict the deaths of named characters, unless it is in some way key to the narrative (i.e. Serizawa's self-sacrifice in *Godzilla*). Even then, the deaths typically occur off-screen—they are relatively clean and antiseptic. Mothra and her representatives rebuke the capitalists with words, but Godzilla rebukes them with violence. By staging Kumayama and Torahata's grisly deaths in *Mothra vs. Godzilla*, the filmmakers present an attack on unchecked capitalism in 1960s Japan.

The final thirty minutes of the film are a diptych of *kaijū* battles. Godzilla's destruction of the Shizunoura Happy Center draws to a close and his attention shifts to the egg. He attacks the dome housing the egg. Just as Godzilla is about to destroy the egg, Mothra appears. The monsters' themes wax and wane in the soundtrack based on the results of their fight. Eventually Godzilla wins out, the Horror theme rising in the mix as he strikes Mothra's wing with his radioactive breath. With her last bit of strength she wobbles through the sky, and collapses next to her egg accompanied by her cue.

After Mothra's death, the self-defense forces prepare for Godzilla's attack. At the command, "Tank units, take offensive" a medium-tempo variation of the Horror theme featuring upper brass enters the underscore.[112] Airplanes dive-bomb the monster, corralling him into electrified power lines. Strings enter in the underscore, playing the Horror theme in a low register at a more lugubrious pace. The score alternates between these two as the military and Godzilla battle, with Godzilla's effects and music winning out in the sound design, paralleling the monster's victory over the self-defense forces and their failed trap.

The movie cuts to the protagonists surrounding the egg. The fairies sing the cue Mahara Mosura; the lyrics are in Filipino and the tune is a simplified fragment of the Mothra motif—it includes voice, auxiliary percussion, as well as chanting and punctuative yodeling. The film cross-cuts to the Infant Island natives dancing and performing a similar chant. The music acts as a prayer infusing the ovoid with a mysterious light. Godzilla approaches the egg, and the impotent military cannot stop him. Villagers crowd into a boat, fleeing the monster. But a group of schoolgirls are stranded on a nearby island.

At the same time, the fairies continue praying to the egg, as if cheering it on. As they finish their song, the egg cracks and two larvae emerge.[113] The Mothra motif appears in the score, telling us that the larvae are indeed baby Mothras. The larvae instinctively head to the island to protect the schoolgirls from Godzilla. The final *kaijū* battle features the larvae attacking Godzilla in creative ways, including a string attack (cocooning material) and a tag team of tail-biting. The music and effects follow the ebb and flow of the battle, until the baby Mothras finally defeat Godzilla, the Mothra motif swelling in the score as the larvae chirp victoriously.[114]

In the conclusion, an orchestral version of the Sacred Springs cue underscores the protagonists' musings on recent events. The tuneful melody implies a concern for the suffering that continues on Infant Island, and by extension, around the world due to militarism and continued nuclear testing. As the larvae and the fairies depart, Junko wonders if they ought to thank the fairies. Sakai replies, "The only way to thank them is to make a better world." Prof. Miura concurs, "Yes, free from distrust."[115] The group waves goodbye from a hilltop. As "The End" appears on the screen the tune cadences on a major mode chord, implying resolution of the situation and hope for the future. Ifukube in this way transformed Mothra's lament into an optimistic dream.

What can viewers glean from the analysis of *Mothra* and *Mothra vs. Godzilla*? We believe that throughout both works, the filmmakers align Mothra with the feminine, via the little ladies and the egg. They also associate her with the primitive and the natural. Although the depiction of the Infant Island natives is troubling and problematic for contemporary audiences, the portrayal speaks to both Japan's perceived role in 1960s Asia and to the film's critique of the modernized world. In particular, Mothra represents an alternative to big business and its wanton destruction of the environment. The movies imply that industrial capitalism, like science and militarism, repeatedly fails to consider the disastrous repercussions of certain actions. Mothra acts as both castigator and savior of humanity, a role that in future films she increasingly shares with her adversary, Godzilla. In the end, the true monsters in the Mothra films and many other *kaijū eiga* of the 1960s are humans themselves. Humanity, in its hubristic refusal to acknowledge the past, is doomed to repeat it.

5

The Decline of Cinema
and Rise of Monsters

By the mid–1960s, a new era was on the horizon for the Japanese film industry. The early salad days of Godzilla and Mothra were at an end and an uncertain future lay ahead. This chapter focuses on the trials and tribulations film studios faced in the mid–1960s and their reaction to events lying largely beyond their control. It was by no means certain that Godzilla, Mothra, their new competitor Gamera, and a host of other monsters would survive the 1960s—yet through ingenuity, business acumen, and sheer will, the monsters and the film industry survived, though they did not thrive. Although budgets collapsed and talent flocked to other industries, *kaijū eiga* nevertheless generally sustained their ecological commentary during this bleak period for the Japanese film studios. In fact, as *kaijū eiga* became focused on a loyal band of child fans, they attempted to instill environmental awareness in the fertile minds of a new generation.

Television and the Tokyo Olympics

Throughout the mid–1960s into the 1970s, the Japanese film industry suffered a notable decline. Scholars credit the rapid sales of television sets leading up to the 1964 Tokyo Olympics as the predominant cause for the collapse of the cinema studios.[1] Prior to the Olympics, a growing number of Japanese families purchased televisions to view the games. This increase in the affordability and availability of TVs in Japan was made possible by the rapid industrial expansion of the high-speed economic growth period of the same time. Subsequently, this in turn led to a rapid expansion of and investment in TV programming. Former moviegoers abandoned cinemas in favor of watching television sets in the comfort of their own homes. This caused a decline in the financial feasibility and profitability of Japanese cinema corporations.

Television made its debut in Japan in 1953 with the commencement of public and commercial broadcasting by the Japan Broadcasting Corporation *Nippon Hōsō Kyōkai*, or NHK. Originally conceived as a national radio network during the late Taishō era (1912–1926), NHK gained worldwide notoriety during the Asia-Pacific War via its infamous "Tokyo Rose" propaganda broadcasts intended to demoralize Allied forces. As the Allied Occupation of Japan began winding down in the early 1950s, however, NHK made the leap to television programming.[2]

In *A Hundred Years of Japanese Film*, the inimitable Donald Richie discusses the impact of television on the Japanese film industry. In one of his most telling though sensationalist comments about the rise of TV, Richie asserts: "Television [...] damaged the Japanese film industry much more than had either the 1923 earthquake or the 1945 fire-bombings."[3] With this statement, Richie proclaims that the invention and proliferation of TV devastated Japanese film studios more than the 1923 Great Kantō Earthquake, which was responsible for the near total destruction of the greater Tokyo area and over 100,000 deaths and the 1945 bombing raids on Tokyo by American air forces using napalm and other incendiaries, which also resulted in over 100,000 deaths.[4] By comparing the devastation caused by television to the Japanese film industry to these two horrific historical events, Richie conveys the severity and ultimate blow to the movie studios in no uncertain terms.

In 1958, the film industry in Japan reached its apex in terms of ticket sales, marking over one billion tickets sold. In 1960, the studios released their highest combined number of movie productions, for a total of 537 feature-length films.[5] Following these two apices, the industry entered an abrupt and lengthy decline. But sales of television sets in Japan were rising. Whereas in 1960, just under 55 percent of Japanese households possessed a television set, that number skyrocketed to 95 percent by 1965.[6] The leading incentive for television purchases was the Tokyo Olympics, which held its opening ceremony on October 10, 1964.[7]

The 1964 Olympics marked the first time the games were ever held in an Asian country.[8] The Japanese government and many of its citizens viewed the games as the international rebirth of the new Japanese nation—a veritable democratic phoenix rising from the radioactive ashes of World War II imperialism. Tokyo had been slated to host the Olympics in 1940, but the games that year were cancelled due to the war, pushing off Tokyo's turn to bask in the athletic limelight for over a generation. But by 1964, the Japanese economy was barreling along and the high-speed economic growth period of the country's industrial revitalization was in full swing. The Japanese organizing committee accentuated the confluence of the games with Japan's global renaissance. They chose Sakai Yoshinori, a university student born near Hiroshima on the very morning of the atomic bombing, as the nation's standard-bearer to light the flame for the Tokyo Olympics.[9]

By the time organizers doused the Olympic torches, the severity of television's blow to the Japanese film industry was becoming increasingly apparent. By 1965, ticket sales plummeted to only 372 million. Ten years later, in 1975, sales fell to a mere 187 million. A similar dip in the number of motion pictures produced by Japan's major studios paralleled the decline in ticket sales. Although production reached its apogee in with 537 films in 1960, by 1965 the number of films released dropped to 483.[10] The precipitous decline continued unabated over the course of the next decade, with only 405 films produced in 1975.[11] By the mid–1970s, only a shambles of the once prosperous and proud Japanese film industry remained, as capital, talent, and funding flowed into the burgeoning television business.

Although the downtrend leveled out towards the end of the 20th century, the slump persisted; in the year 2000, studios produced only 282 films.[12] One way that Japanese film corporations combatted their impending financial collapse was through the increased production and proliferation of *kaijū eiga*. Monsters like Godzilla, Mothra, Gamera, and a wide array of other lesser-known creatures attracted loyal childhood followings. They in turn helped keep the film industry afloat for a time during the lean years of the 1960s and 1970s. There is no single clear and definitive reason for the success of the "monster boom," but various theories on entertainment, the nature of fantasy, and capitalism can be used to help clarify the appeal of monster films at the time.

The "Monster Boom"

In the mid–1960s the Japanese film studios realized that their profits would continue to dwindle unless they adapted to the *fait accompli* of television predominance, which was already cutting into the proverbial piece of the *kaijū* action, with shows like the Tsuburaya Eiji creation *Ultraman*. At the time, the industry was heavily dominated by six main studio corporations: Tōhō, Daiei, Tōei, Nikkatsu, Shōchiku, and Tōhō's affiliate and subsidiary Shin-Tōhō.[13] By the 1970s, several of these studios had collapsed, filed for bankruptcy, or were acquired by competitors. Others began to shift their focus to other venues besides the silver screen, in some cases targeting their capital and investment towards television productions, theme parks, and other attractions and media.[14]

Film studios also combatted plummeting revenues and dropping theater attendance by means of new movie features and formats. Some of these attractions included color films (opposed to the predominantly black-and-white television broadcasts of the time), widescreen productions, odd-length features, star-studded casts, double-billed showings, softcore pornography, and monsters.[15] Of all these ploys, monster movies became a hit for several studios, especially among children. Three of the most successful monsters were Tōhō's Godzilla and Mothra franchises and Daiei Company's Gamera series. Although Tōhō, Daiei, and other studios created other monsters as well, this trio of *kaijū* developed into long-running franchises (and eventually household names) that helped their respective studios stay afloat for a time in the late 1960s and 1970s.[16] Godzilla, Mothra, and Gamera also managed to stand the test of time, and gain a loyal following of not only children but also foreign camp and kitsch film enthusiasts around the globe.

As discussed in Chapter 3, the *kaijū eiga* debuted in Japan in 1954 with the release of Tōhō's film *Godzilla*. Though an amalgam of the fantasy, horror, and science fiction genres, the monster movie *Godzilla* was intended to be viewed as a serious and prescient social and political commentary in Japan. In 1955, following on the success of the original *Godzilla*, Tōhō Studios released the second Godzilla film, *Gojira no Gyakushū* (*Godzilla Raids Again*).[17] While still aspiring to the sober commentary of its predecessor, *Godzilla Raids Again* nonetheless commenced what would soon become a staple of Japanese monster movies—two or more monsters battling against each other, with Japan caught in the middle. Aside from Godzilla's return to the silver screen, *Godzilla Raids Again* featured the debut of Anguirus, a massive, armored-dinosaur-like creature, another Tōhō monster that would appear throughout numerous future features of the Godzilla series.

Even before the cinematic decline of the mid–1960s, Tōhō was willing to bring in whatever extra funding it could through licensing their monster films to international studios and production companies. As noted in Chapter 3, Edmund Goldman, the owner of the small Manson International distributing company, inquired at Tōhō's Los Angeles office in Little Tokyo about purchasing the rights to *Godzilla*. Tōhō jumped at the interest, and accepted Goldman's paltry $25,000 offer without reservations.[18] Various American producers and distributors then juggled the rights for the film, until it was decided to heavily edit the original masterpiece, cast Raymond Burr, and dub it into English for a 1956 release as *Godzilla, King of the Monsters*.[19]

Like the Japanese film industry as a whole in 1958, the Godzilla series reached its own financial peak in 1962 with the release of *Kingu Kongu tai Gojira* (*King Kong vs. Godzilla*), which pitted Hollywood's giant ape against Japan's indigenous movie monster. Cultural appropriation is occasionally a two-way street—while Hollywood studios were busy altering Japanese monsters like Godzilla for American audiences, Tōhō was likewise morphing the American icon Kong to fit more seamlessly into the *kaijū eiga* genre. *King Kong vs. Godzilla* proved popular among audiences in both countries, but critics offered scant praise for the American version of the film, which was poorly edited by John Beck and released by Universal-International in 1963.[20] Although Beck's version altered elements of the film's story and received the now standard bad dubbing, there is no truth to the widespread belief that the Japanese and American versions feature different conclusions. Godzilla does not triumph in Japan and Kong in America; both iterations feature the same ambiguous draw—Kong swims out to sea while Godzilla returns to the ocean's depths.[21]

The America versus Japan script for the movie proved to be a winning formula for Tōhō, and *King Kong vs. Godzilla* became the only installment in the series to outsell the original *Godzilla*—whereas theater attendance for *Godzilla* topped out at some 9.61 million tickets sold, *King Kong vs. Godzilla* attracted 12.55 million theatergoers in Japan alone.[22] By 1964, however, when the next film in the Godzilla series was released, ticket sales had plummeted by nearly half.[23] Throughout the latter half of the 1960s, revenue and production values of the films in the Godzilla series continued to fall. Television had taken its toll on the Japanese film industry, and the films began targeting an ever-younger fan base.

If we can say that a wave of monster films flooded Japan in the 1960s, then 1966 and 1967 were without doubt the crest of that wave. According to Yuasa Noriaki, the main director of the Gamera series, "following Tōhō's *Godzilla*, every film company tried to compete with its special effects, but only our studio—Daiei—continued to make one film a year for seven years."[24] Tōhō Studios, Daiei Company, and other Japanese production companies released a plethora of *kaijū* films during this short period, including a bevy of new monsters and creatures, many of which only appeared in a single film.

In 1966, Daiei released *Daikaijū Kettō: Gamera tai Barugon* (*Gamera vs. Barugon*) and the entire *Daimajin* trilogy, while Tōhō Studios screened *Furankenshutain no Kaijū: Sanda tai Gaira* (*The War of the Gargantuas*) and *Gojira, Ebira, Mosura: Nankai no Daikettō* (*Godzilla vs. the Sea Monster*). The cinematic tsunami increased in intensity the following year, when in 1967 Daiei produced *Daikaijū Kūchūsen: Gamera Tai Gyaosu* (*Gamera vs. Gyaos*), and Tōhō released *Kingu Kongu no Gyakushū* (*King Kong Escapes*) and *Kaijū-tō no Kessen: Gojira no Musuko* (*Son of Godzilla*). The "monster boom" even spread to other studios that year, with Shōchiku screening *Uchū Daikaijū Girara* (*Space Monster Guilala*) and Nikkatsu producing *Daikyojū Gappa* (*Gappa*).[25] While many of these *kaijū* witnessed their first and last feature films during this period, Godzilla, Mothra, and Gamera continued starring in movies into the following decades.

Pre-Millennial Monsters?

During the "monster boom" years, Japanese studios pandered *kaijū eiga* to a loyal childhood audience. But why were monsters so popular with children? Tsutsui discusses the origin of his own personal interest in Japanese monsters. He relates: "When I was nine, I wanted to be Godzilla. I wanted to drag my big reptilian feet through a crowded city. I wanted to swat a helicopter with a scaly hand and crumple a commuter train with my powerful jaws. I wanted to ignite a chemical plant with my radioactive breath."[26] Tsutsui goes on to posit: "I've always felt that the joy of Godzilla movies [...] is that they are pure and simple fun. Who can beat 90 minutes of suspended disbelief, moral certainty, and guiltless revels of gratuitous destruction? The Godzilla films were made to be engrossing, exciting, humorous, perhaps a little thought provoking, and—above all—enjoyable."[27] These characteristics of the Godzilla series are, of course, subjective (and it should be noted that these same features apply to the Mothra and Gamera franchises as well), but these themes and motifs are not exclusive to monster movies. So how can we explain the special appeal of Godzilla, Mothra, Gamera, and other *kaijū* in the "monster boom" of the 1960s and 1970s? Anthropologist Anne Allison's work sheds some light on this theoretical question.

Throughout her book *Millennial Monsters*, Allison connects the notions and theories of the fantasy genre with capitalism. These two features are clearly both at work in the films of the "monster boom"—movies featuring immense, prehistoric, radioactive beasts are clearly works of science fiction and fantasy (with an occasional dash of horror), and their use to bolster the failing economic fortunes of Japanese cinema studios falls into the realm of capitalism. In *Millennial Monsters*, Allison adopts a theoretical approach to discuss the success of certain Japanese popular culture products around the turn of the 21st century. The products Allison refers to are predominantly characters and creatures from Japanese games, movies, graphic novels, television shows, and other pop culture media. She discusses how certain cultural products exhibit the traits of fantasy and utilize both the theories of "polymorphous perversity" and post–Fordism.[28]

According to Allison, the notion of "polymorphous perversity" is a Freudian psychological theory defined as "pleasure that [...] extends over multiple territories [and] can be triggered by any number of stimuli."[29] Meanwhile, the capitalist theory of post–Fordism contrasts itself with the earlier economic model of the assembly line, popularized and extensively utilized by industrialist Henry Ford in the early 20th century. Unlike Ford's lack of customization (as the joke goes, a person could purchase a Ford Model-T automobile in any color they wanted, as long as it was black), Allison argues that the Freudian theory of "polymorphous perversity," taken in tandem with the capitalist theory of post–Fordism, enables cultural products to appeal to a wider range of consumers.

Allison provides several examples to illustrate her theories in practice by the way of Japanese cultural products, namely the anime *Sailor Moon* and the *Pokémon* franchises. Both *Sailor Moon* and *Pokémon* exemplify Allison's stated phenomenon—they appeal to a wide range of consumers by offering variety and choice. A consumer, whether a child or otherwise, can find their own kindred spirit, so to speak, given the numerous choices and options presented by a wide assortment of *Sailor Moon* characters and almost myriad *Pokémon* creatures.[30]

Allison's theories can also be applied to the monsters of the Godzilla, Mothra, and Gamera franchises. Like Allison's examples, these movie monsters along with their related and allied creatures offer a wide array of choices and kindred spirits for the viewer and consumer, particularly the child-dominated audiences of the time. For example, children interested in dragons may feel drawn to King Ghidorah, youngsters with a disposition toward dinosaurs, Anguirus, and children afflicted with an entomological itch (or perhaps girls who simply like butterflies), Mothra.[31] When coupled with the belief that monster films represent what is simply a formula for good entertainment, Allison's theories on the connection of fantasy and capitalism help explain the incredible appeal and subsequent success of the movie monsters. Taken along with other factors, such as the relatively cheap production costs of the formulaic and episodic *kaijū eiga*, a fairly clear picture of the reasons behind the rise of monsters in Japan in the 1960s and 1970s begins to emerge.

Yoshikuni Igarashi provides an even clearer view of the "monster boom." In his book *Bodies of Memory*, Igarashi analyzes the rise of monster movies in the 1960s, positing that the *kaijū* productions of the Godzilla series changed with Japan, as the films moved away from the war commentary and monstrous horror of the original *Godzilla* into the high-speed economic growth period of the 1960s. Like Japan's bright economic outlook at the time, Igarashi asserts, Godzilla films became effusively optimistic as they targeted a new generation of child viewers.[32]

Beginning in 1964, the year of the Tokyo Olympics, Godzilla morphed from villain to hero. No longer a menace to the Japanese people, Godzilla instead became their indefatigable protector. In the words of veteran Godzilla and Mothra franchise actor Takarada Akira: "Godzilla is not a narrow actor. He can play many different characters. He can be comical. He can be serious. He has known both the bitter and the sweet."[33] These alterations further aided Godzilla, like Daiei's child-protecting monster Gamera, in his appeal to children. The monster Godzilla transformed from being a terrifying threat to a friendly, nurturing beast.

Eventually, the "monster boom" proved unsustainable. As Steve Ryfle notes, "the mighty nuclear monster [Godzilla] that once invoked Japan's greatest fears and faced an assembly line of worthy adversaries was powerless against the economic forces that were destroying the once proud Japanese movie business."[34] Through the theories and analyses of *kaijū* offered by Tsutsui, Allison, and Igarashi, the reasons for the success of monster movies can be better understood—they were a combination of good, engrossing entertainment and a well-crafted and cunningly-employed capitalistic medium, that changed with Japan during the optimistic years of the high-speed economic growth period to appeal to a wide array of Japanese children consumers.

Godzilla's Offspring and Japanese Children

The "monster boom" of the latter half of the 1960s presaged several new trends in *kaijū* cinema, many of which were manifested in 1967's *Son of Godzilla*. As the title suggests, *Son of Godzilla* features the debut of Godzilla's unusual offspring Minira (also known as Minya or Minilla).[35] Clearly, by 1967, Tōhō Studios realized that targeting and cultivating a childhood audience was the obvious way to encourage a loyal following. Furthermore, in shifting their focus to juvenile viewers, Godzilla's creators emphasized the importance of environmental protection to the malleable minds of a new generation.

Scholarly examinations of the film and the character Minira are equally derisive. In Tsutsui's view, Godzilla's offspring is nothing more than "a shapeless, mid-gray, squeaky voiced, more-fetus-than-infant monster introduced [...as] an entirely cynical appeal to the kiddie market."[36] Galbraith quips: "*Son of Godzilla* might've been a good little film if they hadn't bothered to include the title creature."[37] Ryfle presents a more mixed interpretation, asserting: "[Minira] is undeniably comical and charming, but his impact upon Godzilla's characterization is troublesome [...] This look inside the Godzilla family is fun and funny in its own right, providing some laughs for kids and adults alike, but it detracts from the straightforward and serious sci-fi story."[38] Although Minira's debut certainly affected the portrayal and general understanding of the monster Godzilla, there are nonetheless other aspects of the film worth considering. Interestingly, not only do Godzilla and Minira mirror the franchise's new audience (parents accompanying their children to the theater), the picture also boasts a new environmental appeal relevant to late-1960s Japanese society.

Son of Godzilla is set on the tropical Solgell Island somewhere in the South Pacific, where a team of Japanese researchers works under the auspices of the United Nations.[39] The team intends to carry out a weather experiment; they plan to alter Solgell Island's climate as part of a broader U.N.-backed science project. Two of the film's primary characters, Dr. Kusumi Tsunezo (Takashima Tadao) and journalist Maki Gorō (Kubo Akira), discuss the planned experiment over a meal:

> DR. KUSUMI: As a journalist, you should know how overpopulated the world will be in another century.
> MAKI: Yes.
> DR. KUSUMI: Do you know what the problems will be?
> MAKI: The main problem would be feeding all of the people.
> DR. KUSUMI: Yes, because of this we must use areas like the Siberian tundra, African desert, and South American jungle. Of course, they're useless in their present state, but if we could convert them into fertile lands, we could eliminate the chance of famine.[40]

The Japanese team plans to alter the island's weather by launching a freezing device followed by a radioactive heating device. The project and the film itself is prescient to several environmental concerns not only in late-1960s Japan but globally in the 21st century: overpopulation, desertification, destruction of the rainforests, and climate change.

Although subtle, the team's conversation mirrors similar humanity versus nature themes noted in earlier chapters, as well as several ideas presented in the original *Godzilla*. Like the monster Godzilla, created by human science in the form of nuclear testing, global overpopulation—by definition, a human-generated problem—becomes the new nemesis. The threat, whether Godzilla or overpopulation, is confronted by Japanese scientists with ingenious new technologies, like Dr. Serizawa's oxygen-destroyer or Dr. Kusumi's weather control experiment. To solve society's problems, nature is once again called into thrall to serve human needs.

Not only does Kusumi mirror Serizawa, his plan is similarly myopic, arrogant, and oblivious to the toll nature will ultimately pay. Serizawa defeats Godzilla but wipes out all life in Tokyo Bay in the process, whereas Kusumi stands ready to totally transform huge swaths of the planet into agricultural land. Kusumi calls tundra, desert, and jungle "useless"; although these terrains may not be agriculturally productive, they are nonetheless active and vibrant ecological regions, boasting wide arrays of plant and animal life.[41] Kusumi plans to sacrifice them all for the sake of feeding an ever-expanding human population.

As monster movie viewers first learned when watching Cooper's *King Kong* over thirty years before the release of *Son of Godzilla*, humanity's attempts to control nature never end well, for either humanity or the natural world. Like Kong's escape from servitude and subsequent rampage through New York City, Kusumi's own attempt to harness nature for humanity's desires backfires. The weather experiment suffers a glitch, and rather than transforming Solgell Island into an idyllic agricultural paradise, the team unleashes radioactive storms and a blistering 70°C (160°F) heatwave. In their cavalier haste to create a Xanadu, the scientists instead open a nightmarish Pandora's Box. As a result of the radiation, the island's already unusual animal life greatly transforms, and praying mantises nearly the size of Godzilla appear. Whereas American nuclear testing unleashed Godzilla in 1954, by 1967 Japanese scientists create radioactive abominations of their own.[42]

The remainder of *Son of Godzilla* involves sequences intended to appeal to Japanese children and the adults accompanying them to the theater. There are several scenes of the island's "native" woman Matsumiya Saeko (Maeda Bibari) tossing Minira large pieces of fruit. Godzilla teaches Minira life skills, such as using his own radiation breath, while the little scamp causes mischief for his saurian father. Finally, *Son of Godzilla* boasts numerous monsters for the film's audience, including battles between not only Godzilla and the enlarged mantises, but a final decisive conflict wherein Godzilla and Minira work together to defeat the film's primary *kaijū* villain, the giant spider Kumonga. The film concludes with the Japanese science team repeating their experiment, leading to an atypically melancholic conclusion where Godzilla and Minira huddle together for warmth while snow begins to fall on the tropical island.

Two years after the release of *Son of Godzilla*, the series became even more child-oriented with the debut of *Ōru Kaijū Daishingeki* (*All Monsters Attack*) (1969).[43] Although the film was directed by original *Godzilla* director Honda Ishirō, it clearly targeted the childhood audiences which now dominated the Godzilla series fan base. Due to cost overruns on some of Tōhō's other pictures in 1969, as well as the faltering health of the studio industry in general, the budget for *All Monsters Attack* was drastically diminished.[44] The film's production relied heavily on stock footage, a cacophonous and seemingly out-of-place score, and a new child star named Ichirō (Yazaki Tomonori).

The production of *All Monsters Attack* employed numerous advertising schemes and cost-saving measures. For example, the majority of the monster special effects in *All Monsters Attack* were made of recycled film from recent Godzilla pictures. The film also boasts an unusually short running time of seventy minutes. Likely a result of its truncated length, *All Monsters Attack* was released as part of a double-billed feature along with the film *Kūsō Tengoku* (*Fancy Paradise*), a *kaijū* comedy about an anthropomorphic frog named "Gamara" (in an overt parody of Daiei's chief monster Gamera). The film led some reviewers to mourn what they considered the devolution of the Godzilla franchise. With more than a touch of wistfulness, film critic Phil Hardy lamented that *All Monsters Attack* was "a sad occasion."[45] Despite (or perhaps because of) the budgetary cuts, the film attempted to appeal to younger audiences through the child character Ichirō and Godzilla's own offspring Minira (returning from 1967's *Son of Godzilla*), who are both taught valuable life lessons by the elder Godzilla about self-reliance and standing up to bullies.[46]

The box office performance of *All Monsters Attack* was very poor, even for the Godzilla series at the time, with an anemic 1.48 million seats sold.[47] This represented barely more than one-tenth the number of tickets sold when compared to 1962's *King Kong vs. Godzilla*, only seven years earlier. According to David Kalat, the predominant reason the film drew such abysmally low crowds was because "although the appeal of the Godzilla movies lies in the monster scenes, [*All Monsters Attack*] delivers very little in this regard."[48] The dreadful dubbing of the international release of *All Monsters Attack* greatly contributed to the marginalization of the *kaijū eiga* genre abroad, with an adult voice actor straining to portray the boy Ichirō as a whining child.[49] Moreover, the American distributor of the picture, Maron Films, was forced to retitle and cancel planned screenings of the film twice. When negative reviews of the picture reached potential moviegoers, the distributor ultimately sold the rights to the film to television broadcasters.[50]

The critical reception and poor ticket sales of *All Monsters Attack* hit a point so low it nearly decimated the Godzilla series. In order to remain financially feasible, the franchise began to increasingly rely on cost-saving measures and new gimmicks to keep audiences entertained and returning to the cinemas. This sometimes led to what has been called "pulling out all the stops" to keep fans, particularly Godzilla's loyal childhood base, interested and engaged. These ploys in many cases led to Godzilla doing new, ostensibly exciting, but widely ridiculed feats in each movie.

Although the Godzilla pictures of the 1970s became more outlandish, they nevertheless continued the franchise's general engagement with ecological issues and overarching themes comparing nature vis-à-vis science and technology. The best case study of this trend is undoubtedly *Gojira tai Hedora* (*Godzilla vs. Hedorah*) (1971), which we will discuss in a later chapter. Other pictures of the 1970s also continued environmental themes. In *Chikyū Kōgeki Meirei: Gojira tai Gaigan* (*Godzilla vs. Gigan*) (1972), for example, a cockroach-like alien race flees its own environmentally devastated planet to seek refuge on the relatively clean Earth.[51] Unfortunately for the alien-invaders, due to their over-reliance on technology, they lose control of their subjugated space monsters and destroy themselves, allowing Godzilla and Anguirus to save Japan and the planet. Before their demise, the aliens make sure to note that if humanity does not change its ways, Earth could also become unable to support life, like the aliens' own toxic world.[52]

New environmental messages continued throughout the remainder of the late-Shōwa era Godzilla films. The following year, in *Gojira tai Megaro* (*Godzilla vs. Megalon*) (1973), a subterranean race of Seatopians, disturbed by underground nuclear testing, summon and unleash the giant cockroach Megalon.[53] Next, for the twentieth anniversary of the Godzilla franchise, Tōhō Studios released *Gojira tai Mekagojira* (*Godzilla vs. Mechagodzilla*) (1974). *Godzilla vs. Mechagodzilla* and its sequel *Mekagojira no Gyakushū* (*Terror of Mechagodzilla*) (1975) both contrast the natural and the technological, the biological and the synthetic.[54] In these films, Godzilla battles his mechanical doppelgänger—developed by a race of über-technological, ape-like aliens—emerging victorious on both occasions.[55] In the former picture, Godzilla even joins forces with the Okinawan deity-monster King Caesar, uniting the biological with the spiritual in their defeat of the mechanical. This motif continues our earlier discussion of the lingering historical connection between nature and Japan's religious tradition of Shintō, while also critiquing the country's over-reliance on technology. However, despite Tōhō's best efforts, these films failed to resuscitate the series, and finally after *Terror of Mechagodzilla* sold a record low 970,000 tickets, the studio decided to temporarily shelve the saurian behemoth.[56]

As noted earlier, Tōhō Studios was not the only company to produce monster pictures during this period. One of Tōhō's major competitors was Daiei Company. As Daiei, like Tōhō, continued to hemorrhage viewers and revenue in the 1960s, they took a page from the rival studio's path to success. In response to the Godzilla series, Daiei created their own popular movie monster: Gamera. Daiei's turtle-monster made his debut in 1965 in *Daikaijū Gamera* (examined in the next chapter), only one year after the Tokyo Olympics, and before the full effects of television's impact on the film industry were entirely apparent.

Like the Godzilla films of the latter part of the 1960s into the 1970s, Daiei's Gamera series relied heavily on child protagonists throughout the run of the monster series, beginning with Gamera's first outing. In several ways, the Gamera films more overtly catered to children than those of the Godzilla series. For example, one of Gamera's aliases used throughout the series is "Friend of All Children." Gamera served the role as protector of Japan's children, defending them from evil monsters and alien invaders alike. The big-screen terrapin's penchant for protecting children is quite explicit in all of the Gamera films, with one movie villain even going so far as to say: "Gamera has formidable destructive power, but there is a weak point, and that is his unusual and overpowering kindness to children."[57] Like the character Ichirō in *All Monsters Attack* and child characters in other Godzilla pictures in the 1970s, the films of the Gamera series featured children in starring roles in every franchise installment. Finally, Daiei's monster even possesses his own Gamera Theme Song, sung by a chorus of children; it appears during key monster battle action sequences throughout the films. In the song, the singing children expound on Gamera's might and strength, taunting "space monsters" from "Mars, Venus, and any other stars" to come and deal with Gamera's "jet-propulsion attack."[58] Gamera's theme song (sometimes with additional verses) appears in several installments of the series, always intoned by a non-diegetic child chorus in a sing-along type manner. Clearly, Daiei invited children viewing the films not only to buy tickets, but to immerse themselves in an interactive, child-focused, *kaijū* experience.

Despite the focus on attracting juvenile audiences, Japanese film studios also attempted to appeal to other demographic groups as well, in an attempt to maximize the potential profits from each *kaijū eiga* installment. In the cutthroat atmosphere of the "monster boom" era, directors, crew, and talent never knew when the plug might be pulled on their cinematic livelihoods. The only way to ensure survival, even if only for a brief time, was to provide a steady income for their respective studios by selling as many seats as possible, and not solely to children. After all, children did not purchase their own tickets, nor did they drive themselves to the theaters. In order to keep the financially dependent children flowing into theater seats, both Tōhō Studios and Daiei Company would also need to attract, or at least not repel, the teenagers and adults accompanying them to the cinemas.

This behind-the-scenes still from Daiei Company's *Gamera vs. Guiron* (1969) showcases the importance of children on both sides of the silver screen during the "monster boom" era. From left to right: Tom (Christopher Murphy), Officer Kondo (Ōmura Kon), Tomoko (Akiyama Miyuki), Akio (Kajima Nobuhiro), and Tom's mother Elza (Edith Hanson) (Daiei Company).

Sex Sells—But Sex and Monsters Sell More

As one study notes, "Sex never had much of a role in the Godzilla films, even before they became pure kiddie fare."[59] Indeed, throughout the entire Shōwa-era series, only a single romantic kiss was depicted on-screen—and even that was a rather bloodless and sterile affair between spacewoman Namikawa (Mizuno Kumi) and American astronaut Glenn (Nick Adams) in 1965's *Kaijū Daisensō* (*Invasion of Astro-Monster*).[60] However, although it may be *literally* true that sex played little part in the *kaijū eiga* genre, the allure of sex nevertheless proliferated throughout the films of the "monster boom" period.[61] Moreover, this expansion of sexuality in *kaijū eiga* proceeded hand-in-hand with the continuing juxtaposition of technology and science with humanity and nature.

From the mid–1960s through the mid–1970s, studios like Tōhō and Daiei began incorporating a new character type into monster pictures to lure older, ostensibly male theatergoers. We have chosen to label this stock character "the temptress." Unlike the more demure and classical female characters that appear in Japanese monster movies of the 1950s and early 1960s, the temptresses are blatantly sexualized: they tend to be young, conventionally attractive women who wear tight, alluring (and oftentimes revealing) outfits. Moreover, the temptress tends to be a character that occupies a space outside of mainstream Japanese society (such as hippies, cyborgs, or most commonly, aliens). In this way, they represent a sexualized Other, free from the otherwise strict constraints of Japanese gender relations, even during the sexual revolution contemporaneous with the "monster boom" period.[62]

Furthermore, as we noted in earlier chapters, although many female characters in early *kaijū eiga* tended to play stereotypical roles like "women who needed to be rescued, or women who existed primarily to be 'love interests,'" others exhibited a strong connection to nature.[63] This phenomenon was most directly and obviously embodied in the Mothra franchise's Twin Fairies. As we pointed out in Chapter 4, the Twin Fairies channeled the feminine, the magical, and Mother Nature in their connection to the *kaijū* Mothra. However, by the "monster boom" years, this connection between the feminine and nature began to falter. Instead, rather than channeling the mystical and the natural, the temptress characters began to embody the technological and the artificial.

There are numerous examples of temptress-like characters in *kaijū eiga*, and some appear in the films we focus on in this book. Because of this, we want to consider the trope of the temptress more closely, and connect their appearance to our overall discussion of the seemingly interminable conflict between nature and technology. In the 1950s, the earliest *kaijū eiga* featured demure female characters in static roles.[64] This trend began to transition in the early 1960s; the Twin Fairies in the Mothra films are not overtly sexual creatures, but their skimpy outfits, doll-sized figures, and overall foreignness that borders on magical are all qualities absorbed into the stock character of the temptress in later *kaijū eiga*. Saeko (Maeda Bibari) in 1967's *Son of Godzilla* represents a form of proto-temptress—she is not magical like Mothra's priestesses, but she lives primitively in a Solgell Island cave, wearing revealing, tropical attire.[65]

As the late 1960s transitioned into the early 1970s, the temptress characters flourished. For example, in 1969's *Gamera tai Daiakujū Giron* (*Gamera vs. Guiron*) two intentionally-seductive alien cannibals named Barbella (Kai Hiroko) and Florbella (Kasahara Reiko) serve as the film's primary villains.[66] In 1971, both *Gojira tai Hedora* (*Godzilla vs. Hedorah*) and *Gamera tai Shinkai Kaijū Jigura* (*Gamera vs. Zigra*) featured temptresses in the countercultural Miki (Mari Keiko) and the spacefaring Woman X (Yanami Eiko), respectively.[67] Finally, in 1975's *Terror of Mechagodzilla*, the cyborg Katsura (Ai Tomoko) saves Tokyo after falling in love.[68] Katsura's role as the temptress is doubly clear—not only does her allure transfix other characters, the film itself features a frontal nudity shot of Katsura's breasts, which Tōhō even used in promotional material to market the film.[69]

Katsura serves as a perfect example of the connection between the sexualized temptress and the loss of innocence. Echoing the Godzilla-as-nature versus Mechagodzilla-as-technology aspects of *Godzilla vs. Mechagodzilla* and *Terror of Mechagodzilla*, Katsura also embodies this motif. In the latter picture, Katsura is injured only to be "saved" by alien technology—although she appears the same externally, the alien doctors replace her internal organs with mechanized parts, turning her into a literal cyborg. The aliens then use Katsura to control the *kaijū* Titanosaurus, a once-natural creature pressed into the service of science and technology. However, in the end, nature wins out. Katsura rejects her computer programming in favor of her love for a Japanese biologist and her country. However, her "natural" innocence lost, Katsura can only win by sacrificing herself.

Here, we can glean yet another societal critique embedded within *kaijū eiga*'s environmental commentary. As women's liberation made strides in the 1960s and 1970s, the genre's overall portrayal of female characters shifted decisively. Women shed their earlier connection to nature and maternity, replacing it with sexuality and technology. Simultaneously, rather than acting as Japan's nurturing saviors (as Mothra's Twin Fairies did previously), many of these technological temptresses instead took up the role of villainesses.

The temptress characters represent a dramatic shift from static, reticent female roles to empowered, sexual beings, but whether this transition is beneficial or detrimental is left largely ambiguous. In fact, this question has stirred much academic debate. For example, as Jason Barr relates, "some feminist critics have argued that the 'bad' women who appear so frequently in the 1960s and 1970s *kaijū* franchises may actually be good [...because] they are functioning as independent and strong females for their audiences."[70] However, as Barr opines, "It's difficult to imagine that a female character who, for example, kidnaps small children and tries to destroy the world will provide an 'inspiring sight of proud and dominant women.'"[71] In sum, then, although the temptress characters are generally subversive, it is unclear if they are worthy of aggrandizement.

We can only speculate as to why temptress characters proliferated during the "monster boom" years, but it seems likely that in addition to attracting children with monster battles, Japanese film studios decided to dabble in sexploitation to draw teenagers, fathers, and all other interested parties to the theaters as well. Tōhō Studios and Daiei Company were not alone in this regard—around the same time, other Japanese studios entered the burgeoning softcore pornography market with gusto. For example, another Japanese studio, Nikkatsu, started a long-running series of sexploitation films known

The villainous spacewomen Barbella (Kai Hiroko, left) and Florbella (Kasahara Reiko) in a publicity still from 1969's *Gamera vs. Guiron*. Like the emergence of child characters during the "monster boom," a new type of technological "temptress" character also proliferated *kaijū eiga* productions during this era (Daiei Company).

as *roman poruno* in 1971. The effort resulted in surprisingly well-regarded classics like *Danchizuma Hirusagari no Jōji* (*Apartment Wife: Affair in the Afternoon*) and the titillatingly titled *Joshikōsei Repōto: Yūko no Shiroi Mune* (*Coed Report: Yūko's White Breasts*).[72] Meanwhile, a few years later, director Ōshima Nagisa was challenging Japanese censors' definition of pornography with his socially astute historical film *Ai no*

Korida (*In the Realm of the Senses*) (1976).[73] Clearly, monster films were not the only genre where sex was booming in the late 1960s and early 1970s.

While it is difficult to determine exactly how temptresses were viewed at the time, we can gain a glimmer of insight by examining how *kaijū eiga* critics and fans discuss these characters. In a provocative essay in the short-lived publication *Kaijū Review*, one commentator notes that the inclusion of such characters "panders to [a] male fantasy."[74] Indeed, previous academic studies of the *kaijū eiga* genre seem likewise entranced by the temptress. In *Japanese Science Fiction, Fantasy, and Horror Films*, Stuart Galbraith describes Woman X as "a sexy female alien."[75] In *Japan's Favorite Mon-Star*, Steve Ryfle seems unable to help referring to the cyborg Katsura as "sexy yet icy cold," as well as noting the display of her "fake tits" (a prosthetic prop) in the infamous aforementioned scene.[76] Finally, even William Tsutsui seems seduced by the temptress, noting the presence of "shapely brain-eating aliens" in the Gamera franchise.[77] That *kaijū eiga* scholars cannot help but remark on the temptresses' bodies speaks to Tōhō and Daiei's effective integration of sexploitation elements into *kaijū eiga*.[78]

Fans, too, seem transfixed by the *kaijū eiga* temptress. One of the most hypersexualized characters is undoubtedly Yanami Eiko's Woman X in *Gamera vs. Zigra*. In the film (discussed in Chapter 9), she sports not only a form-fitting metallic spacesuit, but also a bikini and a dangerously short, hot pink miniskirt. One fan chose to bestow on Woman X the moniker "Space Babe to end all Space Babes."[79] Furthermore, in the popular television series *Mystery Science Theater 3000* (1988–1999), the show's cast makes several snarky jokes regarding temptress characters in the Godzilla, Mothra, and Gamera franchises. Among their more memorable remarks are: "We'll have the hottest prom dates of all," "Massive babe-age," and "'You forget space is curved' and so am I."[80] It seems clear that the inclusion of temptresses in *kaijū eiga* was not a fluke— even if juvenile viewers remained the primary audience, studios intentionally targeted more than just children during the boom years.

Despite the initial success of Tōhō's Godzilla and Mothra franchises and Daiei's Gamera series, the "monster boom" and concomitant "temptress boom" of the 1960s and 1970s eventually proved unsustainable. Their numerous victories against megalomaniacal alien invaders, villainous cyborgs, and a host of other adversaries aside, Godzilla, Mothra, and Gamera all succumbed to the financial pressures exerted on the Japanese film industry. After starring in five motion pictures throughout the 1960s, Mothra appeared in her final film of the Shōwa era in 1968's *Kaijū Sōshingeki* (*Destroy All Monsters*). Gamera's ignominious end occurred after the release of *Gamera vs. Zigra*, the franchise's seventh installment, in 1971 and the subsequent collapse of Daiei Company. Likewise, Godzilla reached the end of the road in 1975, following the dismal ticket sales of *Terror of Mechagodzilla*. Although all three franchises would reappear in various incarnations and reboots throughout the remainder of the 20th century and into the 21st century, this demise marked the end of the monsters' initial runs.

Given the declining quality, sales numbers, and eventual end of the Godzilla, Mothra, and Gamera series, it may seem paradoxical to state that a "monster boom" occurred in the latter half of the 1960s into the 1970s. Nevertheless, monster franchises provided a steady stream of revenue for their respective studios. Their formulaic and episodic nature made them relatively cheap and easy to produce, and despite their falling ticket sales they were nevertheless made and released quickly and in rapid succession, usually at the rate of at least one film per year from each series.[81] This allowed the film studios to remain financially feasible and fiscally salient, at least for a time—it was because of the low costs and prolific production of *kaijū* films that the "monster boom" was able to occur.

6

Daikaijū Gamera
Consuming Natural Resources

Daiei Company released *Daikaijū Gamera* on November 27, 1965, the year after the Tokyo Olympics. The film became the leading installment in a series of Gamera films, which share many similarities with Tōhō's Godzilla series. Like Godzilla and Mothra before him, Gamera gained international popularity following the release of the edited and altered *Gammera the Invincible* in the United States in 1966. Although Gamera never truly attained equal footing with his Tōhō Studios counterparts, the monster turtle nevertheless achieved lasting fame both in Japan and around the world. In this chapter, we show that environmental themes expanded beyond Tōhō monster movies and were incorporated into *kaijū eiga* productions by competing studios like Daiei Company.

Gamera's Origins: Myths and Legends

Yuasa Noriaki, Daiei's favored director for nearly every film in the Gamera series made during the franchise's initial run, directed the original movie *Daikaijū Gamera*. Yamauchi Tadashi scored the film, and a menagerie of second-rate Japanese and foreign actors filled the roles of stock characters by this point common in the *kaijū eiga* genre, such as scientists, journalists, and government officials. However, unlike prior Japanese monster movies, the first Gamera film established a new trope that would continue throughout the "monster boom" period—the addition of impish children to the cast.

Daiei's Gamera franchise chronically suffered from severe financial constraints. Even though *Daikaijū Gamera* was produced eleven years after *Godzilla*, Yuasa completed the film with a budget barely two-thirds that of Tōhō's cost for the original Godzilla film—only ¥40 million (about $111,000 U.S. dollars in 1965), leading to noticeably lower production values.[1] As a result, the Gamera films have been widely savaged in other studies of Japanese monster movies as derivative and of poor quality, despite their popularity with fans. For example, Stuart Galbraith states: "The Gamera movies are slow-moving, slow-witted, and almost unwatchable, little more than expanded kiddie shows touting special effects only marginally better than what was already flooding Japanese television."[2] Perhaps *Daikaijū Gamera* does not reach the solemn heights of the original *Godzilla*, but it nevertheless provides a poignant commentary on environmental, social, and political issues relevant to the rapidly changing Japanese society of the mid–1960s.

Gamera's creation tale is steeped in both legend and economic pragmatism. In a 2003 interview, Yuasa Noriaki recalled that Daiei's president Nagata Masaichi conceived of Gamera as a way to compete with Tōhō's Godzilla success.[3] Nagata, who remained president until the company folded in 1971, oversaw some of Daiei's most commercially successful and critically acclaimed films, among them Kurosawa Akira's 1950 masterpiece *Rashōmon*, the first Japanese film to win an international award.[4] Nagata developed the initial plans for the Gamera series to help bolster Daiei Company's faltering viewership, as Japanese increasingly eschewed cinema for television.

Eerily similar to Godzilla's prior conception by Tanaka Tomoyuki, Gamera's creation also occurred in the skies over the Pacific Ocean. According to Yuasa, Nagata was inspired to create the monster Gamera while on an international flight from the United States back to Japan. Nagata reportedly spotted a peculiar cloud over the ocean that led him to imagine a giant, flying turtle. Thus, Gamera was born.[5] Given the similarities in origin stories and physical characteristics between Godzilla and Gamera, it is easy to understand why some deride Daiei's franchise as uninventive.

Even Gamera's name owes a debt to Godzilla. As discussed earlier, Godzilla is an Anglicization of the original Japanese name Gojira, a portmanteau of the Japanese words for gorilla, *gorira*, and whale, *kujira*, respectively.[6] Due to the prominence of Godzilla, the suffix "-ra" came to be used to denote any sort of giant monster in Japanese cinema. For example, in order to name the giant sea creature Ebirah that battled Godzilla in 1966, Tōhō simply took the Japanese word for shrimp, *ebi*, and added "-ra" at the end to denote the monstrous crustacean.[7] In this same way, the origin of Gamera's own name is quite clear. Gamera is

Japanese mythology abounds with creatures, monsters, and demons, one of the most common of which is the *kappa*. Daiei Company's monster Gamera mimics many traits and characteristics of *kappa* folklore. Here, one interpretation of a *kappa* is depicted in a woodblock print by the renowned Japanese artist Katsushika Hokusai (1760–1849).

simply the "monsterized" form of the Japanese word for turtle, *kame* or *game*, with the "-ra" suffix attached. Gamera is literally, by his very name, a monster turtle.

As with Godzilla and other *kaijū* before him, the monster Gamera also drew inspiration from the creatures, or *yōkai*, of Japanese mythology.[8] Godzilla has been frequently connected with the water dragon, a monster common throughout East Asian folklore.[9] Gamera also boasts a historical analog in Japanese mythology—the ubiquitous *kappa*, also known as "river goblins" or "water sprites."[10] Although a varied mythology exists surrounding *kappa*, their connection to water, particularly Japan's rivers, lakes, and marshes, remains a constant throughout Japanese folklore. Descriptions of *kappa* range from the decidedly amphibian or reptilian to the nearly humanoid. *Kappa* are often associated with mischief and troublemaking, such as loud flatulence and occasional voyeurism. Sometimes they are suspected of more malevolent crimes, like drowning children and animals. Several stories tell of *kappa* drowning (or at least attempting to drown) horses, as well as their vociferous appetite for cucumbers.[11] Historically, many agricultural communities in Japan celebrated *kappa* as water deities, once again revealing the ongoing connection between Japanese mythology, Shintō religious traditions, monsters, and nature. Moreover, *kappa* appear throughout Japan's theatrical traditions, as villains, antagonists, or general troublemakers in numerous Nō, Bunraku, and Kabuki plays.[12]

Kappa and Gamera share a few specific traits, notably a turtle-like appearance and ability to control water. Ancient Japanese believed that *kappa* could provide ample rainfall for irrigating crops if pleased, or cause droughts or floods if angered.[13] As we will see later, Gamera (at least in his first film) possesses a similar skill. Finally, by drawing inspiration for Gamera from Japanese mythology, the film's producers reminded Japanese viewers of a simpler, natural way life widely associated with Japan's distant past. Whether or not such a time and place ever actually existed is largely irrelevant—in the audience's mind, such nostalgia for an idyllic, legendary past provided a stark contrast to the frenetic, go-go Japan of the mid–1960s.

A New Monster Arises

Following the display of the Daiei company logo, the black-and-white *Daikaijū Gamera* opens to a shot of strategic bombers flying in formation.[14] This establishing sequence highlights the Cold War tensions dominating global affairs in 1965, only a few years after the Cuban Missile Crisis and escalating tensions between the superpowers around the globe. The film introduces the three main human protagonists: Dr. Hidaka (Funakoshi Eiji), his assistant Kyoko (Kiritachi Harumi), and journalist Aoyagi (Yamashita Junichirō).[15] They drive a jeep across a bleak, icy snowscape on the polar ice cap of the Arctic Ocean, arriving at a small "Eskimo Village." Dr. Hidaka introduces himself to the village elder, and the two speak in heavily accented English with Japanese subtitles displayed on the side of the screen.[16]

The children in the village begin scurrying, and Dr. Hidaka and the village elder notice the bombers flying in the distance. This prompts Hidaka to comment on the Cold War's global impact to Kyoko and Aoyagi. The scene then cuts to the team's research ship, the *Chidori Maru*, where the captain and his mate also witness the mysterious jet bombers flying overhead. The crew radios a nearby American military base, advising them of the unknown aircraft.

Unlike *Godzilla*, which only added foreign actors like Raymond Burr when it was edited for American audiences, Daiei Company included American and other foreign actors in the film's original release. Despite their abysmal acting abilities, the inclusion of foreign extras in the first Gamera film marks an interesting departure from the trail forged by *Godzilla* a decade earlier. As opposed to *Godzilla*, where the shadow of the U.S. military remains totally absent throughout the film, *Daikaijū Gamera* highlights an American presence in its first few minutes. Moreover, later in the film, the international community assists Japan in its defense against the monster. In this way, the Gamera franchise presents a more realistic assessment of the geopolitical situation and its implications for Japan than other examples of *kaijū eiga*, where an isolated Japan must often fend for itself against the wrath of numerous monster invaders.[17]

The U.S. commander orders his fighter aircraft to investigate the mysterious bombers. "Calling all planes, fighter planes, based in the Arctic Ocean, this is your commander calling, over," he stumbles.[18] The commander tells the fighters to intercept and escort the bombers back to the American airbase, and to shoot them down if they resist. The U.S. military's actions are warrantless. The commander orders his fighter planes to shoot down unidentified aircraft over international waters without any justification. Aside from being necessary to move the film's plot forward, the irrational belligerence of the U.S. military in this scene cannot be ignored. At a time when the United States was escalating its involvement in Vietnam, the film, in its depiction of the trigger-happy air force officer, makes an overt comment regarding American militarism and the global power struggle between the superpowers.

The U.S. Air Force fighters pursue the mysterious bombers. After a particularly aggressive message from the fighters, one of the (presumably Soviet) bombers fires two missiles at a U.S. aircraft. The American plane then responds with a salvo of missiles, disabling one bomber that plows into the ice below. The bomber explodes, detonating a nuclear weapon. A mushroom cloud rises from the impact. Dr. Hidaka and his staff witness the explosion, and Kyoko believes that they have seen an atomic test in the Arctic. Aoyagi disagrees, telling her that the bombers must have been carrying atomic weapons.

A hard cut to a shot of the mushroom cloud that lasts for several seconds follows. The scene is compelling and worthy of contemplation.[19] The soundtrack remains silent as the mushroom cloud roils in the distance in a long shot of the polar snowscape. The lack of sound emphasizes the weapon's devastation; even sound itself is a silenced victim. The mushroom cloud shrouds the sky in darkness. Despite the terrain's bleakness, the shot is strikingly artistic; the snow's brightness sharply contrasts with the darkness of the nuclear blast in the background. This image conveys one of the film's environmental themes before the titular monster even makes his appearance. It clearly juxtaposes the destructiveness and violence of human-made weaponry with the tranquil serenity of the natural world.

Near the atomic blast, fissures begin to form in the ice sheet, and Gamera emerges from the depths. The sounds of cracking ice and blasting steam break the atomic silence.

Low strings and brass enter the soundtrack in a monophonic texture, playing an ascending melody as Gamera claws his way to the surface. Gamera emerges and rises to his feet. A jarring dissonant chord and monstrous roar accompanies the film's title as it appears across the screen.[20] The audience is then treated to a series of close-ups of Gamera as he begins his journey, while an overlay of the film's credits appears on the screen. The musical accompaniment, comprised again of brass, low strings, and percussion, is a pale imitation of Ifukube's Horror theme from *Godzilla*.[21]

Despite the ominous score, Gamera's initial appearance differs markedly from Godzilla's first arrival on the silver screen. Whereas in *Godzilla* the eponymous monster is not seen until nearly thirty minutes into the film, Gamera's appearance occurs significantly earlier. Moreover, Godzilla's arrival is a terrifying experience for Prof. Yamane and the villagers on the slopes of Ōdo Island. Gamera's appearance, though sinister, does not carry with it the immediate possibility of a gruesome death for a major protagonist.

Although nuclear explosions awaken both Godzilla and Gamera, there are substantial differences between them. American nuclear testing rouses Godzilla from his slumber; earlier we directly linked this to the 1954 Castle Bravo test and irradiation of the *Lucky Dragon No. 5* fishing vessel. Unlike Godzilla, Gamera arises not due to an American H-bomb test, but following an accidental (presumably Soviet) nuclear detonation when the bomber crashes. Despite these differences, it is still the U.S. military that is ultimately responsible for disturbing Gamera. Why such differences between the two films? Whereas Tōhō produced *Godzilla* in 1954, less than a decade after the end of the Asia-Pacific War and only two years after the conclusion of the Allied Occupation, Daiei released *Daikaijū Gamera* in 1965, when the war and its aftermath were more distant memories, and both the world and Japan were far different places than they had been only a decade earlier.

As the film continues, Dr. Hidaka and his staff spot Gamera in the distance. Hidaka plans to immediately return to the *Chidori Maru*, but the Inuit village elder presents a gift—a sacred stone showing a depiction of an ancient, massive species of turtle, named "Gamera." The stone presages one of Gamera's unique qualities, his ability to process energy for flight and flame, though the characters at first do not understand its significance. Here, as in *Godzilla* and *Mothra*, *Daikaijū Gamera* instills its titular monster with an ancient legend. Furthermore, like the Ōdo Islanders and Infant Islanders, the film's depiction of the indigenous Inuits connects this mythological origin to "primitive" indigenous peoples, and through them, nature.[22]

The film cuts back to the bridge of the icebreaker, where the captain and crew discuss their fears after witnessing the radioactive mushroom cloud rising in the distance. Interestingly, the crew's fears are not about an imminent nuclear war leading to widespread death and destruction, but about the impact of nuclear testing on the planet itself. One crewman frets that continued nuclear testing will alter Earth's axis of rotation. Another reckons that altered weather patterns will lead to more typhoons striking Japan. Here, the crew's discussion reveals an awareness of the detrimental effects of nuclear testing on the environment, and a concern about its impact on human society.

The scientific accuracy of the crew's statements may be unsound, but the scene effectively depicts the public perception of nuclear testing. In 1961, four years before

Daikaijū Gamera's release, the Soviet Union tested the world's most powerful thermonuclear weapon, the *Tsar Bomba*.[23] This test, carried out over the Arctic island of Novaya Zemlya, produced fifty-eight megatons of destructive force. Fifty-eight megatons is the equivalent of fifty-eight million tons of TNT, one percent of the power output of the sun, or in the Japanese context, almost 4,000 times the power of the atomic bomb dropped on Hiroshima in 1945.[24] It is obvious why the producers of *Daikaijū Gamera*, and the Japanese public at large, were anxious about both the societal and environmental effects of continued nuclear testing in the 1960s.

As the ship's crew scrambles to send a distress signal, Gamera lumbers across the ice toward Dr. Hidaka's icebreaker. Gamera attacks and destroys the *Chidori Maru*. Hidaka, Kyoko, and Aoyagi had not yet returned to the ship, so their lives are spared. Crediting Kyoko for their survival, Aoyagi begins a painful romantic pursuit of her that carries throughout the film. The American airbase receives the icebreaker's SOS warning about Gamera's appearance. In one of the more unintentionally funny scenes of the film, the U.S. commander and his men lethargically discuss the *Chidori Maru*'s final message on the appearance of a sixty-meter (200-foot) turtle. Unsure of the accuracy of the icebreaker's report, the commander dispatches his fighters to investigate the area, where they find neither the ship nor Gamera.

The second act of *Daikaijū Gamera* shifts from the frozen Arctic to bustling New York City. A TV reporter interviews Dr. Hidaka about the emergence of Gamera. Hidaka relates that Gamera is an ancient creature that existed in distant antiquity. He explains that Gamera once lived on the continent of Atlantis, now submerged beneath the Arctic Ocean. Akin to Godzilla's Ōdo Island mythology and Mothra's Infant Island folklore, the connection between *kaijū* and myth is multilayered—not only do the monsters themselves draw inspiration from pre-existing Japanese mythology, they also receive fictitious origin stories within their own cinematic universe.

The film cuts to a brief interlude of an old man walking home and spying a ball of fire whirling about the night sky. At this point, neither the viewer nor the film's characters are aware of Gamera's flying prowess. In an allusion to the many science fiction films released throughout the 1950s and early 1960s, the old man determines that the spinning flame must be a flying saucer. This exemplifies one of several meta-generic scenes that appear throughout *kaijū eiga*, wherein the producers deliberately insert self-referential components to the storyline. *Daikaijū Gamera* functions primarily as a monster movie but makes tongue-in-cheek allusions to other popular related genres, such as science fiction B-movies.

After the scene with the old man misidentifying Gamera as a UFO, the movie introduces an older teacher and a young woman, Nobuyo (Sugata Michiko), walking along the coast of rural Hokkaidō (Japan's northernmost main island) and discussing her younger brother Toshio's (Uchida Yoshiro) passion for turtles.[25] The teacher says that it would be best if Toshio spent less time befriending reptiles and more time interacting with other children. Later that night, Toshio's father orders him to release his pet turtle Chibi (a diminutive prefix meaning very small) into the wild. Despite his sorrowful reluctance, Toshio sets Chibi free in the rocks near the family's lighthouse. After releasing Chibi, Gamera appears. Toshio climbs the lighthouse tower to get a better view of the monster turtle. The boy falls after Gamera damages the lighthouse, and in a scene reminiscent of Kong's delicate handling of Ann Darrow, Gamera gently picks up Toshio and sets him on the ground near his horrified family. Like Kong's predilection for attractive blondes, Gamera reveals his own love for helping small children, a quality that persists throughout the other films of the Gamera franchise.

This sequence touches on another environmental message present in *Daikaijū Gamera*. Both in Japan and around the world, the release of non-native animals—often in the form of abandoned pets—has caused widespread ecological damage.[26] This problem, termed biological invasion, relates to invasive species outcompeting native plants and animals when they are introduced to a new region. Biological invasions are even more acute in isolated ecosystems, like the Japanese archipelago, long separated from the mainland, where unique indigenous and endemic species found nowhere else evolved and thrived. Toshio's pet turtle appears to be a Japanese stone turtle (*Mauremys japonica*), a species that is not native to Hokkaidō.[27]

In 1965, the environmental disruptions associated with invasive species were already known in Japan. Many examples of biological invasions have been recorded in the Bōnin Islands, a chain of small isles lying south of central Honshū, Japan's largest island. For example, domestic cats were brought to the Bōnins by settlers and became feral during the Meiji period (1868–1912), adversely impacting the island chain's native bird population.[28] Around the same time that Toshio was releasing Chibi, a different invasive reptile was being introduced to the Bōnin Islands—the green anole. Spreading rapidly since the early 1960s, the green anole lizard hunts the island chain's insect population, negatively affecting not only the Bōnins' natural wildlife balance, but also disrupting the native plantlife pollinated by those insects.[29] *Daikaijū Gamera* stands alone in its subtextual commentary on the environmental toll exacted by invasive species, a theme not encountered in any other *kaijū eiga* we discuss.

After Gamera saves Toshio, the film cuts to Dr. Hidaka, who has just returned to Japan from his interview in New York City. He learns that Gamera has made landfall in Hokkaidō. Hidaka, Kyoko, and Aoyagi, who are conveniently already at the airport, immediately head north to assist the Japanese armed forces in their defensive preparations. Meanwhile, Toshio futilely searches for Chibi and becomes distraught over his lost pet.

Gamera continues his march across Hokkaidō, heading towards a power plant. Japanese soldiers prepare to defend the plant from the monstrous turtle. When Dr. Hidaka arrives, he asks the workers to explain the plant's geothermal power. An employee obligingly explains (directly to the camera, and hence the viewer) how geothermal power creates electricity from the planet's own abundant heat. Geothermal power is an environmentally-sound means of energy production, being both clean and renewable. By extolling the virtues of geothermal power, *Daikaijū Gamera* integrates a pedagogical moment of environmental relevance into the monster movie format. However, geothermal power is also something of a mixed bag for Japan—while Japan's geology makes it perfectly situated for providing abundant geothermal power, it is that same geology along the Pacific Rim that causes Japan's volatile volcanic and earthquake activity.[30] Mother Nature is a harsh mistress.

The inclusion of a geothermal power station in *Daikaijū Gamera* cannot be considered a coincidence; it is clear that director Yuasa and the film's production team wanted to feature a scene praising the benefits of clean, renewable energy to the viewer. At the time of the film's release, there was not a single operating geothermal plant in Japan, with the first such station only coming online the following year, when the Matsukawa plant in northern Honshū began operation in 1966.[31] By the early 21st century, Japan was producing more geothermal power than all but five other countries, but when *Daikaijū Gamera* was released such a dependence on clean energy was still only a hope for the future, not a reality.

An army officer asks Dr. Hidaka if it would be possible to defeat Gamera using the heat of the geothermal vents below the power station. The doctor replies that if a nuclear blast was unable to harm Gamera, the heat from the vents will certainly fail as well. At this point, the film directly compares the dangers of atomic testing to the fundamental power of nature itself. Atomic testing is in essence humanity's attempt to harness the inherent power of nature—atomic energy is in fact quite natural on some levels; the sun and every star in the sky illuminate the universe through nuclear fusion. Up until the first atomic detonation in 1945, nature was without doubt both the most beneficial and destructive force throughout all of human history. Hidaka, as the film's moral mouthpiece, concludes that humanity's attempts to exploit nuclear power are a greater danger than unbridled nature itself. This message would likely be particularly poignant to Japanese viewers living in a land long plagued by geological and weather-related catastrophes, ranging from earthquakes and volcanoes to typhoons and tsunamis.[32]

Dr. Hidaka then surmises that electricity may defeat Gamera. The army surges electrical power through the station but when Gamera touches it, it has no effect. A similar gambit failed against Godzilla in his debut film, so it is unsurprising that this sequence was included in *Daikaijū Gamera*.[33] Here, Daei Company shows viewers that their monster turtle is at least as potent as the radioactive dinosaur from Tōhō Studios. With the collapse of the electrical perimeter, the JSDF opens fire on Gamera. The colossal chelonian becomes enraged and begins toppling buildings and structures. When the dust settles, it is unclear who is more responsible for the leveling of the geothermal power station, Gamera or the Japanese military. Gamera then inhales the flames of the burning ruins, baffling Hidaka and other observers.

In the following scene, Dr. Hidaka travels to Hokkaidō University where he confers with a prominent paleontologist, Professor Murase (Hamamura Jun). Murase recounts the mythological origins of Gamera, noting tales of fire-eating turtles in the writings of Plato and other ancient texts. He muses that Gamera is able to transform inorganic matter into organic, meaning that human-made weapons and nuclear arms are all useless in defeating the monster. Gamera, then, is a living processing plant that consumes natural resources for energy and vitality—not unlike humanity itself.

Back at the remnants of the geothermal power station, the Japanese military launches an airstrike against Gamera. Unlike Godzilla's retreat following a fighter attack in *Godzilla*, Gamera seems unperturbed by the planes and continues to happily ingest the flames. Following the airstrike's failure, the Japanese commander decides the only way to stop Gamera is to request American military assistance, specifically tactical nuclear missiles. Here another divergence from *Godzilla* occurs; as noted earlier, in that film the U.S. military neither appears nor provides any support in fighting the *kaijū*. Thankfully, Dr. Hidaka, Prof. Murase, and Toshio (who for some reason is hanging around with the soldiers near the battlefield), convince the Japanese commander to forgo the use of nuclear weapons. They are concerned that the radioactivity will only increase the monster turtle's power. "Gamera welcomes flames; radioactivity would only make him happy," Prof. Murase declares.[34] Toshio thanks the scientists for saving Gamera, telling them that Gamera is not really destructive. The boy, however, is an unreliable judge of character.

A soldier informs the scientists that the geothermal station has been completely destroyed. Hidaka and Murase consider their options. Dr. Hidaka reasons that if Gamera consumes energy and heat, perhaps using the opposite would be effective. He reveals that the Japanese military has a secret weapon called "deep-freeze," that freezes everything it touches.[35] (One might ask how a zoologist is privy to such high-level military secrets, but *Daikaijū Gamera* does not answer this intriguing question). The commander informs the scientists that the military has developed this new weapon in order to freeze plants and animals in tropical jungles. Whatever the questionable military purpose of deep-freeze, it is certain that it would cause widespread ecological damage were it ever to be used (similar to Dr. Serizawa's oxygen-destroyer that obliterated all life in Tokyo Bay). There is undoubtedly also a connection between the fictitious deep-freeze and the U.S. military's unrestricted use of the toxic chemical herbicide and defoliant Agent Orange, much of which was stored on Okinawa, during the contemporaneous Vietnam War.[36]

Again, *Daikaijū Gamera* portrays the military-industrial complex, American, Japanese, or otherwise, as ecologically inconsiderate. The military shot down a bomber, precipitating an atomic explosion. It contributed to the destruction of a geothermal power station, and developed an environmentally destructive weapon with little obvious military or defense benefit. In this way, *Daikaijū Gamera* thematizes the military's capricious willingness to sacrifice the environment. Moreover, Hidaka's awareness of the deep-freeze weapon indicates the collusion between scientists and the military, a collusion that still deeply concerned postwar Japan.

With the scientists' approval, the military deploys deep-freeze against Gamera, immobilizing him. While frozen, soldiers place dynamite below the *kaijū*, causing him to collapse on his back. As the inverted Gamera starts to thaw, the protagonists believe that victory is at hand. But then the monster turtle reveals his most powerful ability; he draws his head and limbs into his shell, and flames erupt causing him to spiral and fly away into the night. Gamera is in fact the "flying saucer" spotted earlier in the film.

The film cuts to Toshio and his sister, now living with relatives in Tokyo following the demolition of their lighthouse home. Toshio laments the loss of his pet turtle, stating confidently that he believes Chibi transformed into Gamera.[37] This comment expands and clarifies the earlier allusion to biological invasion. What initially seemed an extremely minor incident—releasing a tiny turtle into the wild—has become a much larger menace. In Toshio's mind, his tiny pet Chibi transmogrified into the gigantic monster Gamera; although the monster seems to have a capacity for good, the film makes Gamera's destructive potential clear. In the same way, what may originally seem of little ecological significance (such as releasing a non-native pet into the wild), can and oftentimes does become a much graver environmental problem.[38]

The following sequence reveals the extent of Gamera's ability to consume and destroy. First, we see Dr. Hidaka working in his headquarters with photographs of Gamera sightings around the world on display.[39] Gamera is no longer only a Japanese problem at this point, but a global one. Once again, this strongly contrasts with the plot of *Godzilla*, where the monster poses a threat solely to the Japanese nation. Next, Hidaka gives a lecture where he announces new findings about Gamera, including that the giant turtle consumes all sources of energy, from fossil fuels and minerals to radiological elements as well. In a particularly interesting scene, the heads of Japan's atomic energy agency discuss the need to protect the country's stockpiled nuclear material: "We must hide Gamera's favorite food," one board member states.[40] Another scene at a Japanese fish market shows idle workers with no seafood to clean or sell—they discuss how there are no fish left to catch and muse that something is terribly wrong with the planet. Next, a news broadcast reports not only the fishing shortages, but also unexplained tidal disruptions and flooding throughout the country.

These scenes all support Prof. Murase's theory that Gamera is a biological factory converting natural resources into energy. Raw materials literally fuel the monster. This proclivity for the consumption of natural resources also reinforces Gamera's association with Japan's *kappa* mythology. Like a reimagined *kappa*, Gamera has an insatiable appetite—he consumes so many fish that Japanese fisheries run dry.[41] Moreover, akin to a displeased *kappa*, Gamera causes widespread tidal disruptions and flooding. However, unlike the traditional *kappa*, known for its desire to consume small children, Gamera instead presents a penchant for both befriending and rescuing them in times of danger. Like Godzilla's nearly simultaneous transformation from villain to hero, Gamera's own departure from conventional *kappa* lore can also be explained by the collapsing fortunes of the Japanese film industry, and their resulting need to appeal to devoted child audiences.

Following Gamera's cataclysmic globetrotting, a group of international advisers arrive in Tokyo to help the Japanese confront and defeat Gamera. The international threat of Gamera and subsequent ecological calamity prompts a thaw in Cold War hostilities. Interestingly, the representatives of both the United States and the Soviet Union speak clear, if somewhat stumbling, Japanese.[42] Upon holding a summit with Hidaka, Murase, and others, the international advisers declare that the best hope for defeating Gamera is a mysterious and secret Japanese government project known as "Z-Plan."[43] The American and Soviet scientists pledge to provide Japan support to complete the project quickly.

Following the summit, Gamera returns for the genre-requisite attack on a major Japanese city, in this case Tokyo. Gamera begins his assault with some ironic humor; returning from his world trip, he commences his reign of terror by leveling Haneda Airport, Japan's main international airport when the film was produced. Aside from the inherent comedy of the flying turtle landing at the airport, there is perhaps further environmental commentary hidden here as well. Haneda Airport was notoriously over-capacity in the mid–1960s, and the fumes and noise associated with the airport were infamous throughout Tokyo and Japan.[44] The capacity and noise pollution problems of Haneda led directly to the development of Narita Airport, today Japan's main international hub, the construction of which was publicly announced the following year, in 1966. The film's creators likely enjoyed Gamera's cathartic destruction of the loathed airport.

The monster turtle Gamera destroys Tokyo's Haneda Airport in this promotional image for *Daikaijū Gamera* **(1965). Cast members (from left to right) Kyoko (Kiritachi Harumi), Dr. Hidaka (Funakoshi Eiji), and Toshio's sister Nobuyo (Sugata Michiko) look on in genuine horror (Daiei Company/Photofest).**

Following Gamera's incineration of Haneda Airport, the film cuts to an eclectic scene of go-go dancers and patrons partying in a downtown Tokyo dance bar, "Club Beat."[45] The soundtrack features diegetic surf rock, with numerous close-ups and pans of young Japanese dancing the night away. The sequence includes several low-angle shots of the adolescent dancers, making the viewer feel immersed in the dance party; one can almost smell the sweat, alcohol, and cigarette smoke choking the noxious air. Police show up at the club, ordering an evacuation, but the partygoers are unaware of what Gamera is and refuse, announcing defiantly: "Nothing's going to stop this shindig, so let's dance!"[46] Here, *Daikaijū Gamera* comments on what its creators undoubtedly viewed as a form of social pollution—in this case the wild, carefree, party-going youth. Gamera's imminent arrival is announced by the shaking of the camera, at first being indistinguishable from the tremors of a major earthquake. The police officer condemns the dancers for their foolishness and stupidity, and Gamera soon crushes the building while debris rains down from the ceiling upon the horrified crowd.

After summarily dispatching the dance party, Gamera storms through downtown Tokyo, toppling buildings and crushing vehicles. Gamera knocks down a building with "New Tokyo" emblazoned in neon English across the side.[47] Another jest on the part of Gamera's creators, the image implies Gamera's rejection of America's influence on the reconstructed metropolis. The monster then topples Tokyo Tower, before he breathes fire down on fleeing crowds, immolating people and buildings alike. This image, easily the film's most brutal, inverts to a shot of negatively processed film as the victims burn. The inversion of black and white, light and dark, power and futility is all implied in this single shot.[48] Humanity's foolhardy creation and use of nuclear weapons has awakened a slumbering nightmare, more powerful than any human weapon. Thanks to the inversion technique, this scene is one of the few in *Daikaijū Gamera* to powerfully portray the atomic bomb experience.

Despite superficial similarities, the special effects technique behind Gamera's fire-breath is quite different from Godzilla's. In *Daikaijū Gamera*, Gamera's fire-breath is created with a flame thrower in the Gamera suit's mouth. Godzilla's radioactive ray looks more like a fine mist in *Godzilla*, and in later installments the effect was simply added to the footage in post-production.[49] Gamera's rampage concludes with a montage sequence featuring scenes of destruction—burning oil refineries, sunken fishing trawlers, derailed trains—certainly reminiscent to moviegoers at the time of the destruction of Japanese cities by the Allied bombing campaign in the final months of the Asia-Pacific War.

The American and Soviet scientists assure Dr. Hidaka that Z-Plan will be completed on schedule, but that Gamera must be kept occupied until work is finished the following day. Hidaka, drawing on his zoological knowledge, states that he believes Gamera's violence is due to a lack of energy supply. The audience learns that Gamera is currently at an industrial coal combine snacking on flames, and that oil will be transported to keep feeding the conflagration until the international team finishes Z-Plan preparations.

A sequence of Gamera and Toshio at the coal combine follows. While the workers slave away to ensure that the fires keep Gamera distracted for a further twenty-four hours, the misguided Toshio arrives in order to visit Gamera, whom he still views as his good-natured erstwhile pet, Chibi. Toshio hops onto one of the oil cars being pushed towards Gamera, causing a tense scene where a worker rescues Toshio from a grisly demise.[50] The flames continue to burn and keep Gamera occupied long enough for Z-Plan to be completed on Ōshima, an island just outside Tokyo Bay.[51] Once again, the film portrays Gamera as a remorseless consumer of natural resources, devouring the very fossil fuels and other energy sources that power Japanese society. Gamera uses his energy to cause widespread destruction; the monster embodies the inexorable expansion of human civilization into formerly pristine areas.

Once again, the mischievous Toshio causes trouble, stowing away on a cargo freighter carrying the last of the Z-Plan materials to Ōshima while Dr. Hidaka devises a scheme to tempt Gamera to the outlying island. A small flotilla of tankers and other vessels spray oil as they sail to Ōshima (this cannot be good for ocean life), luring Gamera with a trail of flame towards the still-mysterious Z-Plan awaiting him. Gamera finally arrives at Ōshima, making landfall nearly simultaneously with a typhoon. Although the torrential squalls douse the fires attracting the terrible terrapin, the island's volcano fortuitously begins to erupt, securing the monster's continued interest in the island.

The thematic and cinematic elements of this sequence situate Gamera as a natural force. Like Godzilla, Gamera is a malleable and sometimes contradictory icon—part reimagined *kappa*, consumer of resources, and force of nature. Over the course of the film, Gamera is connected with multiple natural afflictions that plague the Japanese: tidal waves, earthquakes, typhoons, and volcanoes. The cinematic composition of this scene further reinforces this point. Upon arriving on Ōshima, the foreground of the shot frames Gamera with the torrential rains of the typhoon, while the erupting volcano looms in the distant background.[52] Moreover, Hidaka's assistant Kyoko even mutters in dismay that it is impossible to defeat nature.

The following day, once the storm has passed, the entire cast watches from the Z-Plan control room as Gamera is lured to the center of a large platform. Once in place, a giant dome encloses the monster turtle, and an enormous rocket launches him into space. A narrator intones that because Gamera could not be killed on Earth, Z-Plan was devised to send him to Mars.[53] The group rejoices. The films ends with Toshio telling Hidaka that he wants to become a scientist one day so that he can travel to Mars to visit Gamera. The movie ends.

In his first film, Gamera represents a shifting metaphor on nature and the environment in Japan, depicted through the lens of the *kaijū eiga* genre. An analytical viewing of *Daikaijū Gamera* reveals several discrete environmental messages. Much like Godzilla and Mothra before him, Gamera is a fluid symbol representing multiple messages simultaneously. The film presents such disparate ecological themes as atomic testing, the threat of nuclear war, biological invasion, the ecological destructiveness of the military-industrial complex, Japan's reliance on dirty fossil fuels, and the inherent power of nature itself.

Furthermore, *Daikaijū Gamera* anticipates the environmental critiques evident in *kaijū eiga* of the 1970s, notably the high costs of economic prosperity and industrial pollution. Although the idea is not yet fully formed (industrial pollution would increase even more dramatically in the later 1960s), Gamera is portrayed as an insatiable consumer of natural resources. The monster turtle gobbles up Japan's fisheries, coal, oil, and anything else that will produce energy. There are even fears that Gamera will attempt to ingest Japan's reserve of nuclear material. The monster turtle presents an insatiable lust for consumption of all kinds. Yuasa Noriaki's film implies that Japanese socio-economics during the high-speed economic growth period of the mid–1960s were equally monstrous.

Finally, the film promotes scientific literacy and environmentalism among its target audience. Gamera and the JSDF destroy a geothermal power plant, but not before some obvious didactic exposition. Clearly, the film's creators intended to educate the audience on the feasibility of clean, renewable power, even before any such plants were operational in Japan. Later, the young Toshio declares his intent to become a scientist so he can travel to Mars to visit Gamera. In this way, *Daikaijū Gamera* encourages child viewers to pursue careers in the sciences. The film is thoroughly optimistic—although it depicts industrial society's destructiveness, it also reveals the hope of harnessing nature's abundant energy to build a harmonious and sustainable society.

Gammera the Invincible *(1966)*

There are three distinct versions of the original Gamera film. Daiei Company's original *Daikaijū Gamera*, an altered and edited version entitled *Gammera the Invincible* (1966) released in the United States by World Entertainment the following year, and a third iteration simply named *Gamera* (1987) released on home video by Sandy Frank.[54] Stuart Galbraith presents the most in-depth and widely circulated critical analysis of the Gamera series in his book *Japanese Science Fiction, Fantasy, and Horror Films*.[55] However, Galbraith concentrates his discussion on the poorly dubbed Sandy Frank home video version of Gamera's original film, while also briefly mentioning the other American edit, *Gammera the Invincible*.[56]

Due to the confused state of the scholarship, it is worth differentiating the various versions of the original Gamera film. The Sandy Frank *Gamera* that Galbraith analyzes remains visually similar to *Daikaijū Gamera*, but poorly-dubbed dialogue once again alters much of the original film's intent. Additionally, the Sandy Frank version Anglicized the character names: Toshio became Kenny, Kyoko turned into Katherine, Chibi was altered to Tibby, and so on. Sadly, this version of the original Gamera film is probably best known to most casual North American audiences—it was frequently broadcast on TV in the 1980s and was lampooned on two separate episodes of the popular science fiction comedy series *Mystery Science Theater 3000*.[57]

Although *Daikaijū Gamera* features several scenes containing foreign extras, these were removed from World Entertainment's *Gammera the Invincible* and replaced with largely similar scenes featuring more professional (but certainly past their prime) American actors. Dick O'Neill portrays the creatively named General O'Neill, Brian Donlevy plays General Arnold, and Albert Dekker fills in as the U.S. Secretary of Defense.[58] Although an improvement over the foreign extras cast in *Daikaijū Gamera*, Galbraith best describes the performances of the new American actors as "men in the unhappy twilight of their careers."[59]

Furthermore, additional scenes inside the Pentagon and U.N. Headquarters were also filmed to give the edited movie an American perspective, as with *Godzilla's* earlier transformation into *Godzilla, King of the Monsters*. The dubbed dialogue in *Gammera the Invincible* is not a faithful translation of the original script, and the meaning and intent of several scenes is inscrutable. For example, rather than declaring that his missing pet turtle Chibi turned into Gamera, Toshio instead states that the giant chelonian scared the tiny turtle away, completely eviscerating the film's subtextual commentary on biological invasions. Other scenes were also excised to make room in the film's running time for the new American footage, substantially altering the original Japanese film, and once again blunting or completely removing the environmental commentary of yet another *kaijū eiga* for international viewers. Yet, thanks to Mill Creek Entertainment's 2014 restoration and release of the Gamera films in their original language and format, scholars and fans alike can now appreciate the series' contribution to environmental awareness.

7

1970s Japan
"A polluter's paradise"

Despite its many benefits, Japan's high-speed economic growth of the 1960s was not without negative consequences. By the early 1970s, the Japanese people were living in one of the most industrially productive yet highly polluted landscapes on Earth. *Kaijū eiga* began directly confronting Japan's industrial excesses, as they did with earlier environmental crises in Japan since the postwar era. Before embarking on our discussion of pertinent films, we trace Japan's industrial development and environmental experience from World War II through the 1970s. Rapid economic expansion coupled with little to no environmental regulation led to toxic pollution levels throughout the Japanese archipelago.

A War on Nature

A history of the environmental situation in 1970s Japan must begin in 1945 (if not earlier), with the end of the Asia-Pacific War and Japan's subsequent occupation. Although the dynamic between the Japanese people and their natural environment ebbed and flowed over time, from exploitive forestry in the pre-industrial era to Japan's first pollution crisis at the Ashio Copper Mine in the Meiji period, World War II proved catastrophic for the Japanese people and their environment.[1] As a result of the war, Japan was left utterly destroyed not only militarily and economically, but also industrially and environmentally. Taken together, the militarized economy, mobilization for war, deprivations and hardships of the war years, and intensive and extensive Allied bombing campaign drastically altered Japan's physical landscape. Although some rural and provincial regions of Japan escaped the war mostly unscathed, Japan's great metropolitan areas were nearly entirely razed by the war's end.

Japan's ultimate defeat in World War II was the culmination of the nation's imperial endeavor, which found its earliest beginnings in the Meiji period and eventually led to a series of wars in mainland Asia before Japan's total war against the Allied Powers starting in December 1941. By the time Japan surrendered little remained of the once-mighty Japanese empire. Allied forces controlled most of Japan's overseas possessions and the Japanese home islands had been bombed into submission. In addition to the atomic bombings of Hiroshima and Nagasaki, American air forces had subjected Japan's cities and industrial centers to an intense strategic bombing campaign.[2] When U.S. General Douglas MacArthur arrived in Japan to oversee the occupation, the island nation was a devastated shambles of its prewar self.

The scale of Japan's defeat became apparent to the Allies immediately after the formal surrender. Only nine days after the signing ceremony, MacArthur held a press conference where he stated that Japan had plummeted to the level of "a fourth-rate nation."[3] In a communiqué from special envoy Edwin Locke, Jr., to President Truman, the presidential aide reported, "the American officers now in Tokyo are amazed by the fact that resistance continued as long as it did."[4] Locke went on to quantify the devastation of Japan: "the entire economic infrastructure of Japan's greatest cities has been wrecked. Five million of Tokyo's seven million population have left the ruined city."[5] A later analysis by the U.S. Strategic Bombing Survey reinforced Locke's preliminary diagnosis, determining that Allied officials had greatly overestimated Japan's industrial output and wartime potential near the war's end. Moreover, the Allied bombing campaign had devastated the Japanese landscape far more than anyone—on either side—had acknowledged.

During the war, Allied bombings razed a high percentage of Japanese cities and factories and nearly 40 percent of the country's railway infrastructure was no longer operable.[6] The devastation was nearly as bad for Japan's motor vehicles, with nearly 25 percent beyond repair. Additionally, bombings destroyed 33 percent of industrial machinery. Worst of all—and arguably most important to a resource-poor island nation—was the destruction of Japan's fleet of military, merchant, and fishing ships. Wartime losses of seagoing vessels took a heavy toll, with approximately 80 percent sunk or damaged by September 1945.[7] Such dramatic maritime losses, discussed earlier in Chapter 2, are reflected in *kaijū eiga*'s repeated trope of featuring the on-screen destruction of ships and boats of all types.

During the Allied Occupation, MacArthur's SCAP bureaucracy refined the estimates of Japan's wartime destruction. In early 1946, SCAP estimated that the war cost Japan fully one-third of its total prewar wealth, and one-third to one-half of its total income potential. At the same time, the country's standard of living collapsed. Rural areas measured only 65 percent of their prewar metric, while urban areas (hardest hit by Allied bombings) preserved only 35 percent of their previous standard of living.

The prolonged Allied bombing campaign had devastated Japan's urban centers. Overall, sixty-six major Japanese cities were heavily bombed during the war. Bombings destroyed 40 percent of Japan's prewar urban development and rendered approximately 30 percent of the country's city-dwelling population homeless. The three largest cities—Tokyo, Osaka, and Nagoya—lost 65 percent, 57 percent, and 89 percent of their residences, respectively.[8] Many prominent historic sites, like Meiji Shrine, Osaka Castle, and Nagoya Castle, burned in the infernos. According to Japan historian John Dower: "The first American contingents to arrive in Japan—especially those that made the several-hour journey from Yokohama to Tokyo—were invariably impressed, if not shocked, by the mile after mile of urban devastation they encountered."[9] *Kaijū eiga* contain numerous visual links to Japan's wartime destruction. From the burning of Japanese cities to more direct metaphors like the repeated razing of historic Japanese castles, monsters like Godzilla, Anguirus, and Tōhō's incarnation of King Kong reenact scenes of wartime devastation.[10]

The destruction of Tokyo was especially horrific. One event in particular, the American firebombing raid on March 9, 1945, destroyed vast swaths of the wood-built city with incendiary devices, leveling over forty square kilometers (sixteen square miles) in a single night. The event was the deadliest air attack of World War II, in any theater of operation, and caused approximately 100,000 deaths and consumed the homes of at least one million Japanese civilians. Military historian Conrad C. Crane recounts: "Victims died horribly as intense fires consumed the oxygen, boiled water in canals, and set liquid glass rolling down the streets. The B-29 crews [...] wore oxygen masks to avoid vomiting from the stench of burning flesh."[11] As we noted in Chapter 3, the firestorm ignited during Godzilla's attack on Tokyo in the 1954 film evoked the audience's memories of not only the atomic bombings, but other wartime catastrophes like the Tokyo firebombing as well.

Not only did the war have a devastating impact on the Japanese urban landscape, it also destroyed much of the archipelago's natural environment. A study in the journal *Environmental History* notes, "Despite the obvious scars left by American bombing, the more indirect effects of war—and specifically of the economic mobilization for war—seem to have had the more profound consequences for the environment in Japan."[12] Following aggressive expeditions into China throughout the 1930s, the Japanese government strove to supplement its reserve currency by increasing exports—they did so by rapidly expanding (and overfishing) tuna and crab catches, greatly increasing whaling as far away as the Southern Ocean, and extensively logging Japan's forests.[13] Although these exports helped shore up Japan's balance sheet before World War II, they nonetheless caused numerous environmental problems and resource shortages on the home front.

In December 1941, Japan's mobilization for total war exacerbated the environmental and ecological damage. The logging increased in pace. Over the course of the war's four years approximately 15 percent of Japan's forest cover totaling some nine million acres was depleted for use as timber, charcoal, wood pulp, and an unsuccessful experiment to make oil from pine roots. Imperial Japan's attempt to distill oil from pine roots was both particularly destructive and indicative of the scarcity of natural resources. In the final two years of the war, Japanese civilians established 34,000 stills and produced 70,000 barrels of pine oil every month.[14] According to one economist of wartime Japan: "Monumental piles of roots and stumps lined many of the roadways [...] Mountainsides were stripped of every tree and sapling."[15] Despite the montane devastation, the denuding of Japan's pine forests was all for naught—Japanese scientists never perfected their "arboreal alchemy."[16] Such extensive deforestation caused other secondary environmental problems, including a proliferation of insect infestations, considerable erosion, and increased cases of flooding.[17] Deforestation and its related ill effects develop as major environmental themes in some *kaijū eiga*, especially the *Rebirth of Mothra* trilogy discussed in Chapter 11.

Although Japan's forests bore the brunt of wartime scarcity, Japan's animal life did not escape harm. Agricultural animals that competed with humans for food such as horses, pigs, chickens, and rabbits decreased in population, while others with auxiliary benefits (like wool) such as sheep and goats increased in number.[18] Moreover, in order to supplement the populace's protein requirements, the Japanese government encouraged the netting and consumption of songbirds. During the total war years of World War II, as many as fifteen million songbirds were trapped and consumed by the Japanese people each year—when the Allies arrived in Japan, the only common bird sightings were crows and a small number of sparrows.[19]

The wholesale destruction of the Japanese environment, both the human and the natural, during the war years fundamentally changed the already complex relationship between the Japanese people and nature. The deprivations of the war years and the early postwar period led many Japanese to yearn for a return to prosperity and economic growth, effectively trumping any residual bonds the people felt for their natural environment after the war. This new human-environment interaction had a significant impact on Japan's postwar environmental policy.

In addition to the direct and indirect consequences of the war years, it is also important to reflect on another element distinct to Japan. Two syncretic belief systems dominate Japanese culture: Buddhism (imported from mainland Asia) and Shintō (Japan's indigenous ethnic religion).[20] Both have long histories of an abiding respect for and deep connection with the natural world. Shintō rituals honor a multitude of diverse spirits known as *kami*. For the most part, *kami* tend to be connected with mythological characters (like the Sun Goddess), important historical figures and ancestors (like the Emperor Meiji), and nature (like Mount Fuji). In particular, awe-inspiring natural objects, such as massive cypress trees, immense boulders, and majestic mountains have long been considered sacred places where *kami* reside.[21]

In Chapter 1, we connected *kaijū eiga* to Shintō and Japanese theatrical and cultural traditions. However, in addition to this historical connection, *kaijū eiga* themselves sometimes overtly reference the intersection of monsters, nature, mythology, and Shintō. For example, in the original 1954 *Godzilla*, the Ōdo Islanders treat the monster Godzilla as a maleficent *kami*, and hold an exorcism ceremony to placate the mysterious beast.[22] In 1974's *Godzilla vs. Mechagodzilla*, a traditional Okinawan *shisa* statue is embodied in the monster King Caesar, the benevolent protector-deity of the Okinawan people. Finally, and perhaps most overtly, in 2001's *Gojira, Mosura, Kingu Gidora: Daikaijū Sōkōgeki* (*Godzilla, Mothra, and King Ghidorah: Giant Monsters All-Out Attack*), three monsters are directly stated to be guardian *kami* of Japan, complete with their own forest shrine.[23]

For anyone who has visited a Shintō shrine in Japan, the connection between nature, religious traditions, and the Japanese past is readily apparent.[24] For example, Meiji Shrine, one of the nation's most prominent, sits among 170 acres of woods and gardens, even though it is located in the heart of Tokyo.[25] Meiji Shrine, like nearly every shrine, epitomizes this deep connection between the natural world and the Japanese people through their native religious tradition.[26] However, despite their religious and cultural importance, not even renowned Shintō shrines fully escaped the environmental destruction of the war years. In one piteous example, an ancient stretch of cryptomeria trees (commonly known as Japanese red-cedar) planted at Nikkō Shrine in the mid–1600s were felled for the war effort.[27]

Although deforestation affected the sylvan setting of some Shintō shrines, Japan's loss to the Allies had much greater impact on Shintō itself. After the Meiji Restoration of 1868, what was once a loose system of Shintō shrines and practices was institutionalized by the imperial government, and converted to what has been described as a state cult.[28] This state cult was likewise "a bulwark of emperor-centered ultranationalism" and the Allied Occupation thoroughly dismantled it.[29] In December 1945, General MacArthur issued the Shintō Directive, which banned the use of any public funds for Shintō, severing it from the Japanese government. Although SCAP thought that ending government-controlled Shintō would cause the religious tradition to wither, the non-profit National Association of Shrines sprouted in its place in February 1946.[30] Nevertheless, SCAP's actions unsettled the existing Shintō establishment and disrupted one of the Japanese people's time-honored connections with the natural world. Taken in tandem with the ecological destruction and degradation of the war years themselves, this disarray further contributed to the changing relationship between Japanese society and the environment in the postwar era.

The widespread environmental destruction of the war years, coupled with the destitution and scarcity endemic to total war and the postwar period, and joined with the disruption of Japan's formerly organized Shintō religious tradition, unsettled the complex relationship between the Japanese people and nature. Throughout the postwar period, political and industrial leaders prioritized economic growth over ecological preservation, and the Japanese populace largely accepted the industrial pollution that accompanied rapid re-industrialization. These conditions led to severe pollution and wholesale destruction of the environment throughout the struggles of the 1950s and the boom years of the 1960s. In the following section, we provide data regarding industrial pollution in order to contextualize the state of the Japanese environment by the early 1970s, setting the stage for the pollution protest *kaijū eiga* reflective of that time.

Toxic Land, Diseased Seas and Polluted Air

During the occupation, SCAP compelled the Japanese government to restructure and "democratize." Additionally, Article 9 of the 1947 Constitution, drafted by SCAP personnel, explicitly banned the formation of a Japanese military.[31] As a direct result of these fundamental changes, Japanese factories were extensively retooled and redirected. Prior to defeat, 90 percent of Japanese industry was geared toward military production. Following the promulgation of the new constitution this was no longer viable.[32]

The newly reconstructed factories, which became the basis for Japan's high-speed economic growth in the 1960s, instead focused on the production of consumer products for both the domestic and global markets. The market was flooded with consumer products and capital from overseas sales. This created a positive feedback loop—prices fell, more people were able to purchase the goods, so more factories were built and more workers moved to the cities to find employment, growing the market ever more for the sale of additional goods.[33] Although production levels had collapsed near the end of the war, by the mid–1950s production in major sectors of the economy had rebounded and even surpassed the industrial output of the war years.[34] This system of rapid growth enabled Japan to reach a sustained Gross National Product (GNP) growth rate of over 10 percent throughout the 1960s.[35]

By the dawn of the 1970s, heavy industry was extensively polluting Japan's land, air, and water. Most industry was concentrated along the Pacific Ocean and Inland Sea coasts, stretching from Tokyo through Nagoya to Osaka. This industrial core coexisted with one of the densest human populations in the world. To put this in perspective, the entirety of Japan covers approximately the same land area as the state of California, roughly 400,000 square kilometers. However, about 80 percent of Japan is too rugged to be considered habitable under normal circumstances, leaving only about 20 percent suitable for regular human activity.[36] In this remaining land area, slightly over 100 million Japanese lived in the early 1970s, and 44 percent of that population, or around 44 million people, were crammed into the much smaller area of central Honshū located between Tokyo and Osaka.[37]

During the 1970s, heavy industries in these areas imported vast amounts of crude oil, iron ore, and coal. Production of steel along the coast of the Inland Sea reached seventy million tons in the 1970s, an amount equal to the combined output of both the United Kingdom and France during the same period.[38] Expansion of heavy industry and production of industrial and chemical products increased dramatically from the 1960s through the early 1970s, to a point where over 20 percent of the coast of the Inland Sea was occupied by factories.[39]

A comparison of production over the years illustrates the rapid growth of industry in Japan. For example, in 1965 (when *Daikaijū Gamera* premiered) Japan produced approximately 696,000 automobiles, but by 1970 that number increased by more than four-fold to 3,179,000 vehicles built.[40] Although many were exported abroad, the number of registered automobiles polluting Japanese roadways skyrocketed from 441,000 in 1960 to 6,777,000 in 1970, at the same time the number of trucks jumped from 1,322,000 to 5,460,000.[41] Likewise, electricity production nearly doubled, and petroleum importation increased from 83,000 kiloliters in 1965 to over 195,000 kiloliters in 1970.[42] Industrial output of consumer goods also barreled ahead: between 1960 and the end of the 1970s, the number of construction excavators built shot from a paltry 1,217 to 57,063 only two decades later. Moreover, the number of TV sets manufactured went from 3,578,000 in 1960 to 16,327,000 per year by the close of the 1970s.[43]

Severe environmental destruction on an astonishing scale accompanied this economic growth. The amount of industrial pollution produced led Japanese historian Hashimoto Michio to refer to pre–1970s Japan as "a polluter's paradise."[44] Processing plants dumped enormous amounts of industrial byproducts and waste into rivers and waterways and spewed smog into Japan's air. Some industries, such as rayon-to-pulp textile production, emitted nearly twice the amount of waste into the environment as they produced in finished products.[45] Most of these byproducts were poured into riparian and coastal zones or belched into the atmosphere unfiltered, as scrubbing or filtering methods were either unavailable or deemed too costly by most corporations. This toxic environmental degradation of Japan's land, water, and air became the focus of *kaijū eiga* productions in the early 1970s.

Throughout the 1950s and 1960s, high-profile industrial poisoning of human populations began occurring.[46] These cases of industrial poisoning led directly to the deaths of thousands and harmful side effects and birth defects in tens of thousands more. Four major industrial diseases acquired notoriety in Japan during this time: Itai-itai Disease, Minamata Syndrome, Niigata Minamata Syndrome, and Yokkaichi Asthma. The Mitsui Group's mining and smelting operations in Toyama Prefecture caused the Itai-itai Disease (literally "it hurts, it hurts") by dumping cadmium into the local river.[47] Meanwhile, the Shōwa Oil Refinery petrochemical plant pumped sulfur dioxide into the air around the port city of Yokkaichi. In a nearby area, schoolchildren were told to "breathe as little as possible" due to the fumes; in another local town, nearly half the children contracted a new breathing disorder coined Yokkaichi Asthma.[48] Minamata and Niigata Minamata Syndromes were both the result of methylmercury poisoning transmitted through water pollution.

The Minamata Syndrome was particularly horrific. The illness led to extreme neurological damage. A Chisso Corporation industrial plant directly caused it when it began dumping heavy amounts of mercury into the sea near the fishing town of Minamata.[49] By the 1970s, industrial pollution had become an environmental and even economic problem on a nationwide scale, "compromising the viability of the fishing industry [...and] destroying the natural viability of the human environmental support system."[50] Mishima Akio, in his gripping account of the Minamata incident portrayed in *Bitter Sea*, depicts the environmental nightmare: "Dead fish were found floating on the surface of the water, and cats began dying in convulsions [...] The white bellies of dead fish dotted the water. The stench of rotting fish and shellfish, mingled with the noisome fumes of factory effluent, hung in the air like a miasma."[51] Because of mercury pollution, people and animals throughout the region suffered severe neurological effects, ranging from involuntary muscle spasms and numbness to damaged vision, hearing, and speech. Severe cases led to insanity, paralysis, and eventually death within weeks of the onset of symptoms from acute mercury poisoning.[52]

Although mercury levels in the waters of Minamata Bay were extraordinarily high, the levels found in fish, shellfish, and other marine life were even more lethal. The levels of mercury and other pollutants increased the higher one traveled up the food chain, due to an effect known as bioaccumulation. Due to this principle, as mercury traveled through organisms up the Minamata food chain, each higher rung exhibited ever-higher doses of mercury poisoning. For example, bivalves such as mussels and oysters ingested the plankton growing in the mercury-ridden waters, which in turn were eaten by local fishermen and their families, passing on in even higher levels by pregnant mothers to their unborn and nursing children. As Brett Walker explains in his examination of industrial diseases in Japan, "Sadly, the unborn children of Minamata inhabited the highest link in the food chain: they served as the final destination of, and hence repository for, Chisso's deadly toxins."[53] The Japanese Ministry of the Environment later determined through extensive investigation that over 10,000 individuals in Kumamoto, Kagoshima, and Niigata Prefectures were affected by the disease and received financial and medical compensation from the responsible corporations.[54] But Minamata was not the only example of extensive tragedy for both humans and marine life.

Fish and Ships: Poisoned Food

The importance of the sea to the Japanese people cannot be overstated. The ocean serves as a setting in many examples of *kaijū eiga*, and its importance only grows in the pollution-oriented monster films of the 1970s. Despite Japan's small geographic size, the country has the sixth longest coastline in the world, totaling some 29,751 kilometers. As an archipelago with four main islands as well as many isles, inlets, bays, and seas, nature endowed Japan with a coastline far more extensive than other, much geographically larger countries like the United States, Australia, or China.[55] As noted in Chapter 2, a deep and abiding connection exists between the Japanese nation and the sea. This intrinsic connection, a result of its distinctive geography, stretches back to the mythological origins of the Japanese people themselves—according to Shintō legend, the deities Izanami and Izanagi stuck a spear into the ocean depths, and from the brine dripping from its tip the islands of Japan formed.

Oceans and seas are literally the lifeblood of Japan. The Japanese people have always depended on the bounty of the sea to supplement their diet; they consume more fish and other seafood per capita than any other nation or region on Earth. On average, Japanese rely on thirty kilograms (sixty-six pounds) of seafood per person per year, whereas Scandinavians place a distant second at fifteen kilograms (thirty-three pounds) annually for every person.[56] Additionally, as a resource-poor island, Japan in the modern era has depended on shipping and overseas trade to both export goods abroad and to import a wide array of raw materials. Whether for food or trade, Japan's island geography forever links its people with the sea.

Although land and air pollution by the 1970s was detrimental, the degradation of the seas—including their essential fisheries—was dramatic and acute. Japan historian Conrad Totman describes the situation succinctly: "The most devastating problem that fishermen faced in the postwar era was the rampant pollution of their fisheries as industrial development roared ahead, spreading ever more widely about the realm."[57] However, before many Japanese became aware of the plight of their seas and fisheries, the same laissez-faire attitude about pollution applied to the oceans. To ensure strong economic growth in the 1950s and 1960s, people willingly sacrificed the natural environment, including Japan's vital and bountiful seas.

As noted above, resource-poor Japan relied heavily on imports, particularly oil, to fuel its economic engine. Throughout the 1950s and 1960s, crude oil imports grew dramatically, and ever-larger tankers were built to carry more and more oil. As more tankers steamed through Japan's waters, so too did more oil spill into its seas, inlets, and bays. In 1966, for example, one study determined that oil pollution in the Inland Sea ruined seventy-three fisheries, resulting in ¥578 million in damage.[58] Despite these environmental costs, public opinion barely changed. In January 1967, the president of the Idemitsu Kōsan oil company blustered: "The oil spills from supertankers and the foul-smelling fish that those in the opposition movement talk about are just trifling matters."[59] This statement reveals that while a nascent environmental movement existed, it lacked authority.[60]

Coastal waters in Tokyo Bay also degraded significantly. The Tokyo side of the bay was already extensively deteriorated from the development of the metropolis, but until the postwar period the Chiba Prefecture side of the bay had remained fairly pristine. By 1958, effluent pollution from factories like the Honshū Paper Company regularly spewed into Chiba's waters.[61] Although the government later required the paper factory to install a water-purification system, the situation in Tokyo Bay declined, and by 1962 fishermen operating out of Tokyo gave up all fishing rights in return for an indemnity.[62]

The sullying of Tokyo Bay continued and in 1972 a joint report from the Tokyo, Chiba, and Kanagawa prefectural governments declared that the bay was nearly a "dead water body" devoid of active marine life.[63] As we discussed in Chapter 3, when Dr. Serizawa deployed his oxygen-destroyer to save Japan from Godzilla he simultaneously extinguished Tokyo Bay's animal life. By the early 1970s, the Japanese managed to wipe out the bay's ecosystem even without the help of the scientist's fictitious weapon.

Pollution, pungent odors, and dead fish came to define Tokyo Bay; meanwhile, the bay itself steadily shrank as land reclamation and landfill projects lined its shores. Like factories, the number of reclamation projects increased prodigiously in the postwar period. According to one study, a total of 18,000 hectares of land were reclaimed from the sea during the twenty-eight year period between the end of World War II and 1973, only slightly less than the 19,000 hectares reclaimed during the nearly three centuries of the Tokugawa period (1603–1868).[64] Such ventures were a large factor in Japan's industrial development of the 1960s and 1970s—one such project is depicted in 1964's *Mothra vs. Godzilla*.[65] Massive drainage and reclamation enterprises contributed to the stress placed on Japan's littoral zones and fisheries, exacerbating the problem created by industrial waste and pollutants.[66]

On the Osaka side of the Inland Sea, the case was as hopeless as Tokyo's. Osaka's tremendous growth and expansion produced pollution that destroyed the fishing shoals in the sea's eastern waters. Landfill reclamation projects also crowded the coastline, altering the natural geography and ecology while providing more room for increased industrial expansion and yet further pollution.[67] In 1969, Osaka fishermen abandoned their fishing rights just as their brethren in Tokyo had seven years earlier.[68] Throughout the 1960s, red tides swept the waters of the Inland Sea. Comprised of massive blooms of plankton in the pollutant-rich waters, red tides wiped out wild fish and marine creatures. By 1968, the damage to the Inland Sea's fisheries totaled approximately ¥3.4 billion.[69] In June 1970, a report by the Yamaguchi prefectural government determined that several portions of the Inland Sea near Hiroshima Bay were at the precipice of becoming a "dead sea."[70]

The same proved to be the case for other toxic pollutants and heavy metals that poured into other Japanese bodies of water during this period. In northern Kyūshū, the Yahata steel mill heavily polluted a long estuary known as the Dōkai-wan from the postwar era and into the early 1970s. Conrad Totman notes: "By 1970, the Dōkai-wan was virtually lifeless."[71] Although local authorities attempted to resuscitate the estuary by limiting industrial pollution and requiring factories to implement filters and other environmental protocols, the marine life of the area was nearly entirely extinguished.

The magnitude of Japan's environmental problem became so obvious that public opinion and government policy began to swiftly change. Perhaps one of the best indications of the mindset of a populace is the push for government action on an issue. In July 1971, the same month that both the Godzilla and Gamera franchises premiered installments directly addressing industrial pollution (discussed in Chapters 8 and 9), the Japanese Environment Agency was formed.[72] Miki Takeo, the agency's director and future prime minister, stated in the official *Japan Environment Summary*: "The deterioration of the environment is an increasingly grave issue. There has emerged amongst the nation a strong doubt about the wisdom of placing high priority to economic growth. The cries of the people demanding to regain their healthy, bright, and rich living environment are being raised like a swelling of the tide."[73] The state of the Japanese environment, and public opinion calling for government action, must have been strong indeed for a government minister to make such a direct and unequivocal statement.

The subsequent year, a public opinion poll published in the second volume of the journal echoed Miki's sentiments: "50 percent of those who replied to questions in a recent public opinion survey were in favor of elimination of pollution and protection of nature even if economic activities had to be sacrificed, compared with 20 percent who attached greater importance to economic development than to environmental protection [...] 70 percent felt that destruction of nature was going on around them, and 53 percent were of the view that pollution would become worse in the coming years."[74] Both Miki's emphatic statement and the results of the poll clearly show a desire for cleaning up the Japanese environment, even if the result was a downturn in the economic growth rate.

By 1971, several Japanese environmental groups had formed, largely in response to debilitating diseases resulting from toxic industrial waste. Yet they remained "scattered, small, and locally oriented."[75] These environmental advocates tended to focus on compensation issues for those afflicted with debilitating diseases caused by industrial pollution, rather than advocating for changing industrial and economic practices on a national scale. For example, one of the most prominent groups worked towards achieving social justice and material compensation for the victims of the Minamata Syndrome.[76] Whereas other democratic, industrialized nations witnessed the formation of large national umbrella organizations to lobby for environmental protection, Japan had no such political formations at this time.[77] The government began to respond with environmental protection legislation in the early 1970s, while pollution-related lawsuits slowly wound their way through the byzantine Japanese legal system, usually resulting in convictions for the wrongdoers and compensation for the victims.[78]

The Japanese fishing industry managed to sustain itself throughout this period despite the widespread degradation of its traditional fishing zones. First and foremost, the fishermen fought back against polluting industries through the use of protest movements and compensatory lawsuits. In the early years of the 1970s, such strategies were beginning to bear fruit as public opinion shifted away from supporting unencumbered economic growth toward a more balanced environmental and ecological approach. At the same time, the fishing industry itself changed to meet the demands of this new world, by expanding deep-sea fishing, aquaculture production, and shifting to less-polluted coastal areas.[79]

In the early 1970s, Japanese schools began to teach their students about pollution and its related problems, preparing a new generation to face the environmental issues left by the prior one. At the same time, books, films, and lectures about industrial pollution and its consequences spread throughout Japan.[80] The Godzilla and Gamera franchises of the early 1970s both emphasized the desperate state of Japan's environment, especially its seas and sea life. Turning from the single-issue movements toward one of general environmental protection and natural conservation, these *kaijū eiga* reflected a new nation-wide dialogue on Japan's environment-be-damned economic growth. By understanding the ecological situation at the time, a more thorough appreciation of both films is now possible.

8

Smog, Sludge and Hippies
Godzilla vs. Hedorah

Gojira tai Hedora (*Godzilla vs. Hedorah*) debuted in Japan in July 1971 and premiered internationally the following year under the alternate title *Godzilla vs. the Smog Monster*.[1] The environmental message presented in the film departs considerably from earlier *kaijū eiga*. *Godzilla vs. Hedorah* shifted the focus of the Godzilla franchise from nuclear fears to the crippling toll of rapid industrialization and its toxic pollution. When *Godzilla vs. Hedorah* opened, Japan's natural and human environments had transformed into ecological nightmares. The public and politicians were finally starting to take notice. The film therefore depicts a change that occurred simultaneously in Japanese society—the nuclear anxiety of the postwar period became supplanted by the suffocating results of Japan's own economic success.

A Historiography of Hedorah

Godzilla vs. Hedorah elicits strong opinions from scholars and critics alike.[2] Not only is the film widely panned, but "fans consider *Godzilla vs. the Smog Monster* one of the weakest Shōwa offerings."[3] Although many have largely ignored *Godzilla vs. Hedorah*'s contributions to the Japanese environmental debate, the film made a concerted attempt to raise the issue of Japan's 1970s pollution epidemic through a popular medium.[4] Failing to absorb this context, many viewed the picture as campy and occasionally ridiculous. Given the time and place in which the film was created, however, it is clear that *Godzilla vs. Hedorah* attempted to address a grim issue at the forefront of the minds of many Japanese.

Why have critics, fans, and other authors dismissed *Godzilla vs. Hedorah*? By the 1970s, Godzilla had transcended Japanese cinema and was an international movie icon. Despite this fact, the dubbed versions of *kaijū eiga* abroad failed to provide contextualization for foreign moviegoers and often left audiences baffled and confused. *Hedorah* presents a particularly poignant example of this affliction, and foreign audiences around the globe were left bewildered by what many viewed as a nonsensical and silly film.

Despite its inclusion in some compendiums of fan literature and its mention in passing by some writers, *Godzilla vs. Hedorah* has been largely ignored. The popular press and *kaijū eiga* fans have approached *Hedorah* with either outright dislike or cautious curiosity. More often, the film has been treated as a pariah for its entirely unique style. Generally, new director Banno Yoshimitsu's filming techniques, which have been characterized as everything from "peculiar" to "bizarre" to "avant-garde," led to the film being viewed with confusion and bewilderment.[5] Some of the features of Banno's film that clash with the pre-established ideas of what *kaijū eiga* audiences generally expect are: strange and unconventional camera shots and techniques; a cacophonous and jarring musical score; animated segments; assorted disturbing montages; vivid and gruesome death sequences (including one of a major character); and even a psychedelic drug-induced scene at a discotheque.

The first major widely circulated retrospective review of *Godzilla vs. Hedorah* appeared in the 1978 book *The Fifty Worst Films of All Time* by Harry Medved.[6] As its title suggests, Medved's review is less than kind. He bases his assessment on the poor English dubbing of the film, picking some of the worst (and consequently most amusing) translations to use as quotes. Medved begins his assessment with a selection of critical reviews panning the film. For example, he quotes *Monster Times*: "One of the worst monster films ever ... an idiotic kiddie show! ... The theme song can drive you right up a ceiling."[7] Medved himself includes numerous snide remarks such as: "[Hedorah] capsizes two Japanese ships in a scene that looks as if it may well have been filmed in a bathtub."[8]

Medved's book not only lacks information as to why a pollution monster would be considered a poignant threat in early-1970s Japan, it also misses the deeper disillusionment represented in the film. Medved concludes by awarding "a year's supply of LSD or any other hallucinogen [...] to the Japanese monster film industry—and in particular Tōhō Corporation for [their] fertile imagination."[9] Numerous fan reviews and analyses note *Godzilla vs. Hedorah*'s inclusion on Medved's list, and its undeserved reputation as a bad film has transformed into almost an article of faith, due in part to Medved's book. Even Banno Yoshimitsu himself, in his 2014 autobiography, cites his film's inclusion on Harry Medved's list and lightheartedly quips, "in over 100 years of film history, it is an honor to be considered among the fifty worst."[10]

Later *kaijū eiga* writers largely echo Medved's superficial take on the 1971 picture. In *Japan's Favorite Mon-Star*, Steve Ryfle calls *Godzilla vs. Hedorah* "a piece of camp nostalgia" and awards the film a mere two out of five stars.[11] In his exhaustive examination of Japanese movies, Stuart Galbraith savages Banno's film: "*Godzilla vs. the Smog Monster* is an unfortunate pastiche of kiddie fare, clumsy social commentary and standard monster movie shenanigans [...] The results are mostly disastrous, though a tiny contingent of *kaijū eiga* fans argue the picture to be more sophisticated than it actually is."[12] We disagree. Galbraith's flippant assessment is flawed, given that his critical review is based entirely on the poorly-dubbed American version of the film and lacks historical context.

Takahashi Toshio, a well-regarded Japanese scholar of Godzilla films, ignores *Godzilla vs. Hedorah* almost entirely. In fact, the only prominent mention of Hedorah to be found in any of his volumes appears in a chart comparing the features of the films of the series.[13] Takahashi is not alone in this regard, since nearly every analysis dealing with Godzilla in both English and Japanese has either derided or ignored the important environmental and social commentary present in *Godzilla vs. Hedorah*. In this case, the silence is deafening—the absence of *Godzilla vs. Hedorah* from Takahashi's work, perhaps the most prevalent of all Japanese scholarly analyses of Godzilla, reveals the utter marginalization of the film.

In light of the nearly two decades that passed between their respective productions, *Godzilla vs. Hedorah* raised different issues and emits a new ambiguity, ambivalence, and social malaise not present in *Godzilla*. Japan rose from the ashes of defeat in 1945 only to rush into the soot and smog of pollution by 1971. Thus, it is no longer American science in the form of nuclear weaponry that rains destruction on Japan, but Japanese industry and economic progress itself. This economic growth simultaneously brought Japan great prosperity but also environmental destruction on a remarkable scale. For this reason, among others, *Godzilla vs. Hedorah* presents a sense of uncertainty not found in the original *Godzilla*. Gone were the days when Japan could blame America for its social ills and collective psychoses. By 1971, the shoe, as the saying goes, was on the other foot.

In order to properly understand and interpret *Godzilla vs. Hedorah*, it is important to view the film through three different lenses: its place within the genres of fantasy, horror, and science fiction, particularly as a *kaijū eiga*; the movie's theatrical and financial constraints due to the crash of the Japanese film industry in the late 1960s and early 1970s; and the societal and environmental conditions of 1970s Japan. Failure to view *Hedorah* with an understanding of this background leads to a misinterpretation of the film, its intent, and its success in conveying an earnest message to a popular audience. When viewed through these lenses, however, it becomes apparent that *Godzilla vs. Hedorah* provided the film's original audience with a grave warning and call-to-action about the dismal state of Japanese society and the environment in the early 1970s.

A New Director, a New Direction

Tōhō's young director Banno Yoshimitsu was largely responsible for the abrupt change of course for the Godzilla series charted by *Godzilla vs. Hedorah* in 1971. Although Godzilla creator and producer Tanaka Tomoyuki was looking for a long-term replacement for veteran director Honda Ishirō, who had directed nearly the entire series since 1954, *Godzilla vs. Hedorah* would prove to be Banno's only Godzilla film. Despite his short tenure, however, Banno left a mark on the franchise that few fans and viewers have forgotten.

Banno Yoshimitsu studied art history at Tokyo University and began his film career after joining Tōhō in 1955.[14] At Tōhō, Banno apprenticed under internationally renowned director Kurosawa Akira as assistant director for several major productions, including *Kumonosu-jō* (*Throne of Blood*) (1957), *Kakushi Toride no San Akunin* (*The Hidden Fortress*) (1958), and *Warui Yatsu Hodo Yoku Nemuru* (*The Bad Sleep Well*) (1960).[15] In 1970, he began working on a natural disasters documentary with Tsuburaya Eiji, the special effects master who brought Godzilla to life in 1954. Banno was on location with Tsuburaya filming the famed Naruto Whirlpools off the coast of Shikoku when Tsuburaya suffered a heart attack and was forced to return home to recuperate.[16]

Banno finished the nature documentary in Tsuburaya's stead, and it proved a great success. He presented his film as part of the Mitsubishi Pavilion at Expo '70 in Osaka. While living in Osaka for six months during the exposition, Banno commuted monthly back to Tōhō Studios in Tokyo. Over the course of his several long commutes, Banno saw "cities like Yokkaichi covered in black smog," with "the sea filled with foam from dumped detergents and air that smelled like rotten eggs."[17] Tanaka Tomoyuki had produced the Mitsubishi Pavilion at Expo '70—he was so impressed with Banno's contribution that Tanaka informed him he would be interested in having Banno direct the next film in the Godzilla series.[18]

Banno's time at the helm of the series, however brief, produced one of the most controversial and memorable Godzilla pictures ever filmed. Banno knew he wanted to approach the series and Godzilla in a different way from his predecessors. He began his first major directing experience without the guidance of Tanaka, who was hospitalized throughout production.[19] An unseasoned production team joined Banno—Nakano Teruyoshi filled the special effects post after the death of Tsuburaya Eiji, and Manabe Riichirō replaced Ifukube Akira as composer of the film's score.[20]

The choice of Manabe as the composer proved one of the film's most interesting and unique developments, leading to a score that is starkly different from the earlier films of the series. Representing several new musical styles of the 1970s, Manabe's compositions contrast harshly with the more classical marches of Ifukube. Manabe drew on a variety of instrumental timbres, including Moog synthesizer, handsaw, electric bass, and drumset. Similarly, the score explores a range of popular genres including everything from college folk and Group Sounds to psychedelia and free jazz.[21]

Manabe's unique and eclectic score has been widely panned throughout *kaijū eiga* literature. Galbraith bluntly states: "The music, by [Manabe Riichirō], is very poor. Besides the obnoxious Godzilla theme and the bad rock numbers, the score features wildly inappropriate instruments like a jew's harp."[22] Kalat also describes the new compositions, saying: "Manabe's irritating score leaps about between wildly different tempos, featuring a horn fanfare, a patriotic march, and a twangy mouth harp."[23] Despite such prevalent critiques, Manabe's eclectic style complements the new directorial and specials effects plans of Banno and Nakano, respectively. The new production staff began work on *Godzilla vs. Hedorah* with the blessing of producer Tanaka, who later regretted his decision.[24]

In addition to witnessing severe pollution on his frequent journeys between Tokyo and Osaka in 1970, Banno also credits Rachel Carson's 1962 book, *Silent Spring*, one of the landmark works leading to the formation of modern environmentalism, for inspiring him.[25] In several retrospective interviews and his memoir, Banno stated his reasons for creating a pollution monster in *Godzilla vs. Hedorah*. In one such interview, Banno asserted: "I wanted to have [Godzilla] battle not with something like a giant lobster, but the most notorious thing in current society."[26] Banno believed that the Godzilla series had slid into a period of troubled films throughout the 1960s—including a fight with the colossal crustacean Ebirah—and he intended to change the course of the Godzilla series. In a 2007 interview, Banno reiterated his reason for making *Godzilla vs. Hedorah*. He declared: "At that time the rapid elevation of the nation's economic strength created a huge pollution problem. So I asked Tanaka, 'What about a pollution monster?' He agreed."[27]

Unfortunately for Banno and his new staff, trends in the Japanese film industry were already working against them before they entered production. By the late 1960s and early 1970s, Japan's movie industry had been faced with budget crises and declining viewership for several years. These economic forces, mostly due to the rise in popularity of television (discussed more fully in Chapter 5), resulted in crippling budget crunches at Tōhō across the board.

After Expo '70 concluded on September 13, 1970, the new production crew—Banno, Nakano, and Manabe—assembled to begin production.[28] They began work on *Godzilla vs. Hedorah* with a shoestring budget, knowing they would have to pull out all the stops (including making Godzilla fly) to keep audiences interested and the Godzilla series financially feasible. To make matters worse, Tōhō initially provided Banno with a budget roughly half that of recent Godzilla pictures, compelled him to shoot the entire film in thirty-five days, and only supported one production team for both the drama and special effects scenes.[29] To help extend his diminished budget, director Banno also opted not to use any big-name Godzilla series regulars in his film's cast.[30] Yet despite these limitations, Banno and his team created a Godzilla film drastically different from any other in the franchise, yet one saturated with social commentary and political relevance. *Godzilla vs. Hedorah* would prove to be a *kaijū eiga* protest film of a different order.

Godzilla vs. Hedorah: *The Price of Pollution*

In *Godzilla vs. Hedorah*, a local fisherman brings a mysterious creature, seemingly a saltwater tadpole, to Dr. Yano Tōru (Yamauchi Akira).[31] Dr. Yano, a marine biologist, lives with his wife Toshie (Kimura Toshie) and their young son Ken (Kawase Hiroyuki). Ken, as a child protagonist, ostensibly serves as a proxy for the many young viewers. A new type of character—the hippie—in the form of Ken's bohemian uncle Yukio (Shibamoto Toshio) and his psychedelic girlfriend Miki (Mari Keiko) rounds out the cast. Unlike nearly every other example of *kaijū eiga*, there are no major journalist characters in the film, and the media in general are critiqued as part of the Japanese power structure.

A larger version of the tadpole creature begins attacking Japanese tanker and freighter traffic (like Godzilla, Mothra, Gamera, and other monsters before him) in the seas around Japan.[32] Dr. Yano and his son Ken investigate Suruga Bay, where the monster attacks both of them. The monster's chemical composition badly burns Yano's face. After performing several experiments on the creature, Yano determines that it is made of minerals and comes to life in pollution. Ken dreams that Godzilla will protect Japan from the creature, which he dubs Hedorah, from the Japanese *hedoro*, or sludge.

Hedorah morphs from a marine creature into a quadruped and fights Godzilla at Suruga Bay's harbor industrial complex, where Hedorah is forced to withdraw. Later, Hedorah mutates a second time into an airborne disc, flying over Japan emitting a sulfuric acid mist and briefly incapacitating Godzilla. Finally, as Hedorah continues to grow larger with the more pollution and toxic waste it consumes, it morphs into a biped larger than Godzilla, and the two meet in battle atop Mount Fuji. After a prolonged battle, Godzilla eventually defeats Hedorah with some small help from the military and Dr. Yano, and Japan is again safe.

Godzilla vs. Hedorah is a film rife with commentary on several levels. The movie lambastes the dire situation faced by Japan in the early 1970s. At a crossroads, Japan must decide whether to continue its undeterred economic expansion regardless of environmental costs, or focus on developing a more sustainable and ecologically-minded economy. Although the film most directly addresses industrial pollution, it touches on numerous other social issues as well, including: the role and power of the government in Japan; the impotence of the JSDF for Japan's protection; the pervasiveness of television in daily life; and the place of the counterculture and hippies and their inability to bring about meaningful change.

From its outset *Hedorah* is clearly an environmental call-to-action, leaving little room for debate or subtleties as to the film's main message. Banno's picture conveys its conservationist appeal through its obvious anti-pollution plot, character dialogue, visual imagery and scene composition, as well as music and score. The film opens with composer Manabe's cacophonous overture and a pollution montage sequence, similar in appearance and theme to other pollution protest films like the more widely known (but later) *Soylent Green* (1973). The music then changes to the theme of the film, "Return the Sun!" Banno wrote the lyrics, Manabe composed the music, and actress and singer Mari Keiko (who portrays the character Miki) performs the song.[33]

Banno states in his autobiography that he considered it vital to create "an entirely new theme song" for his film.[34] "Return the Sun!" exemplifies the film's juxtaposition of nature and pollution, as well as its dire environmental appeal.[35] The song reflects on the disappearance of wildlife like birds, fish, and various insects, before noting the proliferation of deadly elements and compounds like mercury, cobalt, sulfuric acid, and oxidants. The song concludes by noting that all living things will disappear as mountains and fields fall silent, before calling for a return to nature.[36] "Return the Sun!" features jarring lyrics that vacillate wildly between natural imagery and technical names for pollutants and heavy metals; to emphasize the point it reprises three times throughout the film. Initially appearing during the opening credits, the film alternates between psychedelic nightclub shots of the singer, character Miki, with brightly-colored oil effects in the background and shots of floating sludge, dead fish, and belching smokestacks. The montage opening theme song sequence ends with a shot of a broken clock floating on a bed of sludge, indicating that for Japan's environment, time may be running out.[37] This opening overture is a microcosm of what the rest of the film will entail: 1970s social, political, and environmental commentary.

Immediately after the viewer is battered with disturbing images of pollution and acid rock, the film cuts to a shot of vibrant chrysanthemums and Mount Fuji accompanied by the sound of chirping birds. The shot is both naturally idyllic and quintessentially Japanese at once—the chrysanthemum represents the national seal of Japan and the imperial family, and Mount Fuji, another internationally recognized symbol of the Japanese nation, appears clearly in the background.[38]

The boy Ken plays with Godzilla toys in his yard, and is connected to this natural innocence by walking between the chrysanthemums in the foreground and the looming grandeur of Mount Fuji in the distance. Not only are Ken's Godzilla figures wonderfully meta-generic, they reinforce the growing connection between children and *kaijū* in the Japanese film industry.[39] The camera pans and rotates to follow Ken, who is first framed by the flowers and mountain, and then by an industrial complex and numerous smoke-stacks spewing fumes. A shot of a plastic, mechanical bird, making the chirping sounds that the viewer assumed to be from actual, living birds appears on-screen. The juxta-position of these images and sounds contrasts the organic and bucolic with the synthetic and industrial.

The chrysanthemums at the Yano family's home are a recurring theme throughout the movie, exemplifying one of the film's environmental messages. Whereas the first scene showing the flowers appears well before the arrival of Hedorah, their second appearance occurs after the start of the sludge monster's reign of terror and destruction. When they reappear, distant industrial factories frame a shot of the flowers. Their colors are noticeably duller and less vibrant than at the beginning of the film. The final appear-ance of the chrysanthemums occurs as Hedorah flies over the Yano's house on his way to Mount Fuji just prior to the climax of the film. Hedorah's sludge and sulfuric mist blanket the home and garden, covering Ken's Godzilla toys in waste and wilting the once brightly-colored chrysanthemums.[40] The flowers wilt and die in a fast-motion sequence. Hedorah, the embodiment of Japanese industrial pollution and the problems of unregulated economic progress, destroys the chrysanthemums, symbols of the Impe-rial family and a natural and beautiful Japan.

In addition to utilizing imagery that evokes an emotional connection to the Japa-nese nation, *Godzilla vs. Hedorah* also conveys its sobering message via subtle references to the first *Godzilla*. Early in the film, when Hedorah destroys an oil tanker, images of the burning ship strongly resemble shots of the destruction of several fishing boats and trawlers in *Godzilla*. These images are one of several attempts by Banno Yoshimitsu and the film's production team to pay tribute to the franchise's vanguard, while at the same time making clear their intentions to mirror the first film's serious intent. The instances throughout the film that mimic the original indicate that industrial pollution, through Hedorah, should be considered the equivalent of the earlier anti-nuclear fears exhibited in *Godzilla*.

Another sequence echoing *Godzilla* begins with a shot of the Yano family aquar-ium. Without cutting away from the aquarium, Dr. Yano stands up in front of it, creating a clear visual reference to Dr. Serizawa in the original *Godzilla*. Like Serizawa, who wears an eyepatch, Yano's face is now bandaged because of his earlier encounter with Hedorah in the bay, mimicking Serizawa's appearance.[41] However, unlike Serizawa's wartime injury that can be linked to the United States, Hedorah wounds Yano, placing the blame squarely on the industrial pollution of the Japanese nation. The presence of the aquarium makes the homage doubly clear, visually reminding the viewer of Ser-izawa's oxygen-destroyer experiments.[42] Neither Serizawa's nor Yano's fish survive either film—all meet an unpleasant demise. Serizawa is responsible for the death of his own fish while testing his oxygen-destroyer. In *Hedorah*, the smog monster kills Yano's fish with his sulfuric mist as he flies over the family's house. Nonetheless, in both films Japanese progress and modernity are the culprits and nature pays the ultimate price.

The use of color offers another example of the film's visual and aesthetic connec-tions to the original *Godzilla*. While Honda shot the 1954 film in black-and-white, subsequent movies (with the exception of its direct sequel *Godzilla Raids Again*) were shot in color. This use of color was highly noticeable throughout these films, as many took place in colorful tropical, alien, or otherwise exotic locales.

Despite being shot in color, *Godzilla vs. Hedorah* echoes the achromatic imagery of *Godzilla*. The cinematography frequently employs chiaroscuro, a technique juxtaposing light and dark, visually alluding to its 1954 predecessor and the horror genre more generally. Many scenes take place at night, and a drab palette dominates the film. In most daytime scenes, the film even seems to have been washed out, giving the *mise-en-scène* a brown, grimy tinge. One scene, the hippie party atop Mount Fuji, is filtered through a sepia-tone effect. In contrast, the cinematography shows nature in vivid color; shots of the bright pink and yellow chrysanthemums and Dr. Yano's tropical fish exemplify this divergence. In the discotheque sequences, the hippies wear boldly garish and flamboyant clothing. Yet, like the flowers and the fish, Hedorah kills many of the hippies. Thus, film's palette assumes symbolic weight; Hedorah's pollution destroys the few sources of brilliant hues.

In addition to its *mise-en-scène* and cinematography, the narrative of *Godzilla vs. Hedorah* imparts an anti-pollution message. Early in the film, the child Ken dreams that pollution attacks Japan and only Godzilla can save them. In Ken's dream, Godzilla arrives with a radiant sun, another symbol of Japan like the chrysanthemums and Mount Fuji, dominating the background. As the monster moves towards a floating mass of waste and sludge, another of Manabe's interesting, eclectic tunes plays. The moving isle of debris, dead fish, bottles, and cans covers coral reefs, obscuring fish and other aquatic creatures. Ken recites a poetic monologue, while the text appears on-screen superimposed over the shots of sludge and waste:

> Genbaku, suibaku, shinohai wa umi he
> Dokugasu, hedoro, minna minta umi he suteru
> Oshikko mo
> Gojira ga mitara okoranai kana
> Okorudarōnai
> Ni nen ichi kumi
> Yano Ken

> Atomic bombs, hydrogen bombs, radioactive fallout, go into the sea
> Poison gas, sludge, all are thrown into the sea
> And urine
> Won't Godzilla get angry if he sees this?
> He certainly will
> Second Grade, Class One.
> Yano Ken[43]

An interesting feature of Ken's poem is that it appears on-screen in simple Japanese, relying nearly entirely on *hiragana* and *katakana* without using *kanji*, as though written by a young child.[44] Ken directly carries the film's environmental message to the children viewing the film. Following Ken's poem, Godzilla proceeds to destroy the floating waste with his fire-breath, as composer Manabe's new Godzilla theme, comprised of bass guitar and multiple ascending gestures in the brass, plays. Although translation does not do justice to the medium of poetry, the message of Ken's words remains clear.

After noticing the popularity of *manga* and comics shortly before he began work on the film, Banno decided to incorporate animated sequences throughout *Hedorah* in order to reach the young audience members.[45] In a 2002 interview, Banno noted: "I really did try to do new things to get my message across. I included animation scenes in the film, for the children."[46] The animated sequences act as interludes interspersed throughout the film. In one particularly interesting animated short, an anthropomorphized factory (complete with eyes and arms) plucks plants from the ground with massive pincers.[47] The more plant life the factory consumes, the larger it grows. Eventually, Hedorah arrives and lands atop the factory, inhaling its smoke. Here, the destruction of nature is directly connected to the expansion of industry, which directly feeds the destructiveness of the pollution monster Hedorah, all in the form of an animated short meant to impart its environmental message to Japanese children.

Several other experimental animation sequences further the film's themes—far from being childish or light, they are as grim as the live-action portions. For example, one segment depicts Hedorah clutching a bleeding whale while he drinks oil from a tanker; dead fish litter the surface of the sea and smoke, factories, and the word *gokigen* ("cheerful") dominate the background.[48] Another sequence shows Hedorah carrying a banner that reads "anti–Hedorah oxygen masks now on sale."[49] However, the oxygen masks prove ineffective, as two animated women wearing them immediately succumb to Hedorah's toxic fumes. Presumably, the same industrialists polluting Japan's environment are now selling the oxygen masks—simultaneously accepting no responsibility for the destruction they have caused while also continuing to profit from it.

Meanwhile, Ken's father, Dr. Yano, conducts experiments to determine Hedorah's origins. He breaks off pieces of the mysterious tadpole given to him by the fisherman early in the film, placing them in different types of water. Yano determines that unlike all other life on the planet, the supposed tadpole is composed of minerals like rocks and diamonds. Ken, awakened from his dream, joins his parents and tells them about his premonition that Godzilla will come to defend Japan. Yano discovers that smaller pollution-born creatures can join together in polluted water. After telling Ken that Hedorah has the potential to grow larger than Godzilla, Yano declares: "Hedorah is born out of sludge [...] We must act before it is too late."[50]

Unlike most other post–1954 films in the Godzilla series, *Godzilla vs. Hedorah* does not trivialize the damage the monsters inflict on populated areas. In many other films in the franchise, widespread destruction and catastrophe seem to exact a very minor human toll, and few, if any, deaths occur on-screen. *Hedorah* was the first subsequent Godzilla film after the original to show—in graphic detail—the humans killed during the course of the monsters' battles, and it does so repeatedly and on a large scale.[51] The first deaths are shown during the battle between Godzilla and Hedorah at the Suruga Bay industrial complex. During the battle, a piece of Hedorah's sludge kills several businessmen playing *mahjong* in a nearby building. The audience observes their sludge-drenched corpses slumped over a gaming table, while the *kaijū* mêlée continues.

Grisly deaths also abound following Hedorah's air attack on the country. Now shaped like a flying disc, Hedorah soars over cities emitting a sulfuric acid mist. The camera cuts to show the skeletal remains of the dead, their flesh burned off by sulfuric acid, lying in the streets.[52] Another sequence features a man's burned face beginning to melt. The sequence ends with a shot of the remains of a construction worker below the collapsed ruins of his worksite. The smog monster killed them all. The gruesome portrayal of death and decay contrasts with the relatively sterile and antiseptic results of monster attacks in the other post–*Godzilla* films of the series. The images of these corpses echo the photographs taken in the aftermath of the atomic bombings of Hiroshima and Nagasaki. In this way, Banno associates the threat of industrial pollution with wartime horrors and postwar nuclear fears.

The climactic brawl on Mount Fuji represents the last of the numerous sequences depicting human deaths. As Hedorah moves toward a group of partying hippies, led by Ken's enthusiastic uncle Yukio and the trippy Miki, the smog monster's sludge suffocates Yukio and most of the other flower children. Interestingly, the film does not dwell on the death of this major character, and Ken and Miki seem unperturbed by Yukio's sudden demise.[53] It does not go un-avenged.

Smog Monsters and Social Commentary

Godzilla vs. Hedorah succeeds as a dark, bleak film. The film's conclusion provides the viewer with few comforts. Although the smog monster Hedorah lies defeated, the underlying causes of the environmental problems are left unresolved, and the film critiques both the Japanese state and the alternative counterculture as being woefully unprepared to face the dilemma. This conundrum leaves the viewer with the distinct impression that unless the issues presented by the film are addressed it will all occur again.

Hedorah not only comments on Japan's pollution crisis, the film also lashes the Japanese power structure for being unresponsive and incompetent, the scientific elite for being unable to correctly address the problems, and even the countercultural hippies for being self-absorbed and ineffective. Throughout *Godzilla vs. Hedorah*, the film's creators critique the Japanese state as represented by the government, the police, the media, and the military. Dangerously incompetent government officials and TV broadcasters exacerbate the problems caused by Hedorah.

The first instance of government ineptness occurs as Hedorah makes landfall at the Suruga Bay factory complex. In a brief segment, a police officer tells a caller to stop being a fool, and informs him that Hedorah cannot leave the water, effectively ignoring an early warning of the large-scale destruction that would follow.[54] Later, a TV program informs the Japanese people that Hedorah is only a threat at night and on smoggy or overcast days. While Ken rides a roller coaster with Yukio and Miki (who remain completely oblivious to the true threat posed by Hedorah) the monster appears and sprays a poisonous mist onto the Japanese populace. It is a bright and sunny day, one during which Hedorah should not be a threat according to the scientist and journalist on the television broadcast. They are proven completely incorrect. The populace of Japan, duped by their belief in government reliability, is caught completely off-guard by Hedorah's second attack, leading to thousands of casualties.

Another casualty of Hedorah's sulfuric vapor attack is a gym class of high school girls taught by Mrs. Yano. Although only a brief scene in the film, Mrs. Yano's exercise class reflects a direct reference to a contemporaneous event in Japan. In July 1970, one year before *Godzilla vs. Hedorah*'s release, a group of school girls collapsed from smog fumes.[55] By including this scene in the film, director Banno, like Honda and Tanaka before him, drew on current events for inspiration.

Viewers also witness the government and JSDF's impotence at the film's climax. Although an earlier TV announcement stated that the government believed Hedorah could be defeated with oxygen bombs, this turns out to be completely ineffectual, and leads to the death of several JSDF helicopter crews. The most glaring of the film's critiques of the government revolves around the military's construction of a set of giant electrodes invented by Dr. Yano. As the final battle commences atop Mount Fuji, Yano telephones the JSDF to ask about the readiness of the devices, only to find that they remain unprepared to launch the attack. Yano convinces his wife to take him to the site on Mount Fuji, lamenting that "all living things are in danger."[56]

As the Yanos arrive at the JSDF station, the commander reports that the electrodes are finally in working order. Engulfed in their final mêlée, Godzilla and Hedorah knock down the electrical lines supplying the station's power. The JSDF begins repairing the downed lines and Hedorah moves between the electrodes. Godzilla then fires his atomic breath into the powerless devices, activating them. Hedorah smolders, turning into a desiccated pile of sludge, but as Godzilla begins to dismantle its remains, a smaller Hedorah blasts out from the dried shell in an attempt to make a getaway.

In a scene that has been widely criticized (even called "the low point of ridiculous behavior"), Godzilla reveals a new ability—he flies.[57] Knowing he cannot let Hedorah escape, Godzilla uses his atomic breath to propel himself through the air after the fleeing Hedorah. After catching the smog monster, Godzilla returns his adversary to the electrodes. By this point the hapless JSDF has restored power, but as soon as they activate the weapons, the system fails because of a blown fuse. This prompts the commander to query: "What's wrong with everybody?"[58] The commander's question is apt on many levels, applying to his current situation, as well as the Japanese power structure more generally. Godzilla then reactivates the electrodes, delivering the *coup de grâce* to Hedorah. So as not to make the same mistake again, Godzilla tears Hedorah into small bits and then activates the electrodes with his atomic breath a final time, while a re-orchestrated version of "Return the Sun!" appears in the soundtrack.

Although *Godzilla vs. Hedorah* savages Japan's government, military, and media, the alternative—the hippie counterculture—is shown to be no real alternative at all. The character Yukio's death, as the apparent leader of the hippies and symbol of bohemianism, mirrors the treatment of the counterculture throughout the film. As we have noted in our examinations of other *kaijū eiga*, sometimes environmental concerns blur with social critiques—in this case, *Hedorah* depicts the hippies as a form of social pollution, not equal with the threat posed by industrial pollution, but nonetheless deserving derision. In several scenes throughout the film, Yukio, Miki, and the other elements of the counterculture, despite being well-intentioned, are portrayed as oblivious, ineffectual, and occasionally counterproductive.

Early in the film, Banno casts a critical eye on the counterculture. Yukio and Miki party at the nightclub. Miki dances on a table wearing a revealing one-piece spandex outfit patterned with fish, shells, and crustaceans. Miki represents an interesting twist on the technological temptress character—although she is covered in natural imagery of sea life, it is a farce—she wears a synthetic spandex jumpsuit, and is surrounded by the industrial imagery of the nightclub, while the band plays loud electric instruments. Yukio sits at her feet tossing back drinks. Miki sings a reprise of the film's environmental theme, "Return the Sun!"[59] Dancing animated skeletons and bright neon-colored oil effects are projected on the wall behind her.[60] In a 2014 interview, director Banno stated that he chose to include the nightclub sequence in order to use "a lot of that era's modern trends in the film."[61] The psychedelic oil effects were popular at the "Mugen" nightclub in Tokyo's Minato ward in the early 1970s, and Banno invited the club's staff to Tōhō Studios to participate in the scene's production.[62]

Meanwhile, in cross-cuts, the fight between the monsters rages above the subterranean nightclub and Yukio begins to hallucinate as Miki's performance comes to a crescendo. Yukio imagines that Miki and the other bohemians have transformed into fish. Close-ups of Yukio's face clearly show the nature of his drug-induced confusion. The imagined fish heads bear a striking resemblance to traditional Nō theater masks. Moreover, the band playing Miki's diegetic musical accompaniment wear an updated version of *kamishimo*—formal garments also worn by musicians in traditional Nō dramas.[63] The discotheque patrons are oblivious to the ongoing battle between Godzilla and Hedorah taking place above, until a slimy appendage of Hedorah comes crawling down the stairs. It then retreats, leaving a behind a group of very frightened, rebellious, and inebriated youths and a pitiful, sludge-covered kitten.

The viewer returns to the nightclub later in the film. Yukio discusses what the hippies should do in response to Hedorah's attacks. A sketch of Hedorah atop Mount Fuji behind him, Yukio declares: "Hedorah has won, but it's our own punishment because we created it [...] It'll be great, we'll get a million young people and throw a huge go-go party on Mount Fuji! Right before Hedorah gets to it!"[64] Without even attempting to resolve the situation, yet certain of Japan's imminent ruination, Yukio and his comrades give up. This scene also represents the dramatic nadir of the film—Hedorah terrorizes Japan and now looms atop Mount Fuji's summit, victorious.

As the film's climactic battle begins, the flower children drive cars up Mount Fuji for their bonfire party to the sound of folkish, acoustic guitar music, revealed to be diegetic guitar played by Yukio.[65] As mentioned earlier, Banno filmed this sequence in sepia-tone, and although Yukio promised that over one million youths would attend, little more than one hundred are present, revealing the movement's disarray and apathy. When someone mentions to Yukio that so few of their compatriots have come, the film bursts into color as Yukio shouts: "Let's not complain! Green pastures will always exist in our hearts. Let's sing! Let's dance! Let's send our energy into space!"[66] The film shifts from sepia-tone to vivid color and an acid rock band jams in the background. Yukio waxes philosophical about the lost beauty of nature, further connecting the use of color with natural imagery by director Banno. The hippies dance to the exuberant music while a group of elders stand behind tall grass watching them, like some viewers, bewildered. The characterization of the hippies as naïve and irresponsible throughout the film represents a harsh criticism of the counterculture youth.

Like its recrimination of the hippie leader Yukio, the film also condemns the psychedelic Miki. Throughout *Godzilla vs. Hedorah*, Miki exudes both raw sexuality and innocence. Although she performs the film's title song "Return the Sun!" in her kaleidoscopic spandex jumpsuit, she likewise seems unaware of the true horror posed by Hedorah. For example, while Dr. Yano examines the remains of Hedorah that he collected following the battle at Suruga Bay's harbor, he discusses his findings with his family. Miki states that she believes the sparks emitted by Hedorah as a result of Godzilla's atomic breath attack during the battle were beautiful, apparently unaware of the human death toll and threat to her own life. Everyone promptly ignores her. Miki later queries, again oblivious to the deaths caused by the sludge monster, "if Hedorah lived off our smoke wouldn't that clean the air for us?"[67] Dr. Yano simply replies that Hedorah is a horrible monster, and his sulfuric acid mist will make Japan's pollution problem far worse.[68]

After Godzilla vanquishes the smog monster, the film ends with two intriguing images. The penultimate shot displays famed Japanese artist Hokusai's *Great Wave Off Kanagawa* woodblock print. Produced before Japan's major period of industrialization, it shows several men rowing a small boat during a squall, with Mount Fuji looming in the distance. Aside from the film's narrative, the juxtaposition of Japanese natural imagery and industrial and societal excess represents one of the film's stylistic achievements. The natural setting of Hokusai's *Great Wave Off Kanagawa* is a false consolation for viewers at the end of a gritty and disturbing film. The print shows a view of a pristine and powerful nature, undisturbed by human activity, providing a sense of hope for an emotionally battered viewer.

The final shot undermines this optimism. *Godzilla vs. Hedorah* concludes with an image of Hedorah in polluted water and text that warns of the smog monster's return. Audiences are left, like in the original *Godzilla*, to wonder if Japan is truly safe. Although Hedorah lies defeated, the underlying environmental problems remain unresolved. *Godzilla vs. Hedorah* strikes out at the dismal state of the Japanese environment in 1971, but also attacks the incompetent Japanese government, the bumbling military, the out-of-touch scientific elite, as well as the self-absorbed hippies. In sum, Banno Yoshimitsu's *Godzilla vs. Hedorah* is a bleak and poignant entry in *kaijū eiga* history.

Toward a Cleaner Future

Godzilla vs. Hedorah debuted in Japan on July 24, 1971, to generally poor reviews. Although it had one of the strongest showings of the 1970s for a Godzilla film, even surpassing the heavily marketed *Godzilla vs. Mechagodzilla* of 1974 (the twentieth anniversary of the series), the numbers paled in comparison to the ticket sales of the 1950s and early 1960s. *Godzilla vs. Hedorah* sold 1,740,000 seats in Japan, but the only major newspaper to give it a favorable review was the *Asahi Shinbun* (*Asahi News*).[69]

As a result of the film's eclectic, avant-garde style, Tōhō Studios blacklisted Banno Yoshimitsu from ever making another Godzilla film. In an argument with the director, Godzilla's creator Tanaka Tomoyuki reportedly told Banno he "ruined the Godzilla series."[70] Although much of the literature written on *Godzilla vs. Hedorah* points to the infamous scene where Godzilla flies as the source of Tanaka's displeasure, Banno himself gives a different account. In a retrospective interview, Banno claimed he only used the flying scene after clearing it with Tanaka's agent, and instead declared, "I think he probably didn't like the psychedelic atmosphere he saw on set with the fish heads, he probably worried what sort of weird movie I'd make next!"[71]

With Tanaka's death in 1997, however, Banno's prospects began to improve. Tōhō approached him about directing a new IMAX Godzilla movie, initially planned for release in 2007.[72] The film was never made, but Banno continued to be active at Tōhō Studios and in the Godzilla franchise.[73] He was never able to direct another Godzilla film, but Banno served as an executive producer for the American reboot of the franchise, *Godzilla* (2014), produced by Legendary Pictures (discussed in Chapter 12).[74] While Godzilla does not battle pollution directly *per se*, the franchise's recurring environmental and ecological themes even appear in this Hollywood adaptation of the monster series. Although Banno continued to declare his intention to revive Hedorah for a subsequent Godzilla film, he passed away in May 2017.[75]

Barely a year after *Godzilla vs. Hedorah*'s release in Japan, the film was released internationally. Removed entirely from the context of its production, however, it baffled many foreign viewers. Famed *New York Times* film critic Vincent Canby reviewed the film upon its U.S. release in 1972, criticizing what he perceived to be a homoerotic relationship between Ken and Godzilla, instead of discussing the film's compelling environmental commentary.[76] Tsutsui comments on Canby's assertion in his monograph, stating: "Canby obviously felt the same-sex nature of this relationship more noteworthy than the interspecies, boy-and-beast element, which certainly seems more curious to me."[77] That Canby and Tsutsui joust over such trivialities while largely ignoring the film's broad conservationist message seems most curious of all.

Perhaps the most telling example of the misinterpretation of *Godzilla vs. Hedorah* outside Japan occurred in Germany, where the film was billed as *Frankensteins Kampf gegen die Teufelmonster*, or "Frankenstein's War against the Devil Monster."[78] Around the same time, the storied *Famous Monsters of Filmland* magazine declared: "Those Japanese wrestlers are at it again in a moving pic that will leave you groggy!"[79] These and other misrepresentations of the film abroad led to its marginalization by critics and fans, eventually contributing to Harry Medved's review of the film in his 1978 book and yet another article by Vincent Canby in 1979, wherein he states that "[In *Godzilla vs. Hedorah*] the monster becomes a mechanical joke."[80]

Godzilla vs. Hedorah represents powerful, vociferous critique of the human cost and destruction of Japan's natural environment caused by its economic miracle. The movie makes a direct environmental appeal; it is disillusioned with the ineffective Japanese power structures and the sympathetic yet oblivious counterculture to deal with Japan's pollution epidemic. Via narrative, experimental music, and cinematography evocative of the late 1960s and early 1970s, Banno Yoshimitsu's *Godzilla vs. Hedorah* mirrors the gravity of the original *Godzilla*.

In his autobiography, Banno states that he believes *Godzilla vs. Hedorah* contributed to the nation's changing environmental mood.[81] Within Japan, the problem of pollution became less acute throughout the remainder of the 20th century, due to greater public awareness and increased government regulation of industry. Globalization and other economic factors helped mitigate Japan's pollution problems, as the country moved towards a service-based, post-industrial economy in the 1980s and beyond. Though beneficial for the nation and nature (at least within Japan), the Japanese environment's dire past has faded from discourse both at home and abroad. This collective amnesia contributed to the widespread misunderstanding of the film, as well as other contemporaneous *kaijū eiga* bearing similar environmental appeals.

9

Gamera vs. Zigra
A Tale of Space Invaders and the Sea

The same month *Godzilla vs. Hedorah* debuted, July 1971, Daiei Company released *Gamera tai Shinkai Kaijū Jigura* (*Gamera vs. Zigra*).[1] Akin to previous entries in the franchise, *Gamera vs. Zigra* paralleled trends in the Godzilla series. Like *Godzilla vs. Hedorah*, *Gamera vs. Zigra* offers an ecological critique focused on industrial pollution and its detrimental effects on the natural world. In particular, this final film of the original Gamera series highlights the environmental degradation of marine life and the overall health of the seas, a topic apropos to 1970s Japanese society. But unlike the relatively nuanced commentary offered by *Godzilla vs. Hedorah*, *Gamera vs. Zigra* presents a more transparent message, leaving few subtleties for its child-based audience.

Gamera's Final Showdown?

Thanks to the profitability of *Daikaijū Gamera* in 1965, Daiei Company decided to produce a Gamera film every year during the latter half of the 1960s into the early 1970s.[2] After the original film premiered in black-and-white (an attempt to cut costs and visually mimic 1954's *Godzilla*), the remaining films of the Gamera franchise appeared in vibrant color.[3] Moreover, in addition to utilizing the bright colors incumbent within the fantasy genre, the Gamera films began embracing ever more outlandish, technological, and alien plots, solidifying the franchise's place within science fiction as well.

The Gamera franchise quickly departed from first film's mild somberness, instead opting to appeal directly to Daiei Company's expanding base of child viewers. For example, in *Daikaijū Kettō: Gamera tai Barugon* (*Gamera vs. Barugon*) (1966), released only six months after Gamera's first big-screen appearance, Gamera not only gains the ability to fly through the vacuum of outer space, he also follows the tried-and-true *kaijū eiga* trope of battling other monsters.[4] In this case, Gamera's adversary Barugon proves to be a giant lizard-like creature that hatches from a dazzling, mysterious egg (not unlike Mothra's egg and larvae). Due to the commercial success of *Daikaijū Gamera*, Daiei Company doubled the budget for *Gamera vs. Barugon* to ¥80 million (nearly $225,000 U.S. dollars), making it the most costly production of the entire Gamera series.[5]

As the series progressed, Gamera battled a wide array of ever-more unusual opponents in exceedingly exotic locales. Additionally, Daiei Company began to emphatically target the franchise's devoted young fans. The most obvious way director Yuasa Noriaki accomplished this was by placing children in starring roles in every film of the series with the lone exception of the franchise's second installment (the only one Yuasa did not direct himself). Unlike the original *Daikaijū Gamera*'s lone child Toshio, later franchise films featured multiple children—both boys and girls—in starring roles.

Interestingly, Yuasa cast not only Japanese children but also Western youngsters in the Gamera films. This inclusion maintained the original film's international overtures. The insertion of non–Japanese actors bolstered Daiei's attempts to market their films for distribution outside of Japan, bringing the moribund studio much-needed revenue from foreign sales. According to Yuasa in a 1996 interview: "[An American International Pictures representative] said that if we wanted success distributing Gamera movies in foreign markets, we should put American boys in them."[6] With this advice in hand, Yuasa cast American children from U.S. military bases for several Gamera pictures.[7] Daiei Company's efforts proved fruitful; after *Daikaijū Gamera* all but the final film of the original series were picked up for U.S. distribution by American International Pictures.[8]

As the decade wore on, children went from merely appearing in Gamera films—like the impish Toshio in the original picture—to dominating the cast. In 1969's *Gamera tai Daiakujū Giron* (*Gamera vs. Guiron*), the monster turtle saves two young boys (Kajima Nobuhiro and Christopher Murphy) from the clutches of the cannibal spacewomen Barbella (Kai Hiroko) and Florbella (Kasahara Reiko).[9] Set on the spacewomen's alien world of Tera, Gamera fights and defeats the giant creature Guiron (shaped like an enormous chef's knife) to save the two boys.[10]

By this point, the Gamera series was shamelessly and directly appealing almost exclusively to the franchise's faithful fan base of Japanese children. Yuasa Noriaki put it even more bluntly: "After the first film was released, we got a lot of information about the reaction of children to that film [...] so from the fourth film we made them like a children's storybook."[11] *Gamera vs. Guiron* itself is an allegorical retelling of the fairy tale of "Hansel and Gretel," with the role of the witch replaced by the cannibalistic temptresses, and the setting moved from the Germanic forest to an alien planet.

By 1970, Daiei Company was struggling to stay afloat and the production budgets for the Gamera franchise steadily dwindled. When *Gamera vs. Zigra* began production, the studio provided Yuasa with a minuscule budget—only ¥35 million yen (or $97,000 U.S. dollars).[12] As with prior Gamera films, Yuasa attempted to keep his film as lean as possible to stay on budget, shooting the special effects scenes in two months and the live-action sequences in only four weeks.[13] Furthermore, although most *kaijū eiga* productions divided the workload between teams responsible for the special effects and drama, Yuasa handled everything on his own in order to minimize personnel costs.[14]

Yuasa and his crew began filming *Gamera vs. Zigra* in the late summer of 1970. Gamera's seventh outing featured three children, and the crew filmed the picture during their summer vacation (generally from late July through late August in Japan).[15] Yuasa cast a Japanese boy star along with two Western girls. The youngsters play the offspring of two marine biologists that work at Kamogawa Sea World, the main setting for the film. Woman X, another sexualized, technological temptress character—like Barbella and Florbella in *Gamera vs. Guiron* and Miki in *Godzilla vs. Hedorah*—rounds out the cast.

Sea Creatures and Sea Villains

Gamera vs. Zigra opens with a shot of a Japanese moon base.[16] A narrator intones that in the late 20th century, humanity has successfully made trips into space, including the establishment of several bases on the Moon. A mysterious, glowing spacecraft appears over the horizon approaching the Japanese base. The narration concludes on an ominous note: "This story is a warning to humankind."[17] The alien spaceship attacks, destroying the Japanese base and firing a special weapon at a fleeing moon buggy, causing it to vanish.

Following the attack, the film's title card appears, superimposed over a shot of the alien spacecraft heading in the direction of the distant Earth. A hard cut to an aerial panorama of Kamogawa Sea World follows, as a non-diegetic child chorus jubilantly sings the Gamera Theme Song while the film's credits roll. As the credits end, a child narrator introduces the viewer to the new marine park in Chiba Prefecture, the film's main setting. Two marine biologists, Dr. Tom Wallace (Fujiyama Kōji) and Dr. Ishikawa Yōsuke (Saeki Isamu), discuss their children as they walk through the main gate.[18]

Next, *Gamera vs. Zigra* introduces the film's child stars, Ken (Sakagami Yasushi), Helen (Gloria Zoellner), and Margie (Arlene Zoellner), cutting between brief vignettes of the children preparing for their day interspersed with sequences of Kamogawa Sea World's animals performing tricks.[19] As we will see throughout the film, *Gamera vs. Zigra* utilizes loveable images of tamed marine life—killer whales, dolphins, seals, and others—to create a sense of empathy for the animals. The film's setting at Kamogawa Sea World enhances this point.[20]

Following a hard cut from the park's seal performance, Drs. Wallace and Ishikawa perform an autopsy on a deceased dolphin, reinforcing the fragility of ocean life and the need to protect it.[21] The duo head out to conduct research on the rocky Japanese coast. The doctors, peering into clouded test tubes, discuss their findings. The following conversation reveals *Gamera vs. Zigra*'s blunt ecological call-to-action:

> DR. ISHIKAWA: These waters will become polluted too.
> DR. WALLACE: Fish and shellfish can't live here then—it's humankind's fault.
> DR. ISHIKAWA: Progress in science destroys nature. We must protect animal life from pollution.
> DR. WALLACE: Of course.[22]

Following a radio broadcast detailing a series of massive earthquakes in Saudi Arabia and Peru, the two decide to break for lunch. The men discover their packed lunches empty; they soon find Ken and Helen secreted away in their small boat.

After the requisite scolding, Ken spots the alien spacecraft dropping into the sea. Fearing for the safety of dolphins and seals at the crash site, the group sets out on the dinghy to survey the area. En route, Gamera suddenly appears flying overhead. Helen declares that she does not like monsters, but Ken reassuringly replies, "Gamera is our friend!"[23] Unlike in *Daikaijū Gamera*, the monster turtle no longer flies like a spinning disc—he now propels himself through the air like a rocket-powered jet.

The spaceship fires a special weapon at the small boat, causing it to dematerialize (just like the moon buggy). The beam does not evaporate the group, but instead transports them into the spacecraft's interior. Ken and Helen quickly understand that they are inside a spaceship, but the adults dismissively tell them that they watch too much television.[24] Woman X (Yanami Eiko), wearing a form-fitting metallic spacesuit, addresses the group, welcoming them to the spaceship from the planet Zigra. A large monster, obscured overhead, goes unnoticed by the children and marine biologists.

To demonstrate the power of Zigra's science, Woman X announces to the world that she will cause an earthquake comparable to the recent ones in Saudi Arabia and Peru. The spacewoman devastates Tokyo with a magnitude 13 quake—she notes that the Great Kantō Earthquake of 1923, that annihilated much of Tokyo, was a mere magnitude 7.9 temblor by comparison.[25] Although the film does not depict the quake, Woman X shows the group live views of the city's utter devastation.[26]

Woman X sends a message to the people of Earth, demanding the planet's surrender. "We on the planet Zigra lived in the sea," she declares, "But cultural progress polluted our waters, and we could no longer live there."[27] A montage sequence depicts Japan's polluted seas, sludge-covered waters, and rampant industrial pollution. Woman X provides a voiceover: "Recently your seas are becoming polluted by sludge too. If we leave Earth to you, sludge will cover your beautiful seas."[28] She then demands humanity's total surrender.[29]

Woman X hypnotizes the marine biologists, but Ken and Helen realize what is happening and flee. It is worth briefly noting that Woman X's powers are not magical; rather they are technological. Her abilities are based on the spacecraft's advanced machinery. This quality reinforces the notion that the sexualized temptress is in some way artificial, an unnatural result of futuristic technology. The children press the spaceship's exotic controls, freezing the spacewoman and setting off a klaxon. They grab their parents, hop in their small boat, and are transported back to the ocean's surface. Unlike Toshio in *Daikaijū Gamera*, the children in *Gamera vs. Zigra* are key to propelling the film's narrative forward.

Back on the spaceship, the large, immobile monster revives Woman X. He telepathically "speaks" to her. The monster—named Zigra, like his planet—orders Woman X to pursue and kill Ken and Helen. Next, Zigra details his plan. Accompanied by a montage sequence of Japanese seafood markets and fishing vessels, thousands of tuna, red snapper, and other fish, the monster intones that while humans live on the land and eat the bounty of the sea, Zigra intends to live in Earth's seas and consume the animals (including humans) that live on the land.[30] The images of fish markets and seafood remind the viewer of Japan's inherent dependence on the sea. By emphasizing this point, Yuasa and the film's production team reinforce the dire importance of the film's environmental message for the Japanese people. In short: without the sea, Japan starves.

Back on the surface, Ken and Helen spot an oil tanker in the distance. Unfortunately for them, Woman X slices through the vessel with her spacecraft. Although Zigra himself does not destroy the tanker, Woman X does so by his command, continuing the trope of monsters destroying ships found throughout the *kaijū eiga* genre. (One wonders how sinking the oil tanker fits into Zigra's plan of keeping the ocean clean, but perhaps as a *kaijū* he simply cannot help himself). As the children scream for help, Gamera arrives to save the day. The monster turtle plucks their dinghy out of the water. Gamera flies with the children in hand, the full-length version of the Gamera Theme Song playing jubilantly, before he drops them off on a small, rocky island.

Ken and Helen wander the stony shore, encountering a disheveled, wizened old man. Ken, shocked, believes they have accidentally traveled back in time. "I'm sorry," Ken beseeches, "We traveled through time from 1971!"[31] Following Ken's plea, the old man quickly pulls a radio out of his satchel, telling the duo to quit dreaming. Like the UFO sightings in *Daikaijū Gamera*, this brief "time travel" sequence also provides an amusing, self-referential nod to the tropes of the fantasy and science fiction genres.

The JSDF establishes an anti–Zigra command center at Kamogawa Sea World. With the doctors still under hypnosis, the military commander questions Ken and Helen as they are the only non-catatonic witnesses to the Zigra spaceship. The children tell the commander that the interior of the spacecraft looks like the ones shown on television programs (another meta-generic reference to both the prevalence of the science fiction genre and of Japanese TV dominance). Questioning the children proves hopeless—Ken divulges that his father makes loud noises when he eats, and Helen complains about the lack of fruit juice at the interrogation. The JSDF officer decides they must attempt to rouse Drs. Wallace and Ishikawa from their catatonic state.

The United Nations decides to attack the Zigra spaceship—once again emphasizing the international worldview of the Gamera series—but the spacecraft quickly annihilates the fighter jets with a devastating laser assault. Following the failed U.N. attack, Zigra transports Woman X to the Japanese coast so she can continue her pursuit of Ken and Helen. The spacewoman stumbles upon a group of young women, and aware of her unusual attire, she hypnotizes them in order to take their clothes. Of course, Woman X dons a very skimpy bikini.[32]

The JSDF commander orders an evacuation of Kamogawa, prompting the populace to flee the city. Meanwhile, the Kamogawa Sea World dolphin trainer and hotel manager bicker over fish. Stuart Galbraith describes this scene as "a desperate attempt by the filmmakers to pad out the running time."[33] However, where Galbraith finds only fodder, we search for deeper meaning. Why are the two men arguing over fish? There is a shortage due to Zigra, and they both need to buy them (the hotel manager for his guests, the trainer for his dolphins). Like the earlier montage sequence of fish markets and trawlers, this scene buttresses the film's ecological message: Japan is killing its seas with pollution, threatening its own vital food supply.

There is also a second, business-related reason for the sequence. As Daiei Company's fortunes declined, the Gamera films began including more frequent product placements. For example, in several franchise installments the child characters wear baseball hats prominently emblazoned with the logos of Japanese baseball teams, all of which receive corporate sponsorship. In *Gamera vs. Zigra*, Ken wears a Yomiuri Giants cap, a popular Tokyo team subsidized by the Yomiuri Group, a large media conglomerate. Likewise, the film's inclusion of Kamogawa Sea World is two-fold. The film's creators use the location to accentuate their ecological message on the importance of protecting ocean life, while at the same time "urging kiddies in the audience to visit Sea World."[34] By including the scene of the hotel manager's quest for fish, the production team showcases Kamogawa Sea World's on-site, luxury hotel, and its staff's commitment to guests.

Following the argument, the dolphin trainer angrily drives back to Sea World and spots Woman X hitchhiking along the highway. He stops to pick her up, agreeing to take her to the Sea World's marine lab with him. The dolphin trainer ogles the space-woman during their brief drive, a momentary male gaze perhaps shared by the fathers and teens in the film's audience.[35] After dropping her off at the laboratory, the trainer watches her depart, entranced and wistful. A group of JSDF soldiers jog past Woman X, all turning to leer as they run past. Finally, the spacewoman realizes she might need another change of clothes, so she hypnotizes a nearby female reporter—to purloin her hot pink miniskirt.

Woman X's role as the temptress continues unabated in the following sequence. Now sporting the magenta miniskirt ensemble, she sneaks into the marine lab in her pursuit of the children. In a particularly sexualized shot, the film's *mise-en-scène* wonderfully captures the dual role of Woman X's character as both villain and temptress. While lurking around the building looking for the children she intends to murder, she watches two soldiers depart a hallway. When they leave, the film lingers for several seconds on a ground-level shot of Woman X's legs, looking up, while the empty hallway fills the rest of the screen. The lurid pink of her miniskirt attracts the voyeur's eye, while grayscale paint, tile, and windows dominate the otherwise drab image.[36]

Woman X overhears the military commander declare that Earth's weapons are

A behind-the-scenes still from *Gamera vs. Zigra*. Woman X (Yanami Eiko) "captures" the film's child stars, Helen (Gloria Zoellner, left) and Ken (Sakagami Yasushi), on location at Kamogawa Sea World. Yanami's sultry Woman X character fills the temptress role by this point common in the genre, while the children pander to Gamera's enthusiastic juvenile fans (Daiei Company).

useless against Zigra, and that the United Nations has rejected the use of H-bombs against the monster. Ken and Helen watch a TV report of Tokyo's destruction (presumably from the earlier earthquake). As in several prior *kaijū eiga*, Tokyo Tower lies in tangled ruins. The broadcast switches to a view of Gamera arriving to help in the fight against Zigra. Meanwhile, as Ken and Helen stare at the destruction on-screen, Woman X slips into the room and sneaks up behind them. Fortunately for the children, the spacewoman clumsily knocks over a toy, alerting them to her presence. A chase ensues.

Woman X's drawn-out pursuit of the children serves four purposes: first, it moves the film's plot forward, leading to the military's eventual discovery of Woman X; second, it allows the film to promote the brand new, but yet unopened Kamogawa Sea World to Japanese moviegoers and potential patrons; third, the scene provides the audience with images of sea life, allowing the viewer to empathize with protecting such creatures; finally, it highlights Woman X's sexual allure as she runs around in her high heels and hot pink miniskirt.[37] (At several points, the viewer even catches a brief glimpse of the spacewoman's underwear).[38]

After briefly escaping from Woman X, Ken and Helen yell for Gamera's aid, and the monster turtle arrives to defend Japan from Zigra. Gamera dives into the sea, beginning an underwater battle with the alien spaceship. In order to make the events appear to take place underwater and stay within his minuscule budget, director Yuasa ingeniously placed a water tank between the camera and the action sequences.[39] After several moves and countermoves, Gamera fires his trademark flamethrower breath at the spacecraft, destroying it. However, the mysterious monster glimpsed earlier within the craft emerges from the wreckage, quickly growing to Gamera's size. The shark-like monster Zigra continues the battle against the giant turtle. Interestingly, Zigra's appearance mimics that of a stylized goblin shark (*Mitsukurina owstoni*), a species of deep-sea shark first identified in Japan in the late 19th century.[40]

Gamera grabs ahold of Zigra and carries the space-shark onto dry land; the battle continues on the coast next to Kamogawa Sea World. Zigra stuns Gamera with a telepathic ray, hypnotizing the monster turtle. Gamera falls into the sea and sinks to the bottom. With Gamera disabled (and possibly dead), Zigra makes a telepathic announcement to the people of Earth. After asserting that humans cannot be trusted to take care of their own ocean, the space monster declares: "I am beautiful and should rule the seas."[41]

Meanwhile, the JSDF commander and his scientific adviser continue to try to revive Drs. Wallace and Ishikawa. The dolphin trainer overhears their predicament, and it reminds him of something he observed with a blind dolphin. The trainer shows the scientific adviser a video feed of his blind dolphin, and explains (directly to the camera) that the dolphin can swim around its enclosure without bumping into any walls. The scientist quickly understands, and explains for the benefit of the trainer and the audience that dolphins are guided by supersonic waves, a form of natural sonar. As with the geothermal power station in *Daikaijū Gamera*, the Gamera franchise provides a didactic moment to its audience in addition to spotlighting the beauty and importance of marine life.

The scientist posits that Wallace and Ishikawa are being controlled by Zigra's own supersonic waves. He disrupts the waves by shouting into a military walkie-talkie, reviving the marine biologists. Pleased with their success, the scientist and trainer share a bit of excitement: "We owe it to the dolphins."[42] Next, the group finds Woman X attempting to hurl Ken and Helen into the killer whale enclosure (where they will presumably meet a gruesome end). Dr. Ishikawa attempts the same radio revival on Woman X, causing her to melodramatically collapse. As JSDF infantry surround the prone Woman X, the audience learns that she is in fact a Japanese astronaut, captured by Zigra from her moon buggy at the start of the film.

At the edge of despair, the adults concede that they have little hope of saving humanity from Zigra. Ken suggests that Gamera can defeat the space monster, and that despite his questionable disposition he might yet be alive. Wallace and Ishikawa determine they have nothing to lose, and volunteer to check on Gamera with their bathyscaphe.[43] Kamogawa Sea World helicopters carry the bathyscaphe to Gamera's position, slowly lowering it into the sea. The marine biologists peer out of their porthole at Gamera's submerged head, and attempt to revive him with sonar waves. Meanwhile, Ken and Helen emerge from a compartment on the bathyscaphe, annoying the busy scientists.

Zigra attacks the submersible, severing its cable to the helicopters above. The bathyscaphe sinks to the ocean floor. The monster shark picks up the craft and carries it to deeper waters, where the JSDF commander fears Drs. Wallace, Ishikawa, and the children perish. In fact, they survive—the scientists determine that as a deep-sea creature, Zigra avoids light; they annoy the monster with the bathyscaphe's searchlights, causing Zigra to hypnotize the group.

Fortunately, a thunderstorm later that night resuscitates Gamera when lightning strikes his exposed foot. Gamera proceeds to the ocean's abyss, where he seizes the bathyscaphe and carries it to the surface. Although the JSDF commander and the scientists' families believe they have suffocated on the underwater craft, it turns out that in their hypnotized state Ken, Helen, Wallace, and Ishikawa used less air, allowing them to survive. After saving the submersible, Gamera and Zigra engage in a conclusory battle.

The monster turtle and space creature begin their pitched battle underwater, where Zigra inflicts several wounds on Gamera with his sharp fins. Gamera, aware that Zigra has the advantage in the sea, grabs the pelagic predator and carries him to the surface. From the shore, the human cast watches as Gamera flies out of the ocean with Zigra in his grip—an orchestral, non-diegetic version of the Gamera Theme Song intones exuberantly.

On land, Gamera has a clear advantage over the deep-sea monster. Gamera pins Zigra to the ground with a boulder, humiliates the space invader by playing the Gamera Theme Song's tune on his back fins with another giant rock (like an enormous piscine xylophone), and torches the shark with his patented flamethrower breath. As Ken and Helen cheer the monster turtle on, he delivers the final blow to Zigra, saving Earth and its children yet again.

Gamera vs. Zigra ends with a final environmental plea. As Ken and Helen bid Gamera adieu, Ken tosses an empty soda bottle into the air in celebration. Dr. Ishikawa reproaches the boy: "Keep the sea clean [...] It's a disgrace for us to pollute the seas."[44] Clearly, the message is intended for not only Ken, but for the children and others viewing the film in Japanese theaters. The film closes with a rousing scene of Gamera in flight, the monster's theme song playing in earnest. A final aerial shot of Kamogawa Sea World and Japan's coast promotes the message of oceanic conservation while also encouraging children and Japanese families to attend the new marine park.

The End of an Era—Daiei's Bankruptcy

Gamera vs. Zigra possesses a lackluster reputation and most scholars ignore the work. The few who deigned to write about the final entry in the original Gamera series have generally panned the film. Tsutsui makes only a passing reference to the 1971 picture, noting: "*Gamera vs. Zigra* [...] also aspired to a serious message, superficially exploring the pressing ecological issues of the day."[45] Barr briefly notes *Zigra*'s anti-pollution message but only provides a single paragraph synopsis of the film's overall plot.[46] Galbraith, in accordance with his generally dismissive attitude of the entire Gamera franchise, asserts: "*Gamera vs. Zigra* is a cheap, depressing little film."[47]

Even fans, who are usually more tolerative of some of the kitschier aspects of *kaijū eiga*, tend to overlook the film's strong environmental message in favor of critiquing its low-budget special effects and focus on children. For example, the scene where Gamera uses a boulder to play his theme song on Zigra's fins was received with considerable dismay. In his satirical "Gamera Autobiography," originally published in *G-Fan* magazine, J. Christian Grymyr recounts the event from Gamera's point of view: "The scene where I played my theme song on Zigra's back was embarrassing for everybody involved [...] My brief fling with the movie's villainess, the beautiful [Yanami Eiko], was the only redeeming value I found in the whole experience."[48]

Although the musical fin sequence gestures towards the absurd, it is important to consider a few points we outlined in prior chapters. As with Godzilla's similarly questionable ability to fly in *Godzilla vs. Hedorah*, one must remember the considerable strain placed on directors to "pull out all the stops" to sell tickets and keep their respective studios afloat. As children dominated *kaijū eiga*'s reliable fan base, directors like Yuasa Noriaki tried to make their films memorable while still conveying important social and environmental lessons. In *Gamera vs. Zigra*, Yuasa created an exciting, interesting, and amusing film, keeping children entertained while providing a pedagogical moment about the importance of protecting Japan's seas and aquatic life.

Heckled by fans and disregarded by scholars, *Gamera vs. Zigra* nonetheless exemplifies *kaijū eiga*'s deep ties to and abiding concern for Japan's environment. The film's "protect the seas" mantra is blunt; the movie's primary juvenile audience needed a straightforward message. Like *Godzilla vs. Hedorah*, Daiei Company's 1971 picture attempted to provide insight into the national debate on industrial pollution and inspire future generations to be environmentally-conscious citizens.

Moreover, the film's main setting at Kamogawa Sea World—far from being just another product placement—encouraged children to care about marine life. It is now a common sight to see throngs of Japanese primary students on school trips to aquariums and zoos throughout Japan.[49] Such visits provide not only educational experiences, but also help children develop empathy with the planet's animal life. It is much easier to care about protecting the oceans when one experiences—in person—the amazing array of life living in the ocean's depths. Although there are now over a hundred aquariums in Japan, many of the country's major aquariums and marine parks did not open until the 1980s or later, well after *Zigra*'s popular appeal to protect Japan's waters.[50]

Despite Yuasa's best attempts to pack Daiei Company's theaters with patrons, the Gamera franchise reached the end of the road in 1971. Yuasa had a premonition of this with the diminishing budgets for Gamera films, but he nevertheless made plans for an eighth Gamera picture, conceptually entitled "Gamera vs. Garasharp." Thanks to the continued financial success of Yuasa's films, Daiei Company originally intended to make the picture, to be released in 1972.[51] The stalwart director hoped to have Gamera face off against a two-headed snake creature inspired by the Godzilla franchise's three-headed dragon King Ghidorah.[52] Unfortunately, Yuasa's vision could not come to fruition. In December 1971, Daiei declared bankruptcy.

After Daiei's collapse, of the original "big six," only Tōhō, Tōei, Nikkatsu, and Shōchiku studios remained.[53] The abruptness of Daiei's closure caught Yuasa Noriaki by surprise. Shortly after returning from a location shoot for *Seijuku* (*Maturity*) (1971), Daiei Company ceased operation. "After I came back from location, Daiei went bankrupt and I got a dismissal notice," Yuasa later recounted, "I grieved for my son Gamera—it was a very strange fate."[54]

A Promising Pivot in Eco-Awareness

Only a few years after both *Gamera vs. Zigra* and *Godzilla vs. Hedorah* premiered, Japan's environmental situation began to markedly improve. As public opinion shifted, factories began installing desulfurization equipment, quickly and significantly improving Japan's air quality. In addition, between 1971 and 1973, Japanese courts handed down major decisions against corporations in each of the "big four" industrial pollution diseases: Itai-itai Disease, Minamata Syndrome, Niigata Minamata Syndrome, and Yokkaichi Asthma, discussed in Chapter 7.[55] These decisions led to not only direct compensation for the victims of industrial pollution in highly publicized cases throughout Japan, they also forced Japanese corporations to take preventative steps to decrease the likelihood of future outbreaks.[56]

In July 1971, the Japanese government formed the Environment Agency, "to integrate administrative policies for the prevention of pollution and protection of nature."[57] The Environment Agency operated under the motto "Conservation of the Environment First and Foremost."[58] With new government actions and legal requirements, the situation began to improve. However, the extensive pollution of Japan's land, air, and seas would take time to get under control. In June 1973, Japan's Deputy Prime Minister Miki Takeo declared: "Controls are being reinforced and many actions taken. Fortunately there are signs of improvement. Some problems, however, have yet to be solved where as some new problems, such as photochemical smog, have come to our attention."[59]

Japan's Diet also convened a special parliamentary session in 1973. During the course of the 71st Special Session of the Diet, which concluded on September 27, 1973, the national legislature passed a bevy of new environmental laws and pollution controls.

Some of the most important laws promulgated following this extraordinary session were: the Chemical Substances Control Law; the Pollution-related Damages Compensation Law; the Seto Inland Sea Environmental Preservation Law; Amendments to Natural Parks Law and Nature Conservation Law; the Urban Greenery Conservation Law; the Factory Siting Law; Revision of the Harbor Law; and Revision of the Public Water Reclamation Law.[60]

Changing economic conditions also contributed to Japan's improving environment. In October 1973, the Organization of Arab Petroleum Exporting Countries (OAPEC) announced an oil embargo against the United States, Japan, and other countries. The embargo led to what historians call the "oil shock," dramatically increasing the price of oil globally. Historians of Japan use the "oil shock" as a marker for the end of Japan's high-speed economic growth period that had been in full swing since the beginning of the 1960s.[61] The resulting economic slowdown, coupled with changing environmental regulations and the major legal victories for pollution victims, led to drastic improvements in Japan's environmental situation.

The "oil shock" contributed to Japan's changing focus from heavy industry and petrochemical products to services and high technology, which would gain greater attention in the following decade. Miki Takeo presaged this remarkable shift in an official announcement in the 1974 volume of the *Japan Environment Summary*, declaring:

> When I ponder over the oil issue, I cannot help feeling keenly aware that Japan has been increasing energy consumption thoughtlessly. We must use the lesson of the current energy crisis to make a fundamental review of the nation's energy-hungry industrial structure. I am convinced that a programmed shift to an industrial structure of the knowledge-intensive type is the course Japan should take and that this is the way for Japan to eliminate pollution at home and contribute to the conservation of the world's limited resources.[62]

Clearly, Miki wanted to not only clean up Japan's industrial pollution, but reform the country's economy as well. It is therefore particularly relevant that later that year, on December 9, 1974, Miki was elected to serve as the 41st Prime Minister of Japan, a duty he would discharge for the following two years. Despite the need for further improvements, Japan's environmental picture dramatically improved over the course of the 1970s.

10

The Bubble and the Beasts
Kaijū Eiga *of the 1980s*

Kaijū eiga of the 1980s continued to engage with contemporary environmental issues, though reimagined by their creators to remain relevant to a changing Japan. We begin this chapter by examining Japan in the 1980s, when the country reached the pinnacle of its economic power and influence in the postwar era. Then we proceed to ecocritical analyses of two films. We examine the Godzilla franchise films *Gojira* (1984) (*Godzilla 1984*) and *Gojira vs. Biorante* (*Godzilla vs. Biollante*) (1989).[1] Thematically, *Godzilla 1984* maintains the anti-nuclear commentary of earlier *kaijū eiga*, while expanding on the issue to address peaceful nuclear power as well as saber-rattling between the superpowers in the late Cold War. *Godzilla vs. Biollante*, on the other hand, introduces a new subject concerning both nature and technology: genetic engineering. In the late 1980s and early 1990s, biotechnology and genetic engineering became matters of global concern, and *Godzilla vs. Biollante* interrogates their philosophical and ethical implications.

"Peak Japan" and the Bubble Economy

Japan in the 1980s was a far different place than it had been only a few decades earlier. The economy boomed, corporate coffers overflowed, and Japanese companies produced valuable exports at an ever-increasing pace. One historian of Japan states that "the decade of the 1980s, in particular, was a remarkable moment of satisfaction and congratulation, unimaginable in the early postwar era and premature in retrospect."[2] Many children of the 1980s will forever connect Japan with the video games and cultural products that became global household names during this era of high technology and economic optimism: Nintendo, Super Mario Bros., the Legend of Zelda, Sega, Sonic the Hedgehog, Studio Ghibli anime productions, Hello Kitty, and electronics like the Sony Walkman, to name but a few. Japanese corporations developed and manufactured these products—from television shows to video games to figurines—for the domestic market as well as the increasingly globalized economy.

Like the proliferation of cultural products, Japanese factories also pumped out manufactured and finished goods, though with considerably more environmental safeguards than in the early 1970s. By the 1980s, automobile companies like Toyota, Honda, and Subaru were outperforming traditional American manufacturers like General Motors and Ford, not only in Japan but in the United States as well. In 1981, the United States pressured Japanese automobile manufacturers into limiting their sales; widespread admiration of the Japanese economy had quickly turned to envy. By the mid–1980s, the value of Japanese goods exported into the United States (Japan's largest trading partner at the time), was nearly double the value of American goods imported into Japan.[3]

From 1981 to 1991, the Japanese economy grew at a rate of over 3 percent a year, a rate surpassing all other large industrialized economies. Meanwhile, between 1985 and 1990, the Nikkei Stock Index surged from 7000 points to over 39,000, while the price of other assets, especially real estate, multiplied many times over.[4] Japanese investors splurged on international property acquisitions, buying office buildings, country clubs, and other real estate holdings. In 1988, the peak year for foreign real estate purchases, Japanese investors spent $16.54 billion on properties in the United States alone. By 1991, that number tumbled to less than a third, clocking in at only $5.06 billion.[5] In hindsight, of course, historians and economists call this period the Japanese asset price bubble (or "the bubble"), but to the casual observer at the time it certainly seemed that Japan was dominating the global economic marketplace.

The spreading affluence created by the bubble also helped erase (or at least ameliorate) social tensions within Japan. As Japanese industrial productivity increased at the fastest rate in the world the unemployment remained below 2 percent. This contrasted sharply with other major developed countries; Western Europe suffered particularly high unemployment, the United States' heavy industry sector collapsed, and the Soviet Union was economically moribund.[6] Because of a relatively even distribution of economic wealth, a large portion of the population identified as middle-class and social activism gradually dissipated into complacent contentment.[7] Although not everyone benefited equally during the economic heyday, "the once loud dissenting voices of militant unionists on the inside of corporations, or citizen activists on the outside, were barely audible."[8]

The hubris of the 1980s ushered in a new political zeitgeist. In the era of "Peak Japan," politicians and academics published manifestos on Japanese power and promise. In 1979, Ezra Vogel, a Japanologist at Harvard University, published his prescient work *Japan as Number One*, in which he argued that the Japanese had established a remarkable society and amazing economic system, worthy of emulation by the rest of the developed world.[9] As many of Vogel's predictions came to fruition in the 1980s, Ishihara Shintarō promulgated a controversial essay that foregrounded Japan's newfound economic power: *The Japan That Can Say No*. Couching his argument in ethnic and racial terms, Ishihara urged his country to take positions independent of its alliance with the United States, including selling high-tech semiconductors and microchips to the ailing Soviet Union.[10] A few years later, in 1993, when the long-term effects of the bubble were not fully comprehended, another Japanese political figure, Ozawa Ichirō, published *Blueprint for a New Japan*. In it, he declared that because of Japan's economic prowess it ought to assume new political and military responsibilities on the world stage. Ozawa's controversial platform unleashed a political firestorm. The CIA translated it and former

U.S. Secretary of State Henry Kissinger, in his usual understated style, commented that the piece was "a book that will stir much debate."[11]

Despite the arrogant predictions of the 1980s, however, the bubble did indeed burst. The economy collapsed just as the 1980s came to a close; between December 1989 and August 1992, the Nikkei shed 65 percent of its overall value. At the same time, exports tumbled, real estate prices buckled, and Japanese corporations halted expansion plans.[12] Tōhō Studios produced *Godzilla 1984* and *Godzilla vs. Biollante* before the bubble economy crumpled, and this period of excess and anticipations of a bright future are readily apparent in both pictures. These films exemplify the spirit of the times in which they were made. New political, economic, and societal issues abound in the works, defining the Godzilla franchise of the 1980s temporally and thematically from its progenitors.[13] Despite these stylistic differences, the environmental undercurrents endemic to *kaijū eiga* persisted.

New Politics and New Concerns: Godzilla 1984

As discussed earlier, the proliferation of television following the 1964 Tokyo Olympics proved to be a watershed moment in the history of the Japanese film industry.[14] Once-mighty film studios like Tōhō and Daiei struggled to remain fiscally salient. After 1964, the studios began bending to the mercurial whims of a diminishing audience in order to avoid bankruptcy. Most major studios experimented with monsters, attracting a loyal following of Japanese (and international) children, but none equaled the longevity and profitability of the venerable Godzilla, Mothra, and Gamera franchises.

But monsters did not save the Japanese film industry. At most, they gave the studios breathing room while they fruitlessly fought against a long and seemingly irreversible decline. Throughout this "monster boom" period, Godzilla morphed from an irradiated terror into a defender of Japan and Earth. Tanaka Tomoyuki, Godzilla's creator, later determined that this change in Godzilla was a miscalculation. A few weeks after the release of *Godzilla 1984*, *People* magazine interviewed Tanaka about the popular monster's renaissance, and he gave them his opinion on the latter films of the Shōwa era. "[Godzilla's] character change was responsible for his decline," he posited, "It was a mistake."[15] Despite Tanaka's claims, however, had Godzilla not evolved from a somber science fiction horror icon to a playful children's monster, Tōhō would have likely pulled the plug on the franchise far earlier. Moreover, *kaijū eiga* of 1960s and 1970s continued the original 1954 *Godzilla*'s tradition of carrying a strong environmental appeal, despite the character changes to the monster himself.

Although Tōhō's original Godzilla series concluded in 1975 following the abysmal ticket sales of *Mekagojira no Gyakushū* (*Terror of Mechagodzilla*), the 1980s gave birth to a new Japan, and breathed life into the saurian, martial terror of Godzilla. In November 1982, Tōhō Studios re-released several of their classic *kaijū eiga* for Japanese audiences, including 1954's *Godzilla* and 1961's *Mothra*.[16] Viewers flocked to the Tōhō theaters in droves, and Tanaka decided the time was right to reboot the Godzilla series. Far from the jovial monster of the later 1960s and 1970s, Godzilla returned to his roots and original destructive fury. No longer was Godzilla the friend of the Japanese people, saving them from the Machiavellian machinations of Seatopians or simian space-invaders. Instead, Godzilla would return as a radioactive, nuclear terror in line with his original role—a saturnine menace slowly stalking and threatening the Japanese nation.

On December 15, 1984, thirty years after the release of the original Godzilla film, the monster returned from his cinematic hiatus.[17] Hashimoto Kōji directed *Godzilla 1984* and Koroku Reijiro provided the score. The film was both critically acclaimed and commercially successful, though it was not a blockbuster hit. The movie took in about ¥1.5 billion ($6.25 million in 1984 U.S. dollars), barely doubling its production costs.[18] In terms of ticket sales, *Godzilla 1984* filled 3.88 million seats in Japan, four times the number of tickets sold less than a decade earlier by *Terror of Mechagodzilla*, the commercial nadir of the series.[19] Most viewers and Godzilla aficionados praised the film for its return to the weightiness of the original film.[20] At the same time, *Godzilla 1984* reflected events and issues relevant in the 1980s.

Godzilla 1984 is a retroactive continuity (or "retcon") film. This means its narrative ignores the existence of all prior Godzilla films except the 1954 original. In this revised storyline, Godzilla returns to Japan for the first time since the monster's initial appearance thirty years earlier. Although the island nation is better prepared to combat Godzilla than in 1954 (with a booming, high-tech economy and powerful new weapons like the *Super X* hovercraft), Godzilla nevertheless devastates Tokyo. Yet again, Japanese scientists prevail—they lure Godzilla to a volcanic isle off Japan's coast and seal him inside.

Godzilla's creator and long-running producer Tanaka Tomoyuki celebrates Godzilla's rebirth in the 1980s. *Godzilla 1984* **premiered after a nine-year hiatus, breathing life into a new Godzilla that matched the issues and complexities thriving during the late Cold War era (Photofest).**

Godzilla 1984 elaborates on the scope of environmental discourse in *kaijū eiga*. In addition to continuing the now common (perhaps even blasé) critique of nuclear power for military use, the film portrays a sinister side to the peaceful use of nuclear energy. *Godzilla 1984* equates atomic power to the destructive potential of nuclear weapons. In this way, the film represents a subversive departure from the status quo—nuclear energy was mainstream and indeed common in Japan by the 1980s. Viewing the film with the benefit of hindsight following the 1986 Chernobyl meltdown and the 2011 Fukushima Daiichi nuclear disaster, it is clear that *Godzilla 1984*'s warnings over the potentially deadly environmental consequences of a nuclear power plant disaster were prophetic.

Godzilla 1984 also resumes the negative portrayal of nuclear proliferation apparent in earlier *kaijū eiga*. For example, the film critically depicts the planned deployment of space-based nuclear weapons (popularly referred to as "Star Wars" defense systems). The film also features a nuclear-powered ballistic missile submarine, one of the most powerful and destructive strategic weapons ever devised by humankind, as an important narrative component. This approach to nuclear energy and weaponry sets the film apart from previous *kaijū eiga*.

Godzilla 1984 opens to a brass-heavy, impressionistic orchestral cue.[21] The credits overlay footage of an erupting volcano, immediately showcasing the force and majesty of nature to the viewer. Building on this natural imagery, the next scene depicts a fishing trawler caught in a terrible late-night squall. This opening shot echoes the first few seconds of *Godzilla*, when the monster attacks and destroys the crew of the *Glory No. 5*. The storm pushes the trawler—the *Yahata-maru*—towards the coast of Daikoku Island. University student Okumura Hiroshi (Takuma Shin) watches in terror with the bridge crew as the volcanic isle erupts and a giant monster (unseen but bellowing Godzilla's unmistakable roar) emerges. The men shield their eyes, scream, and collapse to the deck.

The film dissolves to a jarringly bright daytime shot of a small sailboat, while soft 1980s pop music plays in the diegetic background. The film's primary protagonist, Maki Gorō (Tanaka Ken), spots the derelict *Yahata-maru* adrift.[22] Maki snaps a photograph with his Nikon camera, turns off his Sony radio, and prepares to board the fishing vessel.[23] As he explores the ship, he discovers only Okumura alive. An abnormally large sea-louse attacks the characters; after dealing with it, Okumura tells Maki about the much larger monster he witnessed the prior night. Maki, a reporter, writes a story about the events, while Professor Hayashida (Natsuki Yosuke) visits Okumura in the Tokyo police hospital. Okumura identifies Godzilla (Hayashida shows him stills from the original film). Hayashida warns Okumura that many will doubt his claims, since monsters are a rarity.[24]

Hayashida posits that the sea-louse encountered on the *Yahata-maru* grew to its massive bulk by feeding on Godzilla's radioactive blood. Here, *Godzilla 1984* continues the anti-nuclear commentary so common throughout the *kaijū eiga* genre. Radiation—linked to atomic testing through Godzilla—is altering animal life and the natural order. Hayashida's supposition filters up the chains of command to Prime Minister Mitamura (Kobayashi Keiju). Based on Hayashida's theory, the prime minister enacts a news embargo on Godzilla stories until more reliable information can be ascertained, reminiscent of the proposed news blackout in *Godzilla* thirty years prior.[25]

The importance of the character Mitamura in the film cannot be over-emphasized— his presence illuminates a stirring nationalist sentiment in 1980s Japan. Whereas earlier *kaijū eiga* generally only show lower-level bureaucrats, government officials, and military officers, *Godzilla 1984* depicts the highest levels of political power. Moreover, while prior monster movies often critiqued political and corporate elites, *Godzilla 1984* showers the Japanese power structure with praise.[26] By 1984, not only had Japan emerged as one of the world's three largest economies, government regulations and statutes had successfully ameliorated the environmental pollution crises of the prior decade. Mitamura's powerful aura in the film doubles for Japan's self-assurance during this period, and his stalwart and resolute manner reflect the confidence of the era.

Due to the news blackout, Maki's editor pulls his article and recommends that he visit Prof. Hayashida for more information. Maki arrives at Hayashida's bioscience institute. While visiting the genetics laboratory, Maki meets Okumura's sister, Naoko (Sawaguchi Yasuko), the only major female character in the film. Unlike the temptress characters of the 1960s and 1970s, Naoko harkens back to the more reticent roles portrayed by female characters in earlier monster films, like Emiko in *Godzilla* and Kyoko in *Daikaijū Gamera*. Her characterization reflects the conservative social atmosphere indicative of the 1980s. Naoko's role as the genetics laboratory's "office lady" illustrates this point. Although supposedly Hayashida's student, Naoko's duties include secretarial work, making tea, and doing small errands. While Japanese women made some strides, in the 1980s they were still struggling to achieve equality in male-dominated Japanese society.[27]

Because of the government's news blackout, Naoko remains unaware that her brother is safe. Maki, angry that the truth has been concealed, divulges Okumura's whereabouts while they stroll through downtown Tokyo. The composition of this scene is worth noting in detail. The skyscrapers of the Shinjuku ward frame the pair while they walk.[28] The backdrop conveys the excitement and hubris of 1980s Japan; the gleaming business towers encapsulate the economic spirit of the bubble economy. From an environmental perspective, the images of the shiny glass edifices contrast sharply with the shots of factories, refineries, and chemical plants so common in the films of the prior decades. In this, the *mise-en-scène* reflects Japan's shift from heavy manufacturing to a post-industrial, service-based economy.[29]

Naoko finds Okumura at the police hospital, only to realize Maki's duplicitous intention to photograph their reunion for his newspaper article. As noted in earlier chapters, journalists are among the most common stock characters in *kaijū eiga*. Normally, they fill sympathetic roles—journalists provide a powerful, altruistic, and independent voice detached from scientific, corporate, and governmental power structures. The reporters are genuinely concerned with the welfare of the Japanese people.[30] Yet by the 1980s, journalist characters are no longer portrayed with the same earnest naïveté as in earlier decades. In *Godzilla 1984*, while Maki does seem interested in conveying the truth about Godzilla to the public, he is also ambitious and inconsiderate. Journalists in *kaijū eiga* can now be a positive force, but they may also have their own agenda.

Following the hospital scene, the film makes a hard cut to an underwater Soviet nuclear-powered missile submarine.[31] The sub, a fictionalized variant of the Soviet Delta-class, runs on nuclear power and houses at least twelve submarine-launched ballistic missiles. Such Soviet submarines were equipped with a total firepower of approximately five to ten megatons, approximately 300 to 600 times the destructive force of the bomb dropped on Hiroshima in 1945.[32] This Soviet sub's destructive potential highlights Cold War tensions of the 1980s. The submarine plays a brief but important role in the film; it encounters a mysterious sonar contact that destroys the vessel, igniting a Cold War standoff between the superpowers.

Following reports of the missing submarine, Prime Minister Mitamura solemnly considers his next course of action in a melodramatic close-up. News of the likely conflict appears on TV reports, and the JSDF gathers photographic evidence that Godzilla—not the United States—destroyed the Soviet submarine. Mitamura quickly presents this information to both superpowers, preventing a potential nuclear exchange between the Americans and Soviets. The film's political commentary is clear: unlike the imprudent, war-mongering superpowers, the sagacious Japanese are able to steer the world away from nuclear war.

The government lifts the news blackout and Okumura recounts the tragedy of the *Yahata-maru* on national television. Meanwhile, Maki runs his story about Okumura and Naoko's reunion, creating a rift between him and the siblings. The Japanese cabinet gathers in an underground command center while the JSDF prepares to protect the nation. In the bunker, the defense minister reveals the existence of *Super X*—an armored hovercraft developed to defend Tokyo from Godzilla.[33] *Super X* boasts cadmium missiles and represents many facets of 1980s Japan—it is a highly-advanced defensive weapon, built through Japanese ingenuity and resourcefulness.

Prof. Hayashida theorizes that Godzilla attacked the Soviet submarine for its nuclear material. This reveals a new aspect to the saurian monster—unlike the haphazard maritime marauding in previous Godzilla films, in this incarnation there is a purpose to the attack. Godzilla feeds on nuclear fuel. The professor posits that Godzilla will return to Japan near a nuclear power plant. Hayashida's prediction immediately proves true. Appearing out of the coastal fog like a mythical water dragon, Godzilla towers over a nuclear power plant. The camera slowly pans upward to reveal his full size and immense presence.[34] Godzilla razes the plant.

Godzilla's destruction of the nuclear power station is strikingly reminiscent of Gamera's destruction of the geothermal station in *Daikaijū Gamera*, discussed in Chapter 6. Like Gamera, this incarnation of Godzilla consumes nuclear energy—he tears the nuclear core from the power plant for food. A flock of migrating birds flies overhead and Godzilla turns to follow them out to sea, leaving rubble (but not radiation) in his wake. Although the exposed nuclear core should have caused widespread contamination, Godzilla safely absorbs the radiation, utilizing it as fuel for his future escapades.

Godzilla's attack on the nuclear plant addresses a new environmental issue for the *kaijū eiga* genre. Despite Japan's total rejection of nuclear weapons, the peaceful use of nuclear technology for energy remained mainstream throughout the resource-poor island nation. In fact, Japan began producing domestic nuclear power in 1966, and by the 1980s over three-dozen nuclear reactors were operating throughout the archipelago.[35] Before the 2011 Tōhoku earthquake, tsunami, and resulting catastrophe at Fukushima Daiichi, nuclear power was more generally accepted. *Godzilla 1984*, however, equates atomic power with nuclear weapons, subversively undermining the Japanese consensus and status quo nearly thirty years before the Fukushima tragedy.

Director Hashimoto Kōji confirmed this assessment in an interview about *Godzilla 1984*: "This time the theme is broader—the risk of nuclear energy in all its forms."[36] Furthermore, in an early 1985 interview with *People* magazine, producer Tanaka Tomoyuki declared: "In those days [1954], Japanese had a real horror of radiation, and that horror is what made Godzilla so huge [...] From the beginning he has symbolized nature's revenge on mankind."[37] However, over time the Japanese people became complacent, so Tanaka wanted *Godzilla 1984* to "show how easily an [atomic] incident could occur today."[38] Indeed, less than two years after the film premiered, a nuclear meltdown occurred at the Soviet Union's Chernobyl power station (in present-day Ukraine), proving the film's warning portentous.[39]

Prof. Hayashida speculates that Godzilla, akin to migrating birds, possesses a homing instinct based on Earth's magnetic field.[40] He devises a plan and dispatches Okumura and his old friend Professor Minami (Koizumi Hiroshi) to Mount Mihara on the island of Ōshima.[41] Okumura and Minami conduct generic, ostensibly scientific activities around the volcano's caldera, taking the volcano's temperature and smashing a rock with a hammer. They peer at the lava through a telescope. The viewing is synchronized with a dissonant "stinger" chord played by low brass, hinting at danger.[42]

The film cuts to an aerial shot of Shinjuku accompanied by an upbeat, non-diegetic melody. With this transition, the film visually and acoustically juxtaposes the destructive power of nature in the form of the volcano with the built-up skyline of the metropolitan urban jungle. The shot visualizes another one of the film's messages. Tanaka Tomoyuki explained: "Japan is rich and people can buy whatever they want. But what is behind that wealth? Nothing very spiritual. Everyone's so concerned with the material, and then Godzilla rips it all apart. I suspect that is good for us to see."[43] Despite the strength and promise of Japan in the 1980s, nature is a force unto itself—a compelling notion in a country with a long history of earthquakes, volcanic eruptions, typhoons, and tsunamis.

Hayashida and Minami present their findings to the cabinet, demonstrating the possibility of causing Mount Mihara to artificially erupt. Hayashida theorizes that by manipulating Godzilla's homing instinct, the monster can be lured and then sealed inside the volcano. The scientists' plan presents the viewer with a complicated and contradictory web. Godzilla, a living nuclear weapon awakened by humanity's meddling with nature can be defeated by once again tinkering with the forces of the natural world. The scientists recommend the manipulation of nature in order to defeat the *kaijū*.

Maki, astounded by the volcano scheme, finds it an unusual way to defeat Godzilla. However, Hayashida quickly corrects him; he states that Godzilla, first believed to be a legendary beast, was regarded with awe. "Godzilla is a warning," Hayashida asserts, "I just want to send him home."[44] Unlike in *Godzilla*, where Dr. Serizawa defeats Godzilla with strictly Japanese science (wiping out life in Tokyo Bay as a result), Prof. Hayashida declares that he does not wish to kill the natural force embodied by Godzilla. Instead, he intends to return the monster back to his place of origin, deep inside the earth. In this way, the film represents a dramatic shift from the environmental theme depicted in *Godzilla*—rather than using technology to overpower nature, Hayashida plans to use science to harness and restore nature for humanity's protection.

With the defense plan in place, the film returns to the simmering conflict between the superpowers. American and Soviet envoys meet with the Prime Minister Mitamura and the cabinet. The superpowers present a united front against Japan. The American envoy demands that Japan "must agree to let [them] use nuclear weapons" in its territory.[45] Both superpowers, in their language and demeanor, do not treat Japan as an equal partner—they make decisions before consulting the Japanese government and then demand that the prime minister consent to their predetermined course of action. In other words, "helpless, peaceful Japan, caught between the two Cold War goliaths, emerges as the innocent, morally superior victim."[46]

The cabinet ministers argue about how to proceed. The defense minister compares the use of nuclear weapons to Hiroshima, the finance minister is more concerned about preserving Tokyo (and with it the Japanese economy) than the potential nuclear fallout, and a military officer raises the specter of untested battlefield nuclear weapons being used on Japan as an experiment. Prime Minister Mitamura firmly declares: "Let me state Japan's overall principles. We neither make, possess, nor use nuclear weapons. We cannot permit their use now."[47] The envoys raise their displeasure, but Mitamura continues to lecture them, asking rhetorically: "What right do America and the Soviet Union have to say that we must follow [them]?"[48] Here, the film mixes both environmental and societal commentary over the use of nuclear weapons with the political and economic hubris of the 1980s. As Ishihara Shintarō would later hope in his 1989 book, *Godzilla 1984*'s Prime Minister Mitamura firmly stares down both superpowers and says "no."

The film's political and anti-nuclear message intensifies. After Mitamura refuses the superpowers' demands, the film cuts to two brief vignettes of Soviet and American nuclear-armed satellites. Although such weapons systems were never actually deployed, the film's depiction of them indicates Japanese unease over the growing nuclear tensions of the Cold War in the mid–1980s. The satellites, based on the political debate surrounding President Ronald Reagan's Strategic Defense Initiative announcement in March 1983, portray the next potential step in the development and danger of nuclear weapons.[49]

A JSDF helicopter detects Godzilla in Tokyo Bay. The government announces Godzilla's impending arrival and a split screen montage shows civilians evacuating Tokyo while tense music plays in the underscore. Back at the lab, Maki asks Prof. Hayashida if the military's plan to use *Super X*'s cadmium shells on Godzilla will be effective. Hayashida demurs, saying that although cadmium seals reactor cores at nuclear power plants, he does not believe the missiles will be effective against a living nuclear weapon like Godzilla.

The JSDF units engage Godzilla. In a brutal shot far removed from the sanitized mayhem of most earlier *kaijū eiga*, the monster vaporizes a group of soldiers with his radioactive breath. Godzilla's rampage through the port causes a tidal surge and large waves. The sloshing maelstrom tosses about the Soviet freighter *Barasheebo*—a covert surveillance ship that controls the Soviet satellite. Heavily damaged, the controls for the space-based nuclear missile begin the launch sequence. Although a Soviet officer bravely attempts to disengage the system, an electrical fire incinerates him.[50]

As Godzilla makes his way toward Shinjuku, a *shinkansen* bullet train track entangles him. The saurian *kaijū* derails a train car, peers inside at horrified passengers, and tosses the car aside. The *shinkansen* sequence updates monster cinema's tried-and-true train sequence to 1980s Japan, showing off Japan's renowned and highly-advanced bullet train system while also paying homage to the genre's roots in films like *King Kong* and the original *Godzilla*. The monster then continues his peripatetic march toward Shinjuku, the financial and economic heart of Tokyo.[51]

Hayashida, Maki, and Naoko test their homing-device on Godzilla, proving its effectiveness. At the same time, *Super X* arrives. JSDF gunfire damages the nearby tower housing Hayashida's lab, trapping the protagonists inside while *Super X* engages Godzilla amidst the towers of Shinjuku. Even though the film's creators nearly doubled Godzilla's size from 1954's *Godzilla*, the modern Tokyo skyscrapers dwarf him. The hovercraft fires its cadmium shells directly into Godzilla's mouth, clearly injuring him. After three direct hits, Godzilla slumps into the side of a tower and collapses. Throughout every other *kaijū eiga* discussed in this book (and many others), the JSDF have never been so successful as they are at this fleeting moment—the high technology, strong economy, and political will of 1980s Japan that built *Super X* is a mighty force indeed.

After a long countdown, the malfunctioning control unit on the Soviet freighter fires its orbiting nuclear weapon. A manic and disheveled Soviet premier telephones the Japanese government to warn them of the accidental launch. Prime Minister Mitamura, grimly hearing the news, requests the Americans help in destroying the Soviet missile before it hits Tokyo. The Americans agree and launch their own rocket to intercept the Soviet one. The nuclear missiles detonate above Tokyo, causing an electromagnetic pulse (or EMP). The EMP disables electricity throughout Tokyo and disables *Super X*. Godzilla, however, absorbs radioactive energy from the detonation and destroys the damaged hovercraft. Nevertheless, two important points are worth noting here: first, the Japanese managed to construct a defensive weapon capable of fighting Godzilla, however, due to Soviet and American interference, that weapon is damaged and ultimately defeated; second, Godzilla inflicts the *coup de grâce* on the armored hovercraft by toppling a Shinjuku tower to crush it, thereby using a symbol of Japan's economic progress and power to destroy a similar symbol of the vanity of the 1980s.

In the meantime, Okumura arrives on a JSDF helicopter to rescue the others trapped in the damaged genetics laboratory. He retrieves Hayashida and the homing device, but a strong wind prevents the evacuation of Maki and Naoko. As the chopper zooms away, Maki and Naoko share a tender moment, and romance blossoms (Okumura should not have left his sister with the shiftless reporter). Maki and Naoko descend the damaged skyscraper, and split up as Godzilla approaches.

Hayashida and Okumura arrive at Mount Mihara with their equipment. The JSDF turns on the homing-device, drawing Godzilla out from Tokyo and across the strait to Ōshima. As Godzilla approaches the volcano's mouth, soldiers detonate explosives around the rim. Roaring in shock and defiance, Godzilla slowly slips down the side of the volcano and slides into the lava below. In the command center, the prime minister watches the live footage. The screen's crimson glow illuminates Mitamura; his eyes glisten as he somberly watches the monster's descent. *Godzilla 1984* concludes with

Godzilla slipping into the volcano, one destructive force of nature contained (but not destroyed) by another.

Just as Hollywood changed the original *Godzilla* to *Godzilla, King of the Monsters*, American studios released a heavily-edited version of *Godzilla 1984* as *Return of Godzilla*. Canadian actor Raymond Burr reprised his role as journalist Steve Martin in the widely panned rendition of the film. Burr's scenes were created in much the same way that they were three decades earlier, but unlike *Godzilla, King of the Monsters*, Burr's footage was never made to interact with the Japanese characters of the film. Instead, Martin views the events of the story from afar, at a military command center in the United States. Ubiquitous Dr. Pepper product placements saturate the American shots, making clear the international commodification of the Godzilla franchise.

The American edit also muddles the film's nuclear issues and exchanges the serious commentary on the Cold War's nuclear brinkmanship for a new, highly politicized, right-wing portrayal of the events. For example, in *Return of Godzilla*, editors modified a shot originally depicting both American and Soviet offensive satellites linked to nuclear weapons. They deleted the American satellite leaving the Soviet's offensive weapon alone in space, thus portraying America as morally superior. Additionally, whereas in *Godzilla 1984* Godzilla's rampage causes an accidental Soviet missile launch, the film's American editors added new footage depicting a Soviet officer intentionally firing the nuclear weapon.[52] This adaptation diluted significant political and environmental issues presented in *Godzilla 1984*, ostensibly making the movie more palatable for a Western audience.

Genetic Engineering and Biotechnology
in Godzilla vs. Biollante *(1989)*

Godzilla vs. Biollante premiered in Japan five years after *Godzilla 1984*. The film picks up moments after the conclusion of the prior picture, then flashes forward five years to 1989 Japan.[53] Reflecting one of many generational shifts, producer Tanaka selected the young Ōmori Kazuki to direct the new film and Sugiyama Kōichi composed its score. *Biollante* acts as a direct sequel to *Godzilla 1984* and conveys environmental awareness while highlighting new issues relevant to the late 1980s.[54] As with Banno Yoshimitsu's surrealist vision evident in *Godzilla vs. Hedorah*, director Ōmori brought a new vantage point to the franchise in a film that J.D. Lees, editor of *G-Fan* magazine, has called "perhaps the most poetic of the series."[55]

Godzilla vs. Biollante focuses on the evolving crossroads of high technology, science, and the natural world in the late 1980s: genetic engineering and biotechnology. Ōmori performed extensive research to make a compelling film about the science behind the emerging technology: "Before beginning, I studied for a long time [...] Reading adventure novels, biotechnology and botany textbooks, etc."[56] The film's espionage subplot is drawn from the director's love of James Bond, and was meant to hook viewers into a film with much deeper environmental themes.[57] In an interview with *Markalite* magazine, Ōmori asserted: "My biggest aim in depicting the reality of the world we live in now, is by using the fictitious presence of Godzilla.... In our present reality, there exist nuclear weapons and the Japanese islands. Additionally, there are theories that a new breed of youthful human beings will appear, through genetic engineering."[58]

Godzilla vs. Biollante opens with sinister-sounding low strings and dissonant chords in the brass accompanying the Tōhō logo. This shifts to a screenshot of computer text that displays a multi-tiered Godzilla alarm system with a jagged string melody in the underscore.[59] Via this exposition, the film immediately situates the viewer in the high-tech world of 1980s Japan, showcasing rapidly developing computer technology and the beginnings of the information age. As the alarm sequence concludes, a microscopic shot of Godzilla's cellular structure quickly zooms out to the extended Godzilla Horror motif in the underscore. This sequence introduces one of the primary issues addressed by *Godzilla vs. Biollante*—cellular manipulation and genetic engineering.

A montage of Godzilla's rampage through Tokyo from *Godzilla 1984* acts as a prelude to the opening credits. An American reporter explains the situation to her viewership (as well as the film audience)—Godzilla is trapped in Mount Mihara, the Shinjuku ward remains closed to civilians, crews salvage the remains of *Super X*, and cleanup of radioactive material is underway. The reporter laments: "This city, built with the most modern technology, was destroyed in just one day."[60]

A mercenary for the American biotech conglomerate Bio-Major purloins a sample of Godzilla's skin from the rubble. Japanese authorities confront him; the mercenary and his compatriots quickly dispose of them. Immediately after their successful escape, a mysterious Middle Eastern man in black, the Saradian assassin SSS9 (Manjot Bedi), guns down the Americans.[61] SSS9 saunters off with the case containing the Godzilla cells. Collectively, the opening sequence hints at the deadly competition between international biotechnology companies hoping to profit from Godzilla's genetic bonanza.

SSS9 boards an oil tanker and eventually delivers the cells to officials for the Republic of Saradia, a fictional Middle Eastern country.[62] Dr. Shiragami (Takahashi Kōji) meets with his employer at the Saradia Institute of Biotechnology. Shiragami and the executive discuss (in English) the importance of the institute's work in genetic engineering. The executive notes that Saradia's wealth is dependent on oil exports, and that Shiragami's work can help turn the "vast desert into a granary."[63] Shiragami asserts that with the help of his daughter Erika (Sawaguchi Yasuko), they will be able to create a new form of "super-plant" by manipulating wheat and cactus genes infused with Godzilla's cellular material. Here, as with 1967's *Son of Godzilla* (examined in Chapter 5), scientists disregard the importance of ecosystems that do not directly benefit the human population. All the characters can imagine is turning the ecologically valuable desert into something more "productive." During the conversation, a bomb explodes in the institute's research laboratory, killing Erika. Shiragami finds her lifeless body surrounded by roses from her greenhouse. In the underscore, a quote from the orchestrated version of Debussy's *Claire de Lune* mourns the young woman's demise.

This musical excerpt bridges the film to a scene five years later with Saegusa Miki (Odaka Megumi), a high school student with psychic abilities. It is at this juncture that the Godzilla franchise embraces the paranormal—Miki goes on to star in several Godzilla films of the 1990s. The inclusion of a psychic in the film meshes well with *Biollante*'s overall environmental theme. In much popular fiction, psychic powers and other paranormal abilities are often explained as genetic mutations of the human population (the

X-Men franchise is perhaps the most well-known example); in a film that delves deeply into issues of genetic engineering, biotechnology, and manipulating the forces of nature, the inclusion of character with psychic abilities is surprisingly fitting as it gestures to ideas of human evolution.[64]

Miki and her mentor Ōkōchi Asuka (Tanaka Yoshiko), administrator at the Japan Psionics Center, visit Dr. Shiragami.[65] At Shiragami's request, Miki attempts to form a mental connection with the rose bushes at his home laboratory. It is apparent that Shiragami has somehow attempted to insert his own daughter's DNA into the roses in a misguided attempt to give her new life. Throughout *kaijū eiga* scientists are common stock characters, but *Godzilla vs. Biollante*'s Dr. Shiragami arguably comes closest to the stereotypical "mad scientist" prevalent in the monster cinema genre.[66] He plays the role in an understated, aloof manner, far removed from the typical deranged scientist, and Shiragami is in many ways a sympathetic character. Director Ōmori even considered making an overt reference between Dr. Shiragami and the original *Godzilla*'s Dr. Serizawa, noting: "Although, it had occurred to me, that maybe I should give him an eyepatch, I didn't do it (laughs)."[67]

During Miki and Asuka's visit, two Bio-Major agents in a covert box truck surveil Shiragami's laboratory. On a hill behind the American operatives, SSS9 reconnoiters both the box truck and the lab. The multiple layers of surveillance on the scientist foreshadow the escalating multilateral corporate warfare between Japanese, American, and Saradian biotech enterprises. The Bio-Major operatives wear garish American flag-themed baseball caps and crassly comment on the attractiveness of Asuka and the underage Miki; the film's portrayal of the Americans is not favorable. As Asuka and Miki depart, Miki blurts out that she hears a female voice calling for Asuka, as the camera pans to the roses. Shiragami's genetic experiment to revive his daughter has been partly successful.

Following this, Asuka meets her boyfriend, geneticist Kirishima Kazuhito (Mitamura Kunihiko), at one of the film's more elegant and memorable sets, the Godzilla Memorial Lounge. The lounge features a massive skylight in the shape of Godzilla's foot—damage from his rampage through Tokyo in 1984. As Kirishima discusses the possibility of genetic engineers creating monsters like the chimera of legend, the lounge serves as an allegorical reminder of another monster created by humans, Godzilla himself.

The structure and *mise-en-scène* evince a new understanding of Godzilla. By the late 1980s, the scars of the atomic bombings healed, but nevertheless remained an indelible aspect of the Japanese social fabric. Godzilla—and through him lingering atomic anxiety—remains monstrous, but the horrors have faded into the background. Memories have become memorials. The lounge in this scene is a monument honoring victims while also serving as a testament to Japan's economic accomplishments. In this way *Biollante* indicates that although Japan had recovered from the war's physical and economic devastation, the nation continued to embrace monuments and museums as psychological placeholders of the past.

Just then, a series of minor eruptions rock Mount Mihara. At the Japan Psionics Center, Asuka and Miki discuss the recent dreams of the younger students. In a rousing sequence, multitudes of ESP-sensitive children hold up drawings of Godzilla—the figure of their nightmares. As the students hold their illustrations in the air, Ifukube's original Godzilla March erupts in earnest. Asuka informs the jaded Colonel Gondō Gorō (Minegishi Tōru) of the JSDF's Godzilla Unit about the students' premonitions. Gondō, on the phone with Major Kuroki Shō (Takashima Masanobu), quips: "It's really exciting waiting for a lizard that never shows up!"[68] The following day, Gondō and Kuroki, joined by Asuka and Miki, fly over Mount Mihara on a JSDF chopper. Miki detects Godzilla telepathically. The film then does a hard cut to a computer screen displaying the warning text of the first-level Godzilla alarm.

Colonel Gondō and Major Kuroki inform the prime minister of their discovery, but he receives the premonitions of a telepathic teenager and a psionic school administrator with understandable skepticism. When asked his opinion on the matter, the ambivalent Gondō laconically asserts: "I hope Godzilla shows up, if he doesn't I'll be unemployed."[69] Gondō and Kuroki consider Godzilla's likely return and discuss the military's latest high-tech programs: robots, lasers, and biotechnology.[70] They meet Kirishima at his genetics firm, where he expounds the abilities and power of the program's anti-nuclear energy bacteria. Kirishima asserts that similar to oil-eating bacteria developed in the United States, Japanese scientists have created a bacteria that consumes nuclear material.[71] In Kirishima's explanation, the all-important Godzilla cells re-enter the film—the bacteria can only be artificially produced in a lab, and the nuclear-digesting genes present in Godzilla's cells are vital to the process.

Godzilla vs. Biollante offers an intriguing dualistic portrait of the *kaijū*. Godzilla—a monster created by humanity's nuclear testing—takes revenge on Japan and its people. At the same time, the destructive science that created Godzilla has also created the very key to defeating the monster. This inherent paradox showcases a new view of science in a Japan now far-removed from the atomic bombings of 1945. Moreover, the characters note that the creation of the anti-nuclear bacteria could be used to clean-up potential nuclear meltdowns, as well as destabilize the current world order dominated by the vast nuclear arsenals of the United States and Soviet Union, adding to the film's nuance.[72]

Gondō and Kuroki attempt to recruit Dr. Shiragami. He refuses to work with the Godzilla cells again, citing Erika's tragic death. In the meantime, Kirishima meets with Asuka's father Ōkōchi Makoto (Kaneda Ryūnosuke), the director of the institute that houses the Godzilla cells. Ōkōchi (an amusingly stereotypical, high-powered Japanese businessman) and Kirishima discuss the political and ethical implications of creating the bacteria, and Ōkōchi shows Kirishima the Godzilla cells locked in a secure vault. He warns the geneticist of industrial sabotage on the part of the Ōkōchi Foundation's international competitors. As Kirishima stares enraptured by the frozen Godzilla cells, Ōkōchi reasons: "Japan was devastated by atomic bombs and Godzilla…. It's only fair that we use the Godzilla cells to protect us from our enemies."[73]

Following an earthquake that damages his rose garden, Dr. Shiragami determines that Erika's spirit will die unless he takes action. He informs Ōkōchi that he will help with the bacteria project under the condition that he temporarily stores the Godzilla cells in his personal lab. In an ominous scene (complete with the requisite thunderstorm) the audience learns that the scientist plans to genetically cross Godzilla cells with the roses containing his dead daughter's spirit. What could possibly go wrong?

Shiragami's personal experiments foreground the film's main environmental message: although recent scientific breakthroughs in bioengineering could be used for noble pursuits (such as defending Japan from Godzilla), they are also rife with pitfalls (such as Shiragami's personal crusade to preserve Erika's spirit). The following day at the Ōkōchi Foundation, Kirishima emphasizes this point to Ōkōchi and Shiragami: "I know it is just a simple bacteria we are creating through genetic engineering, but if research continues on its present course genetic technology will produce something far worse than Godzilla."[74] In a hard cut, the film returns us to Shiragami's lab, with a close-up shot of the monster-rose hybrid growing with eerie synthesizer samples of a glass harmonica, cuing the viewer to the unnatural, shocking results of Shiragami's experiments.[75] The unsettling underscore indicates that, for the time being, biotechnology has surpassed nuclear energy as the Godzilla franchise's preeminent concern.

Gondō and Kuroki monitor Godzilla's volcanic prison. The second-level alarm sounds when physical movement is detected beneath the crater. Meanwhile, Shiragami and Kirishima discuss genetics and cell division at their laboratory. The scene provides a pedagogical moment akin to the brief lectures on geothermal power in *Daikaijū Gamera* and marine life in *Gamera vs. Zigra*. After successfully creating the anti-nuclear bacteria, the scientists need only observe the cells multiply. From one cell, the process naturally increases exponentially every half hour, leading to four million cells at the end of a single day. The film clearly intends to impress its audience with the sheer power of biotechnology.

The two American Bio-Major operatives vandalize Shiragami's lab. The depiction of an American corporation conducting industrial espionage on Japanese scientists alludes to the technological prowess of 1989 Japan. The Bio-Major agents discover Shiragami's notes, but the Saradian assassin SSS9 attacks them; massive plant vines join in the fray, now a three-way *battle royale*. SSS9 and one of the Bio-Major operatives escape, but the rapidly growing plant-monster strangles the other agent. The next morning, Kirishima confronts Shiragami about his Godzilla cell experiments while the two survey the wrecked laboratory. Peering through a massive hole in the lab's wall toward nearby Lake Ashi, Shiragami admits he may have committed an error.

The Bio-Major company blackmails the Japanese government, threatening to destroy Mount Mihara and free Godzilla as punishment for developing the nuclear energy-consuming bacteria. In the meantime, Miki senses the imminent emergence of the vengeful vegetation. She leads Asuka to the lake where the monstrous flora resides. Meanwhile, Kirishima receives a call to deliver the anti-nuclear bacteria to Bio-Major before they destroy Godzilla's montane prison. Shiragami dubs his massive creation "Biollante," after a plant in Norse mythology.[76] He confirms that Biollante is a mixture of Godzilla's DNA, rose cells, and his daughter Erika's spirit.

Kirishima and Gondō deliver the bacteria to the Bio-Major agent, but SSS9 shoots the operative before he can disable the explosives on Mount Mihara. Kirishima and Gondō attempt to turn off the control system, but the explosives detonate. As the bomb's timer counts down to zero, Gondō resignedly remarks "Amen."[77] Godzilla emerges from the smoldering remains of Mount Mihara, and the third-level Godzilla alarm flashes across the screen; SSS9 flees with the bacteria, Japan's best hope of defending itself against the *kaijū*. As in 1954's *Godzilla*, Bio-Major's actions make the United States responsible (albeit indirectly) for Godzilla's attack on Japan.

Newscasts warn the Japanese people of Godzilla's return.[78] En route to Tokyo, Godzilla sinks several Japanese frigates. With the JSDF units failing to even slow Godzilla's approach, *Super X-2* launches and engages Godzilla. *Super X-2* boasts heavier weaponry, advanced computer systems, and a state-of-the-art "fire-mirror" made of synthetic diamonds. The hovercraft proves surprisingly successful, and Godzilla dives in retreat.

A journalist attempts to interview Dr. Shiragami about Biollante. The geneticist self-righteously replies: "You criticize scientific experiments without understanding their true value, scientists must look toward the future!"[79] Ironically, immediately after Shiragami's outburst, one of Biollante's vines destroys part of the pier where they are standing, nearly killing them. In the *kaijū eiga* genre, Biollante is unique. She is the result of intentional experiments conducted by humans, whereas Godzilla, Gamera, and Mothra are all monsters accidentally awakened or enraged by human activities.

Biollante beckons Godzilla towards the lake with her unearthly siren song. *Super X-2*, continuing to shadow Godzilla, re-engages him but Godzilla's sustained radioactive breath attacks damage the fire-mirror, forcing a retreat. Later, as workers attempt to repair *Super X-2*, one laments: "Godzilla melted a synthetic diamond mirror, that's beyond our technological limits!"[80] Godzilla arrives at Lake Ashi for his first encounter with Biollante. Much like the feminine Mothra (and the androgynous Hedorah) the monster Biollante goes through several phases. When Godzilla first encounters the botanical behemoth, she appears to be a giant rose with fangs and powerful vines.[81] Biollante proves no match for Godzilla's radiation breath; glowing embers (perhaps pollen) float into the sky as the abominable bloom burns. The visuals underline the monster plant's connection to biotechnology—the soaring embers take the form of a flowing double helix, the shape of DNA molecules.[82] A solemn requiem in the under-score mourns Biollante's demise.

The JSDF loses track of Godzilla and Kuroki determines that he will likely head to a nuclear plant near Nagoya to restore his energy. Instead, Godzilla surfaces in Osaka Bay. Kuroki orders *Super X-2* to slow Godzilla's advance on Osaka, and contacts Miki and Asuka for assistance. Miki uses her psionic abilities to halt Godzilla, fainting in the process.[83] Here, Miki's character represents the *kaijū eiga* genre's shift away from the previously prevalent temptress characters. Unlike the sexualized, technological female, Miki's character calls to mind the feminine, mysteriously magical (yet natural) abilities of Mothra's Twin Fairies. In *Godzilla vs. Biollante*, a Japanese teenage girl stands toe to toe with Godzilla and delays his advance on Japan more effectively than the entire Japanese military and male-dominated power structure.[84]

Godzilla, befuddled by Miki's telepathic forays, turns and proceeds on a more indirect course to Osaka, giving the authorities more time to evacuate the city. Just as the city's civilian population flees, Kirishima and Gondō arrive at the Saradian Oil Company's Osaka headquarters in search of SSS9 and the stolen anti-nuclear bacteria. They ambush an oil company worker (wearing a loud, multicolored pinstripe suit unique to late-1980s fashion) and retrieve the stolen bacteria.

Godzilla runs amok through Osaka; the skyscrapers dwarf the monster as those in Shinjuku did five years earlier. *Super X-2* assails Godzilla while Gondō and other commandos weaponize the bacteria. The monster and the hovercraft square off near Osaka Castle, which surprisingly survives the affair. Godzilla destroys *Super X-2*, but the commandos manage to fire two bacteria rounds into the monster. Gondō fires a third round directly into Godzilla's mouth, causing him to topple the skyscraper where Gondō is positioned. The other protagonists are shocked. It is rare for a likeable, primary character to die in a Tōhō monster film; Gondō, like Serizawa before him, sacrifices himself while unleashing a terrifying new weapon. Once again, *Godzilla vs. Biollante* subtly references the original 1954 film, juxtaposing the anti-nuclear energy bacteria with the oxygen-destroyer and revealing both as troubling threats to humanity and nature.

The following morning, the protagonists discover that the bacteria failed to affect Godzilla. Kirishima determines that Godzilla's low body temperature limits the speed of bacterial reproduction. The JSDF decides to deploy their new M-6000TC "thunder control" system, which generates artificial lightning, to raise the *kaijū*'s body temperature. While not another form of biotechnology, the M-6000TC system certainly reflects yet another human attempt to manipulate and control nature for military purposes, akin to the "deep-freeze" weapon in *Daikaijū Gamera*. JSDF fighter jets seed clouds with silver iodine to create an artificial thunderstorm, while other military units deploy massive platforms on the ground to direct the unnatural lightning.

Godzilla reappears for the film's climactic battle. The nuclear terror attacks the JSDF units and enters the M-6000TC field. After several lightning strikes, the engineered bacteria takes effect and Godzilla becomes lethargic. The military units continue their withering assault, but to little avail. However, just when it seems Godzilla will emerge victorious once more, a stream of glowing sparks drop from the sky and Biollante erupts from the earth beneath Godzilla. Biollante has mutated since her last appearance, and she now appears to be a formidable monster, larger than Godzilla and sporting a far more aggressive bulk and facial structure. Unlike her earlier rose configuration, Biollante's second iteration resembles a vine-covered crocodilian.

Godzilla's radiation breath damages Biollante, but the plant-monster charges Godzilla and her vines lash him. Biollante spews a luminous green acid on Godzilla, and the two grapple. Overcome by the combined effects of the bacteria and his exertion fighting Biollante, Godzilla retreats, stumbling into the sea. The film's message is clear: Godzilla, a symbol embodying the threat of nuclear energy, pales in comparison to the might of genetic engineering represented by Biollante and the manipulated bacteria. Miraculously, Ōkōchi appears out of nowhere the instant Godzilla collapses and informs Dr. Shiragami that their work on the bacteria must continue. Shiragami rebuffs him, asserting: "Godzilla and Biollante are not monsters, the arrogant scientists who create them are the monsters."[85] This statement indicates a conviction that technology and nature are neither good nor bad, but the reckless pursuit of scientific progress without consideration of the potential consequences is the true evil.

In the film's denouement, Biollante dissipates, flowing back into the sky in the form of radiant particles and an image of Shiragami's daughter Erika. SSS9 shoots Shiragami in the chest, ensuring that the scientist can never again work with Godzilla cells, before he is also killed. Godzilla emerges from the water with a roar, departing into the distance.

Kirishima declares: "The water must have lowered his temperature.... Godzilla goes to the sea, Biollante to the sky."[86] The film ends with a narrated plea from Erika reminiscent of Prof. Yamane's warning at the conclusion of *Godzilla*. The credits roll as Godzilla returns to sea, and the camera zooms out to a shot from outer space, with a rose superimposed in the sky above Japan.[87]

Godzilla vs. Biollante depicts the nascent scientific revolution in biotechnology as a dangerous Pandora's Box filled with unpredictable and potentially dangerous consequences. Moreover, the film adds a wrinkle to an environmental analysis of *kaijū eiga* by altering the science versus nature dichotomy present in monster cinema since the genre's origins. In the earliest films, from *Godzilla* and *Mothra* to *Daikaijū Gamera*, science was most often portrayed through nuclear testing and its related human and environmental costs. Later, the dynamic changed its focus from atomic anxiety to industrial pollution and toxicity in *Godzilla vs. Hedorah* and *Gamera vs. Zigra*. In *Godzilla vs. Biollante*, a new and more insidious paradigm shift occurs. Science is not simply placed in opposition to nature; the advent of genetic engineering and biotechnology allow the manipulation of the natural world itself.

Biollante's metamorphosis emphasizes the unpredictable nature of un-tested genetic technology: the natural world constantly evolves, mutates, and transforms, and the consequences of biotechnology cannot be fully predicted in advance. As Dr. Ian Malcolm (Jeff Goldblum), a famous character in the very similarly-themed 1993 Hollywood blockbuster *Jurassic Park* warns: "If there's one thing the history of evolution has taught us it's that life will not be contained. Life breaks free, it expands to new territories and crashes through barriers, painfully, maybe even dangerously, but [...] Life finds a way."[88] Dr. Malcolm's warning, uttered on-screen four years after *Godzilla vs. Biollante* premiered, is nevertheless apropos. Although science has advanced to the point that genetic engineering is possible, it nonetheless remains an enchanting idea beyond humanity's control.[89]

11

Rebirth of Mothra

Daikaijū *and the Environment in the Post-Bubble Era*

Following the implosion of the Japanese asset price bubble, stock values, real estate prices, and Japanese commodities sagged. Instead of heady growth, Japan's economy began to stagnate. Apprehension replaced the economic confidence of the 1980s and Japan seemed a nation adrift. The death of the Shōwa emperor on January 7, 1989, added to the general malaise. The Shōwa emperor had served Japan since 1926, presiding over the nation's defeat, occupation, and economic miracle; his passing and the subsequent ascendance of his son, the Heisei emperor, marked a significant rupture in modern Japanese history. A stalwart figure that had been a constant in the lives of most Japanese was suddenly gone. Around the same time, the Cold War quickly came to an end—the Berlin Wall fell in November 1989, signaling the collapse of communism in Eastern Europe, and the Soviet Union dissolved only two years later in December 1991. With the end of the Cold War, Japanese concern of a potential nuclear war between the superpowers dissipated accordingly. The collective result was an enervation that lasted throughout the 1990s, leading historians of Japan to refer to the era as the Lost Decade.[1] The rebooted Mothra franchise meditated on these new realities.

Mothra in the Post-Bubble World: Reclaiming Nature, Restoring the Family

In the 1990s and early 2000s, environmental worries shifted from the nuclear (which was at the time still a boon to resource-scarce Japan's energy demands), to other issues, namely conservation. This era was a crucial turn inward and reassessment of Japan's position as an international industrialized power. Simultaneously, nostalgia for a pre-industrialized past surged; in this imagined past, the Japanese were more closely connected to nature and rural life. As we have seen in previous chapters, Japan had long associated its national identity with nature and the environment, such as Mount Fuji, cherry blossoms, and the ocean. In this chapter we examine how post-bubble *kaijū eiga*, especially the rebooted Mothra series, portray these social and environmental concerns at the end of the 20th century.

156

In addition to their overall engagement with ecological worries, the Heisei Mothra films emphasize normative family structures. The movies repeatedly draw parallels between humanity's unsustainable harvesting of natural resources, particularly forests, and unstable relationships within a family structure. The films invariably end with harmony restored to both the natural world and the family. In this way, a balanced family unit mirrors a balanced relationship between nature and humanity.

But the family also serves as a metaphor for the nation. Since before World War II, the concept of family was part of a nationalist discourse that imagined the emperor as the patriarchal head of the Japanese family. The idea, rooted in Confucianism, was that stable family structures contributed to stable governing structures.[2] This correlation between nature and family hierarchy at the turn of the millennium echoes these ideologies of nationalism.

Psychologist Hayashi Michiyoshi's publications promoting a return to patriarchal values provide a case in point. While the *Rebirth of Mothra* trilogy hit theaters, Hayashi's writings captured the spirit of the late 1990s.[3] They characterized a popular sentiment that "certain successes of the women's movement were blamed for concrete problems in contemporary society, such as higher divorce rates and the rise in youth crime."[4] It makes sense that during this time of turmoil Japanese cinema encouraged a portrayal of social values that at times obfuscates true culpability for economic and environmental disasters. The Heisei Mothra films' emphasis on a return to nature as well as a return to "natural" family structures of a pre-industrialized Japan represent a conservative nostalgic turn, despite the relatively progressive environmental critique. In our analysis, we consider the ways *Godzilla vs. Mothra* and the later *Rebirth of Mothra* trilogy succeed as penetrating interrogations of ecology as it relates to social and political issues circulating in Japan during the Lost Decade.

Mothra's Revival

Other Tōhō Studios monster films of the 1990s set a precedent for the Mothra franchise's environmental themes. For example, *Gojira vs. Kingu Gidora* (*Godzilla vs. King Ghidorah*) (1991) explicitly addressed worries regarding nuclear pollution as well as the aftermath of Japan's economic conceit of the prior decade. This film provided a foundation for *kaijū eiga* of the 1990s, as well as a blueprint for the Heisei Mothra films. In *Godzilla vs. King Ghidorah* visitors from the future warn the Japanese prime minister that Godzilla will wreak havoc on nuclear power plants, and the resulting radiological pollution will make the nation uninhabitable. Later it is revealed that the time travelers fabricated this story; they played on fears of nuclear pollution in order to achieve their true goal: demolish the Japan of the past so that it will not become a global economic hegemon in the future.

Indeed, as early as 1990 Tōhō bandied about a Mothra script dealing with contemporary environmental issues. The unrealized "Mothra vs. Bagan" demonstrates this desire to revive the giant moth, who had been shelved since 1968's *Kaijū Sōshingeki* (*Destroy All Monsters*). With a script by *Biollante* director Ōmori Kazuki, the film featured the monster Bagan. Thanks to global warming, Bagan escapes his glacial prison and proceeds to attack civilization, only to be thwarted by Mothra.[5] Although this movie never came to fruition, it bespoke themes that would become relevant in the first Mothra movie of the Heisei era, the film *Gojira vs. Mosura* (*Godzilla vs. Mothra*) (1992). David Kalat suggests that the script for the picture was simply a modified version of the Ōmori script, with the dark-colored Mothra named Battra replacing Bagan and Godzilla simply inserted into the mix.[6] Tanaka Tomoyuki served as executive producer for the *Godzilla vs. Mothra* and Okawara Takao directed.[7]

Like the Godzilla films of the 1980s, *Godzilla vs. Mothra* is a retroactive continuity film; in its narrative world, none of the events of earlier Mothra films occurred. Despite this, the movie contains several references to the 1960s Mothra movies. For example, *Godzilla vs. Mothra* features veteran *kaijū eiga* actor Takarada Akira, who appeared in several Mothra films of the Shōwa era.[8] The soundtrack recycles Ifukube and Koseki's music cues, with Ifukube's music often supplementing the film's new score. Sacred Springs, Mahara Mosura, and of course Mothra's Song appear in the soundtrack as do many of the musical motifs from the original *Godzilla*. Even some of the shots parallel those of the original movies, particularly the opening and closing scenes. Akin to 1964's *Mothra vs. Godzilla*, the 1992 film opens with a raging typhoon eroding Infant Island's coastline and sweeping Mothra's egg out to sea. The final scene of the film echoes the end of the 1961 movie, with the group of protagonists standing on an airfield waving goodbye to Mothra and her tiny priestesses. What's more, the 1992 picture blatantly draws on tropes from popular Hollywood movies of the time, particularly the Indiana Jones franchise, just as the original *Godzilla* drew on *King Kong*. *Godzilla vs. Mothra* continues to riff on thematic material presented in the original movies, stressing unrestrained capitalism's negative effects on the environment.

Mothra's return certainly resonated with film-going audiences. *Godzilla vs. Mothra* sold about 4.2 million tickets and grossed ¥2.22 billion.[9] Given the recession of the 1990s, this was an especially strong showing, and *Godzilla vs. Mothra* would prove to be among the most financially successful films of the Heisei Godzilla series, convincing Tōhō Studios to produce additional Mothra franchise films in the later 1990s.[10] By the years of the Lost Decade, more and more Japanese theatergoers were attending foreign films rather than Japanese productions.[11] For example, Steven Spielberg's *Jurassic Park* dominated at Japanese cinemas, earning ¥8.3 billion.[12] However, *Godzilla vs. Mothra* remained the highest-grossing domestic film in 1993. And while nostalgia for the *kaijū* series and the allure of special effects helped attract a large viewership, we think that the movie's extension of themes from the original ones also contributed to its success. The depravity of corporate-government collaborations and their contribution to environmental destruction was both a prevalent and pertinent topic to post-bubble Japan.

In his entry on the film, Kalat critiques *Godzilla vs. Mothra* for its single-sided portrayal of environmental positivism. In his opinion the work "neglects to show much of mankind's environmental abuse" and "assumes the audience's sympathy already lies with the environmentalists."[13] We do not consider this a departure from earlier Mothra films. The Mothra movies have always worked narratively and audio-visually to compel audiences to sympathize with nature.

Kalat also finds that a change in Mothra's origin story undermines the series' moral message. Instead of being a monster goddess for a native tribe on Infant Island, a tribe that has suffered as a result of Japan and other countries' exploitation of the environment, Mothra is a creature of outer space. Only two of her followers, a pair of tiny ladies called "Cosmos," remain. This, Kalat believes, dilutes the idea that the Japanese must swallow their pride, apologize, and even beg Mothra to help them.[14] While he is correct in that such a scene is absent from the 1992 film, we think the main character Fujita Takuya's apology functions as a proxy. This scene of contriteness carries with it a different kind of symbolic weight, one that brings together issues of environmental exploitation, family roles, and nationalism in some interesting ways. A deeper examination of the film illuminates the ways these issues are introduced. They culminate in Fujita's transformation from unrepentant exploiter, ersatz father, and unreliable husband to rehabilitated patriarch and enlightened hero.

Godzilla vs. Mothra: *A Battle with Earth*

Godzilla vs. Mothra commences with a meteorite slamming into Earth, causing several natural disasters including a typhoon.[15] Its impact also awakens Godzilla, who was sleeping in an ocean trench. During the opening credits, viewers receive shots of the typhoon raging in combination with musical motifs from the 1960s Mothra films. A hard cut takes the audience to the ruins of a temple where a young Japanese man in a brown fedora (actor Bessho Tetsuya) chips away at some stones. He reaches into a crevice and grabs a golden idol of what appears to be the Hindu deity Ganesha. As he admires the treasure the temple starts to crumble, and he races up a set of stairs to escape, the steps disintegrating behind him. Police wait at the temple entrance in order to capture the burglar. This opening sequence establishes the film's cinematic parentage; the credits align the movie with the original Mothra movies while the temple sequence alludes to the Indiana Jones franchise.[16] Because of this, audiences can surmise that the young man possesses some qualities similar to Harrison Ford's character: cleverness, sarcasm, and affability.

The police toss the young man in jail. A group of Japanese businessmen and a sole woman come to visit him. Through this, viewers learn the details of the robber; his name is Fujita Takuya, he is thirty years old, divorced, and has not made regular child support payments. The woman is his ex-wife, Tezuka Masako (Kobayashi Satomi). Masako's power suit, heels, and body language visually denote her as a domineering and outspoken character. The men are representatives of Japan's National Environment Planning Bureau and the Marutomo Company, a corporation involved in land development. They have travelled to meet Fujita and make him an offer: charges concerning his temple-robbing escapade will be dropped if he agrees to locate a giant object in the South Sea that recently appeared in satellite photos. Masako goads Fujita into accepting the proposal.

As a female lead, Masako epitomizes trends established in the previous Mothra movies. Although the women in the original films were certainly plucky, they still occupied positions that were less prestigious than their male counterparts. Junko from 1964's *Mothra vs. Godzilla* was an astute character able to convince Mothra to help Japan, yet nonetheless she basically served as Sakai's assistant. Masako is different. She commands more power and respect than her ex-husband and has managed to be a successful mother and bureaucrat for the National Environment Planning Bureau. Yet she still loves Fujita and he, her. Through the character Masako, *Godzilla vs. Mothra* continues to grapple with issues related to gender and power dynamics. However, the way they play out is complicated.

The film shifts to the National Environment Planning Bureau office in Tokyo, where some men joke about Fujita and Masako's relationship before cutting to a scientific headquarters. There, several people man observation stations monitoring Earth's weather patterns and atmosphere. Minamino Jōji (Takarada Akira) leads a group through the control room, explaining the scientists' work and providing the first of many direct comments regarding the environment. He relates, "Well, there have been some terrible changes in the climate recently. Men are destroying the very Earth they live on. We can't go on like this for very long."[17] The meteorite exacerbated environmental destruction originally triggered by humans, most notably a rise in sea levels. This is a major concern for an island nation such as Japan. Another scientist relates that the shifting ocean plates also disturbed the slumbering Godzilla. "What a day," Minamino bemoans, "Godzilla at large again."[18] This early scene markedly places environmental themes at the forefront of the film.

Following this, the movie shows Masako, Fujita, and a representative of Marutomo Company named Ando (Murata Takehiro) en route to Infant Island to locate the mysterious object. As their speedboat approaches, the film replicates an establishing long shot of the island as seen in the 1960s films. Ifukube's tuneful French horn cue from 1964 accompanies the image. The island itself is lush, akin to its depiction in *Mothra*. Trudging through the jungle the characters happen upon an area of the island that has been eroded due to deforestation in service of land development. Fujita, in shock, says, "This is terrible."[19] Masako provides some deeper insight, pointing out, "Men destroy what nature has been creating for billions of years. Someday this will happen to all of Japan."[20] Again, the film stresses the environmental dangers of over-development. Masako's comment is an important warning that connects the destruction of nature with the destruction of Japan itself, a theme that occurs in more concrete ways over the course of the *Rebirth of Mothra* series.

As the group continues their journey, Masako and Fujita bicker, akin to Indiana Jones and Willie's jungle adventures in *Indiana Jones and the Temple of Doom* (1984).[21] The influence of the Spielberg film becomes even more apparent when the trio crosses a vine-woven bridge that slowly frays, forcing them to jump into a river (*sans* crocodiles) below and swim to shore. Fujita realizes they can float down the river to arrive at their destination more quickly. An affecting scene shows the three rowing in an inflatable raft and then zooms out to an aerial shot revealing the vastness of the river and jungle, and the insignificance of the three human interlopers in comparison to nature.[22]

Encountering a waterfall, they decide to camp for the night. While Ando sleeps, Fujita and Masako chat by a campfire; Masako hands Fujita a picture and letter from their daughter, read by the little girl in voiceover. Fujita clearly loves and misses his family, but feels like he cannot adequately provide financial support for them. Thus, he turned to a life of archeological banditry. This scene establishes the crux of the filial narrative that parallels the environmental and *kaijū* narrative threads. Humanity's relationship with nature must be brought back into balance. Likewise, so too must the relationship within the family be restored to its "natural" order.[23]

The following morning the trio finds a cave behind the waterfall, similar to the one Chūjō discovered in *Mothra*. Paintings on the cave wall explain Mothra's origin and show the butterfly-esque beast facing off with a dark mirror image.[24] Light shines through a cross-shaped crevice; a musical burst of Electone and vibraphone accompanies this shot, a clear audiovisual reference to the 1961 film.[25] Excited by the finding, the group continues and finally locates the large object they sought. A harp cue combined with tremolo strings in the underscore hints at the exotic nature of the object and Fujita scrapes the side of the large ovoid.[26] It is an egg of enormous proportions.

A pair of off-screen voices chime in, "It's Mothra's egg; it belongs to Mothra."[27] Masako, Fujita, and Ando quickly pivot, searching for the voices' source. Ando is convinced a sprig of pansies is speaking to them, but then two tiny women (played by Imamura Keiko and Osawa Sayaka) emerge from behind the flowers. As they do so, the Sacred Springs cue appears in the soundtrack.[28] Like their 1960s counterparts, these women speak in unison. They recount:

> We are the Cosmos.... We have been living on Earth since before humans ever existed. Over 12,000 years ago there was a guardian of Earth named Mothra. At that time there was an advanced civilization on Earth and the Cosmos were in perfect order. But then a terrible thing happened. Some scientists created a device to control Earth's climate. This device greatly offended Earth.[29]

Masako interjects, surprised a planet can be offended. The Cosmos explain that Earth is a living being and can therefore be offended or feel that it is in danger. They impart that the climate control device made Earth feel threatened, so it created a dark Mothra, known as Battra, to protect itself from the scientists' creation. Battra destroyed the climate control machine and anything else that endangered Earth. Mothra tried to protect the Cosmos, but she was defeated. Without the climate control device, massive flooding destroyed the Cosmos' civilization. Now the pair of little ladies are all that remain of their people.

The Cosmos' account plays a key role in the narrative and in the film's environmental message. First it establishes a dichotomy between Mothra and Battra. Mothra, with her origins in the stars rather than Earth, is made even more Other than in her initial 1960s incarnation. This provenance contributes to Mothra's divine persona all the same. She is astral and unassailable. Her dark counterpart Battra is, according to the Cosmos, utterly of the planet Earth. Indeed, Battra is the avatar of the anthropomorphized Earth's vengeance. Battra's dynamic evolution as a villainous *kaijū* is crucial. Battra destroyed an entire civilization, yet the monster is not wantonly evil. Battra does not seek to murder or control for sheer pleasure. In a way, Battra is a heroic *kaijū* that protects Earth from its destroyers, humanity itself.

Next, according to the Cosmos the planet is alive and conscious of the harm being done to it. This portrayal of Earth could be taken at face value by child viewers and as a metaphor by adults. The notion compels both groups to consider the ways they contribute to the degradation of the environment. Masako becomes a surrogate for film viewers when, following the Cosmos' story, she observes, "Once again we are endangering the planet in all sorts of ways."[30] Indeed, the Marutomo Company's deforestation project on Infant Island in combination with the recent meteorite impact contributed to the violent weather patterns and exposed Mothra's egg to the elements. The Cosmos fear that not only will Mothra awake; so too will her dark counterpart.

Back at the National Environment Planning Bureau, scientists and politicians eye screens depicting intensifying climate changes. An older onlooker tugs at his collar as if he himself is overheating, and wonders, "What's happening to our planet?"[31] A hard cut to Marutomo Company heavy construction equipment noisily erecting a golf course resort near Mount Fuji serves as a reply.[32] Tradition demands the land surrounding Mount Fuji be treated as sacred, yet the company plans to use it as a backdrop for luxury recreation. Nearby protesters chant slogans like "Save the forest" and carry signs with similar messages. One eye-catching poster depicts a cartoonish Mount Fuji shedding a single tear, the writing above telling us "Mount Fuji is crying."[33] Again the film favors an anthropomorphization of nature, now clarified in its meaning. A major symbol of Shintō religious customs, the development and degradation of Mount Fuji signals Japan's abandonment of traditional values during the bubble years. While the construction chief refers to the protesters as radicals, they appear to be everyday people across the age spectrum. So while *Godzilla vs. Mothra* lacks subtlety regarding its environmental message, it achieves something remarkable: for the first time in *kaijū eiga*, political activism is shown as a viable response to the overdevelopment of land and environmental degradation.

The head of the Marutomo Company (actor Ōtake Makoto) consults with the construction chief and threatens retribution if the project falls behind schedule like the one on Infant Island (which we learn is part of Indonesia). The businessman speaks with Ando, and commands him to acquire the giant egg. He plans to attract visitors to the tropical resort with promises of an astonishing egg exhibit. Under the pretense of protecting it from exposure, the Cosmos agree to relocate Mothra's egg. Masako promises the Cosmos that they will work to warn humanity of the dangers of environmental destruction. A barge tows the egg while the underscore intones a martial variation on the Sacred Springs theme.[34]

In a cross-cut, the Battra larva nears mainland Japan. True to form, the JSDF is unable to prevent Battra's attack. The fearsome worm destroys Nagoya including the castle, which Godzilla crushed nearly thirty years prior in *Mothra vs. Godzilla*. Like Godzilla's rampage through Nagoya in that film, Battra's romp represents nature's vengeance on the seat of Japanese industrial development. The music accompanying Battra's attack is interesting; initially we hear a heavy brass theme and tone clusters in the lower register of a piano.[35] This is reminiscent of the opening material of the Horror theme in the original *Godzilla*. The musical allusion suggests that like Godzilla, Battra is the result of humanity's failure to respect nature.

As Nagoya crumbles, Godzilla approaches the barge hauling Mothra's egg. Fujita wants to release the egg and escape, but Ando prevents him from doing so, saying he must bring it to his boss. Notably, their fisticuffs receive no musical accompaniment, despite the fact that choreographed fistfights typically represent peaks of dramatic action. The lack of music here emphasizes the banality of their argument. Just like Kumayama and Torahata's similar brawl in the 1964 picture, neither of them are worthy of the emotional weightiness music conveys.

Instead, as Godzilla approaches we hear the March theme, and later, as the egg hatches to reveal a Mothra larva, the Mothra motif appears in the score. Godzilla and the Mothra larva fight as the ship tries to escape. Then Battra joins the fray, also attacking Godzilla, the human-made nuclear monster. This is an important quality—both Mothra and Battra are natural *kaijū*, while Godzilla is the result of humans polluting the world with radiation. Thus, in this film, Godzilla is the embodiment of ecological destruction, in a way more akin to Hedorah, the smog monster. The Mothra larva escapes while the Battra worm and Godzilla grapple underwater, falling into a volcanic fissure. For now, the humans are safe.

The trio checks into a hotel, where Ando promptly drowns his sorrows at the bar while Masako and Fujita reminisce about their honeymoon. They share a distrust of the Marutomo Company and Masako notes that this mutual suspicion is the first time they have agreed on something in years. Together, they realize that they must break out of their comfort zone and face their mistakes, personal or, more broadly, the mistakes of humanity. Yet, though it seems Fujita and Masako are close to reconciling, the framing tells us otherwise. We receive a two-shot from outside the hotel of Fujita and Masako chatting.[36] A pillar divides the space between the former lovers, visually indicating that they are still ideologically separated. The shot recalls the cave painting of Mothra and Battra facing each other; both shots indicate the duality of light and dark and the feminine and masculine.

In the morning, Masako and Fujita discover that Ando has kidnapped the Cosmos. He presents them to his boss as a substitute for the lost egg. Marutomo's president is ecstatic, hoping to use the Cosmos in advertisements. Like other Mothra villains, the tycoon objectifies the tiny women, seeing them as a means to acquire capital. However, he does promise to pay the twins, although they are dubious. The promise of compensation seems to break with previous villains, but it is obvious that the president's offer is empty. Like Nelson, Kumayama, and Torahata before him, the Marutomo president clearly does not consider the tiny ladies to be on par with human beings. The businessman tells Ando to find the Cosmos a place to live, suggesting he purchase a dollhouse. The tiny women are literally treated as dolls, as playthings, as objects. In a way, the president's offer of a salary is a dishonest veneer worse than his predecessors' blatant villainy. This interaction, though brief, continues a theme established in the 1960s films regarding gender equality: in the 1990s and beyond Japanese women still faced misogyny in the workplace.[37]

As Masako and Fujita arrive at Tokyo's Narita Airport, Masako worries about the consequences of the missing Cosmos. She fears that Mothra will justifiably attack Tokyo, and notes, "The only reason the Cosmos came was to protect the environment. The only thing the great Marutomo Company is doing is helping destroy it."[38] In the midst of their conversation, Masako and Fujita both spy their daughter, Midori (or "green"), scouring the crowd for her parents. Masako rushes to hug her. Her friends welcome her home and relate that the planet's tectonic plates are shifting due to the meteorite.[39] Fujita fades into the crowd after looking forlornly at his daughter.

The Marutomo Company refuses the National Environment Planning Bureau's request to return the Cosmos. In a bit of foreshadowing, Masako states, "We can just see how Earth is going to punish us all now."[40] An earthquake jostles Tokyo. The sun sets over the Japanese capital and the Cosmos sing the Mothra Song. Although the words and music are the same as the 1960s films, in this case the film provides subtitles translating the fairies' prayer for help.[41] The Cosmos may be foreign, but they are not obscurely exotic. The subtitles work to build even more empathy for them, and by extension, for the monstrous moth. The song beckons the larva, which we see swimming towards Tokyo. After this sequence, the Cosmos go missing. Ando and another Maru-tomo employee search for them underneath a table, a shot that recalls a similar scene in the 1964 movie.[42] Meanwhile, the military plans a blockade of Tokyo Bay to prevent Mothra from entering and destroying the city. They will kill her if necessary. Masako insists that the Cosmos are the only ones who can stop Mothra's attack and she enlists the help of psychic Saegusa Miki (Odaka Megumi) to locate the tiny women.[43]

The film cuts to Fujita in a restaurant with an American businessman. He carries a basket containing the Cosmos. Fujita demands $1,000,000 for the minute women, prompting the American to remove his sunglasses in shock. This scene reveals a few things; we realize Fujita is not yet rehabilitated. In his attempt to sell living beings for profit he proves to be no better than the Marutomo Company. His actions reveal the depth of his selfishness; even if he plans to use his profits to take care of his family, he is placing personal needs before the needs of the nation. Moreover, Fujita's self-interest and profiteering are tied to an American representative. Selfish individualism and immoral monetary pursuits characterize the movie's depiction of the United States and its people. By extension, American influence has negatively affected contemporary Japan.

The JSDF fails to halt Mothra. They launch attacks while she demolishes Tokyo in her search for the Cosmos. Masako, Midori, and Miki cruise the streets of Tokyo, Miki's psychic abilities homing in on the Cosmos' location. The fairies meanwhile beckon Mothra by singing Mahara Mosura, which also receives subtitled lyrics praising Mothra.[44] Music, women, the foreign, and the fantastic—these elements are by now a trope in kaijū eiga. Yet it remains a powerful one; the song here smooths over cuts from the Cosmos to Mothra coming ashore. As Mothra arrives, Ando, upon seeing the car-nage, repents. He recognizes the company's role in bringing about this destruction, though the Marutomo president refuses any blame and defiantly challenges an uncon-cerned Mothra to destroy everything. Here we identify the bifurcation of ethics in cor-porate Japan—the acceptance of blame leads to healing while refusing it leads to more destruction. The president's mad denial of responsibility is childish and illogical, yet his attitude can be found in many global corporations that refute any proof of their contribution to climate change, deforestation, or other environmental degradation.

Masako, Midori, and Miki arrive at a hotel in Akasaka, a robust commercial district in Tokyo. Masako and her daughter enter a hallway as Fujita exits his room with the Cosmos in tow. Midori calls to him. Fujita's expression melts into a smile. He is a loving father gone morally awry. Masako instantly knows what her ex-husband has done and says, "I'm ashamed of you."[45] Midori asks her father to return the Cosmos to Mothra while Fujita angrily chides Masako for endangering their daughter. His hypocritical attack on his ex-wife underlines his selfishness. Midori then comprehends her father is a criminal. Fujita tries to explain, "After this I wanted to start my life over again." Masako asks if this life would be alone or with others. He replies, "I'd like to be with the two of you." She answers, "Well, if you sell the Cosmos it just won't be possible."

But if Fujita returns the Cosmos to Mothra, Masako states, "I believe we can work something out."[46]

This scene is noteworthy for a few reasons. The film pivots on the scene, which is the first to depict the family unit together. At this juncture, family becomes the centerpiece of the narrative. The restoration of the family is dependent on abandoning selfishness and monetary desires. The father must assume a role of responsibility. The reconciliation of the family is also connected with a restoration of national safety—by returning the Cosmos, Mothra will stop her attack on Japan. This sequence shows us Fujita's pivot from ne'er-do-well individual to paternal head. The family becomes a microcosm of Japan's relationship with nature; the parents and children must build a relationship of love and respect just as humans must build a similar one with the planet. Only in this way can a "natural order" be restored.

Fujita releases the Cosmos and they are brought to Mothra, who now waits outside the hotel. The Cosmos soothe the beast. But as the larva departs, the JSDF takes aim at the monster, wounding her. She crawls to safety and builds a cocoon using the National Diet Building as a support. Soon the ziggurat-like structure is wrapped in silk; the image is a symbol of nature enveloping the political, destroying it.[47] The crumbled political landmark represents the government's failure to protect the environment.

As the larva builds her nest, we hear the Sacred Springs cue with strings and a wordless chorus.[48] It signifies Mothra's divinity and adumbrates her nobility that will culminate in the film's denouement. The youthful larva must transform into a formidable beast in order to defend the Japanese people from the threat of Godzilla and Battra. This metamorphosis parallels Fujita's own transformation into a dependable father and husband, one he undertakes at the same moment in the movie.

Ando and the president of the Marutomo Company watch these events unfold on television. The news camera catches a glimpse of the Cosmos, and the president insists he must recapture them. Ando rebukes him, "Don't you understand? Mothra and the Cosmos are special creatures with a special mission. If we use Mothra for our own benefits it will completely destroy Marutomo."[49] Ando's line here continues the moralistic approach evident in this and the later Mothra films regarding corporate relationships to the environment. His words clarify the conviction that destroying the environment for monetary gain is not profitable in the long run.

Just then, the skyscraper shakes and Mount Fuji erupts. The most prominent symbol of both nature and Japan, Mount Fuji becomes an active volcano.[50] Viewable from Tokyo on a clear day, the peak represents a volatile nature reacting to the overdevelopment of land and carefree consumption of resources. Magma explosions and flowing lava threaten nearby villagers. It is as if the mountain itself has become a vengeful *kaijū*.

The movie cuts back to the company president and Ando; the president whines about the failure of both his island project and the one at Fuji. He indulges in self-pity and complains about his suffering. His grumbling reveals to the audience an important aspect of this kind of pedestrian villain. His grievances are petty in comparison to the vast destruction caused by the eruption and oncoming monster battles. The president is more than greedy; he is narcissistic. His selfishness embodies the avarice and excess of the bubble years, a quality now revealed as shallow in the post-bubble era. Ando, discovering his backbone, tells the president, "Earth is angry." He goes on, "This company destroyed Earth, and now it's getting its revenge."[51] Ando departs as we see the president for the last time, throwing a temper-tantrum and saying he does not care. The lack of environmental foresight and concern that characterized (and still characterizes many) corporations is revealed for what it truly entails: immature, inconsiderate selfishness.

Meanwhile, JSDF soldiers and civilian Tokyoites hold vigil over Mothra's cocoon. Miki is among them. With her psychic powers she senses Godzilla's presence. The monster emerges from a fissure in Fuji's craggy terrain. The March theme appears in the underscore as the film cross-cuts to the environmental headquarters. The characters learn that Godzilla and Battra entered the Philippine Trench and traveled beneath the tectonic plate to Japan. Then the movie cuts back to a news helicopter circling Godzilla. In a summary of humanity's ignorance of nature, the broadcaster cries, "It's a creature beyond our understanding."[52]

The Cosmos sing Sacred Springs. Infused with the power of the song, the cocoon hatches and the adult Mothra emerges in a shower of shimmering dust. She departs Tokyo to search for her rival Battra. While swimming to meet Mothra, Battra transforms into a dragon-like moth. All three monsters make their way to Yokohama, a port city north of Tokyo. The combat between the monsters takes place in Minato Mirai, a business district developed in the 1980s that was once home to Mitsubishi Heavy Industries. This location for the battle site is no coincidence; its impending destruction is a critique of hyper-development. The *kaijū* romp and grapple, destroying the iconic Cosmo Clock 21 Ferris wheel in the process.[53] Finally, Battra and Mothra team up against Godzilla. This collaboration helps us understand the monsters' import. Battra embodies nature's vengeance (a characteristic sometimes associated with Godzilla in other films). Mothra, as a counterpart to Battra, represents the beneficial and beautiful aspects of nature when it is respected. Godzilla signifies heedless destruction; he is a human-made perversion of nature and has no true place on Earth. These *kaijū* are more than monsters; they are a reflection on humanity's relationship with the planet in the late 20th century.

Together Battra and Mothra successfully defeat Godzilla. They carry the monster out to sea. Battra is badly injured and grapples with Godzilla while Mothra seals them both in an underwater cell in the middle of the ocean. Yet Earth is not out of danger. The following day, the Cosmos, Mothra, and a group of humans including Fujita, Masako, and Midori convene at an airfield. The scene is similar to the conclusion of the original 1961 *Mothra*. The Cosmos explain that another meteor will collide with the planet. Battra was planning to stop it, but now Mothra will do so. As the Cosmos and Mothra depart a harp plays the Sacred Springs cue in the underscore. A shot of the nuclear family, bureaucrats, and military officials connects the three groups in a triumvirate of social stability that is mirrored by ecological stability.[54] The Cosmos bid the humans to remember Mothra's efforts to preserve their planet. The camera focuses on Midori, who asks her mother if the Cosmos and Mothra will return. Masako smiles and replies, "Sure they will, but until then we must take good care of Earth ourselves."[55] The camera zooms out from its close-up on Midori to her smiling and holding her parents' hands. Fujita, now in a suit, pulls the shorter Masako close to his side, towering well over her. He is the epitome of a youthful patriarch.

The Cosmos and Mothra depart accompanied by the Sacred Springs theme with wordless chorus again. Mothra zooms through the solar system leaving a trail of sparkling dust behind her, intent on protecting Earth from galactic threats. The Sacred Springs motif pervades the film's soundtrack; it occurs more frequently than any other cue, including the Horror theme, March, or Mothra's Song. Sacred Springs represents nature's purity (a quality emphasized by the wordless chorus variation). Its ubiquity in the soundtrack signifies that ultimately, nature will recover from humanity's follies. The music is an optimistic, even utopian, dream for the future. Yet, there is another key point regarding this cue. Unlike the conclusion of 1964's *Mothra vs. Godzilla*, the Sacred Springs cue at the end of the 1992 film does not cadence on a major tonic chord. That is to say, musically, we do not receive a happy ending; instead the melody simply fades away. This was not accidental. The lack of musical closure suggests that Mothra's story and humanity's need to reevaluate its effect on the environment is ongoing. The trilogy of movies known collectively as *Rebirth of Mothra* buttresses this assessment.

Rebirth of Mothra *and Environmental Discourse at the End of the Millennium*

The *Rebirth of Mothra* series generally follows tropes established in *Godzilla vs. Mothra*, though the films vary in manner and degree. The trilogy began in 1996 with *Mosura (Rebirth of Mothra)*.[56] It was the last film to involve producer Tanaka Tomoyuki, who passed away on April 2, 1997. The sequel, *Mosura 2: Kaitei no Daikessen (Rebirth of Mothra II* or literally, *Mothra 2: The Undersea Battle)*, appeared in theaters in 1997 after the success of the first movie.[57] In 1998, Tōhō released the concluding film, *Mosura 3: Kingu Gidora Raishū (Rebirth of Mothra III*, or *Mothra 3: King Ghidorah Attacks)*.[58] This series represents the first time Mothra appeared in standalone vehicles (without Godzilla) since the original 1961 *Mothra*.

One of the most striking adjustments in the *Rebirth* trilogy is the presentation of three fairies rather than two. In the case of these movies, the fairies are known as Elias (instead of Cosmos), and two of them, Lora (Yamaguchi Sayaka) and Moll (Kobayashi Megumi), appear in costumes similar to their 1992 predecessors. Adding to the confusion, Moll and Lora ride a miniature Mothra known as "Fairy." The third Elias, Belvera (Hano Aki), is their dark-clad elder sister and travels on a tiny biomechanical dragon called Garugaru. Belvera has a penchant for mischief that borders on evil. In all three movies, Belvera's actions in an opening sequence precipitate the films' events. The fairies' appearance expands on characters and ideas presented in the original *Mothra*. For example, Lora and Moll also perform a version of the Mothra Song accompanied by full orchestra and synchronized with gestures reminiscent of Southeast Asian dance aesthetics.[59]

In a manner similar to *kaijū eiga* during the "monster boom" era of the 1960s and 1970s, the trilogy's protagonists are children.[60] *Rebirth of Mothra* centers on a combative brother and sister, the second film on a young girl and her two male classmates, and the third tracks the coming of age of a sensitive boy on the brink of young adulthood. These characters are more than moppets; they serve as bridges between *kaijū*, the mystical fairies, and the adult world. The children have access and insight into a kind of magic associated with nature itself. As a result of the concentration on child characters, the films invite the audience (adults and children alike) to observe the cinematic world through the young people's point of view. The focus on children sometimes encourages a heavy-handed didacticism in the films, particularly regarding environmental awareness (similar to the blunt ecological message of *Gamera vs. Zigra* discussed in Chapter 9). Moreover, by allowing child characters to serve as the narrative focal point, the films integrate depictions of post-bubble family life. In a continuation of the metaphor initiated by 1992's *Godzilla vs. Mothra*, the portrayal of familial relations in the *Rebirth of Mothra* trilogy often parallels the depiction of humanity's relationship with the environment.

Another trait shared by the three movies is their rural setting; the movies take place in locations that lie on the Japanese periphery, far removed from the country's major cosmopolitan centers. *Rebirth of Mothra* features the northern forests of Hokkaidō, while the second film is set in the southernmost islands of Okinawa Prefecture. The trilogy's third entry takes place in Fujiyoshida, a suburban city at the base of Mount Fuji, and in the nearby Aokigahara Forest surrounding the mountain. Though not as remote as Hokkaidō and Okinawa, the dense woodland is removed from civilization and has long been associated with the supernatural.[61] These settings act as alternatives to the typical urban locales, such as Tokyo, Osaka, and Nagoya, usually seen in *kaijū eiga*. Thus the films' *mise-en-scénes* orient the respective narratives towards nature and ecological concerns. Each entry conveys an anxiety about preserving the undeveloped environments at these peripheral locations. The movies imply that while the cosmopolitan areas enjoy technological and economic advantages, the less-developed areas must preserve the natural environment, and by extension, serve as oases untouched by post-bubble woes. These pristine locations are vessels for urban nostalgia.

The first movie makes clear this implication. *Rebirth of Mothra*, directed by Yoneda Okihiro, opens with aerial shots of a vast Hokkaidō forest.[62] The sound of trees falling and logging machinery dominate the soundtrack, and shots of forest animals are interspersed with shots of logging machines.[63] In this way, the film establishes deforestation as its focal point. Protesters surround the logging site and a news team investigates the forestry project. The chief of the Hōkoku Logging Company, Mr. Goto Yuichi (Nashimoto Kenjirō), calls his wife at their home in a Honshū suburb to tell her he will need to work overtime again. Mrs. Goto Mako (Takahashi Hitomi) is vexed. She needs more help caring for their two quarrelling children, son Taiki (Futami Kazuki) and younger daughter Wakaba (Fujisawa Maya). Via these opening sequences, *Rebirth of Mothra* draws an analogy between the Goto family's faltering relationships and humanity's dysfunctional relationship with the environment.

Early in the film, the loggers unearth a mysterious fossil. Mr. Goto removes a medallion embedded in the fossil, accidentally breaking a magical seal entombing the monster Desghidorah (Death Ghidorah), an olive-colored incarnation of King Ghidorah. Desghidorah destroyed the Elias civilization, but the last three Elias—Moll, Lora, and Belvera—managed to trap the monster. Mr. Goto finally arrives home late at night and places the ancient seal on a chain; he gives it to his sleeping daughter Wakaba as a present. The seal, however, is enchanted; it allows Belvera, who is estranged from her good-natured sisters, to control Wakaba. Belvera's mischief attracts Moll and Lora to the Goto residence; there they explain the situation to Taiki, who helps rescue his bedraggled mother and eventually his little sister. Belvera manages to escape with the seal, however, and heads to Hokkaidō to release Desghidorah. Mrs. Goto and her children, along with Moll and Lora, travel to Hokkaidō to stop the evil fairy, but are too late. As protesters and a news team look on, Belvera forces Mr. Goto to destroy the mountainside encasing Desghidorah. The monster surfaces from the rubble.[64]

Desghidorah feasts on Earth's energy; he consumes the green forests, turning them into barren wastelands. The *kaijū* is clearly a metaphor for deforestation run amok. Taiki and Wakaba are separated from their parents and must work together to survive Desghidorah's attack. The Elias beckon Mothra for help via song.[65] Mothra arrives, old and weakened, having just laid her egg. Sensing her mother's waning life, the larva hatches prematurely to help Mothra fight Desghidorah. In a rare occurrence, Mothra and her larva appear together. Their battle against the destructive astro-monster implies that a united family (nuclear or national) can combat environmental degradation. During the Mothras' battle, Mr. and Mrs. Goto reconcile and traverse the forest searching for their children. They find Taiki and Wakaba stranded on a burning cliff. Mr. Goto climbs down to rescue them, while his wife clasps his arm to pull him up, encouraging him, "Come on, darling."[66] The sequence represents the moment when the family overcomes the true hardship of rekindling loving relationships. Once stability in the family structure is achieved, it becomes possible for humanity to achieve balance in its relationship with nature.

The film cuts to the larva, who manages to crack a dam (another symbol of humanity's attempt to master nature) and Desghidorah washes away in the crashing flood. The adult Mothra rescues her child, but cannot cling to life much longer. Mothra sinks to the ocean floor accompanied by a wordless chorus singing a variation of the Mothra Song.[67] The scene reminds the viewer that death, as much as life, is part of the natural order of things. The larva heads off to weave its cocoon.

The film transitions to show the Goto family at an overcrowded Hokkaidō hospital. On the news, a reporter relates that Desghidorah has caused widespread damage; pestilential fogs and fires are consuming the land. Vegetation is dying, leading to a decrease in oxygen. Wakaba and Taiki water houseplants in an attempt to revive them. This desperate scene cuts to Mothra's larva, swimming the ocean, a sun silhouetting the worm on the water's horizon.[68] The iconography is plain: Mothra is aligned with the image of Japan's rising sun; the benevolent *kaijū*'s sympathy for nature and its proclivity for self-sacrifice resonates with traditional Japanese values, values that were abandoned during the arrogant bubble years but must now be reclaimed.

The larva's cocooning process supports this promotion of a return to past values. The worm makes its way to the lush island Yakushima in the southern Kagoshima Prefecture. The isle's old-growth forest was named a World Heritage Site in 1993, just a few years before *Rebirth of Mothra*'s release.[69] The larva embeds itself in an ancient cedar tree as the Elias sing a lullaby referencing the natural world.[70] The cedar tree has a long association with Shintō and its branches are painted on the backdrop of Nō theater to signify divine presence. That the larva selects the cedar tree specifically in this location indicates a connection between national identity, traditional values, and environmental preservation.

Upon hatching, the larva, now transformed into a powerful, green-eyed Mothra, handily defeats Desghidorah in aerial battle, though not before the monster destroys vast swathes of the Hokkaidō forest. Mr. Goto, now wheelchair-bound, and his wife observe Desghidorah's destruction combined with the human's deforestation project. She remarks, "This is terrible. What on Earth have we done here?"[71] The camera pans to a long shot of a desolate horizon. Her husband replies, "Nature spent millions of years making all this and we destroyed it in a matter of minutes.... It may not be too late to save the trees and forest. It's going to take many years of hard work."[72] Mrs. Goto ponders, "Maybe when we have grandchildren they can live in a different world. One where people respect the environment. We have to make sure that becomes a reality."[73]

This conversation provides some obvious lessons about stewardship and general optimism for the future despite present challenges. Yet, the weightiness of the situation is completely undermined in the next scene. Mothra, flying overhead with Taiki and Wakaba on her back, sprinkles some of her magical dust on the ashen plains. The landscape revives, verdant fields and wildlife appearing instantly. The "many years of hard work" anticipated by the Gotos have evaporated. Mothra's *deus ex machina* restoration of the forests absolves the humans. They are not held accountable for their contribution to environmental destruction. It is a problematic ending. Though the triumph of Mothra's achievement is perhaps undercut in the closing shot, as the Goto family waves goodbye to Mothra and the Elias. Mr. Goto, the most prominent figure participating in deforestation is physically incapacitated. He sits in the wheelchair while the others stand. The workaholic patriarch has been crippled, but it is through this injury that he is now able to mend his family's bonds and turn away from his career. The damage embodied by this father character conveys the lingering scars of deforestation on the real Japanese landscape.

Rebirth of Mothra II, directed by Miyoshi Kunio, eschews concerns with the family as a metaphor for nationhood in favor of a streamlined message about water pollution. Its focus on children, a hidden lost city filled with treasure, and bumbling adult bad guys brings to mind the Spielberg-penned 1985 film *The Goonies*, directed by Richard Donner. Yet, the addition of *kaijū* and an environmental message differentiates *Rebirth of Mothra II* from Hollywood's many child adventure films. *Rebirth of Mothra II* opens with a shot of Mothra soaring over a pod of dolphins in the ocean. But bubbles beneath the waves hint at danger. The film cuts to hapless fishermen pulling up their nets, almost bursting at the seams with plastic bottles. One bemoans, "They treat the sea just like a garbage dump."[74] Just then, poisonous starfish attack, burning the face of one fisherman with acidic secretions.

After this prelude, the film introduces a little girl named Shiori (Mitsushima Hikari) and her two playful classmates: the rotund Kyōhei (Otake Masaki) and slim Yōji (Shimada Maganao). They encounter a fuzzy sprite with human eyes named Go-go. Two men (encouraged by Belvera) chase the sprite, trying to capture the gold bracelets encircling its tail.[75] The children work together to escape the men only to encounter the venomous starfish.[76] Moll and Lora arrive and explain the presence of the starfish to the children. They relate that long ago a civilization called "Nirai Kanai" existed. The advanced, Atlantis-esque society faced issues of oceanic pollution. Nirai Kanai scientists utilized DNA from marine organisms to create a monster that could feed on garbage and pollution: Dagahra, a water *kaijū* resembling a Komodo dragon. Unfortunately for the ancient civilization, their scientists failed to notice a defect. Dagahra began producing "barem" (the acidic starfish); the barem kill other marine life, destroying the ocean's natural ecosystem.[77] In order to stop Dagahra and the barem, the children must find the lost treasure of Nirai Kanai in the ancient temple that has magically emerged from the ocean. Much like *Godzilla vs. Biollante*, the unanticipated barem reveal that when humanity (or the mythical people of Nirai Kanai) tinker with nature through genetic engineering, they cannot always anticipate the results.

The rest of the film follows the children's hunt for the treasure as the two men pursue them. Battles between Mothra (who arrives at the Elias' behest) and Dagahra are sprinkled between the temple scenes. After escaping several booby traps, the children arrive in a cavernous hall. A holographic image of a Nirai Kanai princess appears and explains that the sprite Go-go is the treasure they seek. Belvera insists that humans are responsible for destroying the planet and deserve to be eradicated. Her sisters contend that humans are also part of the ecosystem and the children are innocent. The argument becomes moot, though, as the temple begins to crumble.

Outside, Mothra is losing the fight with Dagahra; several barem have latched onto her wings. The children, with the help of the villains and even Belvera, escape the temple and see the defeated Mothra. Go-go transforms into a shower of golden sparkles and destroys the barem. A new power infuses Mothra, who transforms into a sleek-finned, metallic version of her natural self and handily defeats Dagahra.[78] Although the film's environmental message is muted by the many action sequences, *Rebirth of Mothra II* concludes with a transparent directive. The humans manage to escape to land and observe the battle and Mothra's triumph. In conjunction with a shot of the children, a voice-over by the Nirai Kanai princess intones, "Children of a new civilization, the future of this planet is entrusted into your hands."[79] The boy Yōji ponders, "Maybe our society is overdeveloped," and Shiori opens her palm to reveal a gift from Go-go before the sprite sacrificed himself to save Mothra. She holds a large pearl that transforms into a tiny planet Earth.[80] With this shot, the film ties its slapstick humor and child-centered narrative into its primary point: the younger generation must be more conscientious stewards of nature than their parents.

The third entry into the *Rebirth of Mothra* trilogy focuses less on environmentalism than the two earlier entries. Yet, taking into consideration the closing message of *Rebirth of Mothra II*, we recognize a relevant theme that carries into the final installment. In *Rebirth of Mothra III*, King Ghidorah transports Japan's children to a membrane-like dome amidst the forest of Mount Fuji, storing the youth for future consumption. The three-headed *kaijū* literally steals the nation's hope for the future, again using the picturesque mountain as an allegory for both nature and Japan.

In the opening of the film, Belvera breaks into an ancient temple and steals a magical medallion known as the "Elias seal." That evening a string of meteorites crash to the earth. A loving blue-collar father beckons his wife and children to watch the meteor shower after they warmly welcome him home.[81] The portrayal of family life here is rare; the Sonoda family has a modest home but plenty of love and the father is not consumed by his job (he drives a fresh fruit, vegetable, and fish delivery truck). Not all is well though. The eldest son, Shōta, has recently stopped going to school.[82] His mother worries that it is because she took on a part-time job to augment the family's income.[83] Despite all the *kaijū* battle action, the true crux of this film is the evolution of Shōta from a shy and perhaps depressed boy into a brave young man.

One of the meteorites destroys a mountain that entombed King Ghidorah. He proceeds to rampage throughout Japan, whisking children out of schools and playgrounds. Shōta remains uncaptured at home; seeing the news he decides to bike to the forest despite his mother's command otherwise. There the Elias call on Mothra to battle King Ghidorah, but she is outmatched. King Ghidorah captures Shōta's younger brother and sister, Shuhei and Tamako. The evil astro-monster also ensnares Belvera and manages to control the mind of the blue-clad Elias, Lora, who becomes his evil puppet. Alone with her miniature Mothra, Moll approaches Shōta for help. She proposes that Mothra travel back in time, to the age of the dinosaurs (that were wiped out by a young Ghidorah). Mothra could defeat the young monster and thus change the timeline. Mothra will be stuck in the past however. Additionally, Moll must use her entire life force to help send Mothra back in time; it will be entirely up to Shōta to enter the dome and rescue the children as well as the remaining Elias.[84] He and Belvera team up to use the Elias seal (that is strengthened by courage, wisdom, and love) to redeem Lora and release the children.

In a cross-cut sequence, Mothra enters the past.[85] There she defeats the young Ghidorah, lopping off his tail. It burrows into the ground, a promise of future menace. Injured, it seems that Mothra will expire in the past but then two prehistoric Mothra larvae materialize and enshroud her in silk. Meanwhile, in the present day, King Ghidorah returns and captures the newly liberated children. Just then, Mothra emerges from a fossilized cocoon. She transforms into a metallic version of herself and battles King Ghidorah above Mount Fuji. Mothra is victorious. Now reconciled, Belvera and Lora use the seal to revive Moll. The freed children sprint over a grassy hill to worried parents gathered at the base of mountain. The *mise-en-scène* unites images of pristine nature with the depiction of restored families lavishing attention on children. Mr. and Mrs. Sonoda embrace their younger children and acknowledge Shōta's transition to adulthood. The conclusion to *Rebirth of Mothra III* subtly alludes to the ideological connection between family and environment while encouraging responsibility, ecological or otherwise, in future generations.

The Mothra franchise of the Heisei period, from her encounter with Godzilla and Battra to her standalone trilogy, echoes many environmental themes of the 1960s Mothra films, but updated for the late 20th century. While the 1992 movie *Godzilla vs. Mothra* deals with the problem of rampant capitalism like the earlier films, it merges this post-bubble critique with a conservative ideology of the family. The post-bubble families portrayed in the 1992 movie and the *Rebirth of Mothra* trilogy mirror various ways Japanese cinema—cinema rooted at the cosmopolitan and corporate center of Tokyo—imagined the restoration of foundational social structures as key to the preservation of ecosystems. The Mothra films weave together themes of the nation, the family, and the natural environment into a rich celluloid artifact from the final years of the 20th century.

12

Prevailing Concerns in the New Millennium

Kaijū eiga did not disappear with the end of the 20th century. Japanese (and international) studios continue to pen and produce monster movies and will likely do so into the foreseeable future. The final years leading up to and following the turn of the 21st century brought with them new environmental issues, and *kaijū eiga* continued to reflect the genre's longstanding interrogation of the relationships between science, technology, nature, and humanity. While many films grappled with matters presented in the previous Heisei-era entries, March 11, 2011, marks a point of rupture in Japan's modern history as well as the history of *kaijū eiga*. On that day, the Fukushima nuclear meltdown began following the Tōhoku earthquake and tsunami, centered off the coast of Sendai in northern Honshū. The temblor, a magnitude 9.0 quake (more powerful than the Great Kantō Earthquake of 1923) and its resulting tsunami, caused the death of nearly 20,000 Japanese and led to widespread food, housing, and power shortages.[1]

The massive tsunami waves reached heights of thirty-nine meters (128 feet) and pushed ten kilometers (six miles) inland from the coast.[2] Among the different cities and facilities struck by the tsunami was Fukushima Daiichi, a nuclear power plant commissioned in 1971 equipped with six reactors. The tsunami and its floodwaters overwhelmed the power station's designed protections, leading to a failure in the plant's ability to pump coolant into the reactors. The resulting explosions and meltdown in three of the power station's reactors over the following days led to the world's most catastrophic nuclear disaster since Chernobyl in 1986.[3] In this final chapter, we will examine how the Fukushima disaster as well as other pressing environmental concerns like global climate change impacted ecological messages of Japanese monster cinema in the late 20th and early 21st centuries.

Gamera Revitalized

Daiei Company's Gamera temporarily ceased appearing in films in 1971, but the monster turtle would be reborn in reboots released at the turn of the millennium. As part of a debt settlement following Daiei's bankruptcy in December 1971, the company's president handed over the rights of the Gamera franchise to one of the studio's creditors.[4] The terrible terrapin re-emerged nine years later in *Uchū Kaijū Gamera* (*Gamera: Super Monster*) (1980). Although veteran director Yuasa Noriaki returned to direct Gamera's first resurrection, he was dismayed by the film's heavy reliance on stock footage.[5] In addition to utilizing primarily stock monster battles from prior Gamera films, the production company also hoped to capitalize on the simultaneous popularity of George Lucas's Star Wars franchise.[6] Theatrical posters for the film feature Gamera in space next to a starship that bears more than a passing resemblance to the Imperial Star Destroyers ubiquitous throughout the space opera.[7]

Gamera: Super Monster proved to be an anomaly, and the monster turtle returned to his cinematic hibernation following lackluster ticket sales and critical reviews. In the mid–1990s, however, around the same time Godzilla and Mothra were experiencing their own rebirths, Gamera once again made his way onto the silver screen. In 1995, the Gamera franchise launched its own Heisei-era renaissance as a reimagined trilogy, starting with *Gamera: Daikaijū Kūchū Kessen* (*Gamera: Guardian of the Universe*). The renewed Gamera trilogy aimed to capture the enthusiasm of Japanese audiences, and fans widely regard them as some of the best entries of the Gamera franchise.[8] It did not hurt that the movies of the 1990s trilogy were blessed with dramatically increased budgets, leading to noticeably higher production values than earlier install-ments.

Like the original Shōwa-era Gamera films, eco-conscious commentary pervades the pictures of the 1990s. For example, *Gamera: Guardian of the Universe*, directed by Kaneko Shūsuke, exhibits several themes and motifs established in earlier *kaijū eiga*, such as continued nuclear anxiety as well as a discussion of genetic engineering.[9] Early in the film, a Japanese ship carrying the radioactive element plutonium, the *Kairyū Maru* (*Ocean Dragon*), strikes a mysterious floating atoll (a slumbering Gamera). This scene provides an interesting twist on earlier motifs within *kaijū eiga*. Unlike the *Lucky Dragon No. 5* and fictional *Glory No. 5*, irradiated by American nuclear testing and destroyed by Godzilla, respectively, *Gamera: Guardian of the Universe* inverts the tale. Here, another similarly-named vessel, now carrying Japanese plutonium, collides with the monster turtle rather than being destroyed by him. The film, by depicting a ship, radioactive material, and an atoll in the South Pacific, also makes a subtle allusion to Bikini Atoll.

Gamera: Guardian of the Universe's two female leads represent another interesting wrinkle in *kaijū eiga*'s evolving portrayal of women. The film's high school student pro-tagonist, Asagi (Fujitani Ayako), receives a mysterious orichalcum amulet that her father collected on the floating atoll.[10] After touching the talisman, Asagi forms a spiritual connection with Gamera, picking up a similar trope linking the feminine with the mag-ical first forged by the Twin Fairies of the 1960s Mothra films.[11] The young, virginal Asagi commands power over nature, a strong contrast to the temptress Woman X of *Gamera vs. Zigra* and other pictures of the 1970s. This reorientation echoes comparable themes regarding the restoration of traditional family roles appearing in the Heisei Mothra films of the 1990s.[12]

The film's other female protagonist, Dr. Nagamine Mayumi (Nakayama Shinobu), ushers in a departure from previous films' portrayals of women.[13] Unlike nearly every other female character in the genre, Dr. Nagamine is a gifted ornithologist, and is not simply included in the film's plot for her romantic connection to male characters (like the classical female roles) or her own sexual allure (like the temptresses). Nor is she magical; she is woman of science. Between Dr. Nagamine's scientific acumen and Asagi's command of the magical, the two female leads utilize both technology and nature to assist Gamera in protecting Japan.

Finally, similar to *Godzilla vs. Biollante, Rebirth of Mothra II*, and the Hollywood blockbuster *Jurassic Park*, the 1995 Gamera picture also dabbles in questions of genetic engineering. The film buttresses Gamera's earlier connection to Atlantis (broached in the franchise's first film). Not only do Asagi's orichalcum amulet and other stone runes hint to Gamera's Atlantean origins, the film provides more backstory on Gamera's mythological past. Explaining to the franchise's fans Gamera's unique ability to fly, the film reveals that Gamera is not a normal animal created by evolution—he was manufactured by the ancient Atlanteans to fight another genetically engineered monster created by the lost civilization. The mysterious disappearance of Atlantis hints at the dangers of dabbling with biotechnology.

Gamera: Guardian of the Universe proved both critically and commercially successful, leading to the production of two more films in Gamera's Heisei-era trilogy. Themes evident in the 1995 picture percolated into both *Gamera 2: Region Shūrai* (*Gamera 2: Attack of Legion*) (1996) and *Gamera 3: Jyashin Irisu Kakusei* (*Gamera 3: The Revenge of Iris*) (1999). Many fans and commentators credit the more mature focus and story of the 1990s Gamera trilogy with its overall success, although the franchise's departure from appealing to children saddened the franchise's original director Yuasa Noriaki. In an interview, Yuasa confided: "One thing I regret [about the new Gamera movies] is that there's not much focus paid to the children's part. It's much more of an adult film than one for children, so I wish they could go back more to that."[14]

Although the renewed Gamera trilogy concluded at the close of the 20th century the monster turtle would not remain in stasis for long. In 2002, the last remnants of Daiei Company merged with Kadokawa Pictures, bringing a new desire to once again reboot the Gamera franchise. The first Gamera film of the new millennium debuted a few years later under Tasaki Ryūta's direction. *Chiisaki Yūsha-tachi: Gamera* (*Gamera the Brave*) (2006) maintained not only *kaijū eiga*'s longstanding tradition of environmental commentary, the film returned the series to the more child-centered stories of Yuasa's Shōwa-era pictures.[15] Unfortunately, Yuasa passed away in June 2004, so he was not able to see Gamera reclaim his juvenile appeal.

Kadokawa Pictures has no plans to let Gamera remain absent from the cineplex for long. As of publication of this book, the first Gamera film of the post–Fukushima era is in production for the monster's (approximate) 50th anniversary.[16] Although the film's special effects are drastically different from prior franchise installments (Gamera will be rendered with computer graphics), the overall storyline favors many elements found in earlier *kaijū eiga*. There is no word yet on whether the new Gamera film will involve Fukushima or other meltdown-related nuclear anxieties, but it would certainly be in keeping with the tradition of the genre.

The Many Incarnations of Godzilla

While Tōhō Studios churned out the Heisei Godzilla and Mothra series (discussed in prior chapters), across the Pacific, Hollywood embraced the Japanese monsters, particularly Godzilla. Two eponymous features, Roland Emmerich's 1998 *Godzilla*, and a subsequent one directed by Gareth Edwards in 2014, gave the saurian behemoth a uniquely American spin. Both films accentuate American military endeavors, heroic victories, and extended computer graphic imagery battle sequences. In Hollywood's quest for blockbuster tentpole features, the effervescence of Japanese monster movies was lost. Yet while a nuanced discussion of environmental issues vanished from the Hollywood films' narratives, some elements of *kaijū eiga's* overall ecological commentary surprisingly remain.

Fans have particularly condemned Emmerich's 1998 *Godzilla*, produced by TriStar Pictures under license from Tōhō; many even refuse to acknowledge the movie as part of the Godzilla canon.[17] While past *kaijū* films occasionally included a romantic couple, they rarely served as the centerpiece of the narrative. In contrast, Emmerich's movie concentrates on a rekindled romance between the main character, Dr. Niko Tatopoulos (Matthew Broderick) and his news reporter ex-girlfriend, Audrey Timmonds (Maria Pitillo). Additionally, the design of Godzilla departed from previous depictions, upsetting many: "Godzilla was not intended to […] be portrayed as a hysterical postpartum velociraptor scampering around Madison Square Garden."[18] TriStar's CGI rendition of the saurian behemoth bears very little resemblance to his Japanese origins, except for a proclivity for maritime mayhem (Hollywood's Godzilla destroys numerous freighters, fishing trawlers, and submarines) and a troubling recasting of his nuclear origins.

1998's *Godzilla* presents an interesting (and disconcerting) bit of legerdemain regarding the monster's atomic provenance. As we have noted throughout this study, in the 1954 *Godzilla*, American nuclear tests in the South Pacific awake the *kaijū*. The monster then attacks Japan, conjuring up the horrors of wartime atrocities and the nation's atomic dread. However, aside from the 1954 picture's obvious science fiction and horror aspects, Godzilla also contains an element of fantasy. Namely, the Japanese are victims, and bear no responsibility for the horrors of World War II.[19] This allowed Japanese viewers at the time to view 1954's *Godzilla* without any deep introspection about their own responsibility for Japan's wartime actions and subsequent occupation.

Hollywood's 1998 picture offers a similar hustle: like Japan's absolution from its own wartime responsibility in 1954, Emmerich's film shifts blame from Godzilla's irradiation to another party—the French. Although France did conduct nuclear tests in the South Pacific throughout French Polynesia, the number and power of these tests paled in comparison to those simultaneously conducted by the American military. Clearly, Hollywood transferred the blame to a different foreign power to ensure that American audiences would not be uncomfortable with their nation's own atomic experiments. The notion of a giant lizard created by the French chomping down fish in Manhattan carries with it significantly less weight than Godzilla's reenactment of America and Japan's postwar relationship.

The 1998 American *Godzilla* also proffers a connection between Godzilla's irradiation and enlargement, nuclear testing, and the Chernobyl meltdown. Dr. Tatopoulos discovers the lingering effects of nuclear radiation due to his research at Chernobyl. The character is introduced studying oversized earthworms in Ukraine—enlarged due to radiological contamination. Dr. Tatopoulos later determines that like creatures around Chernobyl, Godzilla's size and emergence are the result of human activity. This link reproduces similar themes in the Heisei-era Tōhō films, well before Japan's own similar atomic accident at Fukushima Daiichi.

The post–2011 Godzilla features cannot help but reference the triple tragedy of Fukushima. Due in large part to the disaster, the most pressing issue in these films remains nuclear power, if not nuclear proliferation. The spread of radiological contamination across Fukushima Prefecture and the surrounding regions of northern Japan caused panic and fear that tapped into the nation's long history of atomic anxieties. Many people were concerned about irradiated crops and contaminated groundwater, a problem considering Japan's already limited self-produced food supply. Fukushima returned nuclear fears to the forefront of *kaijū eiga*.

The second Hollywood Godzilla film, 2014's *Godzilla*, provides a case in point. It touches on issues of nuclear disaster as well as the environmental impact of excessive mining in its opening sequences. In an early sequence, the film presents a long shot of a uranium mining operation in the Philippines. Persistent mining results in a sinkhole that kills forty miners. The company brings in a scientist, Dr. Serizawa Ishirō (Ken Watanabe) to investigate.[20] His team discovers a cavern housing some ancient, dormant spores, revealed later to be a chrysalis for a new insectoid *kaijū* called MUTO (for "Massive Unidentified Terrestrial Organism"). The MUTO cocoon absorbs radiation and converts it to electromagnetic pulses (EMPs) that cause earthquakes across the region, including Japan. The earthquake damages a nuclear power plant at the fictional city of Janjira, near both Tokyo and Mount Fuji. The sequence re-imagines the Fukushima disaster and the subsequent government conspiracy to obscure the truth from its populace. In this, Edwards's American *Godzilla* continues to draw inspiration from current events and environmental concerns.

The movie also reimagines Godzilla as a slumbering dinosaur. Humanity's use of nuclear power awakens him from an extended hibernation. The film indicates that Godzilla was roused by the radiation of a nuclear submarine, and that the Bikini Atoll and other nuclear tests were actually covert attempts to destroy the awakened monster. The narrative reveals that Godzilla (in this incarnation), is a primordial alpha predator from Earth's distant past, when the planet was naturally far more radioactive than in the present day. Here, Godzilla is not a monster irradiated and enraged by human nuclear tests (either American or French), but a natural force setting the world in order.

However, despite the superficial references to Fukushima and the supposition that Godzilla is an ancient apex predator, the American film presents its environmental concerns as single issues that ostensibly move the plot forward. The remainder of the picture rehashes many of the themes of Emmerich's 1998 picture, following the exploits of an American soldier (actor Aaron Taylor-Johnson) and his concerned wife (actress Elizabeth Olsen).[21] Edwards's movie's enthusiastic portrayal of American military accomplishments recalls other big-budget blockbusters like Michael Bay's *Transformers* (2007) and its progeny. This is not to say that there are no environmental issues relevant to America, Japan, or the world as a whole in the film, but it seems that Hollywood eschewed any kind of political undertones that might estrange possible audiences at home or abroad. Given Fukushima's dramatic impact on Japanese public discourse and other multiple ecological issues relevant to Japan, it was only a matter of time before Tōhō Studios returned the irradiated *kaijū* to his environmentalist roots.

The 2016 *Shin Gojira* (*Shin Godzilla*, literally "New Godzilla"), a reboot of the Godzilla franchise co-directed by Anno Hideaki and Higuchi Shinji, tapped into renewed nuclear fears sparked by the Fukushima tragedy and the government's subsequent failure to act quickly to ameliorate damage.[22] In this film, like its predecessors, the JSDF and Japanese government are ineffective against the irradiated *kaijū*. The movie itself is more sympathetic to military forces than many others in the franchise, excepting *Godzilla 1984*.[23] Like that film, *Shin Godzilla* portrays Americans in a negative light via the Japanese-American character Kayoko Ann Patterson (Ishihara Satomi). A special envoy for the president of the United States, Kayoko is presented as a reprehensible character and an overtly sexual woman, not unlike the temptresses of old. It is only when she starts to feel the draw of her Japanese roots that Kayoko evolves into a sympathetic character.[24]

Like *Godzilla 1984* over thirty years earlier, *Shin Godzilla*'s narrative structure focuses on high-level Japanese government officials, from the prime minister to the cabinet. But something has changed dramatically. Rather than the fawning portrayal of politicians expressed during the heady times of the 1980s bubble, the post–Fukushima film depicts the Japanese government as a byzantine labyrinth of indecisive committees and small-minded bureaucrats. Whereas Prime Minister Mitamura stared down the United States and the Soviet Union in 1984, by 2016 Japanese politicians (many of whom are killed by Godzilla) are portrayed as being consumed by process over action as the *kaijū* decimates portions of Tokyo. While the upper echelons of the political hierarchy are proven incompent, the film heroicizes the low-level government office workers. Thanks to the ingenuity of a group of these hard-working outliers Japan is saved. Altogether, *Shin Godzilla*'s reference to the government's plodding and vacillating response to the Fukushima disaster is clear.[25]

Mothra Returns

Like Gamera and Godzilla, Mothra has also continued to appear in *kaijū eiga* productions of the new millennium. After the success of her *Rebirth of Mothra* Heisei-era trilogy, the monster moth also returned in three Godzilla franchise films of the early 2000s: *Gojira, Mosura, Kingu Gidora: Daikaijū Sōkōgeki* (*Godzilla, Mothra, and King Ghidorah: Giant Monsters All-Out Attack*) (2001), *Gojira, Mosura, Mekagojira: Tōkyō Esu Ō Esu* (*Godzilla: Tokyo S.O.S.*) (2003), and the final picture of the Godzilla Millennium-era films, *Gojira: Fainaru Wōzu* (*Godzilla: Final Wars*) (2004). Despite receiving second-billing to Godzilla in the Millennium films, Mothra and her tiny priestesses remain instrumental to the story arc.

The films of the early 2000s reinforce Mothra's connection to nature. In *Godzilla, Mothra, and King Ghidorah*, Mothra is revealed to be one of three Shintō *kami* that served as guardians of ancient Japan. In 2003's *Godzilla: Tokyo S.O.S.*, Mothra's priestesses demand that Japan dismantle its new anti–Godzilla weapon, a reimagined Mechagodzilla. Mothra considers the new Mechagodzilla to be an unnatural abomination—it is a robot fusing high technology with the bones of the original Godzilla killed in 1954 by Dr. Serizawa's oxygen-destroyer. Finally, *Godzilla: Final Wars* reaffirms Mothra's designation as the protector-spirit of Earth when the narrative reveals that Mothra defended the planet in the distant past from the alien cyborg Gigan.

Godzilla: Final Wars proved to be a financial flop for Tōhō Studios, selling less tickets than any Godzilla franchise film since 1975's *Mekagojira no Gyakushū* (*Terror of Mechagodzilla*).[26] As a result, the production company decided to suspend Mothra (and Godzilla) until the hour was once again right. Although Godzilla was revived in 2016's *Shin Godzilla*, it seemed as though Mothra's potent environmental commentary would need to wait for another time.

Then, the following year, Mothra returned. The benevolent butterfly appeared in the spiritual prequel to Hollywood's 2014 *Godzilla*, *Kong: Skull Island* (2017). The new Kong film, an international production between American Legendary Pictures, Chinese Tencent Pictures, and licensing from Japanese Tōhō Studios, conveys many ecological, political, and military critiques, rebooting the American ape icon for the 21st century world, despite its setting in 1973 on the titular Skull Island. In the film, an U.S. helicopter unit from Vietnam transports Bill Randa (John Goodman) to the remote isle for a chance to violently study its unique geology and ecosystem. As the helicopters drop seismic charges (destroying plant and animal life), Kong ambushes the choppers and massacres their crews and passengers. It turns out that Kong is nature's defense against other monsters as well as humans, like Godzilla from the prior 2014 film.

Mothra appears in a post-credits scene, establishing future installments of Legendary's "MonsterVerse." The film's few surviving characters are shown footage of ancient cave paintings depicting Godzilla, Mothra, Rodan, and King Ghidorah. Although only a teaser, the promise of Mothra's resurrection in international monster cinema is apparent. Yet, perhaps more fascinating is a brief moment in *Kong: Skull Island*; an image of a giant turtle appears during the opening credits. Fans are in a frenzy about the possible inclusion of Gamera in this new *kaijū* conglomeration.[27] Although only a rumor, the potential for Kong, Godzilla, Mothra, and Gamera to appear together in the same film would provide a unique vehicle for conveying the genre's varied environmental messages to fans and viewers of the previously discreet franchises. The possibilities are intriguing.

Japan's Green Monsters

Kaijū eiga evolved over the course of the 20th century and into the 21st, reflecting cultural and political changes in Japan. Although prior studies of the genre by scholars such as William Tsutsui, Susan Napier, Yoshikuni Igarashi, Anne Allison, and Chon Noriega shed light on deeper meanings and subtextual interpretations within Japanese monster movies, they have led to few shared conclusions. As Tsutsui asks, "Can one really expect to find a lucid moral or thematic consistency […] in such a heterogeneous lot of pictures, running from the atomic age through the sexual revolution, the green revolution, and the IT revolution[?]"[28] Throughout this book, we have demonstrated how numerous *kaijū eiga* productions address environmental concerns. This overarching issue unites an otherwise diverse genre.

By now, it should be clear that Japan's *kaijū eiga* genre is not as heterogeneous or schizophrenic as it initially appears. Numerous elements tie *kaijū eiga* together, from their similar roots in Japan's theatrical traditions of Nō, Bunraku, and Kabuki to their ability to draw inspiration from Japan's varied folklore, mythology, and Shintō religious traditions. Most importantly, however, is the genre's ability to convey serious and timely ecological messages to a general audience through a popular medium. Viewing these cultural artifacts through the lens of ecocriticism allows viewers to appreciate the films' environmental appeals.

Over the decades the popularity of the Godzilla, Mothra, and Gamera franchises waxed and waned; film creators re-invented the monsters to reflect the new realities of Japanese society. On some occasions, the genre's environmental didacticism may seem to some viewers as "absurd preachiness" or "moralizing about man's pollution crisis," but these commentators fail to perceive *kaijū eiga*'s rich commentary.[29] Although some examples of Japanese monster cinema's ecological concern occur overtly in plots, background, and character dialogue, others remain deeply buried in the films' subtext.

In the immediate postwar era, 1954's *Godzilla* and its early successors focused on Japan's collective memory of World War II and the atomic bombings of Hiroshima and Nagasaki. While the overriding environmental concern portrayed in *Godzilla* and its progeny was undoubtedly these anti-nuclear fears linked to the bombings and continued nuclear testing by the United States, other more subtle environmental cues also appeared. Early examples of *kaijū eiga* showcased a connection between indigenous peoples and nature. They also juxtaposed science against nature, a conflict dating back to the genre's origins in films like 1933's *King Kong*.

In the early 1960s, Tōhō's Mothra films maintained anti-nuclear themes through the conflation of the fictional Infant Island and ongoing American atomic testing at Bikini Atoll. However, with the passage of time, Hiroshima and Nagasaki's scars gradually faded and the *kaijū eiga* genre began expanding its ecological messaging. In 1961's *Mothra* and 1964's *Mothra vs. Godzilla*, issues of overdevelopment and unbridled capitalism overshadow atomic anxiety. Both films equate human greed and the unregulated pursuit of capital as environmentally destructive. Additionally, the Mothra films added another unique wrinkle to an ecocritical analysis of Japanese monster cinema—Mothra's Twin Fairies channel the feminine, the magical, and the natural, a connection that persisted and fluctuated throughout later films in the genre.

Following the success of the 1964 Tokyo Olympics and the rapid proliferation of television sets throughout Japan, movie companies began to experience ongoing financial woes. One of the many ways studios like Tōhō and Daiei attempted to confront their declining fortunes was by targeting children. During this "monster boom" era, Daiei Company released *Daikaijū Gamera*. When the monster turtle's preliminary film debuted in 1965, Japan's high-speed economic growth period was in full swing, and *kaijū eiga* reflected this new reality. Gamera's first film, like its *kaijū* predecessors, delineated nuclear fears but now in the context of the escalating Cold War. *Daikaijū Gamera* was among the first in the genre to address energy consumption—the colossal

A Godzilla statue peers over the top of a Tōhō Studios cinema in Tokyo's Shinjuku ward. Godzilla represents not only a film franchise, but a globally recognized Japanese cultural product. Godzilla and *kaijū eiga* continue to be relevant into the 21st century in Japan and around the world, especially with the release of 2016's *Shin Godzilla* (photograph courtesy Keri Fisher).

chelonian's lust for natural resources like coal, oil, and fissile atomic materials mirroring Japan's own reckless industrial expansion.

As the high-speed economic growth period reached fever pitch in the late 1960s and early 1970s, Tōhō Studios and Daiei Company once again adjusted monster cinema's environmental commentary to suit changing circumstances. In 1971's *Godzilla vs. Hedorah* and *Gamera vs. Zigra*, nuclear fears largely vanished and became supplanted by a dire call-to-action regarding Japan's perceived transformation from an idyllic island nation to a woeful industrial wasteland. In *Godzilla vs. Hedorah*, Japan's industrial pollution literally congeals into the terrifying smog monster Hedorah, whose sulfuric acid mist and toxic sludge kill thousands of Japanese civilians. *Gamera vs. Zigra* presents a blunt "protect the seas" mantra aimed at Daiei Company's juvenile fan base, attempting to instill conservationist values in the next generation.

Japan's evolution from a manufacturing to service economy along with government regulations ameliorated the country's industrial pollution throughout the later 1970s into the 1980s. With this change, movie producers, directors, writers, and composers reinvented *kaijū eiga* yet again in order to present timely and compelling ecological lessons. Tōhō Studios rebooted the Godzilla series in the 1980s with *Godzilla 1984* and *Godzilla vs. Biollante*. Reimagined for the late-Cold War era, the 1980s Godzilla pictures feature unease over the destructive potential of Japan's nuclear power plants. *Godzilla 1984*'s anti-nuclear message proved both prescient and prophetic; two years later the Soviet Union's Chernobyl reactor suffered a catastrophic meltdown. 1989's *Godzilla vs. Biollante*, on the other hand, manifested not only a concern over potential nuclear disasters, but also an intertwining of several issues dating back to the origins of monster cinema itself. In *Godzilla vs. Biollante*, the dichotomy between nature and science blurs, as Japanese and international scientists experiment with genetic engineering and biotechnology, creating world-altering anti-nuclear energy bacteria and the herbaceous horror Biollante.

When Japan's asset price bubble burst at the close of the 1980s, the Lost Decade of the 1990s that followed became a time of introspection and reevaluation. Tōhō Studios reconceptualized the Mothra franchise to reflect the changing realities of Japan's declining fortunes. With the collapse of the Soviet Union and dissipation of long-standing fears of thermonuclear war, the Heisei Mothra films focused on renewing the Japanese nation by returning to more traditional views of nature and the family. The *Rebirth of Mothra* trilogy posited that if Japanese families and the country's relationship with nature could be returned to balance, Japan itself would witness its own restoration to global economic and cultural prominence.

At the turn of the third millennium, *kaijū eiga* franchises spread beyond Japan, with Hollywood producing their own iterations of Godzilla. Despite massive alterations from the monster's original appearance and intent, the American films nonetheless carried forth Japanese monster cinema's environmental commentary. Following the 2011 Fukushima catastrophe, creators have once again altered *kaijū eiga* to reflect new realities. 2014's American *Godzilla* and 2016's *Shin Godzilla* both return the genre's focus to the dangers of nuclear power and radiological contamination, while infusing the narratives with pro-military sentiments.

Although Fukushima's nuclear pollution dramatically altered the orientation of *kaijū eiga* in 2011, other environmental issues consistently dominate Japanese headlines. Just as radiation from Fukushima threatened crops, so too does climate change affect the nation's ability to produce food for its 125 million people. As Earth's temperature rises, scientists anticipate the quality of rice crops will decrease.[30] Rising temperatures will especially damage Hokkaidō's produce, which accounts for a large portion of Japan's wheat and rice, not to mention the famously delicious "Hokkaidō melon."[31] Moreover, increasing global temperatures will negatively impact the oceans, the lifeblood of Japan. As waters warm, fish typically associated with colder climes, such as salmon, will likely decline in population.[32] Another prominent concern is oceanic pollution, particularly plastic debris. Microplastics, small plastic particles less than five millimeters in diameter, fill Japanese waters at twenty-seven times the global average.[33] These microplastics threaten fish populations and could eventually make their way up the food chain to threaten humans as well.[34]

But there is still hope. Japan's ecological situation has improved since the establishment of the Environment Agency in 1971. Recycling is the norm, not the exception, and it is rigorously enforced. Several technology companies aim to create increasingly environmentally-friendly products, such as hybrid cars and clean energy. Several government agencies and companies have launched promotional campaigns complete with cute mascots in order to inculcate children in ecological efforts.[35] Like many *kaijū eiga*, these corporations and agencies recognize that environmental issues are multigenerational. Organic farming and foods have become increasingly popular in Japan, with education-centered organizations such as MyFarm, Inc. teaching agriculturalists about alternatives to chemical pesticides and fertilizers.[36]

On July 31, 2016, Tokyo elected its first female mayor, the former Environment Minister Koike Yuriko, to office. This marked the first time Japan's largest city had a female leader, and given her devotion to environmental causes, it is a significant one.[37] As Japan's Environment Minister, Koike introduced the "Cool Biz" campaign, which encouraged office workers to dress more casually during the summer months in order to reduce use of air conditioning.[38] As mayor, she continues to maintain a pro-environment stance, as exhibited by her symbolic donning of green headwear.[39]

Finally and most significantly, Japan shut down all of the country's nuclear plants following the Fukushima disaster and has only recently begun to bring some back online. Although Japan was forced to rely on more fossil fuels for its energy needs while the nuclear reactors were offline, carbon emissions remained relatively flat, thanks to popular efforts to reduce electricity consumption.[40] In this, Japan is an exemplar for other countries; conservation is possible through public participation and engagement. Whether this optimism proves sustainable is something to be determined by the actions of the millennial generations.

We do not know how *kaijū eiga* will evolve and engage future audiences. Monster cinema, like the monsters themselves, has proven adaptable and resilient. Given the desperate issues of climate change, pollution, deforestation, biodiversity, and scarcity of natural resources (as well as the ever-present potential for future nuclear disasters), we anticipate the genre will continue addressing ecological concerns. As long as humanity ignores its culpability regarding natural destruction and environmental degradation, *kaijū eiga* will remain a potent medium to carry a somber message to its audience, a message simultaneously fantastic and frightening: nature will have its revenge.

Chapter Notes

Chapter 1

1. For one of the foundational texts on fantasy, horror, and science fiction in film, see Susan Sontag, "The Imagination of Disaster" *Commentary* (October 1965): 42–48.

2. For a seminal study of the anime genre, see Susan Napier, *Anime: From Akira to Howl's Moving Castle* (New York: Palgrave Macmillan, 2005).

3. Donald Richie, *A Hundred Years of Japanese Film* (Tokyo: Kodansha International, 2001), 130.

4. *Sayonara Jupiter* features famed *kaijū eiga* actor Hirata Akihiko in his final film role. He died shortly after the film's release after a prolonged battle with lung cancer.

5. Cyberpunk is a subgenre of the science fiction genre known for the juxtaposition of high technology with a breakdown of the social order; interestingly, many cyberpunk stories tend to be set in Japan—according to William Gibson, author of the influential cyberpunk novel *Neuromancer*: "Modern Japan simply was cyberpunk." See William Gibson, "The Future Perfect," *TIME*, April 30, 2001, accessed July 19, 2016, http://content.time.com/time/magazine/article/0,9171,1956774,00.html.

6. Napier, *Anime*, 41.

7. *King Kong*, directed by Merian C. Cooper and Ernest B. Schoedsack (1933; New York: RKO Radio Pictures, Inc.), DVD.

8. In fact, Kong himself makes appearances in Japanese *kaijū eiga* productions, including *Kingu Kongu tai Gojira* (*King Kong vs. Godzilla*) (1962) and *Kingu Kongu no Gyakushū* (*King Kong Escapes*) (1967).

9. The portrayal of Skull Island's native population is also troubling, a theme that continues in the appearance of other indigenous peoples in numerous *kaijū eiga* productions as well.

10. *King Kong* was released several times, 1952 being the key release in regards to the conception of *Godzilla*. For more information on the release and reception of *King Kong*, see Ray Morton, *King Kong: The History of a Movie Icon from Fay Wray to Peter Jackson* (New York: Applause Theatre & Cinema Books, 2005).

11. Stuart Galbraith IV, *Japanese Science Fiction, Fantasy, and Horror Films* (Jefferson, NC: McFarland, 1994), 9.

12. For an enlightening interpretation of the original *Godzilla* as a contemporary Nō drama, see John E. Petty, "Godzilla: Just Say 'Nō,'" *G-Fan* 99 (Summer 2012): 20–28.

13. We discuss Shintō at greater length in Chapter 7.

14. Donald Keene, *Nō and Bunraku: Two Forms of Japanese Theatre* (New York: Columbia University Press, 1990), 28–31.

15. *Ibid.*, 31.

16. *Ibid.*, 13.

17. *Ibid.*, 140–143.

18. *Ibid.*, 119.

19. In *Chikyū Kōgeki Meirei: Gojira tai Gaigan* (*Godzilla vs. Gigan*) (1972), Godzilla and his compatriot Anguirus do in fact "speak" to each other in simple Japanese through the use of animated word bubbles, but this sole example represents the exception rather than the rule.

20. Jason Barr, *The Kaijū Film: A Critical Study of Cinema's Biggest Monsters* (Jefferson, NC: McFarland, 2016), 30;

21. For an interesting survey of the changes in Godzilla costumes over time, see Robert Biondi, "The Evolution of Godzilla," *G-Fan* 16 (July/August 1995): 24–33. Mothra, Gamera, and many other *kaijū eiga* monsters also evolved as the decades passed.

22. William Tsutsui, *Godzilla on My Mind: Fifty Years of the King of Monsters* (New York: Palgrave Macmillan, 2004), 53–54.

23. Michael Dylan Foster, *The Book of Yōkai: Mysterious Creatures of Japanese Folklore* (Oakland: University of California Press, 2015).

24. Ria Koopmans-de Bruijn, "Fabled Liaisons: Serpentine Spouses in Japanese Folktales," in *JAPANimals: History and Culture in Japan's Animal Life*, ed. Gregory M. Pflugfelder and Brett L. Walker (Ann Arbor: Center for Japanese Studies, 2005): 69–73.

25. Kevin J. Wetmore, Jr., "'Our first kiss had a radioactive taste': Ohashi Yasuhiko's *Gojira* in Japan and Canada," in *In Godzilla's Footsteps: Japanese Pop Culture Icons on the Global Stage*, ed. William M. Tsutsui and Michiko Ito (New York: Palgrave Macmillan, 2006): 128.

26. See, for example, Mark Justice, "Shintō Symbolism in Tōhō's *Daikaijū Eiga*," *G-Fan* 81 (Fall 2007): 30–37.

27. Tsutsui, *Godzilla on My Mind*, 15–16.

28. Sokyo Ono, *Shintō: The Kami Way* (Tokyo: Tuttle Publishing, 1962), 97.

29. Justice, "Shintō Symbolism," 37.

30. Wetmore, Jr., "'Our first kiss,'" 128.

31. Tsutsui, *Godzilla on My Mind*, 14.

32. *Ibid.*, 21.

33. *Ibid.*, 13.

34. *Ibid.*, 13–14.

35. William Tsutsui and Michiko Ito, edits., *In Godzilla's Footsteps: Japanese Pop Culture Icons on the Global Stage* (New York: Palgrave Macmillan, 2006).

36. Chon Noriega, "Godzilla and the Japanese Nightmare: When *Them!* Is U.S." (1987), in *Hibakusha Cinema: Hiroshima, Nagasaki and the Nuclear Image in Japanese Film*, ed. Mick Broderick (London: Kegan Paul International, 1996), 61.

37. Yoshikuni Igarashi, *Bodies of Memory: Narratives of War in Postwar Japanese Culture, 1945–1970* (Princeton: Princeton University Press, 2000), 114.

38. *Ibid.*, 116.

39. *Ibid.*, 118.

40. *Ibid.*, 119–121.

41. Anne Allison, *Millennial Monsters: Japanese Toys and the Global Imagination* (Berkeley: University of California Press, 2006), 45.

42. *Ibid.*, 51.

43. Susan Napier, "Panic Sites: The Japanese Imagination of Disaster from *Godzilla* to *Akira*," *Journal of Japanese Studies* Vol. 19, No. 2 (Summer 1993): 327–351.

44. *Ibid.*, 331.

45. *Ibid.*, 329.

46. *Ibid.*, 331.

47. *Ibid.*, 332.

48. Quoted in Steve Ryfle, *Japan's Favorite Mon-Star: The Unauthorized Biography of "The Big G"* (Toronto: ECW Press, 1998), 159.

49. Takahashi Toshio, *Gojira ga kuru yoru ni—"Shiso to shite no kaijū" no 40 nen* (Godzilla Comes at Night—40 Years of Monster Ideology) (Tokyo: Kōsaidō Books, 1993); Takahashi Toshio, *Gojira no nazo—Kaijū shinwa to nihonjin* (The Enigma of Godzilla—Monster Legends and the Japanese) (Tokyo: Kōdansha, 1998); Takahashi Toshio, *Gojira ga kuru yoru ni—"Shikō wo semaru kaijū" no gendai shi* (Godzilla Comes at Night—Drawing Near a Contemporary History of Monster Thoughts) (Tokyo: Shueisha, 1999).

50. Tsutsui, *Godzilla on My Mind*, 59.

51. Galbraith, *Japanese Science Fiction*, 201.

Chapter 2

1. Los Alamos Scientific Laboratory Public Relations Office, *Los Alamos: Beginning of an Era, 1943–1945* (Los Alamos, NM: Los Alamos History Society, 2008), 53.

2. James P. Delgado, *Nuclear Dawn: The Atomic Bomb from the Manhattan Project to the Cold War* (Oxford: Osprey Publishing, 2009), 61–62.

3. James L. McClain, *Japan: A Modern History* (New York: W.W. Norton & Co., 2002), 512.

4. "Potsdam Declaration: Proclamation Defining Terms for Japanese Surrender Issued, at Potsdam, July 26, 1945." *Atomic Archive*, accessed July 25, 2015, http://www.atomicarchive.com/Docs/Hiroshima/Potsdam.shtml.

5. McClain, *Japan: A Modern History*, 510–512.

6. *Ibid.*, 512.

7. Norman Polmar, *The Enola Gay: The B-29 That Dropped the Atomic Bomb on Hiroshima* (Washington, D.C.: Brassey's Inc., 2004), 23–42.

8. Functionally, there is little difference between uranium and plutonium devices, but uranium is naturally occurring (though extremely rare), and plutonium is a synthetic element that does not occur in nature. See "Why Uranium and Plutonium?" *Atomic Archive*, accessed July 25, 2015, http://www.atomicarchive.com/Fission/Fission5.shtml.

9. McClain, *Japan: A Modern History*, 514.

10. Polmar, *Enola Gay*, 33.

11. Such a wide range of numbers may seem surprising, but several factors must be considered. First, given the disorder at the end of the war, an exact count of Hiroshima's population at the time of the bombing is a rough estimate at best. Second, the horrific nature of the atomic blast meant many bodies would never be found. Third, although many died immediately in the bombing, radiation poisoning left a lingering and difficult to calculate effect on the local population. See McClain, *Japan: A Modern History*, 514.

12. Until this point, the Soviet Union and Japan had maintained an uneasy non-aggression pact, despite the fact that all the other Axis and Allied powers were at war with one another. On August 9, 1945, the Soviet Union launched an invasion of the Japanese possessions of Manchukuo, Korea, and the Kuril Islands, and were poised to cross the strait and land on Hokkaidō as well.

13. Conrad C. Crane and Mark Van Rhyn, "The Atomic Bomb," *PBS*, accessed July 25, 2015, http://www.pbs.org/thewar/detail_5234.htm.

14. "Minutes of the Second Meeting of the Target Committee, Los Alamos, May 10–11, 1945." Available at: http://www.dannen.com/decision/targets.html.

15. Harry S. Truman, *Diary Entry of July 25, 1945*. Harry S. Truman Presidential Library and Museum. Available at: http://www.trumanlibrary.org/flip_books/index.php?tldate=1945-07-25&groupid=3702&titleid=&pagenumber=1&collectionid=ihow.

16. Polmar, *Enola Gay*, 32–33.

17. Nicholas D. Kristof, "Kokura, Japan: Bypassed by A-Bomb," *New York Times*, August 7, 1995, accessed August 2, 2015, http://www.nytimes.com/1995/08/07/world/kokura-japan-bypassed-by-a-bomb.html.

18. John W. Dower, *Embracing Defeat: Japan in the Wake of World War II* (New York: W.W. Norton & Co., 1999), 79.

19. Andrew Gordon, *A Modern History of Japan: From Tokugawa Times to the Present* (New York: Oxford University Press, 2003), 223–225.

20. *Ibid.*, 223–224.

21. David J. Lu, *Japan: A Documentary History, the Late Tokugawa Period to the Present* (Armonk, NY: M.E. Sharpe, 1997), 457–458.

22. Delgado, *Nuclear Dawn*, 149–150.

23. Delgado, *Nuclear Dawn*, 150.

24. For the story of the *Prinz Eugen*, see Ludovic Kennedy, *Pursuit: The Chase and Sinking of the Battleship Bismarck* (New York: Viking Press, 1974).

25. Quoted in James P. Delgado, *Ghost Fleet: The Sunken Ships of Bikini Atoll* (Honolulu: University of Hawai'i Press, 1996), 155.

26. *Ibid.*

27. Delgado, *Nuclear Dawn*, 147.

28. Dower, *Embracing Defeat*, 40–41.

29. Gordon, *Modern History*, 232–233.

30. Mark E. Stille, *The Imperial Japanese Navy in the Pacific War* (Oxford: Osprey Publishing, 2013), 125–131.

31. Delgado, *Ghost Fleet*, 49–50.

32. Quoted in Delgado, *Ghost Fleet*, 155.

33. Fred Herschler, "The Final Voyage of the HIJMS Nagato Battleship," *Bikini Atoll*, February 3, 1998, accessed August 12, 2015, https://www.bikiniatoll.com/nagatolog.html.

34. Delgado, *Nuclear Dawn*, 148.

35. Rose Eveleth, "The Bikini's Inventor Guessed How Much It Would Horrify the Public," *Smithsonian*, July 5, 2013, accessed August 25, 2016, http://www.smithsonianmag.com/smart-news/the-bikinis-inventor-guessed-how-much-it-would-horrify-the-public-6914887/?no-ist.

36. "Atomic Age: The Broken Mirror," *TIME*, July 15, 1946, accessed August 1, 2015, http://content.time.com/time/magazine/article/0,9171,803826,00.html.

37. Samuel Glasstone and Philip Dolan, *The Effects of Nuclear Weapons* (Washington, D.C.: United States Government Printing Office, 1977), 48–50.

38. Delgado, *Nuclear Dawn*, 154.

39. Jonathan Weisgall, *Operation Crossroads: The Atomic Tests at Bikini Atoll* (Annapolis, MD: Naval Institute Press, 1994), 223–224.

40. Delgado, *Nuclear Dawn*, 159.

41. William H. Chafe, *The Unfinished Journey: America Since World War II* (New York: Oxford University Press, 2003), 109.

42. "The Hydrogen Bomb," *Atomic Archive*, accessed August 11, 2015, http://www.atomicarchive.com/History/coldwar/page04.shtml.

43. "The 'Bravo' Test," *PBS*, accessed August 11, 2015, http://www.pbs.org/wgbh/amex/bomb/peopleevents/pandeAMEX51.html.

44. *Ibid.*

45. For a full account of the *Lucky Dragon* incident, see Ralph Lapp, *The Voyage of the Lucky Dragon* (New York: Harper & Bros., 1958).

46. Shōichirō Kawasaki, *Daigo Fukuryū Maru: Present-Day Meaning of the Bikini Incident* (Tokyo: Daigo Fukuryū Maru Foundation Inc., 2008), 11–18.

47. Quoted in Mark Schreiber, "Lucky Dragon's Lethal Catch," *Japan Times*, March 18, 2012, accessed August 11, 2015, http://www.japantimes.co.jp/life/2012/03/18/general/lucky-dragons-lethal-catch/.

48. Schreiber, "Lucky Dragon."

49. Quoted in Dan T. Carter, *The Politics of Rage: George Wallace, the Origins of New Conservatism, and the Transformation of American Politics* (New York: Simon & Schuster, 1995), 359.

50. Cheyenne MacDonald, "Bikini Atoll Is STILL Uninhabitable: Radiation on Island Exceeds Safety Standards Nearly 60 Years After Nuclear Tests," *Daily Mail*, June 7, 2016, accessed March 17, 2017, http://www.dailymail.co.uk/sciencetech/article-3630359/Bikini-Atoll-uninhabitable-Radiation-island-exceeds-safety-standards-nearly-60-years-nuclear-tests.html.

51. Pete Mesley, "HIJMS Nagato," *Lust4Rust*, accessed August 15, 2015, http://www.petemesley.com/lust4rust/wreck-trips/bikini-atoll/wrecks/nagato.php.

52. Delgado, *Ghost Fleet*, 159–160.

53. Igarashi, *Bodies of Memory*, 116.

54. Quoted in Delgado, *Ghost Fleet*, 49.

55. See, for example, *Godzilla 1984* and *Godzilla vs. Biollante* discussed in Chapter 10.

56. "The RIKEN Story," *RIKEN*, accessed March 17, 2017, http://www.riken.jp/en/about/history/story/.

57. Dower, *Embracing Defeat*, 79.

58. Ryfle, *Japan's Favorite Mon-Star*, 21; Moreover, Tanaka himself retained a deep interest in ships and the sea. According to director and former Imperial Japanese Navy officer Matsubayashi Shūe, who collaborated with Tanaka on several Tōhō productions, "Tanaka adored the Navy." Tanaka's interest in depicting naval battles and maritime scenes carried over into the films of the Godzilla and Mothra franchises, beginning with the original *Godzilla*. See Stuart Galbraith IV, *Monsters Are Attacking Tokyo: The Incredible World of Japanese Fantasy Films* (Venice, CA: Feral House, 1998), 67.

59. Tsutsui, *Godzilla on My Mind*, 18.

60. James Kirkup, "Obituary: Ishirō Honda," *Independent*, March 2, 1993, accessed May 20, 2016, http://www.independent.co.uk/news/people/obituary-ishiro-honda-1495298.html.

61. Schreiber, "Lucky Dragon."

62. Author Sean Rhoads observed the model Godzilla while visiting the *Lucky Dragon No. 5* exhibition hall on April 29, 2017.

63. McClain, *Japan: A Modern History*, 539–542.

64. Masakatsu Yamazaki, "Nuclear Energy in Postwar Japan and Anti-Nuclear Movements in the 1950s," *Historia Scientiarum* Vol. 19–2 (2009): 135.

65. Dower, *Embracing Defeat*, 413–415.

66. Yamazaki, "Nuclear Energy," 135.

67. *Ibid.*, 135–136.

68. *Ibid.*, 136.

69. Yamazaki, "Nuclear Energy," 136.

70. *Genbaku no Ko* (*Children of the Atomic Bomb*), directed by Shindō Kaneto (1952; Tokyo: Kindai Eiga Kyōkai), DVD.

71. Yamazaki, "Nuclear Energy," 137.

72. Quoted in Yamazaki, "Nuclear Energy," 137–138.

73. Schreiber, "Lucky Dragon."

74. Yamazaki, "Nuclear Energy," 138.

75. Tsutsui, *Godzilla on My Mind*, 19.

76. Yamazaki, "Nuclear Energy," 138.

77. *Ibid.*, 141–142.

78. *Ibid.*, 142.

79. Eric Johnston, "Key Players Got Nuclear Ball Rolling," *Japan Times*, July 16, 2011, accessed September 1, 2015, http://japantimes.co.jp/news/2011/07/16/news/key-players-got-nuclear-ball-rolling/.

80. Ran Zwigenberg, "'The Coming of a Second Sun': The 1956 Atoms for Peace Exhibit in Hiroshima and Japan's Embrace of Nuclear Power," *The Asia-Pacific Journal* Vol. 10, Issue 2, No. 1 (Feb. 2012): 1–15.

81. *Ibid.*

Chapter 3

1. Portions of this chapter appeared in earlier forms in the following: Brooke McCorkle, "Nature, Technology, and Sound Design in *Gojira* (1954)," (Master Thesis, University of Pennsylvania, 2012); Brooke McCorkle, "Nature, Technology, and Sound Design in *Gojira* (1954)," *Horror Studies* Vol. 3, No. 1 (April 2012): 21–37.

2. Tsutsui, *Godzilla on My Mind*, 110.

3. *Ibid.*, 14–15.

4. *Ibid.*, 22; some sources dramatically overstate the cost of *Godzilla*'s production. Stuart Galbraith claims that ¥60 million was the equivalent of $900,000

U.S. dollars in 1954, while emphasizing that the average Japanese film cost approximately $75,000 to produce. This is incorrect. The exchange rate at the time was 360 yen per U.S. dollar, making $175,000 a more accurate figure. See Galbraith, *Japanese Science Fiction*, 11.

5. John Burgess, "Godzilla Rises Again," *Washington Post*, December 19, 1984, accessed April 14, 2016, https://www.washingtonpost.com/archive/lifestyle/1984/12/19/godzilla-rises-again/39f6262d-796a-47e4-b0d7-dffdb3781433/.

6. Ryfle, *Japan's Favorite Mon-Star*, 21.

7. August Ragone, *Eiji Tsuburaya: Master of Monsters: Defending the Earth with Ultraman, Godzilla, and Friends in the Golden Age of Japanese Science Fiction Film* (San Francisco: Chronicle Books, 2007), 33–45.

8. See our discussion of Nō, Bunraku, and Kabuki in Chapter 1.

9. Ryle, *Japan's Favorite Mon-Star*, 23.

10. Tsutsui, *Godzilla on My Mind*, 27.

11. Donald Richie, "Gojilla Wreaks Havoc on Miniature Tokyo," *Japan Times*, November 4, 1954.

12. For Godzilla's paleontological origins, see Allen A. Debus, "Triumphant Triumvirate: Godzilla's Dinosaurian 'Progenitors,'" *G-Fan* 98 (Winter 2012): 50–56.

13. Ragone, *Master of Monsters*, 39.

14. *Ibid.*, 42.

15. *Gojira* (*Godzilla*), directed by Honda Ishirō (1954; Tokyo: Tōhō Co., Ltd.), DVD.

16. In the course of our research we discovered that throughout *kaijū eiga* female characters are invariably referred to by their given names while male characters are called by their surnames; for the sake of clarity we maintain this pattern.

17. Dower, *Embracing Defeat*, 45.

18. *Godzilla* (9:13).

19. As we will demonstrate throughout this book, journalists and reporters are a trope throughout *kaijū* cinema, and *Godzilla* is no exception. Such characters tend to represent strong, altruistic, independent voices relaying the truth to the Japanese people despite the obstacles they encounter.

20. Wetmore, Jr., "'Our first kiss,'" 128.

21. *Godzilla* (23:51).

22. *Ibid.* (27:04).

23. *Ibid.* (27:24).

24. *Ibid.* (32:40).

25. Unlike in some other films we discuss throughout this book, such as *Daikaijū Gamera* in Chapter 7, the international assistance Japan receives in *Godzilla* remains vague.

26. John Keegan, *The Second World War* (New York: Penguin Books, 1989), 290–307.

27. Noriega, "Godzilla and the Japanese Nightmare," 61.

28. *Godzilla* (49:48).

29. *Ibid.* (50:17).

30. *Ibid.* (54:54).

31. This scene directly relates to not only the universally acknowledged atomic bombings, but also the less well-known Allied firebombing of Tokyo on the night of March 9–10, 1945. See Conrad C. Crane, "Firebombing (Germany & Japan)," *PBS*, accessed March 28, 2016, http://www.pbs.org/thewar/detail_5229.htm.

32. *Godzilla* (59:19).

33. The caged songbirds could also be understood as vengeful reminders of a disturbing wartime sin: the mass trapping and consumption of songbirds. William Tsutsui notes, "The 'official' wartime harvest was approximately 7.5 million songbirds per year, though even the government estimated that the actual figure was at least twice as much." See William Tsutsui, "Landscapes in the Dark Valley: Toward an Environmental History of Wartime Japan," *Environmental History* 8 (April 2003): 302.

34. *Godzilla* (1:00:00).

35. *Ibid.* (1:08:27).

36. Crane, "Firebombing (Germany & Japan)."

37. *Godzilla* (1:12:29).

38. *Ibid.* (1:35:00).

39. David Kalat, *A Critical History and Filmography of Tōhō's Godzilla Series* (Jefferson, NC: McFarland, 1997), 20.

40. Quoted in Burgess, "Godzilla Rises Again."

41. Tsutsui, *Godzilla on My Mind*, 111.

42. Ifukube scored several *kaijū eiga*, including many in the Godzilla series. Even after he retired, future composers continued to use his leitmotifs in their own scores, including 2016's *Shin Godzilla*.

43. Edward Said, *Orientalism* (New York: Vintage Books, 1979), 67–68.

44. David Mazel, "American Literary Environmentalism as Domestic Orientalism," in *The Ecocriticism Reader: Landmarks in Literary Ecology*, ed. Cheryll Glotfelty and Harold Fromm (Athens: University of Georgia Press, 1996), 141.

45. The question of Japan's place in the common East-West dichotomy is a longstanding issue that continues to elicit debate. See, for example, Tawada Yoko, "Is Europe Western?," *Kyoto Journal*, September 20, 2005, accessed March 31, 2017, http://www.kyotojournal.org/backissues/kj-61/.

46. Ryfle, *Japan's Favorite Mon-Star*, 48.

47. Kazuki Tanimoto, "Japan," in *The New Grove Dictionary of Music and Musicians*, eds. S. Sadie and J. Tyrell (London: Macmillan, 2001), 12, 882.

48. Richard M. Siddle, *Race, Resistance and the Ainu of Japan* (London: Routledge, 1996); Brett L. Walker, *The Conquest of Ainu Lands: Ecology and Culture in Japanese Expansion, 1590–1800* (Berkeley: University of California Press, 2006).

49. *Ibid.*, 882–883.

50. Erik C. Homenick, "Biography," *AkiraIfukube.org*, accessed May 14, 2016, http://www.akiraifukube.org/biography.htm.

51. Judith Ann Herd, "The Cultural Politics of Japan's Modern Music: Nostalgia, Nationalism, and Identity in the Interwar Years" in *Locating East Asia in Western Art Music*, ed. Yayoi Uno Everett and Frederick Lau (Middletown, CT: Wesleyan University Press, 2004), 53.

52. *Ibid.*

53. Noriega, "Godzilla and the Japanese Nightmare," 67.

54. William Tsutsui, interview by Brooke McCorkle, September 2007.

55. Ryfle, *Japan's Favorite Mon-Star*, 14.

56. Tsutsui, *Godzilla on My Mind*, 15–16.

57. Joyce E. Boss, "Hybridity and Negotiated Identity in Japanese Popular Culture," in *In Godzilla's Footsteps: Japanese Pop Culture Icons on the Global Stage*, ed. William M. Tsutsui and Michiko Ito (New York: Palgrave Macmillan, 2006), 106.

58. Kobayashi Atsushi, *Ifukube Akira no Eiga Ongaku* (Ifukube Akira's Film Music) (Tokyo: Waizu Shuppan, 1998), 84.

59. Tsutsui, *Godzilla on My Mind*, 103.

60. Tsutsui, Interview.

61. *Ibid.*

62. Quoted in Kobayashi, *Ifukube Akira no Eiga Ongaku*, 88.

63. *Ibid.*, 88–89.

64. *Ibid.*, 89.

65. Larson, *Musique Fantastique*, 133.

66. Many Thanks to Meiji Gakuin University's Centre for Modern Japanese Music for allowing the authors to view the scores for *Gojira* and *Mosura tai Gojira*. These documents enhanced our understanding of music's role in the films.

67. The five-tone scale is commonly known as a pentatonic scale. The use of this scale is a musical trope used as shorthand to portray Asian characters and settings in everything from Puccini's opera *Madama Butterfly* to Carl Douglas's "Kung Fu Fighting."

68. Shuhei Hosokawa, "Atomic Overtones and Primitive Undertones: Akira Ifukube's Sound Design for *Godzilla*," in *Off the Planet: Music, Science and Science Fiction Cinema*, ed. Philip Hayward (Eastleigh, UK: John Libby Publishing, 2004), 51.

69. Ryfle, *Japan's Favorite Mon-Star*, 50.

70. Larson, *Musique Fantastique*, 133.

71. Hosokawa, "Atomic Overtones," 56.

72. Quoted in Larson, *Musique Fantastique*, 133.

73. Hosokawa, "Atomic Overtones," 52. Ifukube reportedly heard this piece while recuperating at a hospital after the war ended. The tune was performed as part of a ceremony welcoming General MacArthur. See Ryfle, *Japan's Favorite Mon-Star*, 49.

74. Hosokawa, "Atomic Overtones," 53.

75. *Ibid.*

76. Sayuri Guthrie-Shimizu, "Lost in Translation and Morphed in Transit: Godzilla in Cold War America" in *In Godzilla's Footsteps: Japanese Pop Culture Icons on the Global Stage*, eds. William M. Tsutsui and Michiko Ito (New York: Palgrave Macmillan, 2006), 54.

77. *Godzilla, King of the Monsters*, directed by Terry Morse (1956; Boston, MA: Embassy Pictures Corp.), DVD.

78. See Tsutsui, *Godzilla on My Mind*, 39–42; Kalat, *Critical History*, 24–34; Guthrie-Shimizu, "Lost in Translation," 51–60.

79. Guthrie-Shimizu, "Lost in Translation," 54. At the time, the exchange rate was set at 360 yen to the dollar, so Tōhō was able to make a sizable profit from the sale.

80. Raymond Burr is more widely known for his later work, particularly as TV lawyer Perry Mason in the eponymous long-running series. Many readers and prior authors mistakenly identify Burr as an American, but he was in fact a proud Canadian, being born and buried near Vancouver, British Columbia.

81. A curious conflation occurs in the sizable flashback sequences. The audience receives several scenes in which Martin was not present.

82. The original version of the film was first screened for the American public in 1982 at a Japanese film series in New York City. See Kalat, *Critical History*, 28–29. It was not until 2006, with the Classic Media release of the two-disc DVD set *Gojira: The Original Japanese Masterpiece*, that the uncut version became widely available in North America. In 2012, the movie was released as part of the esteemed Criterion Collection. This involved a digital restoration of both *Godzilla* and *Godzilla, King of the Monsters*, as well as a new translation for the former's English subtitles.

83. Tsutsui, *Godzilla on My Mind*, 10.

84. Quoted in Marc Shapiro, *When Dinosaurs Ruled the Screen* (East Meadow, NY: Image Publishing, 1992), 33.

85. Ryfle, *Japan's Favorite Mon-Star*, 67.

86. *Gigantis, the Fire Monster*, directed by Oda Motoyoshi (1959; Burbank, CA: Warner Brothers), DVD.

Chapter 4

1. The original American release distributed the latter film under the title *Godzilla vs. the Thing*, a problematic title that not only leaves Mothra nameless but also swaps the billing order of the monsters.

2. Capitalism is by no means the only economic system with dire environmental consequences, but the one most pertinent to the Japanese experience. The planned, communist economies of the former Soviet Union and People's Republic of China also caused widespread ecological destruction. See, for example, "China and the Environment: The East Is Grey," *The Economist*, August 10, 2013, accessed April 8, 2017, http://www.economist.com/news/briefing/21583245-china-worlds-worst-polluter-largest-investor-green-energy-its-rise-will-have.

3. McClain, *Japan: A Modern History*, 571–582.

4. Kate Soper, "Naturalized Woman and Feminized Nature," in *The Green Studies Reader: From Romanticism to Ecocriticism*, edited by Laurence Coupe (London: Routledge, 2000), 139–143.

5. Ōoka Shōhei, *Fires on the Plain* (Boston: Tuttle Publishing, 1957), 14, 66, 69.

6. Soper, "Naturalized Woman," 140.

7. Mikiso Hane, *Premodern Japan: A Historical Survey* (Boulder, CO: Westview Press, 1991), 13–14.

8. George L. Hicks, *The Comfort Women: Japan's Brutal Regime of Enforced Prostitution in the Second World War* (New York: W.W. Norton & Co., 1994).

9. Dower, *Embracing Defeat*, 123–139.

10. *Ibid.*, 346–373.

11. Beate Sirota Gordon played an essential role in the inclusion of gender equality clauses in Japan's postwar constitution, for more information we recommend: Nassrine Azimi, "Constitutionally Sound," *New York Times*, December 14, 2012, accessed March 8, 2016, http://www.nytimes.com/2012/12/15/opinion/global/the-Japanese-constitution.html?ref=global-home&_r=0.

12. Mark McLelland, *Love, Sex, and Democracy in Japan During the American Occupation* (New York: Palgrave Macmillan, 2012).

13. Anne Allison, *Permitted and Prohibited Desires: Mothers, Comics, and Censorship in Japan* (Berkeley: University of California Press, 2000).

14. Jeff Kingston, *Contemporary Japan: History, Politics, and Social Change Since the 1980s* (Malden, Mass: Wiley-Blackwell, 2011), 95–96.

15. Kumagai Fumie with Donna J. Keyser, *Unmask-*

ing Japan Today: The Impact of Traditional Values on Modern Japanese Society (Westport, CT: Praeger, 1996), 82.

16. Vera Mackie, *Feminism in Modern Japan* (New York: Cambridge University Press, 2003), 133.

17. Although SCAP attempted to erase leftist politics in Japan, it remained a vibrant if small voice on the ideological stage.

18. Mackie, *Feminism*, 133.

19. *Ibid.*, 135.

20. *Ibid.*, 146.

21. *Ibid.*, 146–7.

22. *Ibid.*, 147.

23. *Ibid.*, 150–1.

24. *Ibid.*, 151.

25. We discuss these empowered sexual women, whom we refer to as "temptresses," more extensively in Chapter 5.

26. A literal translation of this film's title is *Three Giant Monsters: The Greatest Battle on Earth*, but it is rarely referred to by this name in English; this movie also features a televised performance of the Mothra fairies, in which their song is subtitled.

27. Kalat remarks that the English subtitles refer to Mothra as "he," "she," and "it." This is merely a result of language and poor translations. The Japanese language uses pronouns sparingly, and the movies do not use a specific pronoun in reference to the monsters. See Kalat, *Critical History*, 64.

28. Dante D'Orazio, "Gareth Edwards Returns to Direct 'Godzilla 2' with Rodan and Mothra," *The Verge*, July 26, 2014, accessed May 13, 2016, http://www.theverge.com/2014/7/26/5940259/godzilla-2-confirmed-with-director-gareth-edwards; Jeff Harris, "What to Expect When Godzilla Returns for Its Long-Awaited Sequel?," *Crossmap*, August 10, 2016, accessed April 1, 2017, http://www.crossmap.com/news/what-to-expect-when-godzilla-returns-for-its-long-awaited-sequel-30175; Andrew Liptak, "Legendary Assembles Godzilla vs. Kong Writers Room to Guide Its Cinematic Universe," *The Verge*, March 20, 2017, accessed April 2, 2017, http://www.theverge.com/2017/3/10/14888036/legendary-godzilla-vs-kong-writers-room-monsterverse.

29. Ragone, *Master of Monsters*, 59.

30. *Ibid.*

31. *Ibid.*, 63. Ragone notes that *Mothra* sold over nine million tickets in Japan.

32. Erik Homenick, personal communication with Brooke McCorkle, September 11, 2015.

33. Dower, *Embracing Defeat*, 198.

34. Ragone, *Master of Monsters*, 63.

35. *Mosura* (*Mothra*), directed by Honda Ishirō (1961; Tokyo: Tōhō Co., Ltd.), DVD.

36. There is no "ca" in Japanese, and the name "Rolisica" utilizes the same *katakana* "ka" character as the one used to render "America" in the Japanese syllabary.

37. Moreover the swarthy Nelson (played by Japanese-American actor Jerry Ito) speaks seemingly fluent (albeit accented) Japanese, something more common perhaps for a Russian, given the nation's proximity to Japan. There has been some debate regarding whether or not Ito's poor Japanese was actually dubbed. In the 2009 release of *Mothra* as part of "Icons of Sci-Fi: Tōhō Collection" by Mill Creek Entertainment, it is our assessment that Ito is not dubbed. The synchronization between lips and voice

is too accurate, especially for a genre infamous for its asynchronous dubbing.

38. Kalat identifies Rolisica as a substitute America, but does not consider the Soviet Russia connection. See Kalat, *Critical History*, 62. Yoshikuni Igarashi supports our assessment, noting that the nation's title is a compound of the Japanese pronunciations of "Russia" and "America." See Yoshikuni Igarashi, "Mothra's Gigantic Egg: Consuming the South Pacific in 1960s Japan," in *In Godzilla's Footsteps: Japanese Pop Culture Icons on the Global Stage*, eds. William M. Tsutsui and Michiko Ito (New York: Palgrave Macmillan, 2006), 89. Also keep in mind the 1960 renewal of the Treaty of Mutual Cooperation and Security. The massive protests against the treaty's renewal were in part out of concern for Japan's position politically and geographically between Communist countries and the United States. See McClain, *Japan: A Modern History*, 558, 567–568.

39. Kalat mistakenly reports Fukuda's first name as "Tsinchan." See Kalat, *Critical History*, 61. "Chan" is a diminutive suffix used in the Japanese language when referring to family members (typically children) or people involved in close friendships or intimate relationships.

40. Some might mistakenly assume Shinji to be Chūjō's son. He is not. The movie implies that both of their parents died during the war and the unmarried (or possibly widowered) elder brother has now adopted his younger, mischievous sibling into his household.

41. *Mothra* (18:50).

42. The geography of Infant Island echoes our earlier discussion of nature and the feminine versus science and the masculine. The scientific expedition, in their radiation suits, stand on the barren, masculine peak, while the island's natives and the Twin Fairies inhabit the fecund, feminine valley.

43. *Mothra* (19:15).

44. Igarashi explores the idea of fetishization of the South Pacific Other in these films. See Igarashi, "Mothra's Gigantic Egg," 83–102.

45. This is in contrast to the similar scene in *King Kong*, in which music underscores everything on Skull Island, including "Mickey-Mousing" music synchronized to Denham's expedition stomping through the jungle.

46. Claudia Gorbman, *Unheard Melodies: Narrative Film Music* (Bloomington, IN: Indiana University Press, 1987), 73.

47. *Mothra* (25:40).

48. *Ibid.* (25:50).

49. *Ibid.* (26:20).

50. The Mothra Song is the most prominent motif that appears in *Mothra* and *Mothra vs. Godzilla*. It could be considered a leitmotif of sorts, as it is re-orchestrated for different situations to suit the films' narratives. Generally, though, it functions as a signpost signifying the fairies' prayer to Mothra. In *Mothra vs. Godzilla*, Ifukube creates a specific cue for Mothra that recurs throughout the film. This is discussed later in the chapter.

51. Soper, "Naturalized Woman," 140.

52. Theodor Adorno tackled this idea in "Music and Language: A Fragment." See Theodor Adorno, "Music and Language: A Fragment" in *Quasi una Fantasia: Essays on Modern Music*, trans. Rodney Livingstone (New York: Verso, 1992): 1–8. Other music

scholars have taken up the issue. A few include Steven Feld and Aaron Fox, "Music and Language," *Annual Review of Anthropology* 23 (1994): 25–53; Jean-Jacques Nattiez, *Music and Discourse: Toward a Semiology of Music*, trans. Carolyn Abbate (Princeton: Princeton University Press, 1990).

53. Bonnie Wade, *Composing Japanese Musical Modernity* (Chicago: University of Chicago Press, 2014), 34.

54. Kawakami Genichi, *Reflections on Music Popularization* (Tokyo: Yamaha Music Foundation, 1987), 276.

55. The Electone's ability to sustain a pitch was possibly another reason for its use; the sustain gives more a sense of the vocal.

56. For more on this, see Michael K. Bourdaghs, *Sayonara Amerika, Sayonara Nippon: A Geopolitical Prehistory of J-Pop* (New York: Columbia University Press, 2012), 85–112.

57. The use of blackface is possibly an attempt to recreate the appearance of the tribal natives depicted in *King Kong* (1933).

58. The soundtrack here is an interesting mix of rapid machine gun fire, kettle drums, and very low in the mix, Electone. The "primitive" drums, with the low hollow sound and steady repeating pattern are a rhythmic contrast to the higher pitched, a-metrical machine gun fire.

59. *Mothra* (33:13).

60. Okinawa, a subtropical island, suffered the brunt of a final Allied attack in the Pacific Theater. The island was only annexed as part of Japan in the late nineteenth century. Because of this, Okinawans have a unique history and culture that evolved separate from the Japanese mainland. Over three months, more than 100,000 Japanese died along with 100,000 Okinawans. America suffered the loss of about 72,000 soldiers. See Ted Tsukiyama, "The Battle of Okinawa," *Hawai'i Nisei Project*, accessed August 17, 2016, http://nisei.hawaii.edu/object/io_1149316185200.html.

61. Jason Barr connects the depiction of native peoples in *kaijū eiga* to lingering issues of colonialism and imperialism. See Barr, *The Kaijū Film*, 70–76.

62. *Mothra* (34:08).

63. The area is also home to several well-known theaters including the Kabuki-za, the main theater for the performance of traditional Kabuki theater.

64. Nelson's speech and theatrical production bear many similarities to Denham's Kong show—in both cases capitalists seek to profit from the natural world without its consent.

65. *Mothra* (35:55).

66. *Ibid.* (37:32).

67. "Mothra Song," *Wikizilla*, accessed May 15, 2016, http://godzilla.wikia.com/wiki/Mothra_Song. The tune itself is in a B natural minor mode with a focus on F#. It includes tight vocal harmonies either in unison or a third apart. A semitone vacillation between F# and G, followed by a leap of a fourth (on the lyrics "Mosura-ya") to B provides the cue with a general ABA structure. Here we have discussed the Malaysian lyrics based on the *kana* syllabary appearing in the score for *Godzilla vs. Mothra* (1992), held by the Meiji Gakuin University Archives of Modern Japanese Music.

68. *Mothra* (39:30).

69. *Ibid.* (39:35).

70. *Ibid.* (40:40).

71. *Ibid.* (41:05); Nelson says "Boku no yōsei tachi ga kotoba wakaranai." "Boku no" is a possessive.

72. Elements of this kind of depiction of Japanese women are evident in stage works such as Gilbert and Sullivan's *The Mikado*, Giacomo Puccini's *Madama Butterfly*, as well as postwar Hollywood films like *The Teahouse of the August Moon* (1956), *Sayonara* (1957), and *The Barbarian and the Geisha* (1958). The James Bond film *You Only Live Twice* (1967) continued the trope of the diminutive, complacent Asian woman. Components of this stereotype linger well into the new century in Hollywood blockbusters like *The Last Samurai* (2003) and *Memoirs of a Geisha* (2005).

73. Kalat, *Critical History*, 63.

74. Koopmans-de Bruijn provides an overview of Japanese myths and legends, many of which connect women to nature and the animal kingdom. See Koopmans-de Bruijn, "Fabled Liaisons," 69–73.

75. *Mothra* (1:30:30).

76. Although the term *kamikaze* is best known to Westerners for its reference to Japanese suicide pilots in the Asia-Pacific War, it has far more ancient roots. The original *kamikaze* dates to the late 13th century, when two Mongol fleets under the command of Kublai Khan were destroyed by fortuitous storms while en route to Japan, thereby saving the archipelago from foreign invasion.

77. This cycle of rebirth is also connected to the pseudo-Christian theme in the film.

78. *Mothra* (1:28:50).

79. It is worth noting that Nelson's final action before being gunned down is grabbing and taking a cane from an elderly man.

80. *Mothra* (1:40:00).

81. See, for example, William Howarth, "Some Principles of Ecocriticism," in *The Ecocriticism Reader: Landmarks in Literary Ecology*, edited by Cheryll Glotfelty and Harold Fromm (Athens: University of Georgia Press, 1996), 69–91; Jonathan Bate, "From 'Red' to 'Green,'" in *The Green Studies Reader: From Romanticism to Ecocriticism*, edited by Laurence Coupe (London: Routledge, 2000), 167–172.

82. Galbraith, *Japanese Science Fiction*, 92.

83. *Mosura tai Gojira* (*Mothra vs. Godzilla*), directed by Honda Ishirō (1964; Tokyo; Tōhō Co., Ltd.), DVD.

84. This includes a chromatic ascent from D to G#.

85. The stepwise descent elides from C to B-flat followed by a leap of a sixth up to G.

86. A sweetener is sound added in post-production to enhance the effect of the primary sound.

87. Takarada played Ogata in the original *Godzilla*. Also note, throughout the movie, Junko calls Sakai "I-chan," an affectionate diminutive of his first name, Ichirō. This indicates a very close and perhaps romantic relationship.

88. *Mothra vs. Godzilla* (5:05).

89. For more on the troubling collusion between corporate interests and politicians in postwar Japan, see Jacob M. Schlesinger, *Shadow Shōguns: The Rise and Fall of Japan's Postwar Political Machine* (New York: Simon & Schuster, 1997).

90. *Mothra vs. Godzilla* (6:02).

91. The Heisei Mothra films expand on this theme. See Chapter 11.

92. Interestingly, efforts are underway to revive extinct species like New Zealand's moa, Australia's thylacine, and the woolly mammoth, through a process

called "de-extinction," by utilizing preserved DNA. Similar genetic engineering experiments also appear in our discussion of *kaijū eiga* in Chapter 10. See, for example, Carl Zimmer, "Bringing Them Back to Life," *National Geographic*, April 1, 2013, accessed April 4, 2017, http://www.nationalgeographic.com/magazine/2013/04/species-revival-bringing-back-extinct-animals/; Hannah Devlin, "Woolly Mammoth on Verge of Resurrection, Scientists Reveal," *The Guardian*, February 16, 2017, accessed April 4, 2017, https://www.theguardian.com/science/2017/feb/16/woolly-mammoth-resurrection-scientists.

93. Between this scene and the beach sequence, we receive a brief conversation between the protagonists. They bemoan the futility of fighting Kumayama's claim on the egg given the lugubrious bureaucracy of contestation. This short scene shows how alienated citizens were becoming from the sources of power.

94. This becomes a running gag. Later, Sakai, believing Junko spoke, commands the same: "Don't use a weird voice."

95. *Mothra vs. Godzilla* (13:43).

96. This music becomes the foundation for the cue called Sacred Springs.

97. *Mothra vs. Godzilla* (16:27).

98. As noted above, it appeared in the Overture during the opening credits. It is later revealed to be the opening melody for the cue "Mahara Mothra."

99. Ifukube famously argued for sparse underscoring in movies. This practice allows the orchestral music to have a greater impact. See "Interview with Akira Ifukube,"*Godzilla*, directed by Honda Ishirō (1954; Tokyo: Tōhō Co., Ltd.), Blu-ray. Criterion Collection: 2012.

100. The variation on the Horror theme includes introductory musical material. It features a series of leaps in the trumpet followed by stepwise ascent in the lower brass. This version of the Horror theme becomes common in the later Godzilla films. The orchestration for Godzilla's music is similar to that of the typhoon cue. In this way, both Mothra and Godzilla are connected to nature and its power to destroy.

101. Indeed this tendency is common in scores of Hollywood's Golden Age, including *King Kong*, and beyond. See Gorbman, *Unheard Melodies*, 71–98.

102. *Mothra vs. Godzilla* (41:05).

103. *Ibid.* (43:10).

104. *Ibid.* (44:10).

105. The green portions of Infant Island seem significantly decreased in *Mothra vs. Godzilla* compared to *Mothra*.

106. It also features mixed meter, with bars of 3, 4, a 5 beats interspersed.

107. The lyrics are based on the *romaji* syllabary present in the original score; the translation is drawn from http://wikizilla.org/wiki/Sacred_Springs, accessed April 9, 2017.

108. Like the Mothra Song, this cue features close vocal harmonies typically in parallel thirds or fourths. This all contributes to the sorrowful quality of the duet, though the concluding cadence on a Picardy third (a major tonic chord) could be understood as lingering optimism amidst a pitiful wasteland.

109. The easy exchangeability of Malay and Filipino lyrics for the fairies' songs is problematic. It implies an undifferentiated South Asian other.

110. *Mothra vs. Godzilla* (47:45).

111. The fairies also point out that although Mothra will die, she lives on in her offspring. In a way, the cycle of sacrifice and rebirth reflects the connection with Christianity established in the first movie. However, we think it more fruitful to consider this cycle of death and renewal in terms of nature rather than religion (especially a religion with only superficial ties to the Japanese people).

112. *Mothra vs. Godzilla* (1:06:34).

113. *Ibid.* (1:16:40).

114. *Ibid.* (1:27:10).

115. *Ibid.* (1:28:05).

Chapter 5

1. Richie, *Hundred Years*, 177.

2. Eric Cazdyn, *The Flash of Capital: Film and Geopolitics in Japan* (Durham, NC: Duke University Press, 2002), 184.

3. Richie, *Hundred Years*, 177.

4. For a detailed account of the 1923 earthquake, see Edward Seidensticker, *Tokyo: From Edo to Shōwa 1867–1989* (Tokyo: Tuttle Publishing, 2010), 23–42; the March 1945 fire-bombing raid on Tokyo is discussed in more detail in Chapter 7.

5. Richie, *Hundred Years*, 177.

6. Yoshiro Hoshino, "Japan's Post–Second World War Environmental Problems," in *Industrial Pollution in Japan*, ed. by Jun Ui (Hong Kong: United Nations University Press, 1992), 66.

7. McClain, *Japan: A Modern History*, 562.

8. *Ibid.*, 562–565.

9. *Ibid.*

10. Ryfle, *Japan's Favorite Mon-Star*, 162.

11. *Ibid.*

12. Richie, *Hundred Years*, 177.

13. *Ibid.*, 177–178.

14. *Ibid.*

15. *Ibid.*, 178.

16. Tsutsui, *Godzilla on My Mind*, 60.

17. Although a more accurate translation of the original Japanese title would be "Godzilla's Counterattack," the film is well-known to English-language viewers as *Godzilla Raids Again*, so we will use that title for the sake of simplicity and clarity.

18. Although $25,000 may seem like a small sum, Tōhō must have considered it a boon—*Godzilla* only cost the studio approximately $175,000 to produce.

19. Ryfle, *Japan's Favorite Mon-Star*, 51–53; see Chapter 3 for more detail on the American release.

20. Ryfle, *Japan's Favorite Mon-Star*, 79–81.

21. *Kingu Kongu tai Gojira* (*King Kong vs. Godzilla*), directed by Honda Ishirō (1962; Tokyo: Tōhō Co., Ltd.), DVD.

22. Tanaka Tomoyuki, *Gojira eiga 40-nenshi, Gojira deizu* (Godzilla days: The 40-year history of Godzilla films) (Tokyo: Shueisha, 1993), 304.

23. *Ibid.*

24. Quoted in Galbraith, *Monsters*, 73.

25. Sean Linkenback, *The Art of Japanese Monsters: Godzilla, Gamera and Japanese Science Fiction Film Art Conquer the World* (Gaithersburg, MD: Signature Book Printing, 2014), 104–136.

26. Tsutsui, *Godzilla on My Mind*, 1.

27. *Ibid.*, 11.

28. Allison, *Millennial Monsters*, 6.

29. *Ibid.*, 10.

30. This trend seems to have only magnified in

recent years. The popular children's franchise *Skylanders: Swap Force* has taken Allison's ideas to a whole new level. Unlike *Pokémon*, which had an extensive yet finite number of creatures, *Swap Force* not only features numerous characters, but each half of every character can be "swapped" with other characters in the franchise, magnifying the number of possible creatures (and kindred spirits) by several orders of magnitude. As long as one is willing to continue purchasing new units, which seem to be released with troubling haste, the number of variables is almost infinite.

31. Mothra is generally considered to be far more popular with women and girls than with men and boys. See, for example, "What Do You Like About Mothra?," *Mothra Kingdom*, July 1, 2013, accessed May 20, 2017, http://mothrakingdom.weebly.com/mothra-blog/what-do-you-like-about-mothra.

32. Igarashi, *Bodies of Memory*, 121.

33. "Godzilla, My Old Friend," *G-Fan* 87 (Spring 2009): 8.

34. Ryfle, *Japan's Favorite Mon-Star*, 161.

35. Here, we once again see the use of the "-ra" or "-lla" suffix; Minira is a "miniature Godzilla."

36. Tsutsui, *Godzilla on My Mind*, 56.

37. Galbraith, *Japanese Science Fiction*, 150.

38. Ryfle, *Japan's Favorite Mon-Star*, 141.

39. *Kaijū-tō no Kessen: Gojira no Musuko (Son of Godzilla)*, directed by Fukuda Jun (1967; Tokyo: Tōhō Company, Ltd.), DVD.

40. *Son of Godzilla* (15:15).

41. Humans also benefit from these regions in other ways. The biodiversity of the planet's rainforests provides abundant auxiliary benefits, like medicinal research. See Paul F. Torrence, "Owed to Nature: Medicines from Tropical Forests," *Rainforest Trust*, January 26, 2013, accessed April 11, 2017, https://www.rainforesttrust.org/news/owed-to-nature-medicines-from-tropical-forests/.

42. Perhaps not unintentionally, the Japanese team is technically operating under the control of the United Nations, therefore Japan once again avoids ultimate responsibility for the scientific expedition's actions.

43. This film is likewise known in English as *Godzilla's Revenge*.

44. Ryle, *Japan's Favorite Mon-Star*, 155–156.

45. Quoted in Galbraith, *Japanese Science Fiction*, 185.

46. *Oru Kaijū Daishingeki (All Monsters Attack)*, directed by Honda Ishirō (1969; Tokyo: Tōhō Company, Ltd.), DVD.

47. Tanaka, *Gojira deizu*, 304.

48. Kalat, *Critical History*, 102.

49. The worst dubbing for the film can be found in the Maron Films release, billed as *Godzilla's Revenge*.

50. Galbraith, *Japanese Science Fiction*, 184.

51. Jason Barr interprets the dominant message of this film not as environmentalism, but U.S.-Japan relations. See Barr, *The Kaijū Film*, 96–98.

52. *Chikyū Kōgeki Meirei: Gojira tai Gaigan (Godzilla vs. Gigan)*, directed by Fukuda Jun (1972; Tokyo: Tōhō Co. Ltd.), DVD.

53. For an enlightening look at the life of actor Robert Dunham, the ruler of the Seatopians, see Brett Homenick, "The Last Emperor," *G-Fan* 94 (Winter 2011), 29–34.

54. *Gojira tai Mekagojira (Godzilla vs.*

Mechagodzilla), directed by Fukuda Jun (1974; Tokyo: Tōhō Co., Ltd.), DVD; *Mekagojira no Gyakushū (Terror of Mechagodzilla)*, directed by Honda Ishirō (1975; Tokyo: Tōhō Co., Ltd.), DVD.

55. The ape-like alien race, known as the Simians, was clearly inspired by Hollywood's simultaneously popular *The Planet of the Apes* franchise.

56. Tanaka, *Gojira deizu*, 304.

57. Quoted in Tsutsui, *Godzilla on My Mind*, 183.

58. The third line of the song text could be interpreted in several ways, but we believe this to be the most logical. Daiei's child chorus sings "ka, sui, moku, kin," which would literally be translated as "fire, water, wood, gold." However, these words are likewise the prefixes of the names of days of the week, or more appropriately, planets. Given both the next line of text and Gamera's penchant for fighting alien monsters, this interpretation seems to make the most sense.

59. Tsutsui, *Godzilla on My Mind*, 52.

60. *Kaijū Daisensō (Invasion of Astro-Monster)*, directed by Honda Ishirō (1965; Tokyo: Tōhō Co., Ltd.), DVD. Nick Adams's character is undoubtedly named for original Mercury Seven astronaut John Glenn. For an interview with Mizuno Kumi, see Brett Homenick, "Godzilla's Leading Lady," *G-Fan* 102 (January 2013): 6–12.

61. For more on cinema and the male gaze, see Laura Mulvey, "Visual Pleasure and Narrative Cinema," in *Film Theory and Criticism: Introductory Readings*, edited by Leo Braudy and Marshall Cohen (New York: Oxford University Press, 1999), 833–844.

62. Jane Condon, *A Half Step Behind: Japanese Women of the '80s* (New York: Dodd, Mead & Co., 1985), 59–84.

63. Barr, *The Kaijū Film*, 158.

64. For example, in *Godzilla*, although Emiko is a major character, she remains passive throughout the film, while the male characters carry the plot forward through their actions. Furthermore, in 1955's sequel *Godzilla Raids Again*, the film's female characters continue this trend; they are entirely lacking in initiative, and are remembered not for their own impact on the plot, but only for their relationships to the film's male protagonists.

65. Unlike the Ōdo Islanders, Infant Islanders, or Skull Islanders (among others), Saeko is not a "native" played by a Japanese actress, but rather a Japanese forced to "return to nature" by the war.

66. Temptress Barbella's name was undoubtedly inspired by Jane Fonda's similarly entrancing spacewoman character in Hollywood's *Barbarella* (1968).

67. We will examine these temptresses further in Chapters 8 and 9.

68. For an interesting retrospective interview with Ai Tomoko, the actress who portrayed Katsura, see "Our Living Doll," *G-Fan* 90 (Winter 2010): 10–14.

69. Ryfle, *Japan's Favorite Mon-Star*, 204; the breasts shown are a prosthetic pair, not Ai Tomoko's actual breasts.

70. Barr, *The Kaijū Film*, 156–157.

71. *Ibid.*, 157.

72. See, for example, Jasper Sharp, *Behind the Pink Curtain: The Complete History of Japanese Sex Cinema* (Godalming, UK: FAB Press, 2008).

73. Richie, *Hundred Years*, 201–202.

74. Marshall Crist, "Space Women in the *Kaijū Eiga*," *Kaijū Review* 8 (1995): 13.

75. Galbraith, *Japanese Science Fiction*, 199.

76. Ryfle, *Japan's Favorite Mon-Star*, 201, 204.
77. Tsutsui, *Godzilla on My Mind*, 184.
78. This study, of course, is but another example of their success.
79. Blinkpen, June 11, 2015 (6:57 a.m.), comment on *Gamera vs. Zigra*, "Gamera Is Really Neat, He Is Made of Turtle Meat," *The Return of Talking-Time*, http://www.talking-time.net/showthread.php?t=16931.
80. *Mystery Science Theater 3000* lampoons hundreds of films in fantasy, horror, and science fiction, and remains popular among fans of the genres long after the show's cancellation. In addition to many other Japanese productions, the show's producers filmed episodes covering two Godzilla films (*Godzilla vs. the Sea Monster* and *Godzilla vs. Megalon*), one featuring Mothra (also *Godzilla vs. the Sea Monster*), and five Gamera films (*Gamera, Gamera vs. Barugon, Gamera vs. Gaos, Gamera vs. Guiron,* and *Gamera vs. Zigra*). Several of these films feature temptress characters, and none escape the caustic wit of Joel Robinson (Joel Hodgson), Crow T. Robot (Trace Beaulieu), and Tom Servo (Kevin Murphy).
81. Tanaka, *Gojira deizu*, 304.

Chapter 6

1. Galbraith, *Monsters*, 74.
2. Galbraith, *Japanese Science Fiction*, 115.
3. J.D. Lees, "Mr. Yuasa's G-FEST," *G-Fan* 65 (November/December 2003): 10.
4. Richie, *Hundred Years*, 138–139; Daiei Company entered *Rashōmon* in the Venice Film Festival, winning the coveted Golden Lion award.
5. Lees, "Mr. Yuasa's G-FEST," 10–11.
6. Tsutsui, *Godzilla on My Mind*, 26–27.
7. The suffixes "-lla," "-ra," and "-rah" are all derived from the same Japanese *katakana* character, they have just been transcribed differently in English over the years.
8. For an enlightening examination of *yōkai* and *kaijū eiga*, see Jeromy Van Paasen, "Yōkai and Obakemono: The Monsters of Japanese Legend and Lore," *G-Fan* 88 (Summer 2009): 20–25.
9. Tsutsui, *Godzilla on My Mind*, 15–16.
10. Foster, *Book of Yōkai*, 157–158.
11. *Ibid.*, 160–161.
12. Wetmore, Jr., "'Our first kiss,'" 128.
13. Foster, *Book of Yōkai*, 158.
14. Black-and-white films were considered out of date by 1965, but Daiei Company chose to produce Gamera in the medium to save costs and provide a more forgiving format for special effects. See Lees, "Mr. Yuasa's G-FEST," 13.
15. *Daikaijū Gamera*, directed by Yuasa Noriaki (1965; Tokyo: Daiei Film Co., Ltd.), DVD.
16. Here, we once again see the use of English as a *lingua franca* between Japanese and indigenous peoples.
17. This divergence may be related to the controversial renewal of the Treaty of Mutual Cooperation and Security between Japan and the United States in 1960, for more on this see Chapter 4.
18. *Daikaijū Gamera* (2:40).
19. *Ibid.* (5:02).
20. Gamera's roar seems to be significantly less musical than Godzilla's. Gamera's cry sounds like a

basic composite of a lion's roar and an elephant trumpeting. It lacks the manipulated *musique concrète* aesthetic that Ifukube infused into Godzilla's voice. According to Yuasa Noriaki, Gamera's various roars and snarls were created with a combination of animal sounds and human voices. See Lees, "Mr. Yuasa's G-FEST," 11.
21. This theme recurs throughout the film, usually in connection with Gamera causing mass destruction.
22. Mazel, "American Literary Environmentalism," 141.
23. "1961: World Condemns Russia's Nuclear Test," *BBC*, October 30, 2013, accessed July 15, 2015, http://news.bbc.co.uk/onthisday/hi/dates/stories/october/30/newsid_3666000/3666785.stm.
24. Polmar, *The Enola Gay*, 23–42.
25. Although Gamera is literally an "unidentified flying object," he is not one in the conventional sense of the term.
26. Even if this warning on biological invasions was unintentional, it still serves as a useful allegory for discussing the environmental and ecological problems posed by invasive species.
27. "*Mauremys japonica*," *The Reptile Database*, accessed February 23, 2016, http://reptile-database.reptarium.cz/species?genus=Mauremys&species=japonica&search_param=%28%28genus%3D%27Mauremys%27%2Cexact%29%29%252.
28. Naoki Kachi, "Impacts of Invasive Species on Native Ecosystems in the Bōnin Islands," in *Restoring the Oceanic Island Ecosystem*, ed. by Kazuto Kazakami and Isamu Okochi (Tokyo: Springer Verlag, 2010), 11–14.
29. *Ibid.*
30. Conrad Totman, *Japan: An Environmental History* (New York: I.B. Tauris & Co., 2014), 10–16.
31. John W. Lund, "Characteristics, Development and Utilization of Geothermal Resources," *Oregon Institute of Technology Geo-Heat Center Bulletin* (June 2007), 1–9.
32. Totman, *Environmental History*, 10–16.
33. The use of electricity for defense is a common trope throughout Japanese monster movies; electrical lines are often used to deter monsters from reaching Japanese cities. These attempts invariably fail for various reasons. Perhaps most interestingly, in *King Kong vs. Godzilla* (1962), the electrical defense is actually effective against Godzilla, but it is later discovered that the electricity only increases the strength and aggressiveness of Kong. Later on in the series, however, Godzilla also uses electricity to recuperate his strength. In *Godzilla vs. Mechagodzilla* (1974), Godzilla attracts lightning in a thunderstorm to heal his battle wounds following his initial bloody encounter with Mechagodzilla.
34. *Daikaijū Gamera* (33:55).
35. *Ibid.* (35:00).
36. Jon Mitchell, "Were U.S. Marines Used as Guinea Pigs on Okinawa?," *The Asia-Pacific Journal* Vol. 10, Issue 51, No. 2 (Dec. 2012): 1–9; Jon Mitchell, "Agent Orange on Okinawa—The Smoking Gun: U.S. Army Report, Photographs Show 25,000 Berrels on Island in Early '70s," *The Asia-Pacific Journal* Vol. 10, Issue 40, No. 2 (Sept. 2012): 1–6.
37. *Daikaijū Gamera* (42:45).
38. Kachi, "Impacts of Invasive Species," 11–14.
39. The photographs are striking in that they feature Gamera-as-flying saucer with human-made

monuments symbolizing national accomplishment. Gamera clearly imperils these constructions.

40. *Daikaijū Gamera* (47:55).

41. If only the film had also mentioned an alarming disappearance of cucumbers, the *kappa* analogy would be complete.

42. The Russian's Japanese is much more polished than the stalled delivery of the American scientist. The appearance of foreigners speaking Japanese may indicate Japan's growing significance in world politics.

43. *Daikaijū Gamera* (50:42).

44. Philip Brasor, "Fight or Flight: Narita's History of Conflict," *Japan Times*, December 13, 2014, accessed February 29, 2016, http://www.japantimes.co.jp/news/2014/12/13/national/media-national/fight-flight-naritas-history-conflict/.

45. *Daikaijū Gamera* (52:14).

46. *Ibid.* (52:55).

47. *Ibid.* (53:58).

48. *Ibid.* (55:25).

49. Yuasa chose to utilize the cheaper (though certainly more dangerous) flame-thrower technique because Daiei Company did not possess the optical printer required to add special effects in post-production. See Lees, "Mr. Yuasa's G-FEST," 13.

50. *Daikaijū Gamera* (1:00:45).

51. This is, presumably, Izu Ōshima, an island about 100 km south of Tokyo.

52. *Daikaijū Gamera* (1:12:30).

53. *Ibid.* (1:17:30).

54. Galbraith, *Japanese Science Fiction*, 303.

55. *Ibid.*, 112–115.

56. We acknowledge that, writing as we are in the 21st Century, it is far easier for us to procure and view original Japanese films than it was for Galbraith in the early 1990s.

57. J. Christian Grymyr, "Godzilla & Gamera vs. Tom Servo & Crow," *G-Fan* 36 (November/December 1998), 22–29; Chris Morgan, *The Comic Galaxy of Mystery Science Theater 3000: Twelve Classic Episodes and the Movies They Lampoon* (Jefferson, NC: McFarland, 2015).

58. *Gammera the Invincible*, directed by Sandy Howard (1966; Los Angeles: World Entertainment, Corp.), DVD.

59. Galbraith, *Japanese Science Fiction*, 115.

Chapter 7

1. Conrad Totman, *The Green Archipelago: Forestry in Pre-Industrial Japan* (Athens, Ohio: Ohio University Press, 1989); F.G. Notehelfer, "Japan's First Pollution Incident," *Journal of Japanese Studies* Vol. 1, No. 2 (Spring 1975): 351–383.

2. Conrad C. Crane, *Bombs, Cities, and Civilians: American Airpower Strategy in World War II* (Lawrence: University Press of Kansas, 1993), 120–142.

3. Quoted in Dower, *Embracing Defeat*, 44.

4. *Ibid.*

5. *Ibid.*

6. Hoshino, "Environmental Problems," 64.

7. Dower, *Embracing Defeat*, 45.

8. *Ibid.*, 45–46.

9. *Ibid.*, 46.

10. When Godzilla and Anguirus brawl in 1955's *Gojira no Gyakushū* (*Godzilla Raids Again*), the two

destroy Osaka Castle. In 1962's *Kingu Kongu tai Gojira* (*King Kong vs. Godzilla*), Kong and Godzilla take turns leveling Atami Castle in Shizuoka Prefecture. Many other castles, temples, and shrines are crushed in other *kaijū eiga*.

11. Crane, "Firebombing (Germany & Japan)."

12. Tsutsui, "Landscapes," 298.

13. *Ibid.*

14. *Ibid.*, 300.

15. Jerome Cohen, *Japan's Economy in War and Reconstruction* (Minneapolis: University of Minnesota Press, 1949), 147.

16. Tsutsui, "Landscapes," 300.

17. *Ibid.*, 300–301.

18. *Ibid.*, 302.

19. *Ibid.*

20. The delineation of Buddhism and Shintō was far murkier before the Meiji Restoration of 1868, and we acknowledge that both religious traditions have complex histories in Japan. However, for our present purposes, we do not intend to delve too deeply into these byzantine considerations, instead considering the religious traditions as they are commonly practiced in Japan in the modern era. See, for example, John Breen and Mark Teeuwen, *A New History of Shintō* (Chichester, UK: Wiley-Blackwell, 2010); Kenji Matsuo, *A History of Japanese Buddhism* (Folkestone, UK: Global Oriental, 2007).

21. Ono, *Shintō*, 97–102.

22. Wetmore, Jr., "'Our first kiss,'" 128.

23. *Gojira, Mosura, Kingu Gidora: Daikaijū Sōkōgeki* (*Godzilla, Mothra, and King Ghidorah: Giant Monsters All-Out Attack*), directed by Kaneko Shūsuke (2001; Tokyo: Tōhō Co., Ltd.), DVD.

24. For more on the deep connection between nature and Shintō, we recommend William Coaldrake, *Architecture and Authority in Japan* (New York: Routledge, 1996), 16–51.

25. We noted earlier that Meiji Shrine was destroyed by Allied bombings in World War II. It was rebuilt in 1958.

26. Ono, *Shintō*, 97–102.

27. Tsutsui, "Landscapes," 299.

28. Breen and Teeuwen, *A New History*, 7–13.

29. Dower, *Embracing Defeat*, 82.

30. Breen and Teeuwen, *A New History*, 13.

31. Dower, *Embracing Defeat*, 73–84.

32. Hoshino, "Environmental Problems," 65.

33. Gordon, *Modern History*, 246–248.

34. J.R. McNeill, *Something New Under the Sun: An Environmental History of the Twentieth-Century World* (New York: W.W. Norton & Co., 2000), 96.

35. Hoshino, "Environmental Problems," 66.

36. Totman, *Environmental History*, 9–10.

37. *Ibid.*

38. Hoshino, "Environmental Problems," 66.

39. *Ibid.*, 71.

40. *Ibid.*, 67.

41. Totman, *Environmental History*, 303.

42. Hoshino, "Environmental Problems," 67.

43. Totman, *Environmental History*, 305.

44. Quoted in McNeill, *Something New Under the Sun*, 93.

45. Hoshino, "Environmental Problems," 69.

46. *Ibid.*, 75.

47. Brett L. Walker, *Toxic Archipelago: A History of Industrial Disease in Japan* (Seattle: University of Washington Press, 2010), 127–136.

48. *Ibid.*, 210.

49. Akio Mishima, *Bitter Sea: The Human Cost of Minamata Disease* (Tokyo: Kosei Publishing Co., 1992).

50. Hoshino, "Environmental Problems," 70.

51. Mishima, *Bitter Sea*, 43.

52. *Ibid.*, 73–88.

53. Walker, *Toxic Archipelago*, 147.

54. Ministry of the Environment, "Outbreak & Cause," *Minamata Disease Archives*, accessed October 30, 2015, http://www.nimd.go.jp/archives/english/tenji/e_corner/qa1/1top.html.

55. Central Intelligence Agency, "Field Listing: Coastline," *The World Factbook*, accessed October 30, 2015, https://www.cia.gov/library/publications/the-world-factbook/fields/2060.html.

56. Jeffrey Hays, "Commercial Fishing in Japan: Fishing Industry, Fish Farms and Fishermen," *Facts and Details*, accessed October 29, 2015, http://factsanddetails.com/japan/cat24/sub159/item937.html. In the premodern era, this was even truer, as Buddhist and Shintō beliefs in addition to cultural taboos proscribed the eating of meat from four-legged animals, greatly limiting available sources of protein. Ishige Naomichi, "Food: Another Perspective on Japanese Cultural History," *Nipponia*, March 15, 2006, accessed December 3, 2015, http://web-japan.org/nipponia/nipponia36/en/feature/feature01.html.

57. Totman, *Environmental History*, 266.

58. *Ibid.*, 264.

59. Quoted in Totman, *Environmental History*, 264.

60. Miranda Alice Schreurs, "Democratic Transition and Environmental Civil Society: Japan and South Korea Compared," *The Good Society* Vol. 11, No. 2 (2002): 59.

61. Totman, *Environmental History*, 267.

62. *Ibid.*

63. Nobuko Iijima (edit.), *Pollution Japan: Historical Chronology* (Elmsford, NY: Pergamon Press, 1979), 336.

64. Hoshino, "Environmental Problems," 71.

65. See Chapter 4. Another such landfill project is also depicted in 1989's *Godzilla vs. Biollante* (the construction of Osaka's new offshore international airport), and is noted in Chapter 10.

66. Coincidentally, one such land reclamation project intersects many different issues and events discussed in this book. Tokyo's Yumenoshima (literally "dream island"), an artificial isle created in Tokyo Bay, was originally planned as a site for a new airport to replace the noisy and much-loathed Haneda Airport destroyed in *Daikaijū Gamera*. Since 1976, a park on the island has hosted the museum dedicated to the *Lucky Dragon No. 5*, the unfortunate Japanese fishing trawler irradiated by the American Castle Bravo H-bomb test at Bikini Atoll and featured so prominently in *Godzilla*. Finally, in the 21st century, portions of the artificial island were repurposed as the Shin-Kōtō garbage incineration plant and as sites for the 2020 Tokyo Olympics.

67. Totman, *Environmental History*, 268.

68. Iijima, *Pollution Japan*, 278.

69. Totman, *Environmental History*, 268.

70. Iijima, *Pollution Japan*, 386.

71. Totman, *Environmental History*, 268.

72. McNeill, *Something New Under the Sun*, 97.

73. Miki Takeo, "Foreword," *Japan Environment Summary* Vol. 1, No. 1 (June 1973): 1.

74. "Public Opinion Survey on Environmental Pollution," *Japan Environment Summary* Vol. 2, No. 1 (January 1974): 2.

75. Schreurs, "Democratic Transition," 59.

76. Timothy George, *Minamata: Pollution and the Struggle for Democracy in Postwar Japan* (Cambridge, MA: Harvard University Press, 2001).

77. Schreurs, "Democratic Transition," 59.

78. Totman, *Environmental History*, 269.

79. *Ibid.*

80. *Ibid.*, 265.

Chapter 8

1. Portions of this chapter appeared in earlier forms in the following: Sean Rhoads, "Godzilla the Social Critic: *Kaijū Eiga* and 1970s Japanese Environmentalism," (Honors Thesis, Dickinson College, 2007); Sean Rhoads, "Godzilla the Social Critic: Big 'Green' Monsters and Environmental Commentary in Japanese *Kaijū Eiga* of the 1970s," (Masters Thesis, University of Pennsylvania, 2010); Sean Rhoads, "Godzilla the Social Critic: Part 1," *G-Fan* 97 (Fall 2011): 26–34; Sean Rhoads, "Godzilla the Social Critic: Part 2," *G-Fan* 98 (Winter 2012): 18–28.

2. Galbraith, *Japanese Science Fiction*, 201–204; Kalat, *Critical History*, 112–118.

3. Tsutsui, *Godzilla on My Mind*, 61.

4. Some writers have briefly examined *Godzilla vs. Hedorah*'s ecological message. See, for example, Max Della Mora, "*Godzilla vs. the Smog Monster*: A Fond Look Back," *G-Fan* 25 (January/February 1997), 40–41; Mark Justice, "Save the Earth! Part 2," *G-Fan* 95 (Spring 2011), 20–29.

5. Tsutsui, *Godzilla on My Mind*, 61; Ryfle, *Japan's Favorite Mon-Star*, 162; Kalat, *Critical History*, 118.

6. Harry Medved with Randy Dreyfuss, *The Fifty Worst Films of All Time (And How They Got That Way)* (New York: Popular Library, 1978), 89–93.

7. Quoted in Medved, *Fifty Worst Films*, 89.

8. Medved, *Fifty Worst Films*, 91.

9. *Ibid.*, 93.

10. Banno Yoshimitsu, *Gojira wo tobashita otoko (The Man Who Flew Godzilla)* (Tokyo: Sentan Eizo Kenkyusho, 2014), Kindle edition location 1184–1188; Banno also cites an earlier version of this study to counter his film's inclusion on Medved's list, see Kindle edition location 1191.

11. Ryfle, *Japan's Favorite Mon-Star*, 161–166.

12. Galbraith, *Japanese Science Fiction*, 201.

13. Takahashi, *Gojira no nazo*, 247.

14. Jorg Buttgereit, "Whatever Happened to Yoshimitsu Banno?" *G-Fan* 60 (January/February 2003): 18–20.

15. *Ibid.*

16. Ragone, *Master of Monsters*, 174–175.

17. Banno Yoshimitsu, interview by J.R. Lipartito, "Smog Monster Director EXTRA," *SciFi Japan TV*, September 11, 2014, https://www.youtube.com/watch?v=N1dL7lA7bss&list=UUU03keCaesfRWZPYV1FUxXw.

18. Tim Smith and Yoko Kobayashi, "Yoshimitsu Banno: Behind Hedorah," *Sake-drenched Postcards*, accessed January 20, 2007, http://www.bigempire.com/sake/smog_monster.html.

19. Kalat, *Critical History*, 117.

20. Ryfle, *Japan's Favorite Mon-Star*, 162–163.

21. For more on the popularity of folk music and Group Sounds in the late 1960s, see Bourdaghs, *Sayonara Amerika*, 113–158.

22. Galbraith, *Japanese Science Fiction*, 203.

23. Kalat, *Critical History*, 113.

24. Buttgereit, "Whatever Happened," 19.

25. Banno, *Gojira wo tobashita otoko*, Kindle edition location 951.

26. Quoted in Ryfle, *Japan's Favorite Mon-Star*, 164.

27. Quoted in Smith and Kobayashi, "Yoshimitsu Banno."

28. Banno, *Gojira wo tobashita otoko*, Kindle edition location 967–968.

29. Banno, "Smog Monster Director EXTRA," *SciFi Japan TV*.

30. Brett Homenick, "The Man Who Made Godzilla Fly," *G-Fan* 73 (Fall 2005): 8–15.

31. *Gojira tai Hedora* (*Godzilla vs. Hedorah*), directed by Banno Yoshimitsu (1971; Tokyo: Tōhō Co., Ltd.), DVD.

32. Earlier, we noted the penchant of Japanese *kaijū* to attack and sink fishing vessels and other ships. Hedorah continues this trope by sinking an oil tanker. See Chapter 2.

33. Smith and Kobayashi, "Yoshimitsu Banno."

34. Banno, *Gojira wo tobashita otoko*, Kindle edition location 1133.

35. The song's official title in Japanese is "Kaese! Taiyō wo!" Many readers may be more familiar with AIP's dubbed English-language song "Save the Earth!" For an interesting interview with the American singer of that version who helped transform the song from the Japanese original, see Brett Homenick, "Singing for the Smog Monster," *G-Fan* 81 (Fall 2007): 10–11.

36. *Godzilla vs. Hedorah* (0:57).

37. *Ibid.* (2:40).

38. *Ibid.* (2:55).

39. Stuart Galbraith believes the inclusion of the figurines is an example of "shameless self-promotion," but we disagree. See Galbraith, *Japanese Science Fiction*, 201.

40. *Godzilla vs. Hedorah* (51:50).

41. *Ibid.* (14:45).

42. For more on Dr. Serizawa and his oxygen-destroyer, see Chapter 3.

43. *Godzilla vs. Hedorah* (13:36).

44. Written Japanese utilizes four different writing systems—*hiragana* (simple native Japanese script), *katakana* (native Japanese script for transcribing foreign words and sounds), *kanji* (imported Chinese characters), and *romaji* (occasionally used Latin alphabet).

45. Smith and Kobayashi, "Yoshimitsu Banno."

46. Quoted in Buttgereit, "Whatever Happened," 19.

47. *Godzilla vs. Hedorah* (30:35).

48. *Ibid.* (11:48).

49. *Ibid.* (42:20).

50. *Ibid.* (17:28).

51. Ryfle, *Japan's Favorite Mon-Star*, 164.

52. *Godzilla vs. Hedorah* (41:40).

53. *Ibid.* (57:25).

54. *Ibid.* (21:10).

55. Banno, "Smog Monster Director EXTRA," *SciFi Japan TV*; McNeill, *Something New Under the Sun*, 96–97.

56. *Godzilla vs. Hedorah* (54:15).

57. Tsutsui, *Godzilla on My Mind*, 56.

58. *Godzilla vs. Hedorah* (1:19:00).

59. *Ibid.* (19:08).

60. The *mise-en-scène* and music combine to create an effect reminiscent of Jefferson Airplane's 1967 performance of "White Rabbit" on *The Smothers Brothers Comedy Hour*. Available at: https://www.youtube.com/watch?v=WANNqr-vcx0, accessed August 21, 2016.

61. Banno, "Smog Monster Director EXTRA," *SciFi Japan TV*.

62. *Ibid.*

63. *Godzilla vs. Hedorah* (19:15).

64. *Ibid.* (45:00).

65. Earlier in the film, the government announced a ban on automobile travel. The hippies ignore this pollution-control edict. Moreover, the bohemians ignite a massive bonfire. Taken together, these actions show little concern for the hippies' own contribution to Japan's pollution problems.

66. *Godzilla vs. Hedorah* (49:40).

67. *Ibid.* (34:30).

68. Both Miki and Dr. Yano's wife Toshie are depicted far worse in the dubbed versions of the film. Both have lines that stand as complete *non sequiturs* as well as other idiotic or oblivious statements. The majority of this dialogue is a result of poor dubbing and attempts to match English-language lines with the characters' lips.

69. Tanaka, *Gojira deizu*, 304; Smith and Kobayashi, "Yoshimitsu Banno."

70. Quoted in Ryfle, *Japan's Favorite Mon-Star*, 165.

71. Banno, "Smog Monster Director EXTRA," *SciFi Japan TV*.

72. Smith and Kobayashi, "Yoshimitsu Banno."

73. Banno, "Smog Monster Director EXTRA," *SciFi Japan TV*.

74. *Godzilla* (2014), directed by Gareth Edwards (2014; Burbank, CA: Legendary Pictures), Blu-ray.

75. Gavin J. Blair, "'Godzilla vs. the Smog Monster' Director Yoshimitsu Banno Dies at 86," *Hollywood Reporter*, May 12, 2017, accessed May 21, 2017, http://www.hollywoodreporter.com/news/godzilla-smog-monster-director-yoshimitsu-banno-dies-at-86–1003092.

76. Vincent Canby, "Stop Kidding Around!" *New York Times*, July 23, 1972.

77. Tsutsui, *Godzilla on My Mind*, 171.

78. Linkenback, *Art of Japanese Monsters*, 161–163.

79. "Godzilla vs. the Smog Monster," *Famous Monsters of Filmland* 91 (July 1972): 5, 26–31.

80. Vincent Canby, "A Midsummer Night's Screams," *New York Times*, June 24, 1979.

81. Banno, *Gojira wo tobashita otoko*, Kindle edition location 1015–1016.

Chapter 9

1. The literal translation of the film's title is "Gamera vs. Deep Sea Monster Jigura," but the film is exclusively known as *Gamera vs. Zigra* to English-language audiences; there is an inherent joke in the name "Jigura" in Japanese—it is a rearrangement of the same characters for the word for whale, *kujira* ("ku" and "gu" are variations of the same *hiragana* character), alluding to both Zigra's shark-like nature as well as the origin of Godzilla's own name.

2. "Essential Gamera: A Primer on the Flying G's Eleven Films," *G-Fan* 61 (March/April 2003): 36–39.

3. Lees, "Mr. Yuasa's G-FEST," 13.

4. *Gamera vs. Barugon* is occasionally known by the title *War of the Monsters*, the name of its original release in North America.

5. Galbraith, *Monsters*, 74.

6. Quoted in David Milner, "Noriaki Yuasa Interview," *Kaijū Conversations*, July 1996, accessed July 13, 2016, http://www.davmil.org/www.kaijuconversations.com/yuasa.htm.

7. *Ibid.*

8. "Essential Gamera," 36–38.

9. *Gamera vs. Guiron* is alternately known as *Attack of the Monsters* to English-language audiences. It is also worth noting that the Japanese title refers to Guiron not as a *daikaijū*, but as a *daiakujū* or "giant evil beast." Finally, one cannot help but wonder (and assume) that temptress Barbella's name was inspired by Jane Fonda's similarly entrancing spacewoman in 1968's *Barbarella*.

10. *Gamera tai Daiakujū Giron* (*Gamera vs. Guiron*), directed by Yuasa Noriaki (1969; Tokyo: Daiei Film Co., Ltd.), DVD.

11. Quoted in Galbraith, *Monsters*, 74.

12. Galbraith, *Monsters*, 74.

13. *Ibid.*, 92.

14. Lees, "Mr. Yuasa's G-FEST," 12.

15. Brett Homenick, "Gamera's Gals," *G-Fan* 83 (Spring 2008): 16–19.

16. *Gamera tai Shinkai Kaijū Jigura* (*Gamera vs. Zigra*), directed by Yuasa Noriaki (1971; Tokyo: Daiei Film Co., Ltd.), DVD.

17. *Ibid.* (1:30).

18. It is unusual, to say the least, that Dr. Tom Wallace is played by decidedly Japanese actor Fujiyama Kōji.

19. Several sources report that the role of Helen was played by Arlene Zoellner, but this incorrect. Arlene was originally cast for the role, but was replaced in favor of her younger sister Gloria Zoellner. Arlene was then added to the script as Helen's older sister. See Homenick, "Gamera's Gals," 16–19; Kasahara Reiko, formerly the cannibalistic spacewoman Florbella in *Gamera vs. Guiron*, reappears in a different role in *Gamera vs. Zigra*. Far from desiring children's brains, she plays the younger sister of Dr. Ishikawa, helping take care of Dr. Wallace's daughters while his wife gives birth to a new baby.

20. The very conceit of Kamogawa Sea World (it is not affiliated with the American marine parks of the same name) as an institution exhibits humanity's attempts to harness and profit from nature. The film does not delve into the ethics of keeping and training animals in captivity to entertain humans. In this pre-PETA era, it is possible the contradiction with the film's pro-environmentalist message simply did not occur to Yuasa and the others. As of publication the park remains open and purports to "provide a place where our visitors will be amazed by the beauty of sea life and learn about the importance of it and its surrounding environments through exhibitions representative of the natural world and performances by our sea animals." See "Vision and Research Activities," *Kamogawa Sea World*, accessed August 7, 2016, http://www.kamogawa-seaworld.jp/english/research/.

21. *Gamera vs. Zigra* (7:18).

22. *Ibid.* (8:18).

23. *Ibid.* (12:12).

24. Like many fantasy and science fiction films, the children of *Gamera vs. Zigra* are more readily able to comprehend the fantastic. The films of Steven Spielberg in the following decade exhibit this quality, as does the *Rebirth of Mothra* series addressed in Chapter 11.

25. For an interesting examination of the lasting effect of the 1923 quake on Japanese society, see Alex Bates, *The Culture of the Quake: The Great Kantō Earthquake and Taishō Japan* (Ann Arbor: Center for Japanese Studies, 2015).

26. *Gamera vs. Zigra* (17:50).

27. *Ibid.* (18:25).

28. *Ibid.* (19:03).

29. Woman X's dialogue provides yet another example of the pitfalls of critiquing the English-dubbed versions of films rather than the Japanese-language originals. Stuart Galbraith mocks *Gamera vs. Zigra* by quoting certain nonsensical dialogue. According to Galbraith, in the dubbed version of the film Woman X claims that Zigra's seas were polluted by "Earth science." In fact, she declares that "cultural progress" polluted the planet's waters. Of course, it would be impossible for human science to pollute the seas on a distant planet, but the aliens' own progress could certainly be responsible. Galbraith should send his complaints to the foreign dubbers, not Daiei Company. See Galbraith, *Japanese Science Fiction*, 199.

30. *Gamera vs. Zigra* (22:57).

31. *Ibid.* (28:40).

32. *Ibid.* (37:00).

33. Galbraith, *Japanese Science Fiction*, 199.

34. *Ibid.*, 200.

35. *Gamera vs. Zigra* (40:12).

36. *Ibid.* (41:17).

37. Daiei Company took advantage of filming at Kamogawa Sea World before the park opened to the public. *Gamera vs. Zigra* filmed in the late summer and the marine park opened a few weeks later on October 1, 1970.

38. *Gamera vs. Zigra* (44:40).

39. Homenick, "Gamera's Gals," 19.

40. David Starr Jordan, "Description of a Species of Fish (*Mitsukurina owstoni*) from Japan, the Type of a Distinct Family of Lamnoid Sharks," *Proceedings of the California Academy of Sciences* (Series 3) Zoology Vol. 1, No. 6 (January 1898): 199–201.

41. *Gamera vs. Zigra* (54:54).

42. *Ibid.* (58:28).

43. A bathyscaphe, like a bathysphere, is a stationary submersible attached to a surface platform by cables.

44. *Gamera vs. Zigra* (1:26:55).

45. Tsutsui, *Godzilla on My Mind*, 184.

46. Barr, *The Kaijū Film*, 56–57.

47. Galbraith, *Japanese Science Fiction*, 200.

48. J. Christian Grymyr, "The Gamera Autobiography," *Shrine of Gamera*, accessed July 27, 2016, http://www.shrineofgamera.com/autobiography_05.html.

49. Author Sean Rhoads personally experienced huge crowds of primary school students on school-sponsored field trips at several Japanese aquariums on three different occasions: the Port of Nagoya Public Aquarium in June 2006; the Osaka Aquarium Kaiyukan in April 2015; and the Sumida Aquarium at the Tokyo Skytree in April 2015. None of these aquariums existed until the early 1990s.

50. Japan National Tourism Organization, "Visiting Aquariums in Japan!" *Japan Monthly Web Magazine*, May 2015, accessed July 31, 2016, http://japan-magazine.jnto.go.jp/en/1406_aquarium.html.

51. Lees, "Mr. Yuasa's G-FEST," 14.

52. *Ibid.*

53. Shin-Tōhō folded in 1961.

54. Quoted in Galbraith, *Monsters*, 114.

55. Gordon, *Modern History*, 284.

56. *Ibid.*, 285.

57. Miki, "Foreword," 1.

58. *Ibid.*

59. *Ibid.*

60. "Environmental Protection Laws Passed by 71st Special Diet Session," *Japan Environment Summary* Vol. 1, No. 5 (October 1973), 1–2.

61. McClain, *Japan: A Modern History*, 520.

62. Miki Takeo, "A New Year Message," *Japan Environment Summary* Vol. 2, No. 1 (January 1974): 1.

Chapter 10

1. The Japanese title for the former film is simply *Gojira* (*Godzilla*), identical to the original 1954 film. To avoid confusion, we refer to the film as *Godzilla 1984*. Also note that *Gojira vs Biorante* dropped the prior use of the *kanji* "tai," instead using the Latin alphabet letters "vs."

2. Gordon, *Modern History*, 291.

3. *Ibid.*, 292–293.

4. Jennifer Amyx, *Japan's Financial Crisis: Institutional Rigidity and Reluctant Change* (Princeton: Princeton University Press, 2004), 1–9.

5. James Bates, "Japan's U.S. Real Estate Buying Plunges," *Los Angeles Times*, February 21, 1992, accessed September 19, 2015, http://articles.latimes.com/1992-02-21/news/mn-2588_1_japanese-real-estate.

6. Gordon, *Modern History*, 298–299.

7. *Ibid.*, 300.

8. *Ibid.*

9. Ezra Vogel, *Japan as Number One: Lessons for America* (Cambridge, MA: Harvard University Press, 1979).

10. Shintarō Ishihara, *The Japan That Can Say No: Why Japan Will Be First Among Equals* (New York: Simon & Schuster, 1989).

11. Ichirō Ozawa, *Blueprint for a New Japan: The Rethinking of a Nation* (Tokyo: Kodansha International, 1994).

12. McClain, *Japan: A Modern History*, 600–604.

13. The Godzilla franchise is often divided into different epochs, the most relevant here being the Shōwa and Heisei periods. These names pertain to the reign of the ruling emperor, but in reality do not line up very well. For example, most fans consider *Godzilla 1984* to mark the start of the Heisei period, but the Heisei emperor did not begin his reign until January 8, 1989. See, for example, August Ragone, "The Complete Godzilla Chronology: 1954–2004," *Famous Monsters of Filmland* 274 (July/August 2014), 10–47.

14. For the complete discussion of the impact of television on the film industry, see Chapter 5.

15. Peter Carlson, "The Return of Godzilla," *People*, January 14, 1985, accessed September 30, 2015, http://www.people.com/people/archive/article/0,,20089685,00.html.

16. J.D. Lees and Marc Cerasini, *The Official Godzilla Compendium* (New York: Random House, 1998), 56.

17. Like 1954's *Godzilla*, an extensively edited American version of the film was released as *Return of Godzilla*. Raymond Burr reprised his role as journalist Steve Martin. For an exhaustive examination of the changes between the two versions of the film, see Greg Shoemaker and Allen Perkins, "Godzilla 1985: Screenplay Comparison," *G-Fan* 101 (June 2013), 20–30.

18. Tsutsui, *Godzilla on My Mind*, 65.

19. Tanaka, *Gojira deizu*, 304.

20. Kalat, *Critical History*, 159–172; Tsutsui, *Godzilla on My Mind*, 65–66.

21. *Gojira 1984* (*Godzilla 1984*), directed by Hashimoto Kōji (1984; Tokyo: Tōhō Co., Ltd.), DVD.

22. Although 1967's *Son of Godzilla* (discussed in Chapter 5) also features a journalist named Maki Gorō, there is no indication in either film that the characters represent the same individual.

23. We mention the Japanese provenance of these electronics because their appearance in the film denotes Japan's superior position as a producer of electronic goods in the 1980s.

24. This line indicates the "retcon" aspect of *Godzilla 1984*. In doing so, the creators removed the explained arrival of the second Godzilla in *Godzilla Raids Again* from the franchise's timeline. This leaves the astute viewer with a question: is the monster in *Godzilla 1984* the original Godzilla, resurrected, or is he an entirely new Godzilla? This question remains unanswered, although in the American edit of the film, Raymond Burr's character laconically remarks: "Just for the record, thirty years ago, they never found any corpse." Presumably, this is likely true; the audience definitively saw the original Godzilla disintegrate in 1954. This conundrum exposes one of the many issues that develop by "retconning" such a vibrant and complex cinematic universe. See Kalat, *Critical History*, 170.

25. This action hints at the Japanese government's tendency to limit the distribution of information to its people. This approach tragically remained in effect during the Fukushima disaster of 2011. See "Fukushima Meltdown Apology: 'It was a cover up,'" *Associated Press*, June 21, 2016, accessed August 10, 2016, http://www.cbsnews.com/news/fukushima-Tepco-power-japan-nuclear-meltdown-apologizes-cover-up/.

26. For example, consider the troubling collusion of political and business interests in *Mothra vs. Godzilla* or the inept government and military in *Godzilla vs. Hedorah*.

27. Condon, *Half Step*, 211–221.

28. *Godzilla 1984* (19:20).

29. Interestingly, Tokyo's transforming skyline led to creative changes in Godzilla himself. Whereas the 1954 monster was fifty meters tall, by 1984 Godzilla towers eighty meters in height. If Godzilla's size had not been altered by producer Tanaka, Tokyo's skyscrapers would have dwarfed him, correspondingly diminishing the threat he posed to the city and Japan. As Japan grows, so does Godzilla. Just as Godzilla's size increased to keep pace with the fruits of Japan's economic growth, the filmmakers altered special effects to reflect the high technology of the times. Unlike the franchise's earlier reliance on puppetry and suitmation, *Godzilla 1984* featured a five-meter (six-

teen-foot) tall robotic Godzilla that towered over the sets and actors. Known as the "Cybot," the robotic, cable-controlled Godzilla contained 3,000 computerized parts, and weighed in at over one ton.

30. For example, see the highly altruistic newspaper reporters and photographers in *Mothra vs. Godzilla*, discussed in depth in Chapter 4.

31. For an interesting interview with actor Dennis Falt, the commander of the Soviet submarine, see Brett Homenick, "Meeting Godzilla at Full Fathom Five," *G-Fan* 92 (Summer 2010): 10–13, 55.

32. Captain John Moore, edit., *Jane's Fighting Ships 1987–88* (London: Jane's Publishing Co. Ltd., 1988), 543–544.

33. *Godzilla 1984* (30:30).

34. *Ibid.* (33:18).

35. From 1974 to 1987, more than 30 plants were built thanks to incentives provided by the national government. See Johnston, "Key Players." Also see "Nuclear Power in Japan," *World Nuclear Association*, accessed October 10, 2015, http://www.world-nuclear.org/info/Country-Profiles/Countries-G-N/Japan/.

36. Quoted in Michael Ross, "Godzilla Comes Home for Christmas," *United Press International*, December 17, 1984, accessed August 7, 2016, http://www.upi.com/Archives/1984/12/17/Godzilla-Comes-Home-for-Christmas/6485472107600/.

37. Quoted in Carlson, "The Return of Godzilla."

38. *Ibid.*

39. *Godzilla 1984* questions Japan's use of nuclear power just as *kaijū eiga* of the 1960s and 1970s criticized Japan's reliance on dirty fossil fuels like oil and coal. With the exception of *Daikaijū Gamera*, the films we have covered do not directly point the audience to renewable forms of energy despite repeated indications of the inherent power of nature. It is surprising that while the later films critique humanity's abuse of natural resources, none promote renewable energy options as an alternative.

40. The American editors of *Return of Godzilla* must have found the scientific discussion of homing and magnetism too intricate for non-Japanese audiences. They dubbed the discussion to reveal that Godzilla is simply attracted to birdcalls.

41. Koizumi Hiroshi starred in numerous *kaijū* films throughout his career. He played a scientist in both *Mothra* and *Mothra vs. Godzilla*, as well as several other Godzilla films from the 1950s through the 1970s. Koizumi's character Prof. Minami is not a major character in *Godzilla 1984*, and serves as little more than a nostalgic cameo appearance for an actor well known to Godzilla franchise audiences.

42. *Godzilla 1984* (40:08).

43. Carlson, "The Return of Godzilla."

44. *Godzilla 1984* (44:17).

45. *Ibid.* (45:40).

46. Tsutsui, *Godzilla on My Mind*, 65.

47. *Godzilla 1984* (48:48).

48. *Ibid.* (49:52).

49. Benjamin S. Lambeth and Kevin Lewis, "The Kremlin and SDI," *Foreign Affairs* (Spring 1988), accessed October 11, 2015, https://www.foreignaffairs.com/articles/russian-federation/1988-03-01/kremlin-and-sdi.

50. In the extensively-edited *Return of Godzilla*, the Soviet officer purposely fires the nuclear weapon, one of many right-wing changes employed by the film's American editors.

51. As Godzilla appears in Shinjuku, the film depicts a homeless man pilfering a food and alcohol from a luxurious hotel restaurant. The homeless man's portrayal in *Godzilla 1984* is problematic; he is a derelict left behind by the economic boom of the 1980s, and although his character is both comical and helpful, he is also crude, a drunk, and a thief. Moreover, as Godzilla rampages through Shinjuku, he is self-absorbed in carnal pleasures, ignoring the rampant death and destruction around him. The homeless man exists outside of mainstream Japanese society, representing a similar form of social pollution to the ambivalent countercultural youths portrayed in earlier films like *Daikaijū Gamera* and *Godzilla vs. Hedorah*. Though brief and played for laughs, these scenes hint at the unspoken underclass of 1980s Japan. Simultaneously they suggest that homeless people are in that position due to personal shortcomings rather than disparate economic opportunities.

52. For a detailed account of *Godzilla 1984*'s alteration into *Return of Godzilla*, see Kalat, *Critical History*, 159–172.

53. Several prior studies of the Godzilla franchise include *Godzilla vs. Biollante* as part of the 1990s, due to its American debut in 1992. This is a mistake—the film was produced and premiered in Japan in the 1980s. Although only three years apart, 1989 and 1992 represent two very different historical moments in Japan.

54. *Gojira vs Biorante* (*Godzilla vs. Biollante*), directed by Ōmori Kazuki (1989; Tokyo: Tōhō Co., Ltd.), DVD.

55. Lees and Cerasini, *Official Godzilla*, 62.

56. Quoted in Ryfle, *Japan's Favorite Mon-Star*, 259.

57. The James Bond franchise would also interrogate issues surrounding biotechnology and "gene therapy," but not until over a decade later in *Die Another Day* (2002).

58. Quoted in "Markalite Interview: Director/Screenwriter Kazuki Ōmori," *Markalite* 1 (Summer 1990): 46.

59. Interestingly, although the text is entirely Japanese, Godzilla is referred to using the Latin alphabet moniker "G."

60. *Godzilla vs. Biollante* (2:30).

61. Sources conflict on the name of the actor portraying SSS9. Some suggest "Manjhat Beti," others "Brien Uhl." Our own research led to the conclusion that Manjot Bedi plays SSS9.

62. "Saradia" is likely a contraction of "Saudi Arabia." Like prior Tōhō productions, *Godzilla vs. Biollante* contains a mixture of real and fictional countries and enterprises, blurring the lines between fantasy and reality.

63. *Godzilla vs. Biollante* (7:46).

64. There is also a longstanding connection between the feminine and the paranormal in Japanese tradition and mythology. For example, Shintō priestesses known as *miko* were widely believed to possess supernatural powers to communicate with spirits and conduct séances. Characters exemplifying this belief appear regularly in the Japanese dramatic arts. Moreover, there is a prominent depiction of a female medium communicating with the dead in Daiei Company's acclaimed 1950 masterpiece *Rashōmon*.

65. Asuka is a strong, professional woman, and her character is vastly different from both the classical

females of the 1950s and the temptress characters of the 1960s and 1970s. It is also worth noting that although Asuka is later revealed to be the girlfriend of character Kirishima, she remains an important character in her own right, not merely through her connection to the male scientist. In fact, in many ways, Asuka is even more instrumental to the film's overall plot than her boyfriend.

66. Hirata Akihiko's portrayal of Dr. Mafune in 1975's *Terror of Mechagodzilla* is the only other potential competition for this title.

67. Quoted in "Markalite Interview," 46.

68. *Godzilla vs. Biollante* (15:27).

69. *Ibid.* (17:02).

70. Gondō's statement is worth some discussion. Despite being a likeable protagonist, he nonetheless openly wishes for Godzilla's return, far and away from the solemn warnings of another Godzilla attack by Prof. Yamane at the end of 1954's *Godzilla*. Perhaps Gondō's statement is indicative of the heady outlook of 1989 Japan, intoxicated with its own economic success, far detached from the horrors of the Asia-Pacific War. Or perhaps Gondō cinematically mirrors the hopes of the audience—after all, many *kaijū eiga* aficionados desire viewing the cathartic destruction of miniature cities. Indeed, therein lies the long-lasting appeal of Japanese monster movies at their very core, channeled through Gondō's character.

71. *Godzilla vs. Biollante* (17:58).

72. Kalat, *Critical History*, 176–194.

73. *Godzilla vs. Biollante* (21:39).

74. *Ibid.* (25:03).

75. The cue is high-pitched, airy, and atonal. These aural components work to produce an unsettling effect that parallels the disturbing implications of biotechnology.

76. Steve Ryfle notes that Biollante is named after Violan, "a mythological Norse nymph." However, despite an extensive search for more information on Violan, one is only led back to Ryfle's own book. See Ryfle, *Japan's Favorite Mon-Star*, 254.

77. *Godzilla vs. Biollante* (38:47).

78. One interesting segment features Demon Kakka, a Japanese heavy metal rocker and journalist.

79. *Godzilla vs. Biollante* (47:24).

80. *Ibid.* (57:07).

81. The design of Biollante in this form clearly references gynic imagery. Red petals encircle the plump bloom, the toothsome orifice at its center. The visual allusion to *vagina dentata* has its roots in Japanese folk legend. The famous Kanamara Matsuri, or Festival of the Steel Phallus, of Kawasaki in Kanagawa Prefecture traces its origins back to a myth involving a demon inhabiting a woman's vagina and emasculating her lovers during intercourse. See, for example, "Kanamara Matsuri 2014: What You Should Know About Japan's Penis Festival," *Huffington Post*, April 4, 2014, accessed August 15, 2016, http://www.huffingtonpost.ca/2014/04/07/kanamara-matsuri-http://www.huffingtonpost.ca/2014/04/07/kanamara-matsuri-2014_n_5105892.html. The design might also reflect a continuing anxiety about masculinity and women's rights in Japan.

82. *Godzilla vs. Biollante* (56:22).

83. The showdown between Miki and Godzilla takes place on a floating platform being used for the construction of Kansai International Airport, an artificial island land reclamation project.

84. According to the film's director Ōmori Kazuki, he planned Miki's character to be even more powerful in his original script, and intended to use "her power to raise Godzilla out of the ocean," but this scene was later removed by Tanaka Tomoyuki. See Brett Homenick, "The Man Who Revived Godzilla: Ōmori Speaks Out!" *G-Fan* 78 (Winter 2007): 37.

85. *Godzilla vs. Biollante* (1:35:26).

86. *Ibid.* (1:39:42).

87. This final shot recalls the "star child" at the conclusion of the science fiction masterpiece *2001: A Space Odyssey* (1968), implying that Biollante (and Erika) have evolved to a higher plane of existence.

88. *Jurassic Park*, directed by Steven Spielberg (1993; Universal City, CA: Universal Pictures), Blu-ray.

89. Genetic engineering and biotechnology continue to cause anxiety and stir debate, not only in Japan but around the world. Issues like stem-cell research, cloning, genetically modified organisms (GMOs), and gene therapy continue to raise controversies. See, for example, Rob Stein, "In Search for Cures, Scientists Create Embryos That Are Both Animal and Human," *NPR*, May 18, 2016, accessed August 20, 2016, http://www.npr.org/sections/health-shots/2016/05/18/478212837/in-search-for-cures-scientists-create-embryos-that-are-both-animal-and-human; Ian Sample, "Scientists Genetically Modify Human Embryos in Controversial World First," *The Guardian*, April 23, 2015, accessed August 20, 2016, https://www.theguardian.com/science/2015/apr/23/scientists-genetically-modify-human-embryos-in-controversial-world-first.

Chapter 11

1. Fumio Hayashi and Edward C. Prescott, "The 1990s in Japan: A Lost Decade," *Review of Economic Dynamics* V (2002): 206–235.

2. See, for example, Peter K. Bol, *Neo-Confucianism in History* (Cambridge, MA: Harvard University Press, 2008), 142–144, 236–246.

3. Hayashi Michiyoshi, *Fusei no fukken* (Restoring fatherhood) (Tokyo: Chūkō Shinsho, 1996); Hayashi Michiyoshi, *Shufu no fukken* (Restoring the housewife) (Tokyo: Kōdansha, 1998).

4. Ayako Kano, *Japanese Feminist Debates: A Century of Contention on Sex, Love, and Labor* (Honolulu: University of Hawai'i Press, 2016), 157.

5. Kalat, *Critical History*, 190.

6. *Ibid.*, 197.

7. Okawara went on to direct *Godzilla vs. Mechagodzilla II* (1993), *Godzilla vs. Destroyah* (1995), and *Godzilla 2000* (1999).

8. In addition to *Godzilla* (1954) and *Mothra vs. Godzilla* (1964), Takarada appeared as various characters in *Kaijū Daisensō* (*Invasion of Astro-Monster*) (1965), *Gojira, Ebira, Mosura Nankai no Daikettō* (*Godzilla vs. the Sea Monster*) (1966), and *Kingu Kongu no Gyakushū* (*King Kong Escapes*) (1967). He went on to play a role in *Godzilla: Final Wars* (2004).

9. Kalat, *Critical History*, 202.

10. Lees and Cerasini, *Official Godzilla*, 85.

11. Kalat, *Critical History*, 203. Kalat notes that the major film studio, Nikkatsu, declared bankruptcy in 1993.

12. *Ibid.*, 202.

13. *Ibid.*, 198. Kalat points out that the benefits of real estate development are not addressed and observes that the film's portrayal of negative effects of development are ironic since Tōhō had profited from its own land holdings.

14. *Ibid.*, 200.

15. *Gojira vs Mosura* (*Godzilla vs. Mothra*), directed by Okawara Takao (1992; Tokyo: Tōhō Co., Ltd.), Blu-Ray.

16. The film's first few minutes also hint at contemporary concerns. The possibility of a large meteorite impacting the planet was a very real worry; the Shoemaker-Levy Comet broke apart in the summer of 1992 and was on trajectory to strike Jupiter two years later. Many wondered what might happen if such an object hit Earth. The temple sequence, on the other hand, addresses the issue of cultural preservation. The message is very clear: pilfering artifacts from indigenous peoples, past or present, for monetary gain is immoral.

17. *Godzilla vs. Mothra* (10:06).

18. *Ibid.* (10:54).

19. *Ibid.* (13:30).

20. *Ibid.* (13:41).

21. *Indiana Jones and the Temple of Doom*, directed by Steven Spielberg (1984; Hollywood, CA: Paramount Pictures), DVD.

22. *Godzilla vs. Mothra* (16:45).

23. We present no judgment on the worthiness of the film's conservative family message, leaving ethical and political viewpoints to the reader.

24. An homage to this and other Mothra cave sequences appears in a post-credits scene in Hollywood's *Kong: Skull Island* (2017).

25. *Godzilla vs. Mothra* (19:31).

26. *Ibid.* (21:05).

27. *Ibid.* (21:30).

28. *Ibid.* (21:45).

29. *Ibid.* (22:05).

30. *Godzilla vs. Mothra* (23:23). Although the subtitles translate Masako's comment as a reference to "men" the actual term she uses is "atashi-tachi," which means "we" or "us."

31. *Godzilla vs. Mothra* (24:03).

32. The construction of golf courses was common during the bubble economy. Although older, the Fuji Golf Course does indeed exist; there golfers can enjoy luxurious restaurants, hot springs and golfing, which can run up to ¥30,900 on peak days. See http://www.fuji-gc.com/english/course/.

33. *Godzilla vs. Mothra* (24:34).

34. *Ibid.* (28:19).

35. *Ibid.* (29:23).

36. *Ibid.* (44:22).

37. Kano, *Japanese Feminist Debates*, 126–132, 140–172.

38. *Godzilla vs. Mothra* (46:31).

39. These characters seem to be Masako's sister and brother-in-law.

40. *Godzilla vs. Mothra* (48:02).

41. *Ibid.* (48:48).

42. *Ibid.* (49:47).

43. Miki originally appeared in 1989's *Godzilla vs. Biollante*, discussed in Chapter 10.

44. *Godzilla vs. Mothra* (54:22).

45. *Ibid.* (57:57).

46. *Ibid.* (58:41).

47. *Ibid.* (1:05:20).

48. The wordless chorus is a musical trope historically associated with the fantastic, sleep, nature, and the divine. See Jean-David Jumeau-Lafond, "Le chœur sans paroles ou les voix du sublime," *Revue de Musicologie* 83:2 (1997): 263–279.

49. *Godzilla vs. Mothra* (1:06:09).

50. Mount Fuji last erupted in 1707.

51. *Ibid.* (1:07:48).

52. *Ibid.* (1:11:28).

53. Cosmo Clock 21 was completed in 1989 and is the result of the bubble years' frivolity and excess.

54. *Ibid.* (1:37:17).

55. *Ibid.* (1:38:38).

56. *Mosura* (*Rebirth of Mothra*), directed by Yoneda Okihiro (1996; Tokyo: Tōhō Co., Ltd.), Blu-Ray.

57. *II*), directed by Miyoshi Kunio (1997; Tokyo: Tōhō Co., Ltd.), Blu-Ray.

58. *Mosura 3: Kingu Gidora Raishū* (*Rebirth of Mothra III*, or *Mothra 3: King Ghidorah Attacks*), directed by Yoneda Okihiro (1998; Tokyo: Tōhō Co., Ltd.), Blu-Ray.

59. It is also worth noting that Lora, Moll, and Belvera are fantastic-sounding, non-Japanese names.

60. We surmise that the use of child characters as well as slapstick elements were a way to attract young people to the movie theater during a time of economic hardship.

61. Aokigahara is commonly known as the "suicide forest" in Japan and abroad. For example, in the Hollywood horror film *The Forest* (2016), a young woman (actress Natalie Dormer) searches the woodland for her missing twin sister, facing many supernatural forces along the way.

62. Yoneda had experience working as the second unit director on several of Kurosawa Akira's later films, including *Ran* (1985), *Dreams* (1990), *Rhapsody in August* (1991), and *Madadayo* (1993). The vivid cinematography featuring vast landscapes in these films perhaps influenced Yoneda, who also directed 1998's *Rebirth of Mothra III*.

63. *Rebirth of Mothra* (2:13).

64. *Ibid.* (36:20).

65. *Ibid.* (42:27).

66. *Ibid.* (1:05:45).

67. *Ibid.* (1:11:37).

68. *Ibid.* (1:17:08).

69. "World Heritage Nomination—IUCN Summary: 662 Yakushima (Yaku Island) (Japan)," *United Nations*, March 1993, Accessed August 1, 2016, http://whc.unesco.org/archive/advisory_body_evaluation/662.pdf. The justification for naming it a World Heritage Site included the arguments that the island provided "outstanding examples representing significant ongoing geological processes and biological evolution...contains unique, rare, or superlative natural phenomenon, formation, or features of exceptional natural beauty ... [and represents] the most important and significant habitats where threatened species of plants and animals still survive." 19–20.

70. *Rebirth of Mothra* (1:21:37).

71. *Ibid.* (1:36:53).

72. *Ibid.* (1:37:04).

73. *Ibid.* (1:37:27).

74. *Rebirth of Mothra II* (4:00).

75. Earlier in the film, the men are shown illegally diving for oysters. They are clearly of dubious moral character.

76. A curious decision in the film involves the mys-

tical healing powers of Go-go's urine. A starfish burns one of the boys; Go-go relieves himself on the boy's wound, curing it. This mystifying action occurs later in the film as well; Go-go heals the adult men, who have a change of heart and help the children escape the crumbling ruins of the ancient city.

77. *Rebirth of Mothra II* (22:22).
78. *Ibid.* (1:27:27). This version of Mothra is sometimes known as Aqua Mothra.
79. *Ibid.* (1:35:48). Only the children are able to hear the princess's voice.
80. *Ibid.* (1:36:45).
81. *Rebirth of Mothra III* (9:50).
82. The movie implies that he is bullied at school. His younger sister surmises that he does not want to eat the requisite school lunch.
83. *Rebirth of Mothra III* (12:14). This small comment hints at a larger issues facing Japan in the late 1990s; the two-income household increasingly becomes a necessity as the economy continued to sag.
84. During these events, Mr. and Mrs. Sonoda (who endearingly call each other "Mama" and "Papa") hike through the caves of Aokigahara Forest searching for Shōta.
85. *Rebirth of Mothra III* (54:00).

Chapter 12

1. Emily Chung, "Japan Tsunami's Huge Size Blamed on Slimy, Slimy Fault," *CBC News*, December 6, 2013, accessed September 5, 2016, http://www.cbc.ca/news/technology/japan-tsunami-s-huge-size-blamed-on-slimy-slimy-fault-1.2452553.
2. Becky Oskin, "Japan Earthquake & Tsunami of 2011: Facts and Information," *Live Science*, May 7, 2015, accessed September 5, 2016, http://www.livescience.com/39110-japan-2011-earthquake-tsunami-facts.html.
3. Kazuaki Nagata, "Revisiting 3/11: Fukushima's Long Shadow," *Japan Times*, February 10, 2016, accessed September 5, 2016, http://features.japantimes.co.jp/march-11-radiation/.
4. Lees, "Mr. Yuasa's G-FEST," 14.
5. Galbraith, *Monsters*, 114.
6. *Gamera gahō: Daiei hizō eiga gojūgo nen no ayumi* (The Gamera Chronicles: A Fifty-Five Year Progression from Daiei's Secret Storehouse) (Tokyo: B Media Books, 1996), 80–82.
7. Linkenback, *Art of Japanese Monsters*, 176.
8. "Essential Gamera," 39.
9. *Gamera: Daikaijū Kūchū Kessen* (*Gamera: Guardian of the Universe*), directed by Kaneko Shusuke (1995; Tokyo: Daiei Film Co., Ltd.), Blu-Ray.
10. Orichalcum is a mythological metal mentioned in Plato's story of Atlantis. The color of orichalcum was said to be a mixture of gold and copper. The metal is no longer known.
11. Interestingly, Asagi's amulet mimics the shape of a *magatama*, a comma-shaped jewel that is also one of the Three Sacred Treasures of Japan. According to Shintō legend, the Sun Goddess Amaterasu gifted a *magatama* jewel to the Japanese emperor, along with a sword and a mirror.
12. For more on the restoration of the traditional family, see Chapter 11.
13. Dr. Nagamine also provides a metatextual link between women and music—actress Nakayama Shi-

nobu was a prominent J-pop singer before launching her acting career.
14. Quoted in Lees, "Mr. Yuasa's G-FEST," 14.
15. *Chiisaki Yūsha-tachi: Gamera* (*Gamera the Brave*), directed by Tasaki Ryūta (2006; Tokyo: Kadokawa Pictures), Blu-Ray.
16. Cameron Koch, "Gamera Is Getting a New Movie for His 50th Anniversary, and It Looks Intense," *Tech Times*, October 9, 2015, accessed September 4, 2016, http://www.techtimes.com/articles/93565/20151009/gamera-is-getting-a-new-movie-for-his-50th-anniversary-and-it-looks-intense.htm.
17. See, for example, Ben Child, "Godzilla to Rampage Again," *The Guardian*, March 30, 2010, accessed September 15, 2016, https://www.theguardian.com/film/2010/mar/30/godzilla-to-rampage-again.
18. Tsutsui, *Godzilla on My Mind*, 10.
19. Allison, *Millennial Monsters*, 45.
20. The character's surname is of course a reference to the 1954 film, though his 2014 incarnation does not wear an eyepatch. His given name is an homage to the original film's famed director, Honda Ishirō.
21. Along with Ken Watanabe, Bryan Cranston and David Strathairn round out the film's otherwise uninspired cast.
22. The film is also billed as *Godzilla Resurgence* in English, but *Shin Godzilla* is the more common moniker.
23. Mark Schilling, "Our Favorite Monster Returns to Terrorize Japan in 'Shin Godzilla,'" *Japan Times*, July 28, 2016, accessed August 26, 2016, http://www.japantimes.co.jp/culture/2016/07/28/films/favorite-monster-returns-terrorize-japan-shin-godzilla/#.V8QZpI78–3M.
24. Mark Schilling, "Shin Godzilla: The Metaphorical Monster Returns," *Japan Times*, August 3, 2016, accessed August 29, 2016, http://www.japantimes.co.jp/culture/2016/08/03/films/film-reviews/shin-godzilla-metaphorical-monster-returns/#.V8QZxo78–3M.
25. Other writers have also connected the slow pacing to inaction over global climate change. See Zac Hestand, "Godzilla as Metaphor for Climate Change in Shin Godzilla," *Film Inquiry*, April 10, 2017, accessed April 22, 2017, https://www.filminquiry.com/climate-change-shin-godzilla/.
26. "Godzilla: Final Wars," *Tōhō Kingdom*, accessed April 22, 2017, http://www.tohokingdom.com/movies/godzilla_final_wars.htm.
27. John Squires, "Did 'Kong: Skull Island' Tease Future 'Gamera' Movie?," *BloodyDisgusting*, March 13, 2017, accessed April 22, 2017, http://bloody-disgusting.com/news/3428029/kong-skull-island-tease-future-gamera-movie/.
28. Tsutsui, *Godzilla on My Mind*, 82.
29. Jason Varney, "1992: Godzilla & Mothra: The Battle for Earth," *Famous Monsters of Filmland* 274 (July/August 2014): 35; Galbraith, *Japanese Science Fiction*, 200.
30. Eric Johnston, "Climate Change Threatens Nation's Agriculture," *Japan Times*, August 6, 2016, accessed August 26, 2016, http://www.japantimes.co.jp/life/2016/08/06/environment/climate-change-threatens-nations-agriculture/#.V8QWJI78–3M.
31. *Ibid.*
32. *Ibid.*
33. Tomoko Otake, "Plastic Debris in Oceans a Growing Hazard as Toxins Climb the Food Chain,"

Japan Times, July 19, 2016, accessed August 26, 2016, http://www.japantimes.co.jp/news/2016/07/19/reference/plastic-debris-oceans-growing-hazard-toxins-climb-food-chain/#.V8Qdro78–3M.

34. *Ibid.*

35. For more on this as well as mascot images, see "Eco-Friendly: 8 Odd Japanese Environmental Mascots," *WebEcoist*, accessed September 10, 2016, http://webecoist.momtastic.com/2013/01/08/eco-friendly-8-odd-japanese-environmental-mascots/.

36. Yuzo Suwa, "Network Promotes Japan's Organic Farming in a Bid to Keep Industry Alive," *Japan Times*, June 27, 2016, accessed September 11, 2016, http://www.japantimes.co.jp/news/2016/06/27/national/network-promotes-japans-organic-farming-in-a-bid-to-keep-industry-alive/#.V9VYe446JSE.

37. Mizuho Aoki, "Former Environment Minister Yuriko Koike Wins Landslide Election as Tokyo's First Female Mayor," *Japan Times*, August 1, 2016, accessed September 11, 2016, http://www.japantimes.co.jp/news/2016/08/01/national/politics-diplomacy/tokyo-elects-former-environment-minister-yuriko-koike-as-citys-first-female-governor/#.V9VcrI46JSE.

38. *Ibid.*

39. *Ibid.*

40. John Timmer, "Japan's Lurch Away from Nuclear Hasn't Caused Fossil Fuels to Boom," *Ars Technica*, September 9, 2016, accessed September 11, 2016, http://arstechnica.com/science/2016/09/japans-lurch-away-from-nuclear-hasnt-caused-fossil-fuels-to-boom/.

Bibliography

Adorno, Theodor. "Music and Language: A Fragment." In *Quasi una Fantasia: Essays on Modern Music*, translated by Rodney Livingstone. New York: Verso, 1992.

Allison, Anne. *Millennial Monsters: Japanese Toys and the Global Imagination*. Berkeley: California University Press, 2006.

_____. *Permitted and Prohibited Desires: Mothers, Comics, and Censorship in Japan*. Berkeley: University of California Press, 2000.

Amyx, Jennifer. *Japan's Financial Crisis: Institutional Rigidity and Reluctant Change*. Princeton: Princeton University Press, 2004.

"Atomic Age: The Broken Mirror." *TIME*, July 15, 1946. Accessed August 1, 2015. http://content.time.com/time/magazine/article/0,9171,803826,00.html.

Azimi, Nassrine. "Constitutionally Sound." *New York Times*, December 14, 2012. Accessed March 8, 2016. http://www.nytimes.com/2012/12/15/opinion/global/the-Japanese-constitution.html?ref=global-home&_r=0.

Banno, Yoshimitsu. *Gojira wo tobashita otoko* (The Man Who Flew Godzilla) Tokyo: Sentan Eizo Kenkyūsho, 2014. Kindle edition.

_____. "Smog Monster Director EXTRA." Interview by J.R. Lipartito. *SciFi Japan TV*. September 11, 2014. https://www.youtube.com/watch?v=N1dL7lA7bss&list=UUU03keCaesfRWZPYV1FUxXw.

Barr, Jason. *The Kaijū Film: A Critical Study of Cinema's Biggest Monsters*. Jefferson, NC: McFarland, 2016.

Bate, Jonathan. "From 'Red' to 'Green.'" In *The Green Studies Reader: From Romanticism to Ecocriticism*, ed. Laurence Coupe, 167–172. London: Routledge, 2000.

Bates, Alex. *The Culture of the Quake: The Great Kantō Earthquake and Taishō Japan*. Ann Arbor: Center for Japanese Studies, 2015.

Bates, James. "Japan's U.S. Real Estate Buying Plunges." *Los Angeles Times*, February 21, 1992. Accessed September 19, 2015. http://articles.latimes.com/1992-02-21/news/mn-2588_1_japanese-real-estate.

Biondi, Robert. "The Evolution of Godzilla." *G-Fan* 16 (July/August 1995), 24–33.

Biondi, Robert, and John Rocco Roberto. "Godzilla in America, Part 6: Save the Earth!" *G-Fan* 16 (July/August 1995): 15–16.

Blair, Gavin J. "'Godzilla vs. the Smog Monster' Director Yoshimitsu Banno Dies at 86." *Hollywood Reporter*, May 12, 2017. Accessed May 21, 2017. http://www.hollywoodreporter.com/news/godzilla-smog-monster-director-yoshimitsu-banno-dies-at-86-1003092.

Bol, Peter K. *Neo-Confucianism in History*. Cambridge, MA: Harvard University Press, 2008.

Boss, Joyce E. "Hybridity and Negotiated Identity in Japanese Popular Culture." In *In Godzilla's Footsteps: Japanese Pop Culture Icons on the Global Stage*, edited by William M. Tsutsui and Michiko Ito, 103–110. New York: Palgrave Macmillan, 2006.

Bourdaghs, Michael K. *Sayonara Amerika: A Geopolitical Prehistory of J-Pop*. New York: Columbia University Press, 2012.

Brasor, Philip. "Fight or Flight: Narita's History of Conflict." *Japan Times*, December 13, 2014. Accessed February 29, 2016. http://www.japantimes.co.jp/news/2014/12/13/national/media-national/fight-flight-naritas-history-conflict/.

"The 'Bravo' Test." *PBS*. Accessed August 11, 2015. http://www.pbs.org/wgbh/amex/bomb/peopleevents/pandeAMEX51.html.

Breen, John, and Mark Teeuwen. *A New History of Shintō*. Chichester, UK: Wiley-Blackwell, 2010.

Brothers, Peter H. *Mushroom Clouds and Mushroom Men: The Fantastic Cinema of Ishirō Honda*. Bloomington, IN: AuthorHouse, 2009.

Burgess, John. "Godzilla Rises Again." *Washington Post*, December 19, 1984. Accessed April 14, 2016. https://www.washingtonpost.com/archive/lifestyle/1984/12/19/godzilla-rises-again/39f6262d-796a-47e4-b0d7-dffdb3781433/.

Buttgereit, Jorg. "Whatever Happened to Yoshimitsu Banno?" *G-Fan* 60 (January/February 2003): 18–20.

Canby, Vincent. "Another 'Godzilla' Movie; Monster Is Now a Good Guy." *New York Times*, July 22, 1976.

_____. "A Midsummer Night's Screams." *New York Times*, June 24, 1979.

Canby, Vincent. "Stop Kidding Around!" *New York Times*, July 23, 1972.

Carlson, Peter. "The Return of Godzilla." *People*, January 14, 1985. Accessed September 30, 2015. http://www.people.com/people/archive/article/0,,20089685,00.html.

Carson, Rachel. *Silent Spring*. Boston: Houghton Mifflin, 1962.

Carter, Dan T. *The Politics of Rage: George Wallace, the Origins of New Conservatism, and the Transformation of American Politics*. New York: Simon & Schuster, 1995.

Cazdyn, Eric. *The Flash of Capital: Film and Geopolitics in Japan*. Durham, NC: Duke University Press, 2002.

_____. "Representation, Reality Culture, and Global Capitalism in Japan." *South Atlantic Quarterly* 99:4 (Fall 2000): 903–927.

Central Intelligence Agency. "Field Listing: Coastline." *The World Factbook*. Accessed October 30, 2015. https://www.cia.gov/library/publications/the-world-factbook/fields/2060.html.

Chafe, William H. *The Unfinished Journey: America Since World War II*. New York: Oxford University Press, 2003.

Chikyū Kōgeki Meirei: Gojira tai Gaigan (Godzilla vs. Gigan). Directed by Fukuda Jun. 1972. Tokyo: Tōhō Co. Ltd. DVD.

Child, Ben. "Godzilla to Rampage Again." *The Guardian*, March 30, 2010. Accessed September 15, 2016. https://www.theguardian.com/film/2010/mar/30/godzilla-to-rampage-again.

Chiisaki Yūsha-tachi: Gamera (Gamera the Brave). Directed by Tasaki Ryūta. 2006. Tokyo: Kadokawa Pictures. Blu-Ray.

"China and the Environment: The East Is Grey." *The Economist*, August 10, 2013. Accessed April 8, 2017. http://www.economist.com/news/briefing/21583245-china-worlds-worst-polluter-largest-investor-green-energy-its-rise-will-have.

Chung, Emily. "Japan Tsunami's Huge Size Blamed on Slimy, Slimy Fault." *CBC News*, December 6, 2013. Accessed September 5, 2016. http://www.cbc.ca/news/technology/japan-tsunami-s-huge-size-blamed-on-slimy-slimy-fault-1.2452553.

Coaldrake, William. *Architecture and Authority in Japan*. New York: Routledge, 1996.

Cohen, Jerome. *Japan's Economy in War and Reconstruction*. Minneapolis: University of Minnesota Press, 1949.

Condon, Jane. *A Half Step Behind: Japanese Women of the '80s*. New York: Dodd, Mead & Co., 1985.

Coupe, Laurence, ed. *The Green Studies Reader: From Romanticism to Ecocriticism*. London: Routledge, 2000.

Crane, Conrad C. *Bombs, Cities, and Civilians: American Airpower Strategy in World War II*. Lawrence: University Press of Kansas, 1993.

_____. "Firebombing (Germany & Japan)." *PBS*. Accessed March 28, 2016. http://www.pbs.org/thewar/detail_5229.htm.

Crane, Conrad C., and Mark Van Rhyn. "The Atomic Bomb." *PBS*. Accessed July 25, 2015. http://www.pbs.org/thewar/detail_5234.htm.

Crist, Marshall. "Space Women in the *Kaijū Eiga*." *Kaijū Review* 8 (1995).

Daikaijū Gamera. Directed by Yuasa Noriaki. 1965. Tokyo: Daiei Film Co., Ltd. DVD.

Davis, Mike. *The Ecology of Fear: Los Angeles and the Imagination of Disaster*. New York: Viking Press, 1999.

Debus, Allen A. "Triumphant Triumvirate: Godzilla's Dinosaurian 'Progenitors.'" *G-Fan* 98 (Winter 2012): 50–56.

Delgado, James P. *Ghost Fleet: The Sunken Ships of Bikini Atoll*. Honolulu: University of Hawai'i Press, 1996.

_____. *Nuclear Dawn: The Atomic Bomb from the Manhattan Project to the Cold War*. Oxford: Osprey Publishing, 2009.

Della Mora, Max. "*Godzilla vs. the Smog Monster*: A Fond Look Back." *G-Fan* 25 (January/February 1997): 40–41.

Devlin, Hannah. "Woolly Mammoth on Verge of Resurrection, Scientists Reveal." *The Guardian*, February 16, 2017. Accessed April 4, 2017. https://www.theguardian.com/science/2017/feb/16/woolly-mammoth-resurrection-scientists.

D'Orazio, Dante. "Gareth Edwards Returns to Direct 'Godzilla 2' with Rodan and Mothra." *The Verge*, July 26, 2014. Accessed May 13, 2016. http://www.theverge.com/2014/7/26/5940259/godzilla-2-confirmed-with-director-gareth-edwards.

Dosen, Ana. "Godzilla's Body: Reviving Memories Through Collective Flesh." *Culture* No. 12 (2015): 121–127.

Dower, John W. *Embracing Defeat: Japan in the Wake of World War II*. New York: W.W. Norton & Co., 1999.

"Eco-Friendly: 8 Odd Japanese Environmental Mascots." *WebEcoist*. Accessed September 10, 2016. http://webecoist.momtastic.com/2013/01/08/eco-friendly-8-odd-japanese-environmental-mascots/.

"Environmental Protection Laws Passed by the 71st Special Diet Session." *Japan Environment Summary* Vol. 1, No. 5 (October 1973): 1–2.

Erb, Cynthia. *Tracking King Kong: A Hollywood Icon in World Culture*. Detroit: Wayne State University Press, 2009.

"Essential Gamera: A Primer on the Flying G's Eleven Films." *G-Fan* 61 (March/April 2003): 36–39.

Eveleth, Rose. "The Bikini's Inventor Guessed How Much It Would Horrify the Public." *Smithsonian*, July 5, 2013. Accessed August 25, 2016. http://www.smithsonianmag.com/smart-news/the-bikinis-inventor-guessed-how-much-it-would-horrify-the-public-6914887/?no-ist.

Feld, Steven, and Aaron Fox. "Music and Language." *Annual Review of Anthropology* 23 (1994): 25–53.

Foster, Michael Dylan. *The Book of Yōkai: Mysterious Creatures of Japanese Folklore*. Oakland: California University Press, 2015.

"Fukushima Meltdown Apology: 'It Was a Cover Up.'" *Associated Press*, June 21, 2016. Accessed August 10, 2016. http://www.cbsnews.com/news/fukushima-Tepco-power-japan-nuclear-meltdown-apologizes-cover-up/.

Fumie, Kumagai, with Donna J. Keyser. *Unmasking Japan Today: The Impact of Traditional Values on Modern Japanese Society*. Westport, CT: Praeger, 1996.

Galbraith, Stuart, IV. *Japanese Science Fiction, Fantasy, and Horror Films*. Jefferson, NC: McFarland, 1994.

_____. *Monsters Are Attacking Tokyo: The Incredible World of Japanese Fantasy Films*. Venice, CA: Feral House, 1998.

Gamera: Daikaijū Kūchū Kessen (Gamera: Guardian of the Universe). Directed by Kaneko Shusuke. 1995. Tokyo: Daiei Film Co., Ltd. Blu-Ray.

Gamera gahō: Daiei hizō eiga gojūgo nen no ayumi (The Gamera Chronicles: A Fifty-Five Year Progression from Daiei's Secret Storehouse) Tokyo: B Media Books, 1996.

Gamera tai Daiakujū Giron (Gamera vs. Guiron). Directed by Yuasa Noriaki. 1969. Tokyo: Daiei Film Co., Ltd. DVD.

Gamera tai Shinkai Kaijū Jigura (Gamera vs. Zigra).

Directed by Yuasa Noriaki. 1971. Tokyo: Daiei Film Co., Ltd. DVD.

Gammera the Invincible. Directed by Sandy Howard. 1966. Los Angeles: World Entertainment, Corp. DVD.

Genbaku no Ko (Children of the Atomic Bomb). Directed by Shindō Kaneto. 1952. Tokyo: Kindai Eiga Kyōkai. DVD.

George, Timothy. *Minamata: Pollution and the Struggle for Democracy in Postwar Japan*. Cambridge, MA: Harvard University Press, 2001.

Gibson, William. "The Future Perfect." *TIME*, April 30, 2001. Accessed July 19, 2016. http://content.time.com/time/magazine/article/0,9171,1956774,00.html.

Gigantis, the Fire Monster. Directed by Oda Motoyoshi. 1959. Burbank, CA: Warner Brothers. DVD.

Glasstone, Samuel, and Philip Dolan. *The Effects of Nuclear Weapons*. Washington, D.C.: United States Government Printing Office, 1977.

Glotfelty, Cheryll, and Harold Fromm, eds. *The Ecocriticism Reader: Landmarks in Literary Ecology*. Athens: University of Georgia Press, 1996.

Godzilla. Directed by Gareth Edwards. 2014. Burbank, CA: Legendary Pictures. Blu-ray.

"Godzilla: Final Wars." *Tōhō Kingdom*. Accessed April 22, 2017. http://www.tohokingdom.com/movies/godzilla_final_wars.htm.

Godzilla, King of the Monsters. Directed by Terry Morse. 1956. Boston, MA: Embassy Pictures Corp. DVD.

"Godzilla, My Old Friend (An Interview with Takarada Akira)." *G-Fan* 87 (Spring 2009): 6–13.

"Godzilla vs. the Smog Monster." *Famous Monsters of Filmland* 91 (July 1972): 5, 26–31.

Gojira (Godzilla). Directed by Honda Ishirō. 1954. Tokyo: Tōhō Co., Ltd. DVD.

Gojira, Mosura, Kingu Gidora: Daikaijū Sōkōgeki (Godzilla, Mothra, and King Ghidorah: Giant Monsters All-Out Attack). Directed by Kaneko Shūsuke. 2001. Tokyo: Tōhō Co., Ltd. DVD.

Gojira 1984 (Godzilla 1984). Directed by Hashimoto Kōji. 1984. Tokyo: Tōhō Co., Ltd. DVD.

Gojira tai Hedora (Godzilla vs. Hedorah). Directed by Banno Yoshimitsu. 1971. Tokyo: Tōhō Co., Ltd. DVD.

Gojira tai Mekagojira (Godzilla vs. Mechagodzilla). Directed by Fukuda Jun. 1974. Tokyo: Tōhō Co., Ltd. DVD.

Gojira vs Biorante (Godzilla vs. Biollante). Directed by Ōmori Kazuki. 1989. Tokyo: Tōhō Co., Ltd. DVD.

Gojira vs Mosura (Godzilla vs. Mothra). Directed by Okawara Takao. 1992. Tokyo: Tōhō Co., Ltd. Blu-Ray.

Gorbman, Claudia. *Unheard Melodies: Narrative Film Music*. Bloomington: Indiana University Press, 1987.

Gordon, Andrew. *A Modern History of Japan: From Tokugawa Times to the Present*. New York: Oxford University Press, 2003.

Grymyr, J. Christian. "The Gamera Autobiography." *Shrine of Gamera*. Accessed July 27, 2016. http://www.shrineofgamera.com/autobiography_05.html.

_____. "Godzilla & Gamera vs. Tom Servo & Crow." *G-Fan* 36 (November/December 1998): 22–29.

Guthrie-Shimizu, Sayuri. "Lost in Translation and

Morphed in Transit: Godzilla in Cold War America." In *In Godzilla's Footsteps: Japanese Pop Culture Icons on the Global Stage*, edited by William M. Tsutsui and Michiko Ito, 51–62. New York: Palgrave Macmillan, 2006.

Hane, Mikiso. *Premodern Japan: A Historical Survey*. Boulder, CO: Westview Press, 1991.

Harris, Jeff. "What to Expect When Godzilla Returns for Its Long-Awaited Sequel?" *Crossmap*, August 10, 2016. Accessed April 1, 2017. http://www.crossmap.com/news/what-to-expect-when-godzilla-returns-for-its-long-awaited-sequel-30175.

Hayashi, Fumio, and Edward C. Prescott. "The 1990s in Japan: A Lost Decade." *Review of Economic Dynamics* V (2002): 206–235.

Hayashi, Michiyoshi. *Fusei no fukken* (Restoring Fatherhood). Tokyo: Chūkō Shinsho, 1996

_____. *Shufu no fukken* (Restoring the Housewife). Tokyo: Kōdansha, 1998.

Hays, Jeffrey. "Commercial Fishing in Japan: Fishing Industry, Fish Farms and Fishermen." *Facts and Details*, August 2012. Accessed October 29, 2015. http://factsanddetails.com/japan/cat24/sub159/item937.html.

Hendrix, Grady. "From Nuclear Nightmare to Networked Nirvana: Futuristic Utopianism in Japanese SF Films of the 2000s." *World Literature Today* (May/June 2010): 55–57.

Herd, Judith Ann. "The Cultural Politics of Japan's Modern Music: Nostalgia, Nationalism, and Identity in the Interwar Years." In *Locating East Asia in Western Art Music*, edited by Yayoi Uno Everett and Frederick Lau. Middletown, CT: Wesleyan University Press, 2004.

Herschler, Fred. "The Final Voyage of HIJMS Nagato Battleship." *Bikini Atoll*, February 3, 1998. Accessed August 12, 2015. https://www.bikiniatoll.com/nagatolog.html.

Hestand, Zac. "Godzilla as Metaphor for Climate Change in Shin Godzilla." *Film Inquiry*, April 10, 2017. Accessed April 22, 2017. https://www.filminquiry.com/climate-change-shin-godzilla/.

Hicks, George L. *The Comfort Women: Japan's Brutal Regime of Enforced Prostitution in the Second World War*. New York: W.W. Norton & Co., 1994.

Homenick, Brett. "Gamera's Gals." *G-Fan* 83 (Spring 2008): 16–19.

_____. "Godzilla's Leading Lady." *G-Fan* 102 (January 2013): 6–12.

_____. "The Last Emperor." *G-Fan* 94 (Winter 2011): 29–34.

_____. "The Man Who Made Godzilla Fly." *G-Fan* 73 (Fall 2005): 8–15.

_____. "The Man Who Revived Godzilla: Ōmori Speaks Out!" *G-Fan* 78 (Winter 2007): 34–41.

_____. "Meeting Godzilla at Full Fathom Five." *G-Fan* 92 (Summer 2010): 10–13, 55.

_____. "Singing for the Smog Monster." *G-Fan* 81 (Fall 2007): 10–11.

Homenick, Erik. "Biography." *AkiraIfukube.org*. Accessed May 14, 2016. http://www.akiraifukube.org/biography.htm.

Hoshino, Yoshiro. "Japan's Post-Second World War Environmental Problems." In *Industrial Pollution in Japan*, edited by Jun Ui. Hong Kong: United Nations University Press, 1992.

Hosokawa, Shuhei. "Atomic Overtones and Primitive Undertones: Akira Ifukube's Sound Design for

Godzilla." In *Off the Planet: Music, Science and Science Fiction Cinema*, edited by Philip Hayward. Eastleigh, UK: John Libby Publishing, 2004.

Howarth, William. "Some Principles of Ecocriticism." In *The Ecocriticism Reader: Landmarks in Literary Ecology*, eds. Cheryll Glotfelty and Harold Fromm, 69–91. Athens: University of Georgia Press, 1996.

"The Hydrogen Bomb." *Atomic Archive*. Accessed August 11, 2015. http://www.atomicarchive.com/History/coldwar/page04.shtml.

Igarashi, Yoshikuni. *Bodies of Memory: Narratives of War in Postwar Japanese Culture*. Princeton: Princeton University Press, 2000.

––––––. "Mothra's Gigantic Egg: Consuming the South Pacific in 1960s Japan." In *In Godzilla's Footsteps: Japanese Pop Culture Icons on the Global Stage*, edited by William M. Tsutsui and Michiko Ito, 83–102. New York: Palgrave Macmillan, 2006.

Iijima, Nobuko, ed. *Pollution Japan: Historical Chronology*. Elmsford, NY: Pergamon Press, 1979.

Imai, Kenichi. "Industrial Organization and the Environment." *Japan Quarterly* Vol. XXIV, No. 1 (January-March 1977): 26–37.

Indiana Jones and the Temple of Doom. Directed by Steven Spielberg. 1984. Hollywood, CA: Paramount Pictures. DVD.

Ishige, Naomichi. "Food: Another Perspective on Japanese Cultural History." *Nipponia*, March 15, 2006. Accessed December 3, 2015. http://web-japan.org/nipponia/nipponia36/en/feature/feature01.html.

Ishihara, Shintarō. *The Japan That Can Say No: Why Japan Will Be First Among Equals*. New York: Simon & Schuster, 1989.

Japan National Tourism Organization. "Visiting Aquariums in Japan!" *Japan Monthly Web Magazine*, May 2015. Accessed July 31, 2016. http://japan-magazine.jnto.go.jp/en/1406_aquarium.html.

Johnston, Eric. "Climate Change Threatens Nation's Agriculture." *Japan Times*, August 6, 2016. Accessed August 26, 2016. http://www.japantimes.co.jp/life/2016/08/06/environment/climate-change-threatens-nations-agriculture/#.V8QWJI78–3M.

––––––. "Key Players Got Nuclear Ball Rolling." *Japan Times*, July 16, 2011. Accessed September 1, 2015. http://japantimes.co.jp/news/2011/07/16/news/key-players-got-nuclear-ball-rolling/.

Jordan, David Starr. "Description of a Species of Fish (*Mitsukurina owstoni*) from Japan, the Type of a Distinct Family of Lamnoid Sharks." *Proceedings of the California Academy of Sciences* (Series 3) Zoology Vol 1., No. 6 (January 1898): 199–201.

Jumeau-Lafond, Jean-David. "Le chœur sans paroles ou les voix du sublime," *Revue de Musicologie* 83:2 (1997): 263–279.

Jurassic Park. Directed by Steven Spielberg. 1993. Universal City, CA: Universal Pictures. Blu-ray.

Justice, Mark. "Save the Earth! Part 2." *G-Fan* 95 (Spring 2011): 20–29.

––––––. "Shintō Symbolism in Tōhō's *Daikaijū Eiga*." *G-Fan* 81 (Fall 2007): 30–37.

Kachi, Naoki. "Impacts of Invasive Species on Native Ecosystems in the Bōnin Islands." In *Restoring the Oceanic Island Ecosystem*, edited by Kazuto Kazakami and Isamu Okochi, 11–14. Tokyo: Springer Verlag, 2010.

Kaijū Daisensō (*Invasion of Astro-Monster*). Directed by Honda Ishirō. 1965. Tokyo: Tōhō Co., Ltd. DVD.

Kaijū-tō no Kessen: Gojira no Musuko (*Son of Godzilla*). Directed by Fukuda Jun. 1967. Tokyo: Tōhō Co., Ltd. DVD.

Kalat, David. *A Critical History and Filmography of Tōhō's Godzilla Series*. Jefferson, NC: McFarland, 1997.

"Kanamara Matsuri 2014: What You Should Know About Japan's Penis Festival." *Huffington Post*, April 4, 2014. Accessed August 15, 2016. http://www.huffingtonpost.ca/2014/04/07/kanamara-matsuri-2014_n_5105892.html.

Kano, Ayako. *Japanese Feminist Debates: A Century of Contention on Sex, Love, and Labor*. Honolulu: University of Hawai'i Press, 2016.

Kawakami, Genichi. *Reflections on Music Popularization*. Tokyo: Yamaha Music Foundation, 1987.

Kawasaki, Shōichirō. *Daigo Fukuryū Maru: Present-Day Meaning of the Bikini Incident*. Tokyo: Daigo Fukuryū Maru Foundation Inc., 2008.

Keegan, John. *The Second World War*. New York: Penguin Books, 1989.

Keene, Donald. *Nō and Bunraku: Two Forms of Japanese Theatre*. New York: Columbia University Press, 1990.

Kennedy, Ludovic. *Pursuit: The Chase and Sinking of the Battleship Bismarck*. New York: Viking Press, 1974.

King Kong. Directed by Merien C. Cooper and Ernest B. Schoedsack. 1933. New York: RKO Radio Pictures, Inc. DVD.

Kingu Kongu tai Gojira (*King Kong vs. Godzilla*). Directed by Honda Ishirō. 1962. Tokyo: Tōhō Co., Ltd. DVD.

Kingston, Jeff. *Contemporary Japan: History, Politics, and Social Change Since the 1980s*. Malden, MA: Wiley-Blackwell, 2011.

Kirkup, James. "Obituary: Ishirō Honda." *Independent*, March 2, 1993. Accessed May 20, 2016. http://www.independent.co.uk/news/people/obituary-ishiro-honda-1495298.html.

Kobayashi, Atsushi. *Ifukube Akira no Eiga Ongaku* (Ifukube Akira's Film Music). Tokyo: Waizu Shuppan, 1998.

Koch, Cameron. "Gamera Is Getting a New Movie for His 50th Anniversary, and It Looks Intense." *Tech Times*, October 9, 2015. Accessed September 4, 2016. http://www.techtimes.com/articles/93565/20151009/gamera-is-getting-a-new-movie-for-his-50th-anniversary-and-it-looks-intense.htm.

Koopmans-de Bruijn, Ria. "Fabled Liaisons: Serpentine Spouses in Japanese Folktales." In *JAPANimals: History and Culture in Japan's Animal Life*, edited by Gregory M. Pflugfelder and Brett L. Walker, 61–88. Ann Arbor: Center for Japanese Studies, 2005.

Kristof, Nicholas D. "Kokura, Japan: Bypassed by A-Bomb." *New York Times*, August 7, 1995. Accessed August 2, 2015. http://www.nytimes.com/1995/08/07/world/kokura-japan-bypassed-by-a-bomb.html.

Lambeth, Benjamin S., and Kevin Lewis. "The Kremlin and SDI." *Foreign Affairs* (Spring 1988). Accessed October 11, 2015. https://www.foreignaffairs.com/articles/russian-federation/1988-03-01/kremlin-and-sdi.

Lapp, Ralph. *The Voyage of the Lucky Dragon*. New York: Harper & Bros., 1958.

Larson, Randall. *Musique Fantastique: A Survey of Film Music in the Fantastic Cinema*. Metuchen, NJ: Scarecrow, 1985.

Lees, J.D. "Mr. Yuasa's G-FEST." *G-Fan* 65 (November/December 2003): 10–14.

Lees, J.D., and Marc Cerasini. *The Official Godzilla Compendium*. New York: Random House, 1998.

Linkenback, Sean. *The Art of Japanese Monsters: Godzilla, Gamera and Japanese Science Fiction Film Art Conquer the World*. Gaithersburg, MD: Signature Book Printing, 2014.

Liptak, Andrew. "Legendary Assembles Godzilla vs. Kong Writers Room to Guide Its Cinematic Universe." *The Verge*, March 20, 2017. Accessed April 2, 2017. http://www.theverge.com/2017/3/10/14888036/legendary-godzilla-vs-kong-writers-room-monsterverse.

Los Alamos Scientific Laboratory Public Relations Office. *Los Alamos: Beginning of an Era, 1943–1945*. Los Alamos, NM: Los Alamos History Society, 2008.

Lu, David J. Japan: *A Documentary History, the Late Tokugawa Period to the Present*. Armonk, NY: M.E. Sharpe, 1997.

Lund, John W. "Characteristics, Development and Utilization of Geothermal Resources." *Oregon Institute of Technology Geo-Heat Center Bulletin* (June 2007): 1–9.

MacDonald, Cheyenne. "Bikini Atoll Is STILL Uninhabitable: Radiation on Island Exceeds Safety Standards Nearly 60 Years After Nuclear Tests." *Daily Mail*, June 7, 2016. Accessed March 17, 2017. http://www.dailymail.co.uk/sciencetech/article-3630359/Bikini-Atoll-uninhabitable-Radiation-island-exceeds-safety-standards-nearly-60-years-nuclear-tests.html.

Mackie, Vera. *Feminism in Modern Japan*. New York: Cambridge University Press, 2003.

"Markalite Interview: Director/Screenwriter Kazuki Ōmori." *Markalite* 1 (Summer 1990): 44–46.

Marx, Leo. *The Machine in the Garden: Technology and the Pastoral Ideal in America*. New York: Oxford University Press, 1964.

Matsuo, Kenji. *A History of Japanese Buddhism*. Folkestone, UK: Global Oriental, 2007.

"*Mauremys japonica*." *The Reptile Database*. Accessed February 23, 2016. http://reptile-database.reptarium.cz/species?genus=Mauremys&species=japonica&search_param=%28%28genus%3D%27Mauremys%27%2Cexact%29%29%252.

Mazel, David. "American Literary Environmentalism as Domestic Orientalism." In *The Ecocriticism Reader: Landmarks in Literary Ecology*, edited by Cheryll Glotfelty and Harold Fromm, 137–146. Athens: University of Georgia Press, 1996.

McClain, James L. *Japan: A Modern History*. New York: W.W. Norton & Co., 2002.

McCorkle, Brooke. "Nature, Technology, and Sound Design in *Gojira* (1954)." *Horror Studies* Vol. 3, No. 1 (April 2012): 21–37.

McLelland, Mark. *Love, Sex, and Democracy in Japan During the American Occupation*. New York: Palgrave Macmillan, 2012.

McNeill, J.R. *Something New Under the Sun: An Environmental History of the Twentieth-Century World*. New York: W.W. Norton & Co., 2000.

Medved, Harry, with Randy Dreyfuss. *The Fifty Worst Films of All Time (And How They Got That Way)*. New York: Popular Library, 1978.

Mekagojira no Gyakushū (*Terror of Mechagodzilla*). Directed by Honda Ishirō. 1975. Tokyo: Tōhō Co., Ltd. DVD.

Mesley, Pete. "HIJMS Nagato." *Lust4Rust*. Accessed August 15, 2015. http://www.petemesley.com/lust4rust/wreck-trips/bikini-atoll/wrecks/nagato.php.

Miki, Takeo. "Foreword." *Japan Environment Summary* Vol. 1, No. 1 (June 1973): 1.

_____. "A New Year Message." *Japan Environment Summary* Vol. 2, No. 1 (January 1974): 1.

Milner, David. "Noriaki Yuasa Interview." *Kaijū Conversations*, July 1996. Accessed July 13, 2016. http://www.davmil.org/www.kaijuconversations.com/yuasa.htm.

Ministry of the Environment. "Outbreak & Cause." *Minamata Disease Archives*. Accessed October 30, 2015. http://www.nimd.go.jp/archives/english/tenji/e_corner/qa1/1top.html.

"Minutes of the Second Meeting of the Target Committee, Los Alamos, May 10–11, 1945." Available at: http://www.dannen.com/decision/targets.html.

Mishima, Akio. *Bitter Sea: The Human Cost of Minamata Disease*. Tokyo: Kosei Publishing Co., 1992.

Mitchell, Jon. "Agent Orange on Okinawa—The Smoking Gun: U.S. Army Report, Photographs Show 25,000 Berrels on Island in Early '70s." *The Asia-Pacific Journal* Vol. 10, Issue 40, No. 2 (Sept. 2012): 1–6.

_____. "Were U.S. Marines Used as Guinea Pigs on Okinawa?" *The Asia-Pacific Journal* Vol. 10, Issue 51, No. 2 (Dec. 2012): 1–9.

Mizuho, Aoki. "Former Environment Minister Yuriko Koike Wins Landslide Election as Tokyo's First Female Mayor." *Japan Times*, August 1, 2016. Accessed September 11, 2016. http://www.japantimes.co.jp/news/2016/08/01/national/politics-diplomacy/tokyo-elects-former-environment-minister-yuriko-koike-as-citys-first-female-governor/#.V9Vcrl46JSE.

Moore, Captain John, ed. *Jane's Fighting Ships 1987–88*. London: Jane's Publishing Co. Ltd., 1988.

Morgan, Chris. *The Comic Galaxy of Mystery Science Theater 3000: Twelve Classic Episodes and the Movies They Lampoon*. Jefferson, NC: McFarland, 2015.

Morton, Ray. *King Kong: The History of a Movie Icon from Fay Wray to Peter Jackson*. New York: Applause Theatre & Cinema Books, 2005.

Mosura (*Mothra*). Directed by Honda Ishirō. 1961. Tokyo: Tōhō Co., Ltd. DVD.

Mosura (*Rebirth of Mothra*). Directed by Yoneda Okihiro. 1996. Tokyo: Tōhō Co., Ltd. Blu-Ray.

Mosura 2: Kaitei no Daikessen (*Rebirth of Mothra II*). Directed by Miyoshi Kunio. 1997. Tokyo: Tōhō Co., Ltd. Blu-Ray.

Mosura tai Gojira (*Mothra vs. Godzilla*). Directed by Honda Ishirō. 1964. Tokyo: Tōhō Co., Ltd. DVD.

Mosura 3: Kingu Gidora Raishū (*Rebirth of Mothra III*, or *Mothra 3: King Ghidorah Attacks*). Directed by Yoneda Okihiro. 1998. Tokyo: Tōhō Co., Ltd. Blu-Ray.

"Mothra Song." *Wikizilla*. Accessed May 15, 2016. http://godzilla.wikia.com/wiki/Mothra_Song.

Mulvey, Laura. "Visual Pleasure and Narrative Cinema." In *Film Theory and Criticism: Introductory Readings*, edited by Leo Braudy and Marshall Cohen, 833–844. New York: Oxford University Press, 1999.

Nagata, Kazuaki. "Revisiting 3/11: Fukushima's Long Shadow." *Japan Times*, February 10, 2016. Accessed September 5, 2016. http://features.japantimes.co.jp/march-11-radiation/.

Napier, Susan. *Anime: From Akira to Howl's Moving Castle*. New York: Palgrave Macmillan, 2005.

_____. "Panic Sites: The Japanese Imagination of Disaster from *Godzilla* to *Akira*." *Journal of Japanese Studies* Vol. 19. No. 2 (1993): 327–351.

Nattiez, Jean-Jacques. *Music and Discourse: Toward a Semiology of Music*, translated by Carolyn Abbate. Princeton: Princeton University Press, 1990.

"1961: World Condemns Russia's Nuclear Test." *BBC*, October 30, 2013. Accessed July 15, 2015. http://news.bbc.co.uk/onthisday/hi/dates/stories/october/30/newsid_3666000/3666785.stm.

Noriega, Chon. "Godzilla and the Japanese Nightmare: When *Them!* Is U.S." In *Hibakusha Cinema: Hiroshima, Nagasaki and the Nuclear Image in Japanese Film*, edited by Mick Broderick. London: Kegan Paul International, 1996.

Notehelfer, F. G. "Japan's First Pollution Incident." *Journal of Japanese Studies* Vol. 1 No. 2 (Spring 1975): 351–383.

"Nuclear Power in Japan." *World Nuclear Association*. Accessed October 10, 2015. http://www.world-nuclear.org/info/Country-Profiles/Countries-G-N/Japan/.

Ono, Sokyo. *Shintō: The Kami Way*. Tokyo: Tuttle Publishing, 1962.

Ōoka, Shōhei. *Fires on the Plain*. Boston: Tuttle Publishing, 1957.

Oru Kaijū Daishingeki (All Monsters Attack). Directed by Honda Ishirō. 1969. Tokyo: Tōhō Co., Ltd. DVD.

Oskin, Becky. "Japan Earthquake & Tsunami of 2011: Facts and Information." *Live Science*, May 7, 2015. Accessed September 5, 2016. http://www.livescience.com/39110-japan-2011-earthquake-tsunami-facts.html.

Otake, Tomoko. "Plastic Debris in Oceans a Growing Hazard as Toxins Climb the Food Chain." *Japan Times*, July 19, 2016. Accessed August 26, 2016. http://www.japantimes.co.jp/news/2016/07/19/reference/plastic-debris-oceans-growing-hazard-toxins-climb-food-chain/#.V8Qdro78–3M.

"Our Living Doll. (An Interview with Ai Tomoko)." *G-Fan* 90 (Winter 2010): 10–14.

Ozawa, Ichirō. *Blueprint for a New Japan: The Rethinking of a Nation*. Tokyo: Kōdansha International, 1994.

Petty, John E. "Godzilla: Just Say 'Nō.'" *G-Fan* 99 (Summer 2012): 20–28.

Polmar, Norman. *The Enola Gay: The B-29 That Dropped the Atomic Bomb on Hiroshima*. Washington, D.C.: Brassey's, 2004.

"Potsdam Declaration: Proclamation Defining Terms for Japanese Surrender Issued, at Potsdam, July 26, 1945." *Atomic Archive*. Accessed July 25, 2015. http://www.atomicarchive.com/Docs/Hiroshima/Potsdam.shtml.

"Public Opinion Survey on Environmental Pollution." *Japan Environment Summary* Vol. 2, No. 1 (January 1974): 2.

Ragone, August. "The Complete Godzilla Chronology: 1954–2004." *Famous Monsters of Filmland* 274 (July/August 2014):10–47.

_____. *Eiji Tsuburaya: Master of Monsters: Defending the Earth with Ultraman, Godzilla, and Friends in the Golden Age of Japanese Science Fiction Cinema*. San Francisco: Chronicle Books, 2007.

Rhoads, Sean A. "Godzilla the Social Critic: Part 1." *G-Fan* 97 (Fall 2011): 26–34.

_____. "Godzilla the Social Critic: Part 2." *G-Fan* 98 (Winter 2012): 18–28.

Richie, Donald. "Gojilla Wreaks Havoc on Miniature Tokyo." *Japan Times*, November 4, 1954.

_____. *A Hundred Years of Japanese Film*. Tokyo: Kōdansha International, 2001.

"The RIKEN Story." *RIKEN*. Accessed March 17, 2017, http://www.riken.jp/en/about/history/story/.

Ross, Michael. "Godzilla Comes Home for Christmas." *United Press International*, December 17, 1984. Accessed August 7, 2016. http://www.upi.com/Archives/1984/12/17/Godzilla-Comes-Home-for-Christmas/6485472107600/.

Ryfle, Steve. *Japan's Favorite Mon-Star: The Unauthorized Biography of "The Big G."* Toronto: ECW Press, 1998.

Sample, Ian. "Scientists Genetically Modify Human Embryos in Controversial World First." *The Guardian*, April 23, 2015. Accessed August 20, 2016. https://www.theguardian.com/science/2015/apr/23/scientists-genetically-modify-human-embryos-in-controversial-world-first.

Said, Edward. *Orientalism*. New York: Vintage Books, 1979.

Schilling, Mark. "Our Favorite Monster Returns to Terrorize Japan in 'Shin Godzilla.'" *Japan Times*, July 28, 2016. Accessed August 26, 2016. http://www.japantimes.co.jp/culture/2016/07/28/films/favorite-monster-returns-terrorize-japan-shin-godzilla/#.V8QZpI78–3M.

_____. "Shin Godzilla: The Metaphorical Monster Returns." *Japan Times*, August 3, 2016. Accessed August 29, 2016. http://www.japantimes.co.jp/culture/2016/08/03/films/film-reviews/shin-godzilla-metaphorical-monster-returns/#.V8QZxo78–3M.

Schlesinger, Jacob M. *Shadow Shōguns: The Rise and Fall of Japan's Postwar Political Machine*. New York: Simon & Schuster, 1997.

Schreiber, Mark. "Lucky Dragon's Lethal Catch." *Japan Times*, March 18, 2012. Accessed August 11, 2015. http://www.japantimes.co.jp/life/2012/03/18/general/lucky-dragons-lethal-catch/.

Schreurs, Miranda Alice. "Democratic Transition and Environmental Civil Society: Japan and South Korea Compared." *The Good Society* Vol. 11, No. 2 (2002): 57–64.

Seidensticker, Edward. *Tokyo: From Edo to Shōwa 1867–1989*. Tokyo: Tuttle Publishing, 2010.

Shapiro, Marc. *When Dinosaurs Ruled the Screen*. East Meadow, NY: Image Publishing, 1992.

Sharp, Jasper. *Behind the Pink Curtain: The Complete History of Japanese Sex Cinema*. Godalming, UK: FAB Press, 2008.

Shoemaker, Greg, and Allen Perkins. "Godzilla 1985: Screenplay Comparison." *G-Fan* 101 (June 2013): 20–30.

Siddle, Richard M. *Race, Resistance and the Ainu of Japan*. London: Routledge, 1996.

Smith, Tim, and Yoko Kobayashi. "Yoshimitsu Banno: Behind Hedorah." *Sake-Drenched Postcards*. Accessed January 20, 2007. http://www.bigempire.com/sake/smog_monster.html.

Sontag, Susan. "The Imagination of Disaster." *Commentary* (October 1965): 42–48.

Soper, Kate. "Naturalized Woman and Feminized Nature." In *The Green Studies Reader: From Romanticism to Ecocriticism*, ed. Laurence Coupe, 139–143. London: Routledge, 2000.

Squires, John. "Did 'Kong: Skull Island' Tease Future 'Gamera' Movie?" *BloodyDisgusting*, March 13, 2017. Accessed April 22, 2017. http://bloody-disgusting.com/news/3428029/kong-skull-island-tease-future-gamera-movie/.

Stein, Mark. "In Search for Cures, Scientists Create Embryos That Are Both Animal and Human." *NPR*, May 18, 2016. Accessed August 20, 2016. http://www.npr.org/sections/health-shots/2016/05/18/478212837/in-search-for-cures-scientists-create-embryos-that-are-both-animal-and-human.

Stille, Mark E. *The Imperial Japanese Navy in the Pacific War*. Oxford: Osprey Publishing, 2013.

Suwa, Yuzo. "Network Promotes Japan's Organic Farming in a Bid to Keep Industry Alive." *Japan Times*, June 27, 2016. Accessed September 11, 2016. http://www.japantimes.co.jp/news/2016/06/27/national/network-promotes-japans-organic-farming-in-a-bid-to-keep-industry-alive/#.V9VYe446JSE.

Swenson, Tommy. "Lucky Dragon 5 and the Terrifying Truth That Inspired Godzilla." *Birth Movies Death*, July 28, 2013. Accessed August 25, 2016. http://birthmoviesdeath.com/2013/07/28/lucky-dragon-5-and-the-terrifying-truth-that-inspired-godzilla.

Symonds, Craig L. *The Battle of Midway*. Oxford: Oxford University Press, 2011.

Takahashi, Toshio. *Gojira ga kuru yoru ni—"Shikō wo semaru kaijū" no gendai shi* (Godzilla Comes at Night—Drawing Near a Contemporary History of monster thoughts). Tokyo: Shueisha, 1999.

———. *Gojira ga kuru yoru ni—"Shiso to shite no kaijū" no 40 nen* (Godzilla Comes at Night—40 Years of Monster Ideology). Tokyo: Kōsaidō Books, 1993.

———. *Gojira no nazo—Kaijū shinwa to nihonjin* (The Enigma of Godzilla—Monster Legends and the Japanese). Tokyo: Kōdansha, 1998.

Tanaka, Tomoyuki. *Gojira eiga 40-nenshi, Gojira deizu* (Godzilla Days: The 40-Year History of Godzilla Films). Tokyo: Shueisha, 1993.

Tanimoto, Kazuki. "Japan." In *The New Grove Dictionary of Music and Musicians*, edited by S. Sadie and J. Tyrell. London: Macmillan, 2001.

Tawada, Yoko. "Is Europe Western?" *Kyoto Journal*, September 20, 2005. Accessed March 31, 2017. http://www.kyotojournal.org/backissues/kj-61/.

Tezuka, Masaaki. *Tōhō Tokusatsu Joyū Daisenzō* (Tōhō Special Effects Actresses Compendium). Tokyo: Yōsensha Co., Ltd., 2011.

Timmer, John. "Japan's Lurch Away from Nuclear Hasn't Caused Fossil Fuels to Boom." *Ars Technica*, September 9, 2016. Accessed September 11, 2016. http://arstechnica.com/science/2016/09/japans-lurch-away-from-nuclear-hasnt-caused-fossil-fuels-to-boom/.

The Tokyo Organising Committee of the Olympic and Paralympic Games. "Olympic Venues." *Tokyo 2020*. Accessed July 7, 2016. https://tokyo2020.jp/en/games/venue/olympic/.

Torrence, Paul F. "Owed to Nature: Medicines from Tropical Forests." *Rainforest Trust*, January 26, 2013. Accessed April 11, 2017. https://www.rainforesttrust.org/news/owed-to-nature-medicines-from-tropical-forests/.

Torry, Robert. " 'You can't look away': Spectacle and Transgression in *King Kong*." *Arizona Quarterly* Vol. 49, Issue 4 (Winter 1993): 61–77.

Totman, Conrad. *The Green Archipelago: Forestry in Pre-Industrial Japan*. Athens, Ohio: Ohio University Press, 1989.

———. *Japan: An Environmental History*. New York: I.B. Taurus & Co., 2014.

Truman, Harry S. *Diary Entry of July 25, 1945*. Harry S Truman Presidential Library and Museum. Available at: http://www.trumanlibrary.org/flip_books/index.php?tldate=1945–07-25&groupid=3702&titleid=&pagenumber=1&collectionid=ihow.

Tsukiyama, Ted. "The Battle of Okinawa." *Hawai'i Nisei Project*. Accessed August 17, 2016. http://nisei.hawaii.edu/object/io_1149316185200.html.

Tsutsui, William. *Godzilla on My Mind: Fifty Years of the King of Monsters*. New York: Palgrave Macmillan, 2004.

———. "Landscapes in the Dark Valley: Toward an Environmental History of Wartime Japan." *Environmental History* 8 (April 2003): 294–311.

Tsutsui, William, and Michiko Ito, eds. *In Godzilla's Footsteps: Japanese Pop Culture Icons on the Global Stage*. New York: Palgrave Macmillan, 2006.

Van Paasen, Jeromy. "Yōkai and Obakemono: The Monsters of Japanese Legend and Lore." *G-Fan* 88 (Summer 2009): 20–25.

Varney, Jason. "1992: Godzilla & Mothra: The Battle for Earth." *Famous Monsters of Filmland* 274 (July/August 2014): 35

"Vision and Research Activities." *Kamogawa Sea World*. Accessed August 7, 2016. http://www.kamogawa-seaworld.jp/english/research/.

Vogel, Ezra. *Japan as Number One: Lessons for America*. Cambridge, MA: Harvard University Press, 1979.

Wade, Bonnie. *Composing Japanese Musical Modernity*. Chicago: University of Chicago Press, 2014.

Walker, Brett L. *The Conquest of Ainu Lands: Ecology and Culture in Japanese Expansion, 1590–1800*. Berkeley: University of California Press, 2006.

———. *Toxic Archipelago: A History of Industrial Disease in Japan*. Seattle: University of Washington Press, 2010.

Weisgall, Jonathon. *Operation Crossroads: The Atomic Tests at Bikini Atoll*. Annapolis, MD: Naval Institute Press, 1994.

Wetmore, Kevin J., Jr. " 'Our first kiss had a radioactive taste': Ohashi Yasuhiko's *Gojira* in Japan and Canada." In *In Godzilla's Footsteps: Japanese Pop Culture Icons on the Global Stage*, edited by William M. Tsutsui and Michiko Ito, 127–138. New York: Palgrave Macmillan, 2006.

"What Do You Like About Mothra?" *Mothra Kingdom*, July 1, 2013. Accessed May 20, 2017. http://mothrakingdom.weebly.com/mothra-blog/what-do-you-like-about-mothra.

"Why Uranium and Plutonium?" *Atomic Archive*. Accessed July 25, 2015. http://www.atomicarchive.com/Fission/Fission5.shtml.

"World Heritage Nomination—IUCN Summary: 662 Yakushima (Yaku Island) (Japan)." *United Nations*, March 1993. Accessed August 1, 2016. http://whc.

unesco.org/archive/advisory_body_evaluation/662.pdf.

Yamazaki, Masakatsu. "Nuclear Energy in Postwar Japan and Anti-Nuclear Movements in the 1950s." *Historia Scientiarum* Vol. 19–2 (2009): 132–145.

Zimmer, Carl. "Bringing Them Back to Life." *National Geographic*, April 1, 2013. Accessed April 4, 2017. http://www.nationalgeographic.com/magazine/2013/04/species-revival-bringing-back-extinct-animals/.

Zwigenberg, Ran. "'The Coming of a Second Sun': The 1956 Atoms for Peace Exhibit in Hiroshima and Japan's Embrace of Nuclear Power." *The Asia-Pacific Journal* Vol. 10, Issue 2, No. 1 (Feb. 2012): 1–15.

Index